The Book of Revelation

Justice and Judgment

Elisabeth Schüssler Fiorenza

Second Edition

Fortress Press   Minneapolis

THE BOOK OF REVELATION
Justice and Judgment

Cover design by Beth Wright
Cover art: © L & M Services B.V. Amsterdam 981004
Sonia Delaunay (1885-1979), Étude de Lumière, 1913. Victoria & Albert Museum, London, Great Britain. Used by permission of Art Resource, NY.

ISBN 0-8006-3161-7

The Library of Congress catalogued the first edition of this work as follows:

Fiorenza, Elisabeth Schüssler, 1938—
    The Book of Revelation—justice and judgment.
    Includes index.
    1. Bible. N.T. Revelation—Criticism, interpretation,
etc. I. Title
BS2825.2.F52 1984 228'.06   84–42920
ISBN 0-8006-1793-2 (pbk.)

Manufactured in the U.S.A.   AF 1-3161

02   01   00   99   98   1   2   3   4   5   6   7   8   9   10

Contents

Preface to the Second Edition   v

Preface to the First Edition   vii

Acknowledgments   viii

Abbreviations   ix

Prologue   1

Introduction:
   Research Perspectives on the Book of Revelation   12

Part One:
Theological Perspectives and Frameworks

1. History and Eschatology in Revelation   35
2. Redemption as Liberation (Rev. 1:5-6 and 5:9-10)   68

Part Two:
Revelation in the Context of Early Christianity in Asia Minor

3. The Quest for the Johannine School:
   The Book of Revelation and the Fourth Gospel   85
4. Apocalyptic and Gnosis in Revelation and in Paul   114
5. Apokalypsis and Propheteia: Revelation in the Context
   of Early Christian Prophecy   133

Part Three:
Literary Vision and Composition

6. The Composition and Structure of Revelation   159
7. Visionary Rhetoric and Social-Political Situation   181

Epilogue:
   The Rhetoricality of Apocalypse and the Politics of
   Interpretation   205

Index of Passages   237

Amos N. Wilder
Ernst Käsemann
Raymond E. Brown

IN MEMORIAM

Preface to the Second Edition

As we ponder the year 2000, articles and books proliferate on the millennial change facing us. Talk about the millennium is connected either with doomsday predictions or with the anticipation of a more just society and world here on earth. Very few are conscious that the cultural discourse on the millennium has its roots in the Book of Revelation, or the Apocalypse of John, and other Jewish apocalypses. The mere mention of the millennium also reminds us that no part of the Bible and its interpretation is more controversial than the Book of Revelation. Literalist fundamentalists read Revelation's multivalent visions as predictions of doom and threat, of punishment for the many and salvation for the elect few. Scholarly scientific readings seek to translate the book's ambiguity into one-to-one meanings and to transpose its language of symbol and myth into propositional language, description, and facts. Both approaches—the popular and the scientific one—end up literalizing the Apocalypse.

The essays in this volume seek to chart a third way of reading that understands Revelation's multivalent language, mythic images, and visions of doom and bliss as a subaltern rhetorical discourse. As do all rhetorical discourses Revelation seeks to persuade and to convince rather than to provide information. It appeals to the imagination and emotions, threatens the "destroyers of the earth," and promises a world different from the world of oppression we know. Apocalyptic rhetoric resorts to images of violence and representations of bliss in order to move its audience to decision. As does all rhetorical discourse, it calls for an ethics of interpretation.

Hence this collection invites readers to become conscious of their own socioreligious presuppositions and learned reading approaches as well as those of scholars and preachers when engaging in the rhetoric of millennium. It seeks to intervene in scholarly as well as popular discourses on the Apocalypse from a liberationist feminist perspective. While I might use a different vocabulary (e.g., I would replace Old Testament with Hebrew Bible) or formulate some sections differently today after working for more than three decades on this biblical book, I believe that the overall interpretive approach developed in these essays still needs to be discussed and recognized if the paradigm shift in Apocalypse studies should continue. It is my hope that this edition will enable a new generation of students to engage the discourses of millennium critically and to arbitrate the rhetoric of Apocalypse competently in the interest of those who cry out for justice.

Preface

This book owes its existence to many people who have over the past twenty years encouraged and supported my research on the Book of Revelation. Francis Schüssler Fiorenza reminded me repeatedly to make my widely scattered essays available in one volume. Without his persistence I probably would have never gotten around to it. I am grateful for his untiring enthusiasm for my work. A special word of thanks is also due to Dr. John A. Hollar, my editor at Fortress Press, who has encouraged the project at every stage and shepherded it through various processes of editing to final completion. His support, encouragement, and friendship over the years have been invaluable.

The John Simon Guggenheim Memorial Foundation made possible uninterrupted research on the Book of Revelation during the 1983–84 academic year. Therefore, I decided to spend a portion of this period to collect, edit, and revise these essays and to write the introductory essay. I am very grateful to the Guggenheim Foundation for their support that made this volume possible.

Much painstaking labor and attention goes into the making of such a volume. I would like to thank the secretaries of the Notre Dame University word processing center for preparing the manuscript, and Therese Boyd, production editor of Fortress Press, for overseeing the production process. Sr. Carol Descoteaux, Ms. Mary Ann Beavis, and Rev. Robert Craft, graduate students at Notre Dame, have checked footnotes and corrected drafts of the manuscript. Ms. Celeste Deroche, my present research assistant at the Episcopal Divinity School, has proofread the galleys and pageproofs. David Wartluft prepared the index. To all of them my sincere thanks.

Ernst Käsemann has taught me to understand apocalyptic in terms of power and Johann Baptist Metz has pointed to its significance for contemporary theology. The book is dedicated to both of them as a token of my appreciation for their theological work.

As usual, a special thank you is due to Christina Schüssler Fiorenza.

Elisabeth Schüssler Fiorenza
Thanksgiving 1984

Acknowledgments

The essays in this volume have been or will be published elsewhere. They appear here, revised, in the following order:

"Research Perspectives on the Book of Revelation." In *The New Testament and Its Modern Interpreters* (ed. E. Epp and G. MacRae; The Bible and Its Modern Interpreters series; forthcoming from Fortress Press and Scholars Press [=Introduction]). Reprinted by permission of the Society of Biblical Literature.

"The Eschatology and Composition of the Apocalypse," *CBQ* 30 (1968) 537–69 [=chap. 1]. Reprinted by permission of the *CBQ*.

"Redemption as Liberation: Rev. 1:5–6 and 5:9–10," *CBQ* 36 (1974) 220–32. Reprinted by permission of the *CBQ*.

"The Quest for the Johannine School: The Fourth Gospel and the Apocalypse," *NTS* 23 (1977) 402–27. Reprinted by permission of *NTS*.

"Apocalyptic and Gnosis in the Book of Revelation and in Paul," *JBL* 92 (1973) 565–81. Reprinted by permission of the Society of Biblical Literature.

"Apokalypsis and Propheteia: The Book of Revelation in the Context of Early Christian Prophecy," in *L'Apocalypse johannique et l'Apocalyptique dans le Nouveau Testament* (ed. J. Lambrecht; BETL 53; Leuven: Leuven Univ. Press, 1980) 105–28. Reprinted by permission of the Colloquium Biblicum Lovaniense.

"Composition and Structure of the Apocalypse," *CBQ* 39 (1977) 344–66 [=chap. 6]. Reprinted by permission of the *CBQ*.

"The Followers of the Lamb: Visionary Rhetoric and Social-Political Situation," in *Discipleship in the New Testament* (ed. F. Segovia; Philadelphia: Fortress Press, 1985 [=chap. 7]).

Abbreviations

AAR	American Academy of Religion
AB	Anchor Bible
Adv. Haer.	Irenaeus, *Against Heresies*
APOT	R. H. Charles, ed. *Apocrypha and Pseudepigrapha of the Old Testament.* 2 vols. Oxford: At the Clarendon Press, 1912.
ANRW	H. Temporini and W. Haase, eds. *Aufstieg und Niedergang der römischen Welt.* Berlin: Walter de Gruyter.
ATANT	Abhandlungen zur Theologie des Alten und Neuen Testaments
BAGD	W. Bauer. *A Greek-English Lexicon of the New Testament and Other Early Christian Literature.* Eng. trans. W. F. Arndt and F. W. Gingrich, rev. F. W. Gingrich and F. W. Danker. 2d ed. Chicago and London: University of Chicago Press, 1979.
BETL	Bibliotheca ephemeridum theologicarum lovaniensium
BEvT	Beiträge zur *EvT*
BFCT	Beiträge zur Förderung christlicher Theologie
BGBE	Beiträge zur Geschichte der biblischen Exegese
BH	*Bibliothèque historique*
BHT	Beiträge zur historischen Theologie
Bib	*Biblica*
BiLe	*Bibel und Leben*
BR	*Biblical Research*
BTB	*Biblical Theology Bulletin*
BZNW	Beihefte zur *ZNW*
CBQ	*Catholic Biblical Quarterly*
CNT	Commentaire du Nouveau Testament
DBSup	*Dictionnaire de la Bible, Supplément*
EBib	Etudes bibliques

EKKNT	Evangelisch-katholischer Kommentar zum Neuen Testament
Eph.	Ignatius, *Letter to the Ephesians*
ET	English Translation
EvT	*Evangelische Theologie*
FRLANT	Forschungen zur Religion und Literatur des Alten und Neuen Testaments
HDR	Harvard Dissertations in Religion
H.E.	Eusebius, *Ecclesiastical History*
HeyJ	*Heythrop Journal*
HKNT	Handkommentar zum Neuen Testament
HNT	Handbuch zum Neuen Testament
HNTC	Harper's New Testament Commentaries
HTKNT	Herders Theologischer Kommentar zum Neuen Testament
HTS	Harvard Theological Studies
ICC	International Critical Commentary
IDBSup	Interpreter's Dictionary of the Bible, Supplement
Int	*Interpretation*
ITQ	*Irish Theological Quarterly*
JBL	*Journal of Biblical Literature*
JEH	*Journal of Ecclesiastical History*
JR	*Journal of Religion*
JRS	*Journal of Roman Studies*
JSJ	*Journal for the Study of Judaism in the Persian, Hellenistic and Roman Period*
JTC	*Journal for Theology and the Church*
JTS	*Journal of Theological Studies*
LTK	*Lexikon für Theologie und Kirche*, 2d ed.
MeyerK	H. A. W. Meyer, Kritisch-exegetischer Kommentar über das Neue Testament
MNTC	Moffatt New Testament Commentary
NICNT	New International Commentary on the New Testament
NovT	*Novum Testamentum*
NovTSup	Novum Testamentum, Supplements
NRT	*La nouvelle revue théologique*
NTAbh NF	Neutestamentliche Abhandlungen, Neue Folge
NTD	Das Neue Testament Deutsch
NTS	*New Testament Studies*
NumSup	Numen, Supplements
Phil.	Polycarp, *Letter to the Philippians*

PTMS   Pittsburgh Theological Monograph Series
1QpHab   *Pesher on Habakkuk* from Qumran Cave 1
4Qpatr   *Blessing of the Patriarchs*
RAC   *Reallexikon für Antike und Christentum*
RB   *Revue biblique*
RelSRev   *Religious Studies Review*
RevExp   *Review and Expositor*
RGG   *Religion in Geschichte und Gegenwart*, 3d ed.
RHPR   *Revue d'histoire et de philosophie religieuses*
RHR   *Revue de l'histoire des religions*
RivB   *Rivista biblica*
RNT   Regensburger Neues Testament
RQ   *Römische Quartalschrift für christliche Altertumskunde
              und Kirchengeschichte*
RSR   *Recherches de science religieuse*
RSV   Revised Standard Version
SBL   Society of Biblical Literature
SBLDS   Society of Biblical Literature Dissertation Series
SBLMS   Society of Biblical Literature Monograph Series
SBM   Stuttgarter Biblische Monographien
SBS   Stuttgarter Bibelstudien
SBT   Studies in Biblical Theology
SE   *Studia Evangelica*
SNT   Studien zum Neuen Testament
SNTMS   Society for New Testament Studies Monograph Series
ST   *Studia theologica*
Str-B   H. Strack and P. Billerbeck, *Kommentar zum Neuen
              Testament*
SUNT   Studien zur Umwelt des Neuen Testaments
TF   *Theologische Forschung*
TLZ   *Theologische Literaturzeitung*
TDNT   G. Kittel and G. Friedrich, eds. *Theological Dictionary of
              the New Testament*
TQ   *Theologische Quartalschrift*
TRu NF   *Theologische Rundschau*, Neue Folge
TS   *Theological Studies*
TSK   *Theologische Studien und Kritiken*
TU   Texte und Untersuchungen
TViat   *Theologia Viatorum*
TZ   *Theologische Zeitschrift*
VC   *Vigiliae christianae*

VD	*Verbum domini*
WMANT	Wissenschaftliche Monographien zum Alten und Neuen Testament
WUNT	Wissenschaftliche Untersuchungen zum Neuen Testament
ZNW	*Zeitschrift für die neutestamentliche Wissenschaft*
ZTK	*Zeitschrift für Theologie und Kirche*

Prologue

The Book of Revelation remains for many Christians a book with "seven seals," seldom read and often relegated to a curiosity in the Bible. For others it has become *the* book of the New Testament, full of predictions for the future and revelations about the present. Such books as Hal Lindsey's *The Late Great Planet Earth* and countless radio and TV programs provide detailed applications of the book's visions to contemporary persons and events. Persons such as the Roman Pontiff, Hitler, Stalin, the Sandinistas, or Khomeini have been candidates for the role of "the beast," while movements such as communism, humanism, or feminism are viewed as the "plagues" of the end time. However, such fundamentalist media-apocalypticism misuses Rev. because it does not either proclaim the apocalyptic promise of justice and salvation to the poor and to the oppressed or challenge the complacency and security of the relatively well-to-do.

Biblical scholarship claims to have moved past such popular readings of Rev. and to understand the eschatological teaching of the book in its historical context of Jewish apocalypticism. It is much divided, however, in the evaluation of such apocalypticism. As an apocalyptic work Rev. is often considered as more Jewish than Christian in its form and theology because it preaches vengeance and judgment but not love. Yet such an assessment reflects more the theological bias of exegetes than it contributes to our understanding of the work, since scholars disagree in their definition of "apocalyptic literature" as well as in their evaluation of apocalyptic theology.

The definition of apocalypticism and of the apocalyptic genre is a thorny problem. The Uppsala colloquium on apocalypticism[1] not only refrained from putting forward a definition of apocalypticism but also indicated that the understanding of apocalyptic writings is often modeled on the "Apocalypse of John." It seems therefore justified to bring together my work on the Book of Rev. that seeks to address the major

1

issues in apocalyptic research but does so in order to elaborate a distinct methodological approach.

The colloquium's distinction between (1) the phenomenon of apocalypticism, (2) the literary genre of apocalypse, and (3) the sociology of apocalypticism and the *Sitz im Leben* of apocalypses corresponds more or less to Paul Hanson's[2] proposed differentiation between *apocalyptic eschatology*, the literary genre of apocalypse, and "the symbolic universe in which an *apocalyptic movement* codifies its identity and interpretation of reality." In a similar fashion I here address the question of the "theology" of Rev., its *Sitz im Leben*, and its literary composition. I am not mainly concerned with a methodological separation of these different areas but with the search for a methodological approach that could integrate them as different aspects of one and the same work. Rather than to isolate a universal apocalyptic genre, to distill an apocalyptic "essence," or to assume a common social milieu for all apocalyptic writings, I propose to look for the integrating center, that is, the distinct historical-social-religious experience and resulting theological perspective that have generated the particular form-content configuration (*Gestalt*) of Rev.[3]

The distinction between form and content, apocalyptic language and eschatological essence, between Jewish tradition and Christian theological perspective is prevalent in the exegetical discussions of apocalyptic in general and the Book of Rev. in particular. Christian apocalyptic texts are expressions of Jewish apocalypticism and therefore do not constitute an independent phenomenon. Typical for such an evaluation is P. Vielhauer's phenomenological approach.[4] Although he discusses Christian texts and writings, his analysis has no room for a specific Christian type of apocalyptic, since he defines apocalyptic as a special expression of Jewish eschatology that is the outcome of the cultural-syncretistic impact of Hellenism as well as a reaction against it. Central contents of Jesus preaching, for instance, the "kingdom of God" or his imminent expectation, link him with Jewish apocalypticism. Nevertheless, Vielhauer asserts, Jesus' authority is not that of an apocalyptist and his preaching has "nothing to do with apocalyptic," because "surveys and divisions of history, numerical speculation and divination" are absent from it. From a tradition-historical and a formal-literary, but not from a theological point of view, Jewish and early Christian apocalyptic represent one and the same phenomenon. Although basic notions of the preaching of Jesus and of Paul are "apocalyptic," they are only remnant expressions of Jewish apocalyptic whereas the "heart" of their message is eschatology.[5]

Although Rev. claims to be a genuinely Christian book and has found its way into the Christian canon, it is often judged to be more Jewish than Christian and not to have achieved the "heights" of genuine early Christian theology. In chapter 1 I focus on this problem when it attempts to adjudicate the question of whether the outline and visions of Rev. depict a historical sequence and follow a salvation-history perspective as it was championed especially by the "biblical theology" school. I argue that for the author of Rev. the sharp distinction between "history and eschatology" is not given, since the resurrection and enthronization of Christ marks the beginning of the eschatological end time. All Christian time and history is "end time." The generative center of Rev. is not the course of history but the experience of the Christian community in the christologically qualified end time. In ever new visions and images the author "interprets" prophetically the concrete situation of Christians in Asia Minor as the short time before the end. Therefore the compositional development of Rev. is not linear-progressive but kaleidoscopic-cyclical.

Since chapter 1 stresses the specific Christian aspect of Rev., it lends itself to the misunderstanding that it seeks to separate the book from its Jewish apocalyptic context. Yet the attempt to delineate the particular Christian perspective of Rev. should not be so misunderstood. Such a delineation of Rev. as something "new" affirms its continuity with Jewish apocalyptic while at the same time maintaining its own distinctive perspective.[6] Distinctiveness does not exclude affinity and continuity with Jewish or Greco-Roman apocalyptic. "New" means only that the characteristic elements of apocalyptic language and perspective have achieved a special constellation or configuration within early Christian apocalyptic in general and Rev. in particular.

This "newness" of early Christian apocalyptic cannot be grasped by constructing a cross-cultural apocalyptic grid or type, nor by distilling the eschatological "essence" from its apocalyptic language and expression. It can only be understood as the reflection of a "new" experience. The creative center of early Christian faith and writings is the experience of Jesus as the resurrected Christ actively present in the Christian community and speaking to it through prophets and apostles. The tension between the past, present, and future of salvation—as William Beardslee[7] has pointed out—has determined the NT literature of gospel, history, and apocalypse, so that in a certain sense all three can be classified as apocalyptic forms. Apocalyptic language is not just the container or form for the Christian communities' faith-experience but it is constitutive of it.

Early Christian apocalyptic therefore stands in continuity with Jewish apocalyptic but represents, so to speak, "a new angle of refraction." In chapter 2, I argue that the understanding of redemption in Rev. is understood in terms of Jewish theology as the exodus and liberation from slavery rather than as the redemption of individual souls. If, as Ernst Käsemann has pointed out, the central question of Jewish and Christian apocalyptic theology is the question of power, then Rev. is clearly an articulation of such a theology.[8]

The author insists that the "Lord" of the world is not the emperor but Jesus Christ who has created an alternative reign and community to that of the Roman empire. Yet over and against a "realized Christian eschatology" Rev. maintains the early Christian apocalyptic emphasis on the "not yet" of salvation. In redemption the community of Christ is gathered and constituted as the domain of God's reign on earth in the end time. Yet salvation is only possible after all dehumanizing powers are overcome and a "new heaven and new earth" has come into being, because salvation means not only the salvation of the soul but of the whole person. Eschatological vision and parenesis have the same function in Rev. They provide the vision of an alternative world and power in order to strengthen Christians in their "consistent resistance" (*hypomonē*) to the oppressive power of the Roman Empire.

The central faith-experience of early Christian apocalyptic theology can be expressed in a twofold way: *either* early Christian writers emphasize the future aspect of eschatological salvation in order to balance the experience of "realized eschatology" *or* they stress the present reality of eschatological salvation over against a future-oriented eschatology. Both early Christian theological emphases, however, share the same Christian apocalyptic faith-experience that in the resurrection and enthronization of Jesus Christ God has already made present eschatological salvation in this world and time. Therefore both Christian apocalyptic emphases— the predominantly futuristic as well as the predominantly realized perspective—should not be played out against each other as "orthodox and heretic" or as "apocalyptic and gnostic" but must be understood in their different orientations to their common christological life-center and social-political "rhetorical situation."[9]

Whereas the first two chapters attempt to assess the theological commonality to and difference from Jewish apocalypticism the next three chapters seek to situate the theology of Rev. within the contexts of early Christian theologies and ecclesial circles in Asia Minor. Since traditionally Rev. is understood as part of the "Johannine tradition and school," in chapter 3 I seek to assess whether and how much it shares in the theological structure and life-center of the Fourth Gospel. I propose here that a careful analysis of Rev. suggests that Pauline, Johannine, and Christian apocalyptic-prophetic traditions and circles interacted with each other in the communities of Asia Minor at the end of the first century C.E.

Since John writes to communities in the Pauline missionary area, in chapter 4 I seek to chart the structural-theological similarities and differences between the response of Paul and that of Rev. to the theological stress on "realized eschatology." It argues that the author of Rev. attempts to correct the "realized eschatological" implications of the early Christian baptismal tradition with an emphasis on a futuristic-apocalyptic understanding of salvation. While I here still work with the widespread interpretative model of "enthusiasts" and "opponents," the theological-historical appropriateness of this model has become more and more questionable. Although the author of Rev. himself employs it, a rhetorical and functional analysis indicates that his apocalyptic theology is rooted in an experience different from his prophetic rivals which has generated his "alternative" prophetic interpretation of the religio-political situation. While the interpretative pattern of "opponents" insinuates that the writer is "in control" and "orthodox" and his "opponents" are in the minority and "deviant," D. E. Aune's discussion of the "function" of apocalyptic literature points out that persons or groups who are powerless or marginalized appeal to visions, trances, and revelations for the sake of legitimization or status enhancement.[10]

Chapter 5 draws conclusions from the insights of the two preceding chapters. Rev. and its author belong neither to the Johannine nor to the Pauline "school" but point to prophetic-apocalyptic circles and traditions in Asia Minor. I argue that at the end of the first century C.E. the local patriarchal offices advocated by the pastoral epistles and Ignatius appear not yet to have replaced the authority and leadership of prophets in the churches of Asia Minor.[11] Rev. does not reflect a rivalry between local officers and prophets but indicates that at least two rival prophetic traditions and circles compete for theological authority and acceptance in these communities.

While the first two parts of the book discuss the kind of theological-historical perspective and ecclesial situation that determine the form-content configuration (*Gestalt*) of Rev., the third part seeks to elaborate how the author expresses his theological perspective in the composition and "visionary rhetoric" of Rev. Chapter 6 seeks to show that the dramatic composition of Rev. is well planned and executed. The early Christian apocalyptic tension between the now of the community and the eschatological future, between the "already" and "not yet" of the end time, is expressed in the literary-structural tension between the forward movement of the narrative, cyclic repetitions, and hymnic proclamations.

The dramatic narrative of Rev. can best be envisioned as a conic spiral moving from the present to the eschatological future. It also could be likened to a dramatic motion picture whose individual scenes portray the persons or actions every time from a different angle while at the same time adding some new light or color to the whole. Sonia Delaunay's expressionist paintings are akin to the dramatic composition of the book. Her picture "rhythm," for instance, contains a number of different-colored circles or half-circles from which radiate lines of color like light that seems to be splintered by a prism. The painting is not static, but its lines indicate a forward movement of the circles of color like a revolving planet. While the evolving circles of color suggest simultaneity, the contrasting colors create a sense of light and movement. In a similar fashion John creates a "literary vision" instead of a sermon and tractate. Yet such a literary composition is not just mythopoeic but also rhetorical. By creating a "new plausibility structure" and "symbolic universe" within the framework of a prophetic-apostolic letter, John seeks to motivate and persuade Christians in Asia Minor. The visions of an "alternative empire and world" seek to encourage Christians in the face of harassment and victimization.

The symbolic universe and world of vision in Rev., I argue in chapter 7, is a "fitting response" to its socio-political "rhetorical situation." It seeks to alienate the audience from the symbolic persuasion of the imperial cult, to help them overcome their fear so that they not only can decide for the worship and power of God and against that of the emperor but also to stake their lives on this decision. The Book of Rev. is written for those "who hunger and thirst for justice" in a socio-political situation that is characterized by injustice, suffering, and dehumanizing power. In ever-new contrast images the rhetoric of Rev. elaborates the opposition between the life-giving power of God and the death-dealing power of Rome without falling prey to a total metaphysical or ethical dualism. Power is "given" to the anti-divine forces for a "short time." All Christians as well as all peoples and nations are called by the "eternal gospel." Moreover, Christians cannot be sure of the final outcome of this struggle for their own salvation; they may not project evil and failure only unto others. All—Christians or not—are subject to the final judgment of the creator-God who will judge according to "one's works."

A critical theological interpretation of Rev. must not just elaborate the "rhetorical vision" of Rev. but must also assess its theological and ethical-political impact.[12] In her contribution to the Uppsala colloquium on apocalypticism A. Yarbro Collins has raised "the question of the moral evaluation and theological significance of the way in which the Book of Revelation resolves its social crisis." In her discussion of vengeance and persecution in Rev. and especially of the "thorough-going and violent attack on Rome" (Rev. 18) she points to the possibility that Rev.

today can function as an outlet for envy, hatred, resentment, vengeful-
ness, and aggression of the weak against the strong. Its only positive
function may be that it could serve "as a reminder to the privileged that
the system which benefits them may be causing real hardship to others."
She concludes:

> Even if a case could be made that the evil in the Roman order outweighed
> the good, one must ask whether prayers (and their equivalent) for the
> destruction or impoverishment of one's enemies should ever be
> encouraged. Justice may seem to call for them at times, but there is also
> the very real danger of becoming like the oppressor in one's opposition.[13]

Yarbro Collins rightly rejects J. Ellul's and W. Stringfellow's interpretation that applies the imagery of Rev. to universal collective human
realities rather than to a particular city and nation. Yet she combines
such an insistence on the historical particularity of the imagery of Rev.
with the assertion that the book speaks about individual human beings
and not simply about institutions. That, however, seems to be a misreading of the symbolic language of Rev. In spite of great diligence, exegetes
are not able to identify any Roman individual, not even the ruling
emperor, with any certainty. The description of Babylon (chaps. 17—18)
and its followers is that of a political-religious collective and of institutional power, and not of individual persons.

Babylon/Rome is not the symbol of the "archetypal enmity" against
God or of "the decadence of all civilization." Babylon/Rome in its
splendor, being carried and supported by the beast, symbolizes imperial
power and cult. In Rev. it is the powerful incarnation of international
exploitation, oppression, and murder. Babylon/Rome is intoxicated not
only with the blood of the saints but with that of all those slaughtered
on earth. Rome's ruthless power and exploitative wealth are enormous
and its decrees are carried out in the provinces that support Roman
oppression.

The central images and theological motifs of Rev. 15:5—19:10[14] are the
splendor, wealth, and power of Babylon/Rome, and the justice of God's
judgments. The whole scene is conceived of in terms of a universal court-
room, in which a "class-action suit" takes place. The plaintiffs are the
saints who represent the class of all those killed on earth (18:24), the
defendant is Babylon/Rome, the charge is exploitation and murder in
the interest of power and idolatry, the judge is God. As was previously
announced in 14:8, Babylon/Rome has lost its lawsuit and therefore its
associates break out in lamenting and mourning, while the heavenly
court and the Christians rejoice. The judge has acknowledged their legal
complaints and claims to justice (18:20) and has pronounced the sen-

tence against Babylon/Rome which will be executed by the beast and the ten horns as divine henchmen. To misread this scene as hate for civilization or as resentment and revenge is a serious misunderstanding of the visionary rhetoric and theology of justice in Rev.

John views Roman power as exploitative, destructive, and dehumanizing because he and some of the Asian communities have experienced poverty, banishment, violence, harassment, and assassination. The outcry for divine justice in Rev. is borne out of the experience that no Christian who was denounced by her or his neighbors could receive justice from a Roman court. Martin Luther King, Jr.'s *Letter from a Birmingham Jail,* for instance, reflects experiences and hopes similar to the theology of Rev. In the crude outline of this letter scribbled on toilet paper in jail, the following three topics emerge: the ethics of Christian commitment that prohibits a Christian from projecting evil only unto others while holding oneself exempt from judgment, the pronouncement of God's judgment on the dehumanizing racist power of White America, and finally a glimpse of the New Jerusalem, echoing King's famous "I have a dream." Admittedly Martin Luther King, Jr., was influenced by the theology of Rev., just as John was influenced by Jewish-apocalyptic writings. Nevertheless, it was his experience of the oppression of his people and his own imprisonment that led him to his theology of justice and judgment. His indictment of racist White America cannot be construed as "hatred of civilization" or as "envy" deficient of Christian love for one's enemies, if the dehumanizing power of racism is understood as evil.

Obviously such an analogy and critical evaluation of the theology of Rev. can only be maintained if the exigency of its "rhetorical situation" is perceived correctly and if it is not just a product of the mind and psyche of the author.[15] Much recent scholarly debate centers around the question whether, because of the increased demands of the imperial cult under Domitian, a full-scale Christian persecution took place as Christian tradition claims and scholarship of Rev. assumes. L. Thompson has rejected the "crisis theory" as unacceptable.[16] He argues that the standard portrait of Domitian found in Roman sources was a product of the rhetoric of Trajan's time that played up the evil nature of the Domitianic past in order to contrast it with the ideal character of the Trajanic present. This may be the case from the perspective of official Roman historiography, but it is not borne out by the experience articulated in Rev. and other NT writings.

How we settle the question may depend on what we mean by "persecution."[17] Roman sources present the later years of Domitian as a reign of terror when informers (*delatores*) and harassment were encouraged by the authorities. Yet the letters of Pliny document that the same harassment, practice of denunciation, suspicion of private associations, and possible execution still existed in Trajan's time. Apparently minor charges could be construed as treason and Christians were particularly vulnerable to such charges. Moreover, the answer to the problem will also depend on whose perspective we adopt. One could argue from the perspective of well-to-do white Americans that no harassment, denigration, discrimination, or oppression of blacks existed at the time of Martin Luther King, Jr., although King was assassinated. The perspective and experience of blacks would be quite different! Similarly, the author of Rev. has adopted the "perspective from below" and expressed the experiences of those who were powerless, poor, and in constant fear of denunciation.[18]

Not the theology for justice and judgment and its "advocacy stance" for the oppressed and powerless, but its envisioning of God and Christ in analogy to the Oriental Great King and the Roman emperor seems to me to be the theological "Achilles' heel" of the visionary rhetoric of Rev. that calls for theological evaluation. In likening God's glory and power to Roman imperial power and splendor, in portraying Christ as the divine "warrior" and "King of kings," Rev. is in danger of conceiving divine power as "power over" in terms of Roman domination. True, the author seeks to transform these images, but it is doubtful whether he was able to do so for many readers. Nurturing and compassionate images of Christ or God, such as those of Rev. 7:16–17 and 21:3–4, function as correctives, but they are not sufficiently strong to determine the image of God and Christ in the overall narrative of the book. Since Rev. is not the only biblical writing that promotes the image of an Almighty Ruler-God, G. Kaufman has called upon theologians to "enter into the most radical deconstruction and reconstruction" of the central Christian symbols for God and Jesus Christ.[19] In the face of nuclear disaster the traditional imagery for God, Kaufman argues, tends to foster militarism and escapism but not human responsibility for the fate of the earth. In a similar fashion feminist theologians have pointed out how much the images of a patriarchal God and all-powerful Lord in heaven legitimate and perpetuate patriarchal domination on earth.

The essays collected and revised for the context of this book represent my work on Rev. over a period of almost twenty years. When in 1964 at the request of Prof. Dr. R. Schnackenburg I began my doctoral work on "priesthood in the NT," I had not even read Rev. in its entirety. I remember that I looked in despair at the three passages referring to priesthood and kingship in Rev. wondering how I ever would have enough material to write a term-paper, not to speak of a dissertation, on these enigmatic texts.[20] Yet twenty years later I am still fascinated with Rev. and with its methodological, historical-theological, as well as literary problems and challenges to biblical scholarship and theology.

I was encouraged to select, revise, and arrange these essays in their present form, in order to make them available to a wider readership of students and scholars who are interested in apocalyptic literature in general and in the Book of Rev. in particular but who are not specialists in this "fringe area" of biblical studies. I hope that this book will familiarize readers with important historical-literary critical and theological problems raised in the study of apocalypticism. In their present context the individual essays can shed light on each other and thus offer a comprehensive articulation of the paradigm shift in interpreting the Book of Rev., to which my research seeks to contribute. As such they can function as a preliminary introduction to my work on the Hermeneia commentary on Revelation, since it will not be possible there to discuss the issues raised here in such an extensive way. Whether or not readers will agree or disagree with the hermeneutical paradigm offered in this book, I do hope that they will join me in the fascination of interpreting one of the most enigmatic but also most challenging books of the NT.

NOTES

1. See the introduction by the editor, David Hellholm, to *Apocalypticism in the Mediterranean World and the Near East* (Proceedings of the International Colloquium on Apocalypticism, Uppsala, August 12–17, 1979; Tübingen: Mohr/Siebeck, 1983) 1–6. See also the "Nachwort" to Hartmut Stegemann, "Die Bedeutung der Qumranfunde," ibid., 526–27.

2. Paul D. Hanson, s.v. "Apocalypticism," IDBSup.

3. See my contribution to the Uppsala colloquium: "The Phenomenon of Early Christian Apocalyptic. Some Reflections on Method," in *Apocalypticism in the Mediterranean World*, 295–316, and Kurt Rudolph's evaluation, "Apokalyptik in der Diskussion," ibid., 777.

4. Philip Vielhauer, "Apocalyptic in Early Christianity, Introduction," in *New Testament Apocrypha* (ed. E. Hennecke–W. Schneemelcher; Philadelphia: Westminster Press, 1965) 2:609; See also his *Geschichte der urchristlichen Literatur* (Berlin: De Gruyter, 1975) 487.

5. For the general discussion of "eschatology" in New Testament studies, see E. Schüssler Fiorenza, s.v. "Eschatology in the NT," IDBSup.

6. I differ here from John J. Collins ("Pseudonymity, Historical Reviews and the Genre of the Apocalypse of John," *CBQ* [1977] 342), who argues that the lack of *ex eventu* prophecy and pseudonymity as well as the epistolary frame of Rev. are "superficial differences which do not reflect a significant change of perspective."

7. William Beardslee, *Literary Criticism of the New Testament* (Philadelphia: Fortress Press, 1970) 27.

8. See my "Religion und Politik in der Offenbarung des Johannes," in *Exegetische Randbemerkungen: Schülerfestschrift R. Schnackenburg* (Würzburg: Echter Verlag, 1974) 261–71.

9. For the notion of "life-center," see Alfred Schutz, *Phenomenology of the Social World* (Evanston, Ill.: Northwestern Univ. Press, 1967), and Karl Mannheim, *Essays on the Sociology of Knowledge* (London, 1962); "The Problem of a Sociology of Knowledge," in *From Karl Mannheim* (ed. K. H. Wolff; New York, 1971) 59–115. In diverse publications Kenneth Burke has stressed the relationship between extra-literary "situations" and literary-rhetorical "strategies." Cf. chap. 7 of this book, "Visionary Rhetoric and Social-Political Situation."

10. D. E. Aune, "The Apocalypse of John and the Problem of Genre," paper presented in the *Seminar on Early Christian Apocalypticism* at the annual SBL meeting in Dallas, 1983.

11. For a fuller discussion, see my book, *In Memory of Her: A Feminist Theological Reconstruction of Christian Origins* (New York: Crossroad, 1983) 245–342.

12. See my forthcoming book, *Bread Not Stone. The Challenge of Feminist Biblical Interpretation* (Boston: Beacon Press, 1985).

13. A. Yarbro Collins, "Persecution and Vengeance in the Book of Revelation," in *Apocalypticism in the Mediterranean World*, 729–49, esp. 746–47.

14. See the discussion of this section in my commentary, *Invitation to the Book of Revelation* (Garden City, N.Y.: Doubleday & Co., 1981) 154–79.

15. J. Gager (*Kingdom and Community* [Englewood Cliffs, N.J.: Prentice-Hall, 1975] 49–57) understands Rev. as mythic therapy, whereas A. Yarbro Collins ("The Revelation of John: An Apocalyptic Response to a Social Crisis," *Currents in Theology and Mission* 8 [1981] 4–12) sees its function as an emotional catharsis of the audience's feelings of resentment and envy against Rome. For a critique of both psychological interpretations, see David L. Barr, "The Apocalypse as a Symbolic Transformation of the World: A Literary Analysis," *Int* 37/1 (1984) 46–50.

16. See L. Thompson, "The Framing Function of the Revelation of John," paper presented in the *Seminar on Early Christian Apocalypticism* at the annual SBL meeting in Dallas, 1983.

17. For a similar argument with respect to the Gospel of Mark, see Luise Schottroff, "Die Gegenwart in der Apokalyptik der synoptischen Evangelien," in *Apocalypticism in the Mediterranean World*, 716.

18. As any analogy so also the one presented here does not completely "fit," since we have much more documentation for the complexity of the North American situation. However, I do think it clarifies my point that any interpretation of historical situations depends on the perspective and experience of the interpreter.

19. Gordon Kaufman, "Nuclear Eschatology and the Study of Religion," *Journal of the American Academy of Religion* 51 (1983) 13.

20. My thesis has subsequently appeared as *Priester für Gott. Studien zum Herrschafts- und Priestermotiv in der Apokalypse* (NTAbh 7; Münster: Aschendorff, 1972) but has never been translated into English.

Introduction:
Research Perspectives on the
Book of Revelation

E. Lohmeyer has summed up scholarly efforts of the research period 1920–1934 with the observation that very few early Christian writings have been so much courted by scholars, while almost completely eluding their methods of interpretation.[1] The elusive meaning of Rev. might be one of the reasons why serious critical scholarship has not focused on the book in the research period 1945–1979. This is obvious if one compares research on Rev., for example, with the number of publications, commentaries, monographs, and conferences on the Fourth Gospel. Nevertheless, in the past ten years interest in Rev. has increased. Except for some outstanding dissertations, however, serious research on Rev. is rather limited and mostly restricted to journal articles and collections of essays.[2] Although a plethora of popular commentaries has appeared,[3] no scientific commentary has been written that would embody the same research breadth as for example the work of W. Bousset, R. H. Charles, I. Beckwith, or E. B. Allo.[4] H. Kraft's new commentary, replacing that of E. Lohmeyer in the Handbuch zum Neuen Testament,[5] approximates best the format of a scientific commentary whereas the most recent commentaries of J. M. Ford, R. H. Mounce, P. Prigent, and J. P. M. Sweet[6] aim at a more general audience or are methodologically deficient.[7]

This relatively negative assessment of scholarly work on Rev. does not imply that the book was neglected or overlooked. Several bibliographical essays indicate that much effort has been exerted to interpret Rev. Rather than duplicate these essays, I shall briefly discuss them and then focus on perspectives and issues in interpretation in order to sketch the paradigm shift[8] that is taking place in scholarly interpretation in this field.

REVIEW OF RESEARCH
ON REVELATION

A. Feuillet's research report appeared in 1963 and covers the time between 1920 and 1960. He discusses the general tendencies and methods of interpretation (Chap. 1), composition and literary structure (Chap. 2), interpretation of Rev. 2—3 and 4—22 (Chap. 3), the doctrine of the book (Chap. 4), date and place of composition (Chap. 5) and the author (Chap. 6). He discusses various problems in Chap. 7: the woman of Rev. 12, the problem of the millennium, and several other studies of special issues. Each of these chapters first reviews the opinions of the commentators, then discusses special studies, and finally concludes with an evaluation.

Although Feuillet's research report introduces an abundance of studies and problems, its selection and discussion of the literature is marred by its traditional, conservative tendencies. For instance, Feuillet argues that Rev. is written by the apostle John who used a secretary. The objection that Rev. 21:14 refers to the twelve as the foundations of the New Jerusalem is rejected with the following argument: "But this is, after all, merely a reference to the will of Christ who has assigned a position of preeminence to the members of the apostolic college."[9] In a similar fashion it is argued that the ecclesiological interpretation of Rev. 12 does not exclude the traditional mariological understanding.[10]

H. Kraft's bibliographical essay[11] is more like an extended book review than a comprehensive research report. Kraft positively evaluates Feuillet's work, discusses the christological studies of Holtz and Comblin,[12] critically analyzes U. B. Müller's *Messias und Menschensohn*,[13] and briefly refers to the studies of Prigent, Jörns, and Schüssler Fiorenza.[14] After a somewhat more lengthy review of Rissi's books,[15] he discusses the studies of Vanni, Lancelotti, and Mussies.[16] In his review of the more popular commentaries he praises that of E. Lohse[17] because of its combination of scientific accuracy with general intelligibility. The review concludes with H. H. Rowley's discussion of apocalyptic literature.[18] Kraft's essay is very selective; it does not aim at a comprehensive discussion of the scholarship on Rev. that could adequately reflect the status of research.

Since O. Böcher's bibliographical essay appears in a series presenting the results of research, one expects a comprehensive review of scholarly methods and interpretations.[19] The small book is divided into two main sections, one reviewing the history of research of Rev. from the eighteenth century until 1974 and the other discussing the main problems of interpretation. The first section reviews the interpretations of the eighteenth and nineteenth centuries and discusses the history of religions approach in the twentieth century, critical Anglo-Saxon exegesis, several Roman Catholic interpretations, Protestant research after Lohmeyer, and the combination of different interpretative methods in Roman Catholic scholarship.

The second section singles out exegetical problems in Rev.: the author and his historical-religious background, date and contemporary historical background, Christ the Lamb, the apocalyptic riders, the 144,000, the two witnesses, the woman of Rev. 12, the satanic trinity, the number 666, the harlot Babylon, the thousand-year reign, and the heavenly Jerusalem. The book concludes with a bibliography containing five hundred entries of publications which have appeared since 1700. For each of the enumerated exegetical-interpretational problems, Böcher consults the commentaries of Bousset, Charles, Lohmeyer, Hadorn, Sikkenberger, Wikenhauser, and Kraft and then concludes with his own evaluative summary.

It is apparent that the small size of the book does not allow for any comprehensive presentation of the *status quaestionis*. Not only does Böcher fail to take into account any of the foreign commentaries which have appeared after 1945 but he also fails to review major articles and essays on Rev. Only one page of the book is concerned with special studies and monographs even though Böcher himself observes that the last three decades of research on Rev. are determined by studies of individual problems.[20] He singles out the following areas of major scholarly interest: history of religions and tradition-historical analysis, questions of form and redaction criticism, contemporary historical and political interpretation, textual criticism and the history of interpretation. He concludes that studies focusing on the theology of Rev. are relatively rare and center on ecclesiological problems. He points out briefly that further research is necessary on the relationship of Rev. to the Fourth Gospel and the Johannine epistles, on the interrelationship between Rev. and Jewish apocalypticism and the Hebrew Scriptures, as well as on the prophetic realism and the specific Christian features of the book. Finally, according to him the political conditions of the language of Rev. and the social and pastoral aspects deserve further exploration.

U. Vanni[21] has authored the most recent bibliographical essays on Rev. His work presents a comprehensive listing of international scholarship on the book since 1963, although his strength lies in his familiarity with French, Italian, and Spanish literature. After a short introductory review of the development of scholarship and bibliographical summaries (I, II, and III), in the next three sections he discusses the hermeneutics of Rev., literary aspects, and the historical-religious milieu of the book. Sections VII–IX mention studies on the relationship of Rev. to the OT, NT, and on the biblical theology of Rev. After a short discussion of commentaries and individual passages, he points to several areas for future research: the literary analysis of Rev., the hermeneutics of the book, its relationship to the OT and NT, its interrelation with Jewish and Christian apocalypticism, and finally the need for a new type of commentary that would integrate and profile present scholarly research on Rev. Since his bibliographical essay also includes articles and essays, it reflects more adequately the present state of scholarship on Rev. than that of Böcher. The limitations of space as well as the nature of a bibliographical essay, however, allow only for an enumeration of problems, not an overall integration.

Two recent English review essays by J. J. Pilch and J. J. Megivern[22] address a more general public. Whereas Pilch provides a short introduction rather than a comprehensive review of the literature, Megivern illustrates that the literature on Rev. ranges from "apocalyptic pornography" to dialectical philosophy. While serious scholarly works are rare, popular and fundamentalist writings abound. No wonder that Rev. is still considered to be the most difficult book in the NT. Scholars seem to have arrived at a consensus that the book does not provide us with any details of church- or world-history nor give us a calendar of future events, while popular interest still focuses on such information. Nevertheless, R. H. Mounce concludes his discussion of the classical approaches to interpretation (the preterist, the historicist, the dispensationalist, and the timeless-symbolic) by insisting that "the predictions of John, while expressed in terms reflecting his own culture, will find their final and complete fulfillment in the last days of history."[23] Although most exegetes have replaced the classical approaches to the interpretation of Rev. with the historical-critical approach, they still maintain a combination of the preterist or futurist interpretation, or insist that Rev. reveals the course of salvation history or timeless historical principles. My first Chapter, "History and Eschatology in Revelation," will discuss these questions and interpretative proposals.

HISTORICAL-CRITICAL ANALYSES

It is universally acknowledged that Rev. has to be understood in its historical-cultural and religious context. Therefore historical-critical methods developed in other areas of NT research have also been employed for interpreting Rev., but have not achieved generally accepted results. The only exception is the textual-critical work of J. Schmid,[24] whose classification of the manuscripts and evaluation of the textual tradition seem to be generally unrivaled.

The grammar and style of Rev. are notoriously difficult because they are full of solecisms and semitisms, repetitions and logical breaks. Nevertheless scholars have not accepted the thesis that Rev. is a rather deficient translation from Hebrew or Aramaic[25] nor that John's language is a ghetto language due to his inability to write Greek, since the text is not interspersed with Aramaic expressions or inconsistent in its linguistic offenses. Lancelotti's study of the author's syntax has substantiated Charles's dictum that while John "writes in Greek, he thinks in Hebrew."[26] However, the bilingualism of the author needs much more careful study before a socio-linguistic evaluation can be attempted.

It is interesting, however, that Hebraisms, not Aramaisms, are typical of the linguistic expression of Rev. This Hebraic character of the language in Rev. is primarily due to numerous allusions to the OT text. Although John never quotes the OT explicitly, he uses it to express in apocalyptic fashion his own visions.[27] H. Kraft has therefore proposed that the author deliberately created a hieratic language that was not spoken anywhere but recreates the sentence melody of the psalms for its liturgical setting.[28] That the author was capable of writing poetic-hymnic language is substantiated by the research on the hymns in Rev. which the author composed using traditional-liturgical language in order to comment on the apocalyptic actions of the book. Even though the attempts to render the text of Rev. in strophic form are not conclusive, they support the assumption that its style and language were intentionally created.

Whereas traditional exegesis attributes the doublets, inconsistencies, and repetitions of the text either to the faulty memory of the author or to the incompetence of a student,[29] historical-critical scholarship, particularly of the nineteenth century, proposes source-critical solutions or postulates various stages of revision,[30] so that in this understanding Rev. manifests the same editorial processes as other Jewish or Christian apocalypses.

Because of the uniform language of Rev., however, contemporary scholarship tends to stress the unity of Rev. and to reject source-critical manipulations.[31] Yet U. B. Müller and J. M. Ford have recently challenged this scholarly consensus. U. B. Müller attempts to separate out sources with the help of christological criteria. He classifies those texts which refer to the messianic judgment of the nations as originally Jewish source texts, while those texts in which Christ relates to the community are Christian. A more far-reaching source hypothesis was put forward by J. M. Ford who argues that two Jewish apocalypses which she attributes to John the Baptist and his school were redacted by a Christian disciple of John. Yet these recent source-critical reconstructions have not received much support.

Source hypotheses tend to be replaced by revision hypotheses,[32] since these can acknowledge that Rev. has a style peculiar to itself and that a final redactor is responsible for the whole work. While M. E. Boismard assumes that the final redactor combined two different works which were written by himself at different times, H. Stierlin proposes three such apocalypses that were fused together by a different redactor at the beginning of the second century. F. Rousseau on the other hand assumes five successive redactions of two Jewish and three Christian strata.[33] Finally, H. Kraft suggests that the same author has revised and expanded an existing pattern (*Vorlage*) consisting of the seven-seal cycle. According to Kraft, however, the final redactor of Rev. was such a skilled artist that he was able to combine and to integrate into his foundational document (*Grundschrift*) disparate traditions and *topoi* in such a way that a unitary composition and optimal configuration of artistic form and theological content was achieved.[34] However, if this is the case, then any reconstruction of the pre-history of Rev. must remain in the sphere of conjecture.

Form-critical and tradition-historical as well as history of religions analyses have concentrated primarily on the liturgical-hymnic materials and motifs and explored their *Sitz im Leben* in Jewish and early Christian liturgy.[35] Special attention was given to the judgment doxology or vindication formula in Rev. 16:4–7,[36] the worthy acclamation and macarisms,[37] the heavenly journey and to prophetic-parenetic forms, especially in the seven letters.[38] Most of these form-critical studies, though, are limited and selective. A comprehensive analysis and systematic evaluation of traditional forms and their redaction in Rev. still needs to be written.

The analysis of small formal units and their traditions must be supplemented by a pattern analysis because the author has modeled whole visions and sections after OT, Jewish apocalyptic, mythological, and early Christian patterns. This procedure can best be traced with respect to OT texts since they are still extant as written-patterns (*Vorlagen*). Such OT patterns are found throughout the book and are derived especially from Exodus, Ezekiel, Isaiah, and Daniel.[39] Other patterns are taken over from Jewish apocalyptic (judgment/salvation, cosmic week, messianic reign), from Near Eastern (divine warrior pattern or the assembly of the gods), from Hellenistic mythological (divine child, sacred marriage, divine polis) or early Christian tradition patterns (e.g., Synoptic Apocalypse or the apostolic letter form). Contemporary scholarship tends to elucidate especially the Jewish apocalyptic and OT matrix of the images and patterns in Rev., but does not sufficiently acknowledge that the cultural-religious milieu of Rev. and its communities is also Greco-Roman and Asian culture.[40] The scholarly attempts to determine the history of religions background and influences of Rev. 12 elucidate how complex and inextricable the fusion and interaction of cultural-religious traditions and influences could be.[41] Therefore, instead of trying to isolate different traditions and backgrounds, scholars might consider that the author, consciously or not, drew on and fused together traditions, motives, and patterns at home in very different cultures and mythologies.

Scholars have also attempted to chart the literary type or model John had in mind when writing his book.[42] It has been suggested that his overall pattern was a Jewish or Christian liturgy, a festal calendar, or a drama. Most often it is assumed that John intended to write a prophetic book or an apocalypse, since Rev. gave the whole literary type (*Gattung*) of apocalyptic literature its name. Yet we do not know whether the author could have been familiar with a definite literary genre "apocalypse."[43] Scholars have not yet succeeded in delineating the literary types of prophecy and apocalypse, nor in identifying essential component elements and stylistic characteristics of an apocalypse.[44] Therefore, it seems best to place Rev. within the wider context of Greco-Roman revelatory literature which would allow us to understand it not just in relation to Jewish apocalyptic literature but also to Gnostic "apocalypses."[45] Such a broad delineation, though, would not define the formal purpose and literary function of the book.[46]

It is generally agreed that the contemporary cultural-political milieu of Rev. is that of western Asia Minor, and that its setting is early Christianity at the end of the first century, since Rev. is addressed to seven Christian communities in Asia Minor.[47] However, some exegetes suggest that either the communities mentioned in Rev. or the author himself was alien to the church in Asia Minor because the book reflects a prophetic community order quite different from that known through the letters of Ignatius. It is suggested that the seven communities were Jewish apocalyptic conventicles within a predominantly Pauline missionary area[48] or that the prophet John, who had emigrated from Palestine-Syria, had nothing in common with these communities.[49] However, these studies assume that the letters of Ignatius, but not Rev., are reflective of the situation of the church in Asia Minor. The issue can only be resolved if a comprehensive study of the interaction between early Christian prophecy and developing local church leadership is written.

John understands himself as an early Christian prophet who also might have been the head of a prophetic circle.[50] The ecclesiastical tradition-historians, however, still debate whether John the apostle, or the presbyter John mentioned by Papias, was the author of Rev. or they propose that Rev. belongs to the same school or circle as the Fourth Gospel and the Johannine epistles.[51] However, the Johannine school hypothesis is based on the a priori assumption that the Johannine writings must somehow be related to each other because the ecclesiastical tradition ascribes them to the same author. John's self-understanding and perception of authority, though, are not apostolic but prophetic (Rev. 1:3). He derives his authority not from his fellowship with Jesus of Nazareth but, like Paul, from the revelation of the resurrected Lord (Rev. 1:9–20). It seems necessary, therefore, that Rev. be discussed not only in the context of the Johannine school but that it also be situated within Pauline and post-Pauline, as well as prophetic-apocalyptic Christian school traditions, as I will argue in the fourth chapter of this book. Such a discussion of Rev. within the context of early Christian developments could shed new light on debated theological-interpretative issues as, for instance, the Christian or sub-Christian character of the book,[52] its understanding of God,[53] Christ,[54] the Spirit, or the self-understanding of the church.[55] The question of whether Rev. is related to prophetic or apocalyptic[56] thought, its relationship to Synoptic[57] and other early Christian traditions or to Gnostic developments[58] appears in a new light when situated within the overall theological and institutional developments of the Christian community in the context of Asia Minor at the end of the first century C.E.

H. Kraft dates the final redaction of the book by comparing the situation of the communities in Rev. with that of Ignatius's letters. Since John and Ignatius argue against two very similar groups of opponents, Kraft concludes that the letters of Rev. and those of Ignatius reflect the same theological-ecclesial situation. Whereas Rev. 13 and 17 were written towards the end of Nerva's reign, the epistles and the final redaction must be dated between 110 and 114.[59] Further studies are needed to test Kraft's claim that the comparison of the opponents in Ephesians, Colossians, the pastoral epistles, and the letter of Polycarp would confirm this conclusion. The attempt to situate Rev. within the context of early Christian development, however, seems to be most promising.

In dating Rev., the letters have always played a major role. Although we have several popular studies of them, no extensive scholarly monograph has been published recently.[60] S. Johnson's review article on early Christianity in Asia Minor[61] suggests many promising avenues for further research, however. Publication of A. T. Kraabel's work on "Judaism in Western Asia Minor"[62] is also long overdue. The archeological discoveries of recent decades would provide the materials for a socio-historical profile of cities like Ephesus, Smyrna, or Pergamum. Similarly Roman presence, especially the imperial cult, needs to be investigated more fully with respect to Rev.[63] Further, mystery cults, private associations, and philosophical schools need to be discussed with reference to Rev. In short, a comprehensive work like that of W. A. Ramsay[64] still needs to be written.

One of the main points of contention in evaluating the relationship of Rev. to the Roman Empire continues to revolve around the question of whether a persecution of Christians took place under Domitian.[65] While the majority of scholars still accept Irenaeus's dating of Rev. at the end of Domitian's reign,[66] others have challenged this majority consensus.[67] They propose that the book was written in the sixties when Jerusalem and the temple were not yet destroyed. J. A. T. Robinson, for instance, argues that internal evidence speaks for a date between 64 and 70. Rev. 11, 17, and 18 link Rev. historically with events in Jerusalem and Rome during these years. Psychologically, Rev. reflects the Neronic program since no such bloody persecution is documented for Domitian's reign. He supports this contention also with a Neronic interpretation of the number 666 and with the *Nero redivivus* legend.[68] However, it is difficult to decide whether a severe persecution is an actual reality or an impending danger, or whether it is just a part of the experience of the author who attempts to shatter the complacency of Christians prospering under Domitian and forgetting the persecution of Nero.[69] Moreover, scholars also debate whether John was exiled to Patmos or whether he had withdrawn to the island for the sake of prophetic experience.[70]

In Rev. 17:9–16 John supposedly points to his own historical standpoint. Yet scholars have not yet succeeded in decoding this information. They do not agree whether or not to begin with Caesar, Augustus, Caligula, or Nero. Some omit the short-term emperors in their count, whereas others suggest that only those emperors who were deified by the Senate should be counted. Another suggestion is that Rev. 17:9–16 was inserted by a later redactor who thereby deliberately predates Rev. Since all these scholarly discussions have not yet arrived at a generally accepted solution, it must be asked whether they misunderstood the language and intention of the author.[71]

In conclusion: The current progress in historical-critical analysis of Rev. moves in a way parallel to that of other NT writings. Just as in other areas the stress on source-criticism and form-criticism has been replaced by a stress on redaction criticism, so in scholarship on Rev. the source-critical and compilation theories of the last century gave way to the scholarly opinion that Rev. is the theological work of a single author. Since linguistic analyses have established that the seven letters form an integral part of the book, Rev. as a whole is no longer seen as a Jewish writing with superficial Christian additions. Instead it must be evaluated as an authentic Christian prophetic-apocalyptic work addressed to the situation and problems of the Christian church in western Asia Minor, as will be argued in the second part of this study.

Nevertheless the judgment of E. Lohmeyer applies also to the research period of the last three decades: After reviewing scholarly efforts to arrive at a definite interpretation of Rev. he concludes that the proposed interpretations are so diverse that the true meaning of Rev. still remains hidden.[72] All scholarly attempts to arrive at a definite one-to-one interpretation of certain passages or of the whole book seem to have failed. This failure suggests that the historical-critical paradigm of research has to be complemented by a different approach that can do justice to the multivalent character of the language and imagery in Rev. The last two chapters of this study will elaborate on such a literary-historical paradigm.

LITERARY-FUNCTIONAL INTERPRETATION

While redaction criticism elucidates the nature and extent of the author's activity in collecting, arranging, and editing traditional forms, sources, and patterns, literary analysis focuses on the compositional activity of the author and the aesthetic power of the work. Traditional patterns, sources, or stages of redaction may not be equated with the literary composition and expression of a work. The author's interests and intentions in writing the work are not something that lie behind the text, but they manifest themselves in the form-content configuration and social function of the book. Such literary analysis does not discard the results of historical-critical research but integrates them into the overall understanding of Rev. as a literary work. The language and overall composition of Rev. are literary and not descriptive-factual. Individual formal units, traditional patterns, and individual passages derive their meaning from the overall composition and its ecclesial-social function.

J. Ellul[73] has made the claim that all scientific studies written in the last fifty years have erred completely because they applied a method to the interpretation of Rev. which is totally inappropriate to the book. According to him Rev. must be understood as a whole and not analyzed verse by verse because each part takes its import in its relation to the whole architecture of the work. Ellul's criticism is justified, but it over-looks the recent literary and structural analyses of Rev. which have attempted to understand the overall composition of the book. While structuralist analyses of the deep structure of the book are rare,[74] schol-arly analyses of the surface-structure abound.[75] Scholars, however, agree that in comparison with other Jewish and Christian apocalypses the over-all organization of Rev. reveals a careful composition and definite plan in which the number seven plays a key role.

One can almost find as many different outlines of the composition as there are scholars studying the book. It is debated whether the apocalyp-tic part Rev. 4—22 is independent of the letters, or whether the letters are an integral part of the architectonic structure of the book.[76] Other issues of debate are whether the book is totally composed in seven cycles that recapitulate each other[77] or whether only the explicitly numbered visions are intended as seven cycles. It is also discussed whether Rev. consists of two rather even sections (1—11 and 12—22) or whether its architectonic pattern is the concentric ABCDC'B'A' pattern. Another issue is whether the narrative is cyclic, linear, or moves in a conic spiral.[78]

Two methodological issues need to be clarified: First, whether or not the structuring of the book is to be reconstrued on purely formalistic grounds[79] or whether a morphological approach that elucidates the form-content configuration of Rev. is more appropriate. Second, the following criteria formulated by architecture criticism need also to be applied to the structural analyses of the book: one must show that the proposed architectonic or compositional structuration is not derived from the tradition, that it is also found in smaller units of Rev., and that it is present in the art and literature of the time. The greatly differing proposals for the structure of the book indicate that the formulation of such internal and external controls is necessary if structural-compositional analyses of the book are not to degenerate further into purely subjectivistic enterprises.

Exegetes and theologians still have to discover what artists have long understood: the strength of the language and composition of Rev. lies not in its theological argumentation or historical information but in its evocative power inviting imaginative participation. The language and narrative flow of Rev. elicit emotions, reactions, and convictions that cannot and should not be fully conceptualized and phrased in propositional-logical language. Since the author does not employ discursive language and logical arguments but speaks in the language of symbol and myth, the often somewhat unsophisticated discussion of the imaginative, mythopoeic language of Rev.[80] needs to be replaced by a literary approach and symbol analysis that would bring out the evocative power and "musicality" of its language, which was written to be read aloud and to be heard.

Such a literary approach would have to integrate literary-aesthetic analysis with historical-traditional research. It should not neglect tradition-historical and form-critical analyses since the author does not freely create his images and myths but reworks traditional materials into a new and unique literary composition. Nevertheless, the meaning of the mythopoeic language in Rev. cannot be derived from its traditions but only from its literary function in its present historical-literary context. To know the author's original reference points and cultural context helps us to approximate the multivalent meaning and emotive power of the book's imaginative language. Such an approximation is only possible, however, when individual passages of Rev. are interpreted within the context of the overall composition and theological perspective of the book.

Already in the eighteenth century scholars recognized that apocalyptic language is poetic language and that Rev. must therefore be interpreted as a work of poetry.[81] Because of the Jewish character of apocalyptic language, however, they advocated a sharp distinction between literary form and theological content in order to maintain the genuine Christian character of Rev. This dichotomy between Jewish apocalyptic language and Christian theological content, which reduces apocalyptic imagery to a mere container or cloak of timeless essences and propositional truth, has ever since marred the discussion of apocalyptic literature. Insofar as exegetes have understood Rev. as a descriptive or predictive account of factual events of the past and the future, or of timeless theological statements and principles, they have tended to reduce the imaginative language of Rev. to a one-to-one meaning. They thus have historicized the sequence of images and visions, objectified symbolic-allegoric expressions, and reduced mythopoeic vision to abstract theological or philosophical principles.

Even those scholars who have championed a literary approach have tended to reduce the meaning of the book to archetypal or ontological concepts.[82] Such a dehistoricization of Rev. neglects the theological interests of the author and the socio-theological function of the book. A purely formalistic literary understanding of Rev. overlooks the fact that John did not write art for art's sake, but had a definite purpose in mind when writing the book. It is therefore necessary to discuss briefly the communicative situation and literary-social function of Rev.

If the theological intention and the social function of a work are not phenomena that lie behind the texts but manifest themselves in the literary form-content configuration of a work, then it is significant that the apocalyptic visions of John are set within the framework of the apostolic letter-form and that they begin with a sevenfold series of apocalyptic letters. The epistolary framework of Rev. is not an artificial and accidental setting for John's mythopoeic vision. John derives the authority of his work not from pseudonymity and fictional timetables, but from the revelation of Jesus Christ which he must communicate as prophetic address. The overall form and communicative purpose of Rev., therefore, come close to those of the Pauline letters although they are quite distinct from them. In writing down the "words of prophecy," John wants to strengthen, encourage, and correct Christians in Asia Minor who were persecuted and still must expect more suffering and harassment (Rev. 2—3; 13:10; 14:12). He does so not simply by writing a hortatory treatise, but by creating a new "plausibility structure" and "symbolic universe" which he communicates in the form of an "apostolic'-prophetic letter.

The main concern of the author is not the interpretation of history but the issue of power. The focal point of the "already" and "not yet" of eschatological salvation is not history but the kingdom of God and the rule of Christ. Therefore the main symbol of Rev. is the image of the throne and its main motif that of kingship.[83] The apocalyptic question "Who is Lord over the world?" is the central issue of Rev. This question is expressed here in mythological and political images and language. Whereas Paul understood the question in terms of the alternative between the lordship of Christ and that of the cosmic powers, Rev. concretizes this alternative in political terms.[84] Christians are the representatives of God's and Christ's eschatological power on earth and, at the same time, are still subject to the political powers of their time. Those rejecting the beast and its cult are excluded from the economic and social life of their time and have to expect captivity and death (13:10–15). Rev. demands unfaltering resistance to the imperial cult because honoring the emperor would mean ratifying Rome's dominion over all people and denying the eschatological life-giving power of God and Christ.[85]

The author appears to formulate this theology in opposition to an enthusiastic prophetic theology that seems to have advocated accommodation to the Roman civil religion (cf. the code words "idolatry" and "immorality" in the letters and the central section of Rev.). His harsh rejection of the Nicolaitans and his denunciation of the beast and its cult have the same function. John can reject any accommodation to Roman civil religion and any participation in the imperial cult because he can "show" that the power of God and Christ will prevail over all anti-divine and anti-human forces. Without question the symbolic universe of Rev. is genuinely Christian. The central function of Rev. is the elaboration of God's and the Lamb's power not only over the lives of individuals but over the whole world and its political powers.

Nevertheless scholars have labeled the author's theological perspective and attempt at "social control" sub-Christian because of his outcry for vengeance. They argue that the preaching of resentment and revenge in Rev. is not compatible with Christian love and forgiveness.[86] However, the demand of Rev. for judgment must be understood as an outcry for justice for those who are exploited and killed today. John thus resounds the call of the prophets to repentance and justice. In doing so he continues the call and promise of the prophet Jesus. Against the forces of economic, political, and religious oppression within the Roman empire the mythopoeic vision of Rev. shows that God's and Christ's reign and salvation are different from those of the dominant culture. The last chapters of Rev. portray a world free of evil and suffering in order to give hope to those who are suffering and oppressed because they will not acknowledge the death-dealing political powers of their time.

CONCLUSION

I have attempted to review major issues and approaches in the interpretation of the Book of Rev. Scholarship on this book is in the process of integrating the historical-critical and literary-critical paradigms into a new literary-historical paradigm of interpretation. Such a paradigm-shift in interpretation is also taking place in other areas of biblical studies.[87] Nevertheless, Rev. may well emerge as one of the most interesting and challenging areas of the NT for developing such a new interpretative approach, since only a literary-historical approach can do justice to the symbolic mythopoeic language as well as to the historical-communicative situation of the book.

Such a new paradigm of research opens up old questions for new explorations and fresh scrutiny. When I started my work on Rev. the majority of scholars agreed that the book was an only slightly redacted Jewish apocalypse. The theology of Rev. was therefore held to be Jewish rather than genuinely Christian and as such to be of little significance for the reconstruction of early Christian theology and life. Therefore, the hermeneutic-interpretative process had to distill the Christian theological essence or existential significance of Rev. from its crude apocalyptic language and mythological imagery. Today, all these opinions are modified and the book seems to emerge more and more as a Christian writing *sui generis*. Such a gradual change in perspective is due to many different developments in NT exegesis and theology. It is especially fostered by a renewed methodological interest in the literary character of NT writings, on the one hand, and the challenging theological questions of liberation theology,[88] on the other hand.

The following chapters address problems that are crucial for such a change in the theological perspective and interpretative paradigm of scholarship on Rev. Part One explores whether the sequence of Rev. is historical-predictive or eschatological-compositional and underlines its central theological problem of suffering and power. Part Two elaborates the Christian vision and the *Sitz im Leben* of Rev. in the development of early Christian theology and community in Asia Minor at the end of the first century C.E. Part Three seeks to understand the theological vision of Rev. in terms of its literary composition as a public open-letter containing revelatory visions and auditions and to elaborate its rhetorical function as the vision of an alternative world. Thus, the chapters of this

book move from a critical discussion of the interpretations of Rev. in
terms of a philosophy or theology of history to a theological-historical
elaboration of its ecclesial-political situation. They end with two essays
(chapter 6 and 7) which seek to integrate historical-theological and
literary-critical interpretation by insisting that the meaning of Rev.
cannot be found behind the text but is given with the text and its rhetorical function.

NOTES

1. E. Lohmeyer, "Die Offenbarung des Johannes 1920–1934," *TRu* 6 (1934) 270.

2. See the following special issues: *Foi et vie* 74/4 (1976); *CBQ* 39/3 (ed. R. Clifford,
1977); *Semeia* 14 (ed. J. J. Collins, 1979); the Proceedings of the Louvain Colloquium
of 1979, *L'Apocalypse johannique et l'Apocalyptique dans le Nouveau Testament* (ed.
J. Lambrecht; BETL 53; Louvain: The Univ. Press, 1980); the conference volume
Apocalypses et théologie de l'espérance. Congrès de Toulouse 1975 (ed. L. Monlobou;
Lectio Divina 95; Paris: Cerf, 1977); and the Proceedings of the International Colloquium on Apocalypticism, Uppsala, August 12–17, 1979; *Apocalypticism in the Mediterranean World and the Near East* (ed. D. Hellholm; Tübingen: Mohr/Siebeck, 1983).

3. See, e.g., P. S. Minear, *I Saw a New Earth* (Washington, D.C.: Corpus Books, 1980);
A. Yarbro Collins, *The Apocalypse* (NTM 22; Wilmington, Del.: M. Glazier, 1979); my
own *The Apocalypse* (Chicago: Franciscan Herald Press, 1976); "The Revelation of
John," in *Hebrews, James, 1 and 2 Peter, Jude, Revelation* (Proclamation Commentaries;
Philadelphia: Fortress Press, 1977); and *Invitation to the Book of Revelation* (Garden
City, N.Y.: Doubleday & Co., 1981).

4. W. Bousset, *Die Offenbarung Johannis* (MeyerK 16; Göttingen: Vandenhoeck &
Ruprecht, 1906, 1966); R. H. Charles, *The Revelation of St. John* (2 vols.; ICC; Edin-
burgh: T. & T. Clark, 1920); I. Beckwith, *The Apocalypse of John* (New York: Macmillan
Co., 1919); E. B. Allo, *Saint Jean, L'Apocalypse* (EBib; Paris: J. Gabalda et Cie, 1933).

5. H. Kraft, *Die Offenbarung des Johannes* (HNT 16a; Tübingen: Mohr/Siebeck,
1974). Cf. E. Lohmeyer, *Die Offenbarung des Johannes* (HNT 16; 6th ed.; Tübingen:
Mohr/Siebeck, 1953).

6. J. M. Ford, *Revelation* (AB 38; Garden City, N.Y.: Doubleday & Co., 1975); R. H.
Mounce, *The Book of Revelation* (NICNT; Grand Rapids: Wm. B. Eerdmans, 1977); J.
P. M. Sweet, *Revelation* (Westminster Pelican Commentaries; Philadelphia: Westminster
Press, 1979); P. Prigent, *L'Apocalypse de Saint Jean* (CNT 14; Paris: Delachaux et Niestlé,
1981).

7. Cf., e.g., the critical review of J. M. Ford's *Revelation* (*CBQ* 38/4 [1976] 555–57)
and P. Prigent's *L'Apocalypse* (*CBQ* 45/3 [1983] 504–6) by A. Yarbro Collins.

8. For the notion of paradigm-shift, see T. S. Kuhn, *The Structure of Scientific Revo-
lutions* (Chicago: Univ. of Chicago Press, 1962); I. G. Barbour, *Myth, Models, and
Paradigms* (New York: Harper & Row, 1974).

9. A. Feuillet, *The Apocalypse* (New York: Alba House, 1964) 107–8.

10. Ibid., 116–17.

11. H. Kraft, "Zur Offenbarung Johannes," *TRu* NF 38 (1973) 81–98.

12. T. Holz, *Die Christologie der Apokalypse des Johannes* (Berlin: Akademie-Verlag,

1971); J. Comblin, *Le Christ dans l'Apocalypse* (Paris: Desclée, 1965).

13. U. B. Müller, *Messias und Menschensohn in jüdischen Apokalypsen und in der Offenbarung des Johannes* (SNT 6; Gütersloh: Gerd Mohn, 1972).

14. P. Prigent, *Apocalypse 12. Histoire de l'exégèse* (BGBE 2; Tübingen: Mohr/Siebeck, 1959); K. P. Jörns, *Das hymnische Evangelium* (SNT 5; Gütersloh: Gerd Mohn, 1971); E. Schüssler Fiorenza, *Priester für Gott: Studien zum Herrschafts- und Priestermotiv in der Apokalypse* (NTAbh 7; Münster: Aschendorff, 1972).

15. M. Rissi, *Time and History* (Richmond: John Knox Press, 1966); idem, *The Future of the World* (SBT 2/25; London: SCM Press, 1972).

16. U. Vanni, *La struttura letteraria dell' Apocalisse* (Aloisiana 8; Rome: Herder, 1971); A. Lancelotti, *Sintassi ebraica nel greco dell' Apocalisse. I: Uso della forme verbali* (Assisi: Coll. Assiniensis, 1964); G. Mussies, *The Morphology of Koine Greek as Used in the Apocalypse of John: A Study in Bilingualism* (NovTSup 27; Leiden: E. J. Brill, 1971). See also his "The Greek of the Book of Revelation," in *L'Apocalypse johannique*, 167–77.

17. E. Lohse, *Die Offenbarung des Johannes* (NTD 11; Göttingen: Vandenhoeck & Ruprecht, 1960).

18. H. H. Rowley, *The Relevance of Apocalyptic* (London: Lutterworth Press, 1963).

19. O. Böcher, *Die Johannesapokalypse* (Erträge der Forschung 41; Darmstadt: Wissenschaftliche Buchgesellschaft, 1975).

20. Ibid., 23.

21. U. Vanni, "Rassegna bibliographica sull' Apocalisse (1970–1975)," *RivB* 24 (1976) 277–301; "L'Apocalypse johannique. État de la question," in *L'Apocalypse johannique*, 21–46.

22. J. J. Pilch, *What Are They Saying About the Book of Revelation?* (New York: Paulist Press, 1978); J. J. Megivern, "Wrestling with Revelation," *BTB* 8 (1978) 147–54.

23. Mounce, *Revelation*, 44–45.

24. J. Schmid, *Studien zur Geschichte des griechischen Apokalypsetextes* (2 vols.; Münchener Theologische Studien 1; Munich: Chr. Kaiser, 1955–56). See also the discussion of J. Delobel, "Le texte de l'Apocalypse: Problèmes de méthôde," in *L'Apocalypse johannique*, 151–66.

25. C. C. Torrey, *The Apocalypse of John* (New Haven, Conn.: Yale Univ. Press, 1958).

26. Charles, *Revelation*, 1: cxliii.

27. See A. Vanhoye, "L'Utilisation du livre d'Ézéchiel dans l'Apocalypse," *Bib* 43 (1962) 436–76; J. Cambier, "Les images de l'Ancien Testament dans l'Apocalypse de Saint Jean," *NRT* 77 (1955) 113–22; F. Jenkins, *The Old Testament in the Book of Revelation* (Grand Rapids: Wm. B. Eerdmans, 1976) 24–25.

28. Kraft, *Die Offenbarung des Johannes*, 16.

29. P. Gaechter, "The Original Sequence of Apocalypse 20—22," *TS* 10 (1949) 485–521; A. Feuillet, "Jelons pour une meilleure intelligence de l'Apocalypse," *EsVie* 84 (1974) 481–90; 85 (1975) 65–72, 209–23, 432–43; 86 (1976) 455–59, 471–79.

30. Cf. the review of the interpretation of Rev. from the Enlightenment to the present, especially in Germany: G. Maier, *Die Johannes-offenbarung und die Kirche* (WUNT 25; Tübingen: Mohr/Siebeck, 1981) 488–648.

31. For a more extensive discussion, see chap. 6 of this book on "The Composition and Structure of Revelation."

32. Most recently Archbishop J. F. Whealon ("New Patches on an Old Garment: The Book of Revelation," *BTB* 11 [1981] 54–59) has argued "that the parts of Rev. enclosed

by the epistolary introduction and conclusion were originally a Jewish apocalypse preserved without major editing."

33. F. Rousseau, *L'Apocalypse et le milieu prophétique du Nouveau Testament: Structure et préhistoire du texte* (Paris: Desclée; Montreal: Bellarmin, 1971).

34. Kraft, "Zur Offenbarung Johannes."

35. G. Delling, "Zum gottesdienstlichen Stil der Johannes-apokalypse," *NovT* 3 (1959) 107–37; Jörns, *Das hymnische Evangelium;* P. von der Osten Sacken, "Christologie, Taufe, Homologie. Ein Beitrag zu Apoc Joh 1, 5, f.," *ZNW* 58 (1967) 255–66; Schüssler Fiorenza, *Priester für Gott,* 173–79; U. Vanni, "Un esempio di dialogo liturgico in Ap 1, 4–8," *Bib* 57 (1976) 453–67.

36. H. D. Betz, "On the Problem of the Religio-Historical Understanding of Apocalypticism," *JTC* 6 (1969) 134–56; P. Staples, "Rev. xvi 4–6 and Its Vindication Formula," *NovT* 14 (1972) 28–93; A. Yarbro Collins, "The History-of-Religions Approach to Apocalypticism and the 'Angel of the Waters' (Rev. 16:4–7)," *CBQ* 39 (1977) 367–81.

37. W. C. van Unnik, " 'Worthy is the Lamb.' The Background of Apoc 5," *Mélanges Beda Rigaux* (Gembloux: Duculot, 1970) 445–61; W. Bieder, "Die sieben Seligpreisungen in der Offenbarung des Johannes," *TZ* 10 (1954) 13–30.

38. U. B. Müller, *Prophetie und Predigt im Neuen Testament* (SNT 10; Gütersloh: Gerd Mohn, 1975); F. Hahn, "Die Sendschreiben der Johannesapokalypse. Ein Beitrag zur Bestimmung prophetischer Redeformen," in *Tradition und Glaube: Festgabe K. G. Kuhn* (Göttingen: Vandenhoeck & Ruprecht, 1972) 357–94; W. C. van Unnik, "A Formula Describing Prophecy," *NTS* 9 (1962/63) 86–94.

39. G. Harder, "Eschatologische Schemata in der Johannesapokalypse," *TViat* 9 (1963) 70–87. A thorough study of the use of the OT by the author of Rev. is not available. For older literature on the topic, see, e.g., H. P. Müller, "Die Plagen der Apokalypse," *ZNW* 51 (1960) 268–79. See also my article, "Die tausendjährige Herrschaft der Auferstandenen," *BiLe* 13 (1972) 107–24; J. Lust, "The Order of the Final Events in Revelation and Ezechiel," in *L'Apocalypse johannique,* 179–83; and M. Wilcox, "Tradition and Redaction of Rev. 21, 9—22, 5," ibid., 205–15.

40. See, e.g., D. Georgi, "Die Visionen vom himmlischen Jerusalem in Apk 21 and 22," in *Kirche: Festschrift für Günther Bornkamm zum 75. Geburtstag* (ed. D. Lührmann and G. Strecker; Tübingen: Mohr/Siebeck, 1980) 351–72.

41. P. Prigent, *Apocalypse 12. Histoire de l'exégèse* (BGBE 2; Tübingen: Mohr/Siebeck, 1959). H. Gollinger, *Das grosse Zeichen' von Apokalypse 12* (SBM 11; Stuttgart: Katholisches Bibelwerk, 1971); A. Yarbro Collins, *The Combat Myth in the Book of Revelation* (HDR 9; Missoula, Mont.: Scholars Press, 1976); A. Vögtle, "Mythos und Botschaft in Apokalypse 12," in *Tradition und Glaube,* 395–415.

42. Cf. the discussion of J. L. Blevins, "The Genre of Revelation," *RevExp* 77 (1980) 393–408.

43. Cf. the contributions in *Apocalypticism in the Mediterranean World.* See n. 2, above.

44. Cf. J. J. Collins ("Introduction: Towards the Morphology of a Genre," *Semeia* 14 [1979] 1–20), whose definition is also determinative for the discussion of Rev. by A. Yarbro Collins ("The Early Christian Apocalypses," ibid., 61–121). However, the former's determination of the "master paradigm" or "genre apocalypse" is definitional-contentual rather than literary-formal.

45. Cf. E. Pagels, "Vision, Appearances and Apostolic Authority," in *Gnosis: Festschrift für H. Jonas* (ed. B. Aland; Göttingen: Vandenhoeck & Ruprecht, 1978) 415–30; P. Perkins, "The Apocalypse of Adam: The Genre and Function of a Gnostic Apoca-

lypse," *CBQ* 31 (1977) 382–95; idem, *The Gnostic Dialogue* (New York: Paulist Press, 1980); Y. Janssens, "Apocalypses de Nag Hammadi," in *L'Apocalypse johannique*, 69–75.

46. Cf. E. Schüssler Fiorenza, "The Phenomenon of Early Christian Apocalyptic. Some Reflections on Method," in *Apocalypticism in the Mediterranean World*, 295–316.

47. See chap. 5 of this book, "Apokalypsis and Propheteia." D. E. Aune seems to be in basic agreement with me. See Aune, "The Social Matrix of the Apocalypse of John," *BR* 26 (1981) 16–32, although he misrepresents my argument.

48. A. Satake, *Die Gemeindeordnung in der Johannesapokalypse* (WMANT 21; Neukirchen-Vluyn: Neukirchener, 1966).

49. U. B. Müller, *Zur frühchristlichen Theologiegeschichte: Juden-christentum und Paulinismus in Kleinasien an der Wende vom ersten zum zweiten Jahrhundert n. Chr.* (Gütersloh: Gerd Mohn, 1976).

50. D. Hill, "Prophecy and Prophets in the Revelation of St. John," *NTS* 18 (1971/72) 408–18.

51. Cf. the most recent attempt by O. Böcher to establish the affinity of Rev. and John's Gospel. O. Böcher, "Das Verhältnis der Apokalypse des Johannes zum Evangelium des Johannes," in *L'Apocalypse johannique*, 289–301. However, this study is methodologically deficient because it does not take into account the specific linguistic character of both works and proceeds as if one could liken "apples to pears" just because they can be subsumed under the general heading and classification of "fruit."

52. Cf., e.g., K. M. Fischer, "Die Christlichkeit der Offenbarung des Johannes," *TLZ* (1981) 165–72.

53. A. Vögtle, "Der Gott der Apokalypse," in *La notion biblique de Dieu* (ed. J. Coppens; Louvain: The Univ. Press, 1976) 377–98; C. Rowland, "The Visions of God in Apocalyptic Literature," *JSJ* 10 (1979) 137–54; T. Holtz, "Gott in der Apokalypse," in *L'Apocalypse johannique*, 247–65.

54. T. Holtz, *Die Christologie der Apokalypse des Johannes* (TU; Berlin: Akademie-Verlag, 1971); J. Comblin, *Le Christ dans l'Apocalypse* (Paris: Desclée, 1965); C. Rowland, "The Vision of the Risen Christ in Rev. 1.13ff.," *JTS* 31 (1980) 1–11; R. Baukham, "The Worship of Jesus in Apocalyptic Christianity," *NTS* 27 (1980/81) 322–41; M. de Jonge, "The Use of the Expression *ho christos* in the Apocalypse of John," in *L'Apocalypse johannique*, 267–81.

55. E. Schweizer, "Die siben Geister in der Apokalypse," *EvT* 11 (1951/52) 502–12; F. F. Bruce, "The Spirit in the Apocalypse," in *Christ and the Spirit in the New Testament* (ed. B. Lindars and S. S. Smalley; Cambridge: At the Univ. Press, 1973) 333–44. For a dualistic definition of the relationship between church and world, see Satake, "Kirche und feindliche Welt," in *Kirche*, 329–49; cf. also C. Wolff, "Die Gemeinde des Christus in der Apokalypse des Johannes," *NTS* 27 (1980/81) 186–97.

56. J. Kallas, "The Apocalypse—An Apocalyptic Book?" *JBL* 86 (1967) 69–80; J. J. Collins, "Pseudonymity, Historical Reviews and the Genre of the Revelation of John," *CBQ* 39 (1977) 329–43. See also P. Prigent, "Apocalypse et Apocalyptique," *RSR* 47 (1973) 280–99.

57. L. A. Vos, *The Synoptic Tradition in the Apocalypse* (Kampen: J. H. Kok, 1965); R. Bauckham, "Synoptic Parousia Parables and the Apocalypse," *NTS* 23 (1977) 162–76.

58. See chap. 3 of this book, "The Quest for the Johannine School," on this question. Cf. also P. Prigent, "L'hérésie Asiate et l'église confessante de l'Apocalypse à Ignace," *VC* 31 (1977) 1–22.

59. Kraft, *Die Offenbarung des Johannes*, 7–8.

60. E.g., W. Barclay, *Letters to the Seven Churches* (Nashville: Abingdon Press, 1957); B. Newman, *Rediscovering the Book of Revelation* (Valley Forge, Pa.: Judson Press, 1968). The results of C. J. Hemer's work ("A Study of the Letters to the Seven Churches of Asia with Special Reference to their Local Background" [Diss., Univ. of Manchester, 1969]) were published as "Unto the Angels of the Churches," *Buried History* 11 (1975) 4–27, 56–83, 110–35, 164–90. Cf. also J. Lähnemann, "Die sieben Sendschreiben in der Johannesapokalypse," in *Studien zur Religion und Kultur Kleinasiens: Festschrift Dorner* (ed. Sahin, Schwertheim, and Wagner; Leiden: E. J. Brill, 1978) 2: 516–39.

61. S. E. Johnson, "Asia Minor and Early Christianity," in *Christianity, Judaism, and Other Greco-Roman Cults* (ed. J. Neusner; Leiden: E. J. Brill, 1975) 2: 77–144.

62. A. T. Kraabel, "Judaism in Western Asia Minor under the Roman Empire with a Preliminary Study of the Jewish Community at Sardis" (Diss.; Harvard Univ., 1968); idem, "The Diaspora Synagogue: Archeological and Epigraphic Evidence Since Sukenik," *ANRW* II.19.1 (1979) 477–510.

63. Cf. E. Stauffer, *Christ and the Caesars: Historical Sketches* (trans. K. Gregor Smith and R. Gregor Smith; Philadelphia: Westminster Press; London: SCM Press, 1955); P. Prigent, "Au temps de l'Apocalypse: I. Domitien; II. Le Culte Impérial au 1er Siècle en Asia Mineure; III. Pourquoi les persécutions?" *RHPR* 54 (1974) 455–83 (= I); 55 (1975) 215–35 (= II), 341–63 (= III).

64. W. M. Ramsay, *The Letters to the Seven Churches of Asia* (London: Hodder & Stoughton, 1904). See also the popular book of E. Yamauchi, *The Archeology of New Testament Cities in Western Asia Minor* (Grand Rapids: Baker Book House, 1980).

65. Cf. the review of the discussion by P. Keresztes, "The Imperial Roman Government and the Christian Church," *ANRW* II.23 (1979) 247–315; K. Aland, "Das Verhältnis von Kirche und Staat in der Frühzeit," *ANRW* II.23 (1979) 60–246.

66. For a careful recent discussion, cf. A. Yarbro Collins, "Dating the Apocalypse of John," *BR* 26 (1981) 33–45.

67. A. A. Bell, "The Date of John's Apocalypse," *NTS* 25 (1978) 93–102.

68. J. A. T. Robinson, *Redating the New Testament* (Philadelphia: Westminster Press; London: SCM Press, 1976).

69. J. P. M. Sweet, *Revelation*, 27.

70. H. D. Saffrey, "Relire l'Apocalypse à Patmos," *RB* 82 (1975) 384–417.

71. E.g., A. Strobel, "Abfassung und Geschichtstheologie der Apokalypse nach Kap. 17, 9–12," *NTS* 10 (1963/64) 433–45; B. Reicke, "Die jüdische Apokalyptik und die johanneische Tiervision," *RSR* 60 (1972) 173–92; for discussion and review of the question, see now A. Yarbro Collins, "Dating the Apocalypse," 35–36.

72. Lohmeyer, "Die Offenbarung des Johannes 1920–1934," 271.

73. J. Ellul, *Apocalypse: The Book of Revelation* (New York: Seabury Press, 1977). Cf. my critical review, *Horizons* 5 (1978) 263–64, and that of A. Yarbro Collins, *CBQ* 40 (1978) 269–70. For a more positive assessment, see J. Megivern, "Jacques Ellul's Apocalypse," *BTB* 11 (1981) 125–28.

74. J. Calloud, J. Delorme, and J. Duplantier, "L'Apocalypse de Jean. Propositions pour une analyse structurale," *Apocalypses et théologie de l'espérance*, 351–81; P. Prigent, "L'Apocalypse. Exégèse Historique et Analyse Structurale," *NTS* 26 (1980) 127–37.

75. For a careful discussion of the literature and a new proposal, see J. Lambrecht, "A Structuration of Rev. 4, 1—22, 5," in *L'Apocalypse johannique*, 77–104; see also F. Hahn, "Zum Aufbau der Johannesoffenbarung," in *Kirche und Bibel: Festgabe für Bischof E. Schick)* (Paderborn: Schöningh, 1979) 145–54.

76. While Lambrecht ("A Structuration") does not integrate the messages in his "structuration" of the book, L. Hartman ("Form and Message. A Preliminary Discussion of 'Partial Texts' in Rev. 1—3 and 22, 6ff," in *L'Apocalypse johannique*, 129–49) presents a text-linguistic analysis and proposes that the seven messages have a double function in the composition: they both involve the reader/listener and present the situation which the following visions address (143–44).

77. G. Bornkamm, "Die Komposition der apokalyptischen Visionen in der Offenbarung Johannis," in *Studien zu Antike und Christentum: Gesammelte Aufsätze* (BEvT 28; Munich: Chr. Kaiser, 1959) 2:204–22; A. Yarbro Collins, *Combat Myth*, 19–32, and her summary statement in "Revelation 18: Taunt-Song or Dirge?" in *L'Apocalypse johannique*, 185–204, esp. 188–92.

78. For a fuller discussion, see chap. 6 of this book: "Composition and Structure of Revelation."

79. U. Vanni, *La Struttura letteraria dell' Apocalisse* (Aloisiana 8; Rome: Herder, 1971) 71.

80. Cf. W. Foerster, "Bemerkungen zur Bildersprache der Offenbarung Johannes," in *Verborum Veritas: Festschrift G. Stählin* (ed. O. Böcher and K. Haaker; Wuppertal: Brockhaus, 1970) 225–36; J. M. Court, *Myth and History in the Book of Revelation* (London: SPCK, 1979).

81. J. M. Schmid, *Die jüdische Apokalyptik: Die Geschichte ihrer Erforschung von den Anfängen bis zu den Textfunden in Qumran* (Neukirchen-Vluyn: Neukirchener, 1969) 87–97. See also chap. 7 of this book, "Visionary Rhetoric," for a more detailed argument.

82. Cf. A. Farrer, *A Rebirth of Images* (London: Dacre Press, 1949); R. Halver, *Der Mythos im letzten Buch der Bibel* (Hamburg: Reich, 1965); H. Schlier, "Zum Verständnis der Geschichte nach der Offenbarung des Johannes," in *Die Zeit der Kirche* (Freiburg: Herder, 1956) 265–74; P. Prigent, "Pour une théologie de l'image: Les visions de l'Apocalypse," *RHPR* 59 (1979) 373–78.

83. Cf. my position in "Religion und Politik in der Offenbarung des Johannes," in *Biblische Randbemerkungen: Schülerfestschrift Schnackenburg* (Würzburg: Echter, 1974) 261–71. See also my books *Priester für Gott* and *Invitation to the Book of Revelation* for a fuller elaboration. P. Prigent ("Le temps et le Royaume dans l'Apocalypse," in *L'Apocalypse johannique*, 231–45) seems not to be aware of my work since he does not refer to it.

84. For the difference between the political perspective of the Zealots and that of John, see W. Klassen, "Vengeance in the Apocalypse of John," *CBQ* 28 (1966) 300–311, and A. Yarbro Collins, "The Political Perspective of the Revelation of John," *JBL* 96 (1977) 241–56.

85. See also H. W. Günther. *Der Nah- und Enderwartungschorizont in der Apokalypse des heiligen Johannes* (Würzburg: Echter, 1980); P. Lampe, "Die Apokalyptiker—Ihre Situation und ihr Handeln," in *Eschatologie und Friedenshandeln: Exegetische Beiträge zur Frage christlicher Friedensverantwortung* (ed. U. Luz; SBS 101; Stuttgart: Katholisches Bibelwerk, 1981) 59–114.

86. D. H. Lawrence, *Apocalypse* (Baltimore: Penguin Books, 1976); A. Yarbro Collins, "Persecution and Vengeance in the Book of Revelation," in *Apocalypticism in the Mediterranean World*, 729–50.

87. See especially the contributions in *Orientation by Disorientation. Studies in Literary Criticism and Biblical Literary Criticism. Presented in Honor of W. A. Beardslee*

(ed. R. A. Spencer; PTMS 53; Pittsburgh: Pickwick Press, 1980); E. Schüssler Fiorenza, "Contemporary Biblical Scholarship: Its Roots, Present Understandings, and Future Directions," in *Modern Biblical Scholarship. Its Impact on Theology and Proclamation* (ed. F. Eigo; Villanova, Pa.: Villanova Univ. Press, 1984).

88. See my *Invitation to the Book of Revelation,* especially the introduction.

PART ONE

THEOLOGICAL PERSPECTIVES AND FRAMEWORKS

1
History and Eschatology
in Revelation

The Book of Rev. was written in the form of a circular letter[1] whose sender and recipients, in contrast with Jewish apocalyptic writings, are explicitly named. Rev. 1:1–3 serves as a superscription and a prologue to the whole letter; the following vv. 4–6 contain the epistolary introduction (*praescriptio*) in a fully developed, stylized form which is similar to the address of ancient letters. The salutation is also similar to the Pauline form as it is expanded in Rom. and Gal.[2] Moreover, it closes with a doxology to Christ (v. 6b). Like the opening *praescriptio* the concluding greetings[3] have a strong liturgical character in their form and terminology. They reaffirm the reliability and authority of the writer's prophetic words and indicate the source of his authority and the intention behind his message.[4] In contrast with Jewish apocalyptic writings, therefore, Rev. is not an esoteric secret work: John receives the command not to seal the book (22:20), which is to be read in the liturgical service (1:3).[5]

For the average Christian, however, Rev. has remained a book with "seven seals" and an "esoteric revelation"—despite its explicit claim to be the revelation of Jesus Christ for Christian communities (1:1). Moreover, the present-day biblical scholar seems to experience the same perplexity as the average Christian. Despite all scholarly efforts, no generally recognized or accepted consensus[6] has been reached in regard to the composition and the theological interpretation of the book. E. Lohmeyer's judgment in 1934 on the results of studies on Rev. remains true today: "There are few primitive Christian writings which as a whole and in detail have received so much attention and yet seem to remain untouched in regard to the secret of their meaning and history."[7] This statement is exemplified by the variety of proposals and solutions offered by scholarly research on Rev. both in the past and present.[8] Besides the fundamentalist view, which assumes that John wrote the whole book either during or after his visions,[9] analyses based on literary criticism[10] and the history of traditions maintain that Rev. is composed of small written or oral units of previous traditions. This critical position attempts to solve the logical difficulties and the obscurity of the composition with its transitions and connections, repetitions and cross references, by presuming different sources or traditional schemata which a later redactor put together more or less skillfully.[11] Today, however, most exegetes assume that Rev. is "as a whole a work of strict composition and of magnificent completeness."[12] This is demonstrated by the uniformity of the vocabulary and style as well as by the unity of its theological conception and the force of its argumentation. John does, indeed, borrow his material from the traditions of his time, especially from Jewish apocalyptic theology, but he works it into an independent literary form and a personal theological conception.[13] The double literary character of Rev. originates, thereby, from the author's independent use of available materials. On the one hand, Rev. appears as an artistic mosaic and on the other hand, as an artificial construction. As a result, Rev. is a great drama[14] of poetical conciseness into which material from the OT,[15] Jewish apocalyptic, and mythological sources[16] has been worked.

A general consensus exists among scholars only as to the purpose of the book: the author seeks to give courage and perseverance to Christians threatened by persecution insofar as he refers to the nearness of the final eschatological salvation. In the following pages the relationship between the literary composition and the theological purpose of Rev. will be examined in an attempt to show how its ecclesiology and its eschatology determine the literary structure of the book.

HISTORY AS
MATERIAL AND FORMAL PRINCIPLE OF
THE INTERPRETATION OF REVELATION

Although Rev. is full of eschatological images and sayings, previous scholars have nevertheless considered and developed history rather than eschatology as the main motive and formal structural principle of the book. The *kirchengeschichtlich* (history of the church) as well as the *zeitgeschichtlich* (history contemporary to the author) and *endgeschichtlich* (final history) interpretations[17] of Rev. are based on the presupposition that the book intends to say something primarily about historical events and to make possible their theological ordering and interpretation. According to the *kirchengeschichtlich* interpretation Rev. presents "a picture of the things that are to come until the end of history from the viewpoint of the Church of Christ." What Rev. "pictures in a symbolic-logical manner finds its correspondence, therefore, in the process of history for the time and Church of John as well as for the following times."[18]

Even the *endgeschichtlich* interpretation,[19] which makes the "eschata" the principle of its interpretation, remains caught in this historical problematic, when it sees in Rev. a description of the sequence of real events which will occur at the end of the world.

Contemporary scholars no longer dream of finding predictions for history or for the future within Rev. They correctly reject, therefore, those interpretations maintaining that Rev. treats the history of the Church, of the world, and of the final times. However, they still retain—as I will argue here—the basic approach and concern of these interpretations insofar as they attempt to show that history is the main theme of Rev. and try to establish it as revelation for our time. Whereas the *zeitgeschichtlich* interpretation understands Rev. as an historical book located within and relevant to the time in which it was written, the *geschichtstheologisch* (theology of history) and the *heilsgeschichtlich* (salvation history) interpretation seek to show what enduring valid truth concerning history is revealed in the visions of John, be it the truth of the world or the truth of the new people of God.[20] Although both methods of interpretation emphasize eschatology, they nevertheless accept history and not eschatology as their fundamental principle of interpretation.[21] On the one hand, they aim to work out a chronological and historical sequence[22] for the visions insofar as they understand the visions concerning final salvation which interrupt the temporal sequence of the apocalyptic events as proleptic in character. On the other hand, they construct a chronology insofar as they try to demonstrate that John understands the history of his time from the perspective of the history of Israel. Consequently, they maintain that this perspective determines the structure of the book.[23] Both interpretations presuppose, therefore, that Rev. describes a continuous way of history from the beginning of the Church to the end of time.[24]

THE PRETERIST INTERPRETATION
OF REVELATION

The consistent *zeitgeschichtlich* interpretation, which has been especially prevalent in France,[25] not only discovers historical references to the author's time in Rev. 2—3 and 12—18, but also attempts to chart a temporal sequence of events for the entire book and its composition. It seeks to rediscover and to reconstruct in Rev. a consecutive history of the primitive church, whereby it connects this "historical" definition of the book with an eschatological and ecclesiological interpretation. According to this view John points to the immediate past or present history of the Christian community to show that the final time has already been inaugurated and is realizing itself in the present. Just as God has acted in the past, so, too, God will destroy the enemies of the church in the eschatological future. The history of the Christian community thereby becomes something which can be surveyed and from which the future can be derived. An example of such a *zeitgeschichtlich* interpretation is the attempt made by M. Hopkins[26] in relying upon A. Feuillet. Hopkins believes that previous interpretations of Rev. have gone in false directions because they have not sufficiently taken into account the factor of the *genus litterarium* (i.e., the genre) of Rev. in determining the structure of the book. "That factor is the historical perspective with a consequent pre-dating of certain events. By this I mean the inclusion of a segment of past history to inspire confidence and thus to serve as a spring board from which to launch the apocalyptic prognostication."[27] According to Hopkins the first eleven chapters of Rev. describe the triumph of the Church over Judaism, so that the author may then assert "that Rome, too, will fail to stamp out the infant Church."[28]

Feuillet,[29] who has developed the basis for such a theological-historical conception of Rev., has expressly raised the question of the book's eschatology and its presuppositions. He has reached the conclusion that Rev. has the same *heilsgeschichtlich* conception which Conzelmann[30] has worked out for the Gospel of Luke. According to this interpretation Luke distinguished more clearly than Mark and Matthew the individual divisions of salvation history. The "time of Israel" is followed by the "time of Christ" and then by the "time of the church." Since the author of Rev. has not written a gospel, he has not given an exposition of the time of Christ. Nevertheless he does differentiate between the time of Israel and the time of the church, insofar as he presents a description of the divine judgment at the end of his outline of both periods of time. The first and prophetical section of Rev. (chaps. 4—11) is therefore, according to Feuillet, an explicit reference to the events described in Luke 21. The theological explication of John is, in Feuillet's view, based on historical events.[31] In order to understand better Feuillet's proposal, it is helpful to refer to Conzelmann's outline of the end time in Luke 21.[32]

The strongest motif in the Lucan presentation (Luke 21) of the final events is, in Conzelmann's interpretation, the delay of the Parousia, which has led to a reflection on the nature and course of salvation history. Instead of the immediate expectation of the end time, Luke develops the notion of successive stages of salvation history.[33] According to Conzelmann, Luke's outline of the course of the final events indicates that the imminent expectation of the end time no longer plays a constitutive role for him; the Lucan presentation is therefore only apparently similar to that of Mark. The temporal reconstruction which Luke undertakes becomes evident in his change of Mark's account. Whereas in Mark 13 the disciples ask about the eschatological fulfillment of time (13:4:

tauta synteleisthai panta) Luke changes the formulation of the question to *tauta ginesthai* (21:7), whereby the *tauta* refers to all the events described in the speech. Furthermore the various temporal references in Luke 21 (v. 9: *prōton, ou eutheōs*; v. 12: *pro de toutōn*) are used to provide a different temporal division from that of the Marcan text.[34] In regard to the contents Luke presupposes that the fall of Jerusalem predicted in Mark 13:14–17 has already taken place, whereas the terrible signs and events (Luke 21:11) are yet to come. From the very beginning Luke concentrates the attention of the reader on these two facts insofar as he connects the question of the disciples with the prophetical threat against the temple (Luke 21:5–6). In particular, it is possible to establish the following sequence of eschatological events in Luke.[35]

1. False announcement of the end (v. 8);
2. Wars and insurrections which hint at the Jewish uprising (v. 9);
3. Siege and destruction of Jerusalem. Judgment upon Israel (v. 24);
4. The disciples are brought before judgment (vv. 12–19). [Here the present time of Luke is reached.]

5. Nation vs. nation; signs in heaven (vv. 10–11; these are taken up again in v. 25);
6. Appearance of the "Son of man" (vv. 27–28) who, however, is not accompanied by angels. The apocalyptic description of the events of the Parousia is reduced in Luke. It is noteworthy that the cosmic crisis does not harm the elect, but brings them liberation (vv. 28, 29–31).

The discourse ends with the warning to be watchful (vv. 34–36).

The affinity of Luke's approach—as proposed by Conzelmann and accepted without question by Feuillet—with Jewish apocalyptic theology is clear. The latter is said to be concerned with history as a closed and exactly divided totality, which the seer can survey.[36] Jewish apocalypses[37] of history describe history constantly as a totality. They do not, of course, give concrete historical data nor do they describe history as a continuous homogeneous process, but rather they use mythological images and divide history into sharply separated periods and segments of time. The reader discerns precisely through these mythological images the meaning of history, its unity, and goal.[38] A good example of this is the "Apocalypse of Weeks" (Book of *Enoch* 93:3–9 and 91:12–17) which divides the whole of history into ten periods; seven of these describe history in its process, and three the eschatological event.

1. I was born the seventh in the first week,
   . . . [alleged viewpoint of the seer].
2. And after me there shall arise in the second week great wickedness,
   . . . [deluge, Noah].

3. And after that in the third week at its close
   A man shall be elected as the plant of righteous judgment,
   . . . [Abraham].
4. And after that in the fourth week, at its close,
   Visions of the holy and righteous shall be seen,
   . . . [Exodus].
5. And after that in the fifth week, at its close,
   The house of glory and dominion shall be built for ever [Temple].
6. And after that in the sixth week all who live in it shall be blinded,
   . . . [division of kingdom].
7. And after that in the seventh week shall an apostate generation arise,
   . . . [here is the *present time* of the author].

8. And after that there shall be another, the eighth week, that of righteousness,
   And a sword shall be given to it that a righteous judgment may be executed on the oppressors,
   . . . [beginning of the eschatological event].
9. And after that, in the ninth week, the righteous judgment shall be revealed to the whole world,
   . . . [judgment against the godless].
10. And after that, in the tenth week in the seventh part.
    There shall be the great eternal judgment,
    . . . [vengeance against angels, new heaven].
    And after that there will be many weeks without number for ever,
    And all shall be in goodness and righteousness,
    . . . .[39]

In this Jewish apocalypse from the flood to the eschatological events, the history of Israel is presented in mythological images, and the present and future are understood and deduced from the past.[40] E. Lohmeyer has called attention to the deeper reason for this historical and futuristic conception of some Jewish apocalyptical writings. According to him Jews understood themselves both as a historical-national unity and as an eschatological people of God. The two aspects belong inseparably together and become evident in their conception of history and eschatology.[41] Therefore, when Jewish apocalyptic writers wanted to prove the correctness of their prophecy[42] for the future, they could do so by establishing the connection between future events and past "salvation history." In Jewish apocalypticism this was generally accomplished when authors placed themselves, with the help of a pseudonym,[43] at the beginning of the history which they would relate in such a way that they could depict past history as future history. In such a manner he corroborated their claim that, just as past history has occurred according to God's plan, so too will the eschatological promises be fulfilled.

To sum up, the following can be established: the *zeitgeschichtlich* or preterist interpretation of Rev. proposed here by Hopkins and Feuillet, the outline of the "Apocalypse of Weeks," and the conception of salvation history as proposed by Conzelmann for Luke formally agree with one another in that they portray past history which has already occurred as future history which is to come. In such a unified conception of history they place their own present time as a future time. The past and present are thus understood as having an inner unity, which as a necessary, periodic, and successive course, is placed in distinction to the eschatological future. The reason for the suffering[44] of God's people in the present time is explained with reference to a divine plan for history. The present is a time of hardship because it is the close of the time of this world, after which will follow the coming eon.[45] Such a portrayal of history, in which past events are portrayed as future events is based on pre-dating,[46] which is achieved with the help of pseudonymity. The Ethiopian Book of *Enoch* as well as other Jewish apocalyptic writings are capable of portraying the past history of their people in the form of future events because their authors have given up their own historical standpoints and have placed themselves with the help of pseudonyms at the beginning of the depicted historical sequence. Even the presentation of Luke (as outlined by Conzelmann) is based upon this device of pre-dating insofar as Luke places in the mouth of Jesus predictions about events in Jerusalem which had already taken place in Luke's time.[47]

But, in contrast to other Jewish and Christian apocalypses, Rev. is not written under a pseudonym;[48] its author and recipients are explicitly named. The writer describes himself simply without any other epithet as "the servant of Jesus Christ," and he belongs to the same historical time and situation as the recipients. He is their "brother and companion in the tribulation, in the kingdom and in waiting for Jesus" (Rev. 1:9).[49] Like that of the Christian communities of Asia Minor his present situation is a time of persecution and eschatological tribulation.

Despite these clear statements of Rev., Feuillet tries to support his own theory by attempting to prove the author's use of the literary fiction of pre-dating and of pseudonymity. According to him the first four of the eight rulers mentioned in Rev. 17:9–12[50] were Augustus, Tiberius, Caligula, and Claudius. The fifth is Nero; the sixth who is now ruling is Titus and the beast, "who was and is not," Domitian. If Feuillet's interpretation of this difficult passage were correct, then the author who wrote in the time of Domitian pre-dated his work to the time of Vespasian so that he could describe both the fall of Jerusalem and that of Rome as future events.

Against this interpretation A. Strobel[51] has pointed out that the assumption of Domitian as the antichrist contradicts the clearly future-directed sense of the passage. Moreover, as Strobel has argued the seer could not possibly have been interested in a presentation of the succession of Roman emperors because the turning-point in world history is for him neither the beginning of the Roman principate nor the golden age of Augustus, but rather the death and resurrection of Christ. "For the apocalyptic writer the cross and resurrection signify both the *telos* of the old eon and at the same time its eminent historical meaning. Everything which happens after (the cross and resurrection) and up to the time (of the apocalyptic writer) is presented as an eschatological appendix and remnant."[52] Strobel begins his enumeration, therefore, with the first emperor who came to power after the death of Christ, namely, Caligula. This enumeration also accounts for *epesan* ("they fell," 17:10),[53] because Caligula was murdered, Claudius was poisoned, and Nero committed suicide; Vespasian and Titus died of fevers. The sixth, presently ruling emperor is then to be identified as Domitian, who was reigning, according to the tradition of the early church,[54] when Rev. was written.

Strobel's interpretation finds its strongest support in Rev. itself, which, on the one hand, has the final time begin with the exaltation of Christ (5:6; 12:5)[55] and, on the other hand, always emphasizes that the time until the end is only "short." For these reasons Feuillet's thesis of the pre-dating of Rev. is untenable. Since pseudonymity and pre-dating constitute the presuppositions of an apocalyptic outline of history, their absence in Rev. deprives every temporal-developmental interpretation of the book of its main support and condition. This does not mean that Rev. has no *zeitgeschichtlich* references whatsoever. These references allow us to see the *Sitz im Leben* of the book; they are, however, not determining the sequence and structure of Rev. in a temporal sense. The author does not aim to present a historical sequence; nor does he seek to justify and deduce the future from history. Rather he understands his book as a prophecy for the present[56] which receives its justification from the future, that is, from the coming of Christ (22:20).[57]

THE GESCHICHTSTHEOLOGISCH INTERPRETATIONS OF REVELATION

Since the consistent *zeitgeschichtlich* interpretation stresses the historical principle and content of Rev., it runs into the danger of neglecting the theological relevance of the book for our present time. The *geschichtstheologisch* interpretations, which center on a philosophy of history, or on an eschatological principle, or on "salvation history," seek to avoid this danger. For although they take seriously the results of the history of traditions and of comparative historical research, they search behind the historical events for that theological truth of the book relevant even for the present time.

First, the *geschichtsphilosophisch* (historical-philosophical) interpretation of Rev. searches for the "fundamental truth"[58] contained in the book. It seeks, thereby, to establish the enduring validity of its revelations. Since "Rev. is the only book whose theme is history, it has an especially inspired insight into history."[59] Although the author displays this history before human eyes, it fundamentally hides its meaning.[60] What this history means can only be learned by a spiritual penetration of history, that is, by an understanding in faith of a vision which transcends history. The true insight into history, therefore, depends upon the "pre-judgment" and the "pre-decision" of faith. According to this *geschichtsphilosophisch* interpretation the seer perceives history as the "process" of critical truth in general and as the paradigm of his own history.

Thus history does not simply repeat itself. "But in the different historical events of various times the same thing respectively takes place. Imperial Rome can be seen as representing the one cruel and drunken world-city of all times."[61] Thus from his examination of his present time, the author of Rev. derives judgments on history in general and a total viewpoint as to the process and goal of history.

Since the visions of Rev. are an expression of a great and everlasting truth, they are always realized more or less clearly in the vast field of human history.[62] The book, therefore, is the prophetic charter of the dialogue which God carries on with humanity in world history.[63] The visions and images of Rev. are types of what lies "behind" the history of the world and what constitutes the meaning of all history. This conception of history, which, however, "only '*cum grano salis*' can be thought of as a 'philosophy of history,'"[64] places the author of Rev. within a broad but related tradition. His "view of history in all its details has its roots in the Old Testament; Jewish apocalyptic provided the trunk; the gospel of Christ and primitive Christian faith provided the crowning tree-top."[65] Against this *geschichtsphilosophisch* interpretation, E. Lohmeyer[66] already has validly pointed out that the author of Rev. was not concerned with the meaning of history but with the apocalyptic judgment of God over the world. It is not legitimate, therefore, to reinterpret the eschatological faith of Rev. into a philosophy or theology of history, even if it seems to be unavoidable for Western thinking since Augustine.[67]

Second, Lohmeyer[68] has attempted to make eschatology and an eschatological understanding of time the principle of his interpretation. For him the boundaries of time are abolished in an eschatological perspective, so that the eschatological future has already become present for believers. Lohmeyer maintains that eschatology as God's judgment is only necessary for the world but not for the Christian community. The end time has significance for the Christian community only as the final manifestation of what has been accomplished in the death of Christ and of what exists from eternity. Since eschatological judgment does not intervene in the eternal relationship of God and Christ with the faithful, every eschatological event becomes a *timeless* event that "was, is, and will come." "Past and future are equally exchangeable because both are dissolved (*aufgehoben*) in the eternity of God and Christ."[69] The composition and eschatological vision of Rev. reveal, therefore, the timelessness of every event in the past and present in "future images." Eschatology is for Lohmeyer the mirror of a tradition traversing all times and the disclosure of what has been determined in this tradition.[70]

Lohmeyer's position represents a progress over other interpretations insofar as it brings eschatology into focus and argues that the community and not world history forms the main reference point of the eschatological perspective in Rev. However, against Lohmeyer's position, T. Holtz has correctly maintained that it negates the worldly and temporal character of the Christian community.[71] If salvation is understood as presently realized in the Christian community, then this community stands above world and time and not within them. Holtz argues that this conception "is basically the 'Greek' approach to the solution of the problem."[72] Lohmeyer remains imprisoned, therefore, in the problematic of the "historical" interpretation when he defines eschatology as "above-timeness" (*Überzeitlichkeit*).

Third, Holtz in turn proposes a Christian *heilsgeschichtlich* understanding of Rev. which is characterized by a dialectical tension between the "already" and "not yet" of salvation. For him the understanding of salvation in Rev. is a combination of the gnostic view of salvation as something above time and history on the one hand and the OT and apocalyptic view on the other hand, which, due to its conception of time as linear, places all salvation in the future at the end of time. "A correct understanding of Rev. depends upon the combination of historical limitation and believed perfection."[73] According to Holtz, Rev. considers the glorification of the Christian community and the victory over the evil powers as having essentially taken place; the eternity of the New Jerusalem is already present. But Rev. also preserves undiminished the "historical" temporal aspect. The Christian community is as a "community underway" threatened by defection and lukewarmness, as well as by the powers opposed to God who desire to destroy it. So until the judgment and Parousia the church too must remain in a temporal mode of existence, which is determined through the "not yet" of the complete perfection and consummation. Holtz accurately stresses that Rev. views salvation as already present in the redemption through Christ, but at the same time final salvation is still to be awaited by the church. This dialectic of the Christian understanding of salvation is not to be dissolved in favor of one aspect.[74]

In my opinion, however, it is questionable whether a unifying center[75] connecting and relating both aspects can be found in the concept of history. If Holtz thinks that the two propositions of faith (the "already" and the "not yet"), whose "contents are so far apart from one another," can find their unity in their "strict reference to history,"[76] then he overlooks that the "already" of the exaltation of the Christian community is not present historically but only eschatologically. The "temporality" of the New Jerusalem, that is, its eternity, is precisely "not yet" present to the Christian community while it lives in time and in the world. The community is, indeed, redeemed, but is precisely as the redeemed community still bound to temporality and worldliness. It can by no means be sure of its salvation and victory. Not the whole community, but only the victorious, those who have overcome the "great tribulation" (Rev. 7:14) and have not worshiped the beast and his image (20:4–6) will have a share in the "temporality" of the New Jerusalem.[77] Only then will those be "exalted" and "glorified" who through redemption already stand under the power of God and the Lamb. Only when Christ has successfully established his heavenly reign on earth will the community participate in his "exaltation" and reign (20:4–6; 22:5). Likewise the reign of Satan has been broken only "in heaven." He can reign over the earth, however, for "a little while." Therefore, the Christian community is "not only placed now in the flux of the development of salvation history," but also remains, like the world, subject to judgment, since "a whole community" can be rejected by Christ (3:5). In other words: while the "already" of Christ's exaltation has occurred in history, the exaltation of the Christian community has "not yet" taken place,[78] since it, unlike Christ, is not yet victorious. The community is, indeed, already under the reign of God, but this reign over the earth will be actively exercised only in the eschatological future.

The question remains to be examined anew: how does the "already" relate to the "not yet" in Rev. so that the temporal and worldly character of the Church is not diminished by considering the eschatological future as a mere manifestation or uncovering of what has already been realized in the present? Now we will attempt to answer this question and to explicate the relationship between the eschatology of Rev. and its composition.

ESCHATOLOGY AS THE PROPER HORIZON
FOR THE UNDERSTANDING
OF REVELATION

The above survey has briefly indicated that previous research on Rev. has generally made the concept of history the formal and material principle of its interpretation. It has presupposed that the author's concern with history has determined the structure of the book. The proponents of this interpretation seek to trace in the sequence of visions a continuous or dialectical line of history. That John wanted to portray the temporal course of events of the end time is even maintained by the *endgeschichtlich* interpretation. However, previous attempts to explain the sequence of visions or the total composition of Rev. either by a linear or cyclic understanding[79] of time have not succeeded in presenting a convincing interpretation, as a quick glance at the variety and multiplicity of proposed solutions[80] can reveal. The central apocalyptic section (4:1–22:5), in particular, creates difficulties for these successive temporal interpretations, because here the author mixes together past, present, and future elements of time. His doublets and his repetition of an entire cycle of visions cannot be satisfactorily explained as a temporal or historical sequence.

If Rev. is not structured according to a "temporal-historical" sequence, then the question arises: are not its contents instead thematically ordered?[81] Hence, I would argue that the main concern of Rev. is not (salvation) history, but eschatology, that is, the breaking-in of God's kingdom[82] and the destruction of the hostile godless powers. The author of Rev. is, indeed, aware of time, but he knows only a "short time" before the eschaton. The eschatology of Rev. is, therefore, not dependent on or legitimated by a certain course of historical events. Rather, time and history have significance only insofar as they constitute the "little while" before the end.[83] This means that in Rev. "history" is completely subordinated to eschatology and receives its significance from the future.[84] Thus it is necessary to analyze the eschatological understanding underlying Rev. and its composition and to explicate how this echatological understanding is related to the central purpose of the book, which is to strengthen and to encourage the Christian communities of Asia Minor.[85]

The Eschatological Expectation of Revelation[86]

The author of Rev. explicitly asks about the time before the final judgment and the measure of its length. In 6:9–11 the souls[87] under the altar, slain for their witness to God's work,[88] cry out:[89] "O Sovereign Lord, holy and true, how long before you will judge and avenge our blood on those who dwell on earth?" They are told that they should wait just a little longer until the number of their fellow servants and their "brethren" who are still to be killed is complete.[90]

1. The Execution of Judgment as the Vindication of the Christian Community. We should note that in Rev. 6:9–11 the author does not ask about the meaning of history and its temporal sequence, but rather about the meaning of the present situation of the community and the date of God's judgment on those dwelling on earth.[91] These are, for the seer, always on the side of the forces hostile to God and to the Christian communities. The description of God's judgment[92] takes up such a large space in Rev. that its whole eschatological presentation culminates in judgment and salvation. Just as the seven visions of the plagues and the "small scroll" climax in an announcement or a portrayal of judgment, so does the whole book. Its apocalyptic section in chaps. 17—20 is concluded with a description of the great harlot's judgment (17—18), with the Parousia of Christ (19:11–21), and with the destruction of the dragon (20:1–3, 7–10). The end events consist of the great world-judgment of all persons according to their works (20:11–13) and of the destruction of Death and Hades (20:14–15). Rev. does not describe, therefore, a continuous development of events from the beginning to the final eschatological judgment and salvation. Rather Rev. consists of pieces or mosaic stones arranged in a certain design, which climaxes in a description of the final eschatological event.[93] The goal and high point of the composition of the whole book, as of the individual "little apocalypses," is the final judgment and the eschatological salvation.

With its judicial terminology the language of Rev. also places emphasis upon judgment. The imminent date set by God for the end is the *kairos* of the judgment of the dead; it is the time of the destruction of those who destroy the earth (11:18). This judgment takes place on the great day[94] of God's wrath (6:17; 16:14); on this day the eschatological "war"[95] between the demonic powers and the Christian community reaches its climax. The eschatological anger of the devil (12:17) and of the nations (11:18) will then be destroyed by God's wrath. In ever new catastrophes[96] the wrath of God is poured out: with the opening of the seven seals (chap. 6), with the blasting of the last trumpet (11:15–18), with the wine of wrath (14:10), with each of the seven bowls of wrath (chaps. 15—16), with the judgment of Babylon (16:19) and with the Parousia of Christ, who himself will tread the wine-press of God's wrath (19:15). All nations (11:18; 14:8; 18:3; 19:15), all ranks (18:9–20), the whole earth (14:9–11), and especially Babylon, the political embodiment of godless power (14:8; 16:9; 17—18) will be smitten. In the "hour of trial which is coming on the whole world" (3:10)[97] only the Christian community will be saved (7:1–8; 11:1–2). In the hour of judgment (14:7) God will finally fulfill the pleas of the martyrs, will avenge the blood of his servants (19:2) and will execute their legal claim (18:20). The Christian community longs for this judgment since its suffering will then be transformed into joy and its oppression into glory. It knows that Christ judges "in righteousness" (19:11) and that God's judgments are "true and just" (16:7).[98]

Since the suffering of the Christian community will find its end and "vindication"[99] only in the judgment of God, the souls of those slain for the word of God seek by their crying-out (6:9) and the living Christian community seeks by its prayers to hasten the final judgment on the world (8:3–5). The death and suffering of the martyrs can be vindicated only through the final judgment because only then will the injustice of the persecuting powers be revealed. Only when the kingdom of God has been established in the cosmos and only when the "great tribulation"[100] has been successfully endured will there be no more hunger, nor thirst, nor persecution, nor grief (7:16–17), but life and rule with God and with the Lamb (22:1–5). The Christian community's situation of suffering demands and determines, in Rev., God's judgment. The question that troubles the author is not that of the meaning of history but rather that of the meaning and termination of the Christian community's suffering. This question is not solved by referring to history (i.e., by arguing that as God has acted in the past, so will God act now) but rather by referring to the future (i.e., by arguing that as God now rules in heaven, so will God rule on earth). Eschatology and ecclesiology are in the theology of Rev. very closely related.[101]

2. The Date or Time of Judgment. To the question of the slain witnesses about the date or time of judgment is given a twofold answer: on the one hand, they are to wait just a "little while," and on the other hand, the persecution of the Christian community is based upon God's will. Both question and answer appear at first glance to correspond to those of Jewish apocalyptic theology which also has questions about the time of the end. *4 Esdras,* for example, refers to the historical plan of God: "For he has weighed the age in the balance, / And with measure has measured the times, / And by number has numbered the seasons: / Neither will he move nor stir things, / till the measure appointed be fulfilled" (*4 Esdras* 4:36–37).[102] In contrast to *4 Esdras,* Rev. 6:11 asserts that the time is "short." Instead of a divine plan of historical events the author of Rev. introduces the imminent expectation.[103]

John does not intend to show as in Dan. 2:28 (LXX) what must occur at the last day (*ep eschaton ton emeron*) but what must happen soon (*ha dei genesthai en tachei*; Rev. 1:1; 22:6). All the visions and images of Rev. are determined by such an imminent expectation, which is the content of the "revelation of Jesus" (1:1). Unlike other apocalyptic writers John is not to seal his book since the time of the end is so imminent. The time until the end is short (6:10). The dragon has only a short time left to exercise his power on earth (12:12; 20:3). When the seven trumpets are blown, then there will be no more time (10:6).[104] The time given by God should be used by the world (14:6)[105] and by the Christian community for conversion and for the veneration of God since the time (*kairos*) is near (1:3; 22:10).[106] This *kairos* is characterized in 11:18 as the time set by God for the judgment of the dead, the rewarding of the Christian community, and the annihilation of those who destroy the earth.

The seer awaits in the immediate future not only the *kairos* of the end and of what he has seen in his visions, but also the return of the Lord, who promises, "I am coming soon" (22:20; 22:8; 2:16; 3:11).[107] The Lord already stands before the door (3:20). He will come soon and bring with him his reward (22:12). Hence, all must be watchful for the Lord will come as a thief (3:3; 16:15). The Christian community does not expect an impersonal end or eschaton, but God, who is the Coming one (*erchomenos*),[108] and Christ, who characterizes himself as the Last (*eschatos*).[109] The Christian community pleading for the coming of judgment is at the same time praying, "Come Lord Jesus."[110] The hope of the Christian community does not find its legitimization and certainty in the occurrence of the final events according to an exactly prophesied plan, in which the end can be determined because it is the final section of a continuous line of apocalyptic history. Rather, the continuity of the present with the past and with the future is seen in the person of Jesus,[111] who comes as one who had historically lived, and who is present now in the midst of the community through the Spirit and prophetic word.

In sum, Rev. does not comfort the community with a reference to God's plan for history but with the assurance of the immediate coming of its Lord to judge the world. John's primary concern is to give a prophetic interpretation of the present situation of the Christian community. By the use of apocalyptic, mythological, and historical materials and by the application of traditional eschatological schemata John qualifies the present time as the "short time" before the end. He knows that the end and the coming of Christ are imminent, but he is also aware that until then only a short but definite time must elapse. Like Mark he knows of a certain "delay of the Parousia."[112] But whereas in Mark

13:10[113] the proclamation of the gospel to all nations is the prerequisite for the end, Rev. links very closely faithful resistance and eschatology. The length of the "short while" is not yet established, but depends upon the community's decisions for martyrdom.[114] The seer therefore warns: "If any one is to be taken captive, to captivity he [or she] goes; if any one is to be slain with the sword, with the sword must he [or she] be slain" (13:10).[115]

3. *The Situation of the Community Until the Final Judgment.* In the short intervening time between the exaltation of Christ and his return in glory the battle between the kingdom of God and the kingdom of Satan will take place on earth. The focal point of this final conflict is the Christian community, which acknowledges and represents during this time the claims of God's rule over the world. Through the blood of Christ the Christian community is ransomed from the world (5:10) and from the rule of the power of sin (1:6) so that it can be a *basileia*[116] for God.[117] The kingdom of God (*basileia tou theou*), which in the eschatological future will be realized in the entire cosmos, is now in and through the reality of the Christian community present on earth in the midst of the worldly demonic powers. The true victory of God becomes manifest in the death of the faithful witnesses, which is only an apparent victory of Satan (11:7; 13:7), since precisely through their death, they have overcome[118] the reign of Satan. The satanic powers battle against the Christian community because it refuses to acknowledge and to worship the beast. Christians are now slain but will rule on earth (5:10) when the powers hostile to God are destroyed. The community can in no way, however, be certain of its victory and salvation, since the final time before the end is a period of decision and probation for both the community and the world.

In contrast to some Jewish apocalyptic writings, Rev. attempts to give meaning to the present suffering of the community not with reference to a divine plan of history, but with an understanding of the present from the horizon of the future, that is, from the coming kingdom of God. The death of Christ was the reason for his exaltation and reign in heaven. Christ then establishes through the eschatological plagues this heavenly reign over the whole world. Just as the victory of the Lamb in death was the prerequisite for his heavenly reign, so also the victory of the Christians in death is the prerequisite for the coming of God's rule on earth (6:9–11), which can become a reality only after the annihilation of the powers hostile to God in judgment. The tribulation of the Christian community is based not on the fact that the time of the world is reaching its end,[119] but rather on the fact that the Christian community is "the sign" that the reign of the satanic powers on earth has been broken through the death of Christ, who through his blood created a new kingdom, a new *basileia* for God. The focal point and center of the "already" and "not yet" is therefore in Rev. not events of history, but God's *basileia* which is now already present on earth in and through the Christian community.

The Composition[120] of Revelation

I have attempted to demonstrate that the three main themes of Rev. are closely related: the establishment of the kingdom of God and Christ in judgment of the world; the imminent expectation, which knows only a short duration of time until the end; finally, the prophetic interpretation of the present situation of the Christian community. What remains to be answered is: how do these three themes concretely determine the contents and outline of the book? How does the author describe the "short time" before the end? How does he characterize the end itself? Finally, how does the author make evident in the formal composition of Rev. that the Christian community is the focal point of his intention and that all apocalyptic statements are directed and ordered to this goal? If the thesis is correct, that Rev. intends not so much to give a survey of history as to present a prophetic interpretation of the embattled situation of the Christian community from the perspective of the eschatological future, then this theological focal point must also manifest itself in the total arrangement and literary composition of the book.

1. The Ecclesial Framework. Rev. has the formal character of a circular letter to the communities of Asia Minor. The sender and receivers are explicitly mentioned. That the communities number seven signifies that they represent the complete Christian community. The use of an epistolary form gives Rev. the character of a prophetic writing intended for the churches in Asia Minor. The author is less concerned with giving an account of apocalyptic visions than he is with bringing his prophetic message to the Christian communities. The author's concern with the present situation of the community rather than with an understanding of history is shown above all and formally in the fact that the prophetic judgment of Christ[121] on the Christian community in the seven letters takes the place normally given to the survey of history in Jewish apocalypses. The "seven letters"[122] follow a basic literary schema:[123] First, the Lord himself speaks[124] and announces his knowledge of the community. Then, he raises indictments against the community. There follows an admonition to do penance[125] which stresses the imminent coming of Christ. Each message closes with an exhortation and with a promise of victory. The constant factors of this scheme are two: (1) the prophetic message and the emphasis on Jesus' knowledge of the community; (2) the witness of the Spirit and "the one who triumphs" (*ho nikōn*), both of which apply to all the communities. The messages are therefore not individual letters, but proclamations[126] of Christ to the whole Church.

The eschatological, concluding section (21:1—22:5)[127] falls into two parts: a prologue (21:1–8), which indicates the content of what follows, and the vision of the New Jerusalem (21:9—22:5), connected with the paradise tradition.[128] The first and third sections of Rev. are closely interlinked because the promises for the victorious in the phrase *ho nikōn*, which conclude each of the "letters," are all taken up again in chapters 21–22.[129] Thus the last and first sections of Rev. stand in close relationship with one another. They frame and encircle with admonitions and promises the middle and central section of the book. They thereby determine the symmetry of the outline of the whole book. In both sections parenesis and vision are closely connected with one another. The concluding section (21:1—22:5) contains a promise and an admonition in the form of visions. The seven letters are likewise parenesis and visions, for the repetition of the characteristics of Christ at the beginning of each letter signifies the incorporation of the letters into the inaugural vision.[130] The concluding section ends with the promise of God's vision that was withheld from Moses (Exod. 33:20–23). It is followed by a promise: "They shall reign for ever and ever" (22:5), which has already been hinted at in 1:6. The image of the redeemed therefore stands at the beginning and the end of Rev. In 1:12—3:22 John looks at the church standing under the protection and under the judgment of its Lord,[131] who speaks to it through the Spirit. In 21:1—22:5 the seer describes with the image of the New Jerusalem the perfected community, to which the whole world belongs (21:14; 15:4).[132] The composition of Rev. therefore builds a bridge from the "now" of the community to that eschatological future announced in the Spirit's promises for the victorious. Through the prophetic word, which the Spirit declares to the churches, the Christian community is oriented toward the imminent coming of the Lord and toward the eschatological future.[133]

2. The Description of the "Little While" Before the End. The "little while," which separates the present time from the eschatological future, is the theme of chaps. 4—16. This apocalyptic main section is subdivided by the visions of the scrolls in chaps. 5 and 10 into two units, which describe the final eschatological time from different "viewpoints."[134] While the scroll with the seven seals has as its theme the heavenly transcendent event of the intervening time in its effects upon the world, the "small scroll" (chap. 10) contains the prophetic word about the "little while" granted for the activity of the dragon and the two witnesses.[135] Since the scroll with the seven seals and the "small scroll" comprise the same period of time, the central section of Rev. is divided not chronologically or temporally, but thematically. The themes of Rev. are divided according to the following subject matter: first, the final time in its significance for the cosmos; second, the eschatological situation of the Christian community. The following will indicate more explicitly this thematic division.

a. Chapter 5, which has as its climax the handing over of the sealed eschatological scroll[136] to the Lamb, forms with chap. 4 the beginning of the apocalyptic vision and the introduction to the middle central section of Rev. The object of the negotiations before the heavenly assembly is the choice of someone worthy to receive and to open the scroll, which lies in the hand of God. The contents of the scroll are clearly "the eschatological catastrophes imposed upon the world by the decision of God."[137] These catastrophes are portrayed in three groups of "seven visions" of cosmic plagues, and they are set in motion by the breaking of the seals. By taking possession of the scroll the Lamb receives the "rank of the eschatological regent of the world, who is to execute the plagues of the final time upon the world, which Jewish and Christian apocalyptic expected to take place before the last day."[138] In the series of the seven cosmic plagues, the eschatological rule of Christ over the cosmos is established. Whereas the visions of the seals note the main characteristics of the final time—antichrist, war, hunger, and death— the visions of the seven trumpets and bowls[139] point to Yahweh's day of wrath as a day of cosmic catastrophes and of demonic onslaughts. According to Rev., the day of Yahweh takes place not in historical events but in supernatural, cosmic occurrences.[140] Here too the sequence of the trumpets and of the bowls is not temporally determined. Instead, the cosmic plagues are characterized as belonging together thematically by their insertion into the whole schema. They complete and consummate the "wrath of God" not temporally but extensively and intensively. Whereas the plagues of the angels with the trumpets strike only a third of the cosmos and of humanity, the bowls of wrath destroy the whole cosmos. Both series of visions begin with a liturgy of judgment (8:2-5; 15:5-8) and conclude with a proclamation of the end.

b. The content of the "small scroll" (10:1—15:4),[141] which has been inserted between the visions of the trumpets and those of the bowls, is explicitly characterized in chap. 10 as a prophetic word. Chapter 10, which like chap. 5 contains a description of an inaugural or commissioning vision, takes our attention away from heaven and directs it toward the earth. Chapter 11,[142] which describes the measuring of the temple and the actions of the two witnesses, occupies a unique position in the composition of the middle section of Rev. both formally and thematically.

Formally, the chapter belong to the series of trumpet-visions, because it comes before the blast of the seventh trumpet (11:15–19) and because its contents belong to the second woe (11:14, cf. 8:13). But it is also formally connected with chaps. 12 and 13 by the mere fact that it stands immediately after chap. 10. In other words: because 11:1–19 has been placed between chaps. 10 and 12, the structural composition of Rev. has become unclear. However, the author has thereby achieved a formal connection of the content of the "small scroll" with the content of the scroll. Just as the beginning of the "small scroll" is connected by means of 11:1–14 with the visions of the trumpets in the preceding chapters, so it is also formally connected with the following visions of the bowls because in 15:1 there is the proclamation of the judgment of the bowls and then in 15:2–8 follows the image of the conquerors, which thematically belongs with the content of the "small scroll." Thus the scroll and the "small scroll" are very closely interlinked.

Thematically, from the viewpoint of its contents, chap. 11 belongs to the visions of the plagues,[143] since the witnesses have power over the cosmos and because they are a torment to those living on earth. On the other hand, chap. 11 corresponds to the contents of chaps. 12:1—15:4 since the affliction of the Holy City and the activity of the witnesses takes place on earth at the same time as the probation period of the Woman in the desert (12:6,15) and as the activity of the antichrist (13:5).[144] While the series of seven visions are of a cosmic nature, the main motive of the "small scroll" is the prophetic interpretation[145] of the situation of the Christian community.[146] John characterizes the present situation of the community by means of the phrase "a time, and times, and half a time" as the eschatological time of tribulation. This number, which in Daniel expresses the duration of the last stretch of time before the appearance of the "Son of man" (7:13,25)[147] has lost all connotation of a certain time span in Rev.

John characterizes the "little while" before the end as the time of eschatological probation of the Christian community (11:1–2;[148] 12:5–14), as the time of the kingly-priestly witnesses (11:3–14), and especially as the time of the activity of Satan on earth, who stands behind the Roman persecution of the Christian community. His activity is manifest in the action of the beast and of the false prophet (12–13). The description of the beast from the abyss is drawn not only from Daniel, but is also influenced by the notion of the antichrist.[149] The beast is the caricature of the Lamb (13:3; 12:14). It has ten diadems upon its horns and has blasphemous names upon its heads (13:1). As Christ has made the redeemed priests for God (1:6), so the beast seduces people to adore the dragon (13:4). For this purpose, it makes use of the false prophet, who uses miracles to seduce the dwellers of the earth into worshipping the beast. It persecutes and hangs a financial boycott over all who do not accept the sign of the beast.[150] This power of the antichrist dominates the whole earth. Only the saints can resist it.

In conclusion: not only Rev. as a whole but also the visions in 10:1— 15:4[151] are divided thematically and not temporally. All these visions comprise the same short space of time before the end, and they qualify it as the time for the probation of the Christian community. Like the series of the seven cosmic visions, this middle section of Rev. has as its climax the proclamation and description of judgment (14:6–20). Rev. 10:1—15:4, with the theme of the situation of the kingly-priestly, prophetic community, forms a distinct unity and constitutes the formal center of Rev. The theme of the eschatological community of salvation not only stands at the beginning and end of Rev. but also constitutes the center of its composition.

3. *The Description of God's Judgment.* The theme of the Christian community defines not only the "framework" and center of Rev. but is also taken up again and again in the visions of judgment, in the interludes, in the songs of praise, and in the admonitions. Likewise the theme of judgment is formally related to the theme of the community and closely interlinked with it through the insertion of the ecclesial, central section into the series of septets. The theme of judgment is broadly developed in the visions of the cosmic plagues and in the last series of visions of the new world. It is also present within the motif of the Christian community, especially in the seven letters, in the admonitions, and in the judgment description of 14:6–20. This theme of judgment always reaches its climax in the announcements of coming salvation for the community and for the world (cf. the promises for the victorious at the end of the letters, the hymns[152] in 11:15–19; 15:2–4; 19:1–8, and the visions of the New Jerusalem). The whole book, and especially the cycles of visions within its apocalyptic section, reaches a climax in the description of judgment and of eschatological salvation. The reader thereby is constantly confronted with the end. The planned but yet unexpected nature of this end is expressed by the use of the number seven for the visions and by the fact that Rev. does not portray a linear course of events. The seer develops out of the last member of a series another series of visions, or he begins a different theme by a new

proclamation or by contrasting imagery (cf. 17:1),[153] which are both connected with the whole book by hints and cross references.

The visions of judgment at the end of the book progress in the same manner as the "scroll visions," namely thematically and not temporally. The sequence of the judgment is prophesied in 14:6–10. The destruction of the satanic powers is described in the reverse order as that of their introduction in chaps. 12—14. The judgment of Babylon is followed by the judgment of the beast and of the false prophets; these are followed by the judgment of the dragon, of the underworld, and of death. Finally the world's judgment[154] takes place. The whole cosmos (heaven, earth, and underworld) is thereby torn away from the satanic powers and is placed under the rule of God. Whereas the seven visions describe the end as the day of God's wrath on which the whole cosmos is affected, the visions of judgment, which are at the end of the book, especially emphasize the establishment of Christ's rule through the destruction of the satanic powers. This establishment of Christ's reign over the whole cosmos takes place, according to Rev., in three steps. First, with his enthronement Christ has taken over the power in heaven (chap. 5) and the dragon is thrown down to earth (12:5). Second, the Parousia is the next step. Satan is banished from the earth. Those who refused to bow to his rule now reign[155] with Christ on the earth[156] (20:4–6). Third, the final stage of the establishment of God's reign consists of the destruction of Satan, the power of death and Hades. Only now can the new creation[157] become a visible reality since the whole cosmos again belongs to God.

Conclusion: I have attempted to show that the author of Rev. does not seek to comfort the persecuted Christian community with reference to past and future history, but with reference to the eschatological reality of God's kingdom. This main theme of Rev. is shortly but precisely expressed in the hymn in 11:15–19 which is composed in the center of the book.

NOTES

1. H. B. Swete, *The Apocalypse of St. John* (3d ed.; 1908; Grand Rapids: Wm. B. Eerdmans, 1951) lxi.

2. E. Lohmeyer, *Die Offenbarung des Johannes* (2d ed.; Tübingen: Mohr/Siebeck, 1953) 9; for a contrary position, cf. W. Bousset, *Die Offenbarung Johannis* (6th ed.; Göttingen: Vandenhoeck & Ruprecht, 1906) 184.

3. The prologue corresponds to the epilogue: 1:1—22:6; 1:2b—22:8; 1:3—22:7; 1:3b—22:10b; 1:8—22:13.

4. J. Sickenberger, *Erklärung der Johannesapokalypse* (2d ed.; Bonn, 1942) 83.

5. Cf. Dan. 8:26; *1 Enoch* 1:2; 93:19; 104:12; *2 Enoch* 33:9.

6. Cf. also G. Delling, "Zum gottesdienstlichen Stil der Johannesapokalypse," *NovT* 3 (1959) 107; T. Holtz, *Die Christologie der Apokalypse des Johannes* (Berlin, 1962) 1.

7. E. Lohmeyer, "Die Offenbarung des Johannes 1920–1934," *TRu* NF 6 (1934) 270.

8. Cf. the research survey presented by W. Bousset (*Die Offenbarung Johannis,* 109–49).

9. H. E. Weber, "Zum Verständnis der Offenbarung Johannis," *Aus Schrift und Geschichte* (Stuttgart: Katholisches Bibelwerk, 1922) 59. For a recent study, see also E. Schmitt, "Die christologische Interpretation als das Grundlegende der Apokalypse," *TQ* 140 (1960) 260.

10. Whereas the "Source Hypothesis" (Weyland, Spitta, Holtzmann) assumes that Rev. is a more or less mechanical compilation of sources, the "Redactional Hypothesis" (Völter, Erbes, and to some extent Vischer) suspects that Rev. is based upon a written text (*Grundschrift*) which was reworked several times before reaching its present form. To the contrary, the "Fragmentary Hypothesis" assumes that the personality of the author stands behind the work. According to this hypothesis, Rev. was not freely created but consists of the reworking of older apocalyptic pieces of tradition.

11. The "Source Hypothesis" is held today especially by M.-É. Boismard (*L'Apocalypse* in *La Sainte Bible* [3d ed.; Paris, 1959]. According to him, Rev. was put together out of two texts: the earlier text was written under Nero, while the later came into existence after 70 C.E. The unity of style and diction of Rev. speaks against such a division of sources: cf. R. H. Charles, *The Revelation of St. John* (ICC; Edinburgh: T. & T. Clark, 1920) 1:lxxxiii. Moreover, it is improbable that the author inserted his own earlier text without correction in a second text. Cf. W. G. Kümmel, *Introduction to the New Testament* (14th ed.; trans. A. J. Matill, Jr.; Nashville: Abingdon Press, 1966) 325. The frequent doublets of Rev. can be explained by an analysis of the composition. Cf. chap. 6 of this book, "The Composition and Structure of Revelation."

12. P. Vielhauer, "Apostolisches, Apokalypsen und Verwandtes," in *Neutestamentliche Apokryphen* (E. Hennecke-W. Schneemelcher; 3d ed.; Tübingen: Mohr/Siebeck, 1964) 2: 438 [ET: *New Testament Apocrypha* (Philadelphia: Westminster Press; London: Lutterworth Press, 1965) 581–642].

13. K. Holzinger (*Erklärungen zu einigen der umstrittensten Stellen der Offenbarung Johannis und der Sibyllinischen Orakel* [Vienna, 1936] 13) goes too far with his suspicion that the author allowed the presence of contradictions in order to startle or even to mislead the reader.

14. Cf. F. Palmer, *The Drama of the Apocalypse* (New York, 1903) 35ff.; V. Burch, *Anthropology and the Apocalypse* (London, 1939); J. B. Bowman, "The Revelation to John. Its Dramatic Structure and Message," *Int* 9 (1955) 436–53; E. Stauffer (*Christ and the Caesars* [Philadelphia: Westminster Press; London: SCM Press, 1955]) presupposes that the outline of the Apocalypse follows the process of the imperial cultic games. Cf. also the survey of R. Halver, *Der Mythos im letzten Buch der Bibel* (TF 32; Hamburg, 1964) 118–26.

15. A. Schlatter, *Das Alte Testament in der johanneischen Apokalypse* (BFCT 16/6; Gütersloh: Gerd Mohn, 1912); cf. also L. A. Vos, *The Synoptic Traditions in the Apocalypse* (Kampen: J. H. Kok, 1965) 16–51.

16. Cf. esp. for chap. 12, H. Gunkel, *Schöpfung und Chaos in Urzeit und Endzeit* (Göttingen: Vandenhoeck & Ruprecht, 1895) 173ff.; F. Boll, *Aus der Offenbarung Johannis: Hellenistische Studien zum Weltbild der Apokalypse* (Stoicheia H 1; Leipzig: Dürr'sche Buchhandlung, 1914).

17. Bousset, *Die Offenbarung Johannis,* 49–108; O. A. Piper, "Johannesapokalypse," *RGG,* 822–34.

18. J. Michl, "Apokalypse," *LTK,* 1: 696.

19. A. Wikenhauser, *Die Offenbarung des Johannes* (RNT 9; 3d ed.; Regensburg, 1959) 21.

20. R. Kraemer, *Die Offenbarung des Johannes in überzeitlicher Deutung* (Wernigerode, 1929); H. M. Feret, *Die geheime Offenbarung des Johannes: Eine christliche Schau der Geschichte* (Düsseldorf: Patmos-Verlag, 1959).

21. Cf. J. Cambier, "Les Images de l'Ancien Testament dans l'Apocalypse de saint Jean," *NRT* 77 (1955) 121.

22. The statement of 1:19 is often related to the outline of Rev. so that chaps. 2—3 report "that which is" and chaps. 4:1—22:5 "that which will take place afterwards." This position is rightly attacked by G. B. Caird (*The Revelation of St. John the Divine* [HNTC; New York: Harper & Row, 1966] 26): "But this is a grotesque over-simplification. Chapters ii and iii, though mainly appraisal, contain both threats and promises; and the remaining chapters include many tableaux which can only denote events already past or present at the time when John was writing. It is better therefore to take the words *what you see* to mean the whole of John's vision."

23. The *heilsgeschichtlich* interpretation emphasizes this continuity of the OT people of God with the church. Cf. M. Rissi, "Das Judenproblem im Lichte der Johannesapokalypse," *TZ* 13 (1957) 241–59; idem, *Die Zukunft der Welt* (Basel, 1966) 74. Rev. 7:1–8; 11; 12; 15:2–5; 21 are therefore interpreted as referring to Israel. Cf. also N. A. Dahl, *Das Volk Gottes* (Darmstadt: Wissenschaftliche Buchgesellschaft, 1963) 191; cf. to the contrary, however, E. Schweizer, *Gemeinde und Gemeindeordnung im Neuen Testament* (Zurich, 1959) 119, who argues that the Christian community is, according to Rev., no longer just the legitimate continuation of Israel but rather Israel itself.

24. Cf. H. Strathmann, *Was soll die "Offenbarung des Johannes" im Neuen Testament?* (2d ed.; Gütersloh: Gerd Mohn, 1947) 14.

25. Cf. Touilleux, *L'Apocalypse et les cultes de Domitien et de Cybele* (Paris, 1935); see also St. Giet (*L'Apocalypse et l'Histoire* [Paris, 1957]), who thinks that he can trace in chaps. 8—11 the course of the Jewish war as described by Josephus.

26. M. Hopkins, "The Historical Perspective of Apocalypse, 1—11," *CBQ* 27 (1965) 42–47.

	Chapter
Introduction: Title and greeting (chap. 1); letters to the seven churches	2—3
HISTORICAL PERSPECTIVE: God's visitation on Israel	4—11

A. Enthronement of the Lamb in the heavenly Liturgy:

without Lamb (OT)	4
with Lamb (NT)	5

B. God's decree regarding Israel:

of punishment, from Synoptic Apocalypse: 7 seals	6
of predestination: sealing of 12 Tribes	7

C. God's judgment on Israel:

the seven trumpets, turning Exodus' plagues on Jews	8—9
Israel's doom: destruction of unmeasured court	10—11

APOCALYPTIC VISION: God's impending judgment on "Babylon"
(Rome)   12—20

  A. Setting:

      Debut of Christianity via Messiah's resurrection—ascension   12
      Cosmic enemy of the New People of God: the two Satanic
      beasts (666)   13

  B. God's judgment on Rome:

      Announcement of impending doom, the 144,000   14
      The 7 bowls (plagues turned on Rome)   15—16
      Description of the fall of Rome (model: Babylon)   17—18

  C. Transition to the cosmic arena: Satan punished   19—20

THE HEAVENLY JERUSALEM: a new universe   21—22

A thorough discussion of this outline is possible only in connection with a detailed analysis of the main apocalyptic section of Rev. Nevertheless one can ask by what right does this interpretation transform the visions of the seals and trumpets, which are unequivocally of heavenly and cosmic character, into a historical event referring only to Israel and not to the whole world? However, to what extent this "historical" outline corresponds objectively to the content and structure of Rev. will not be examined here, since the second part of this essay will present a detailed analysis of the central section of Rev. Therefore only the presuppositions of this outline are of interest here.

  27. Ibid., 42.

  28. Ibid., 43.

  29. A. Feuillet, "Le chapitre X de l'Apocalypse, son rapport dans la solution du problème eschatologique," *Sacra Pagina* XII–XVII (1959) 414–29; idem, "Essai d'interprétation du chapitre xi de l'Apocalypse," *NTS* 4 (1958) 183–200.

  30. H. Conzelmann, *Die Mitte der Zeit: Studien zur Theologie des Lukas* (5th ed.; Tübingen: Mohr/Siebeck, 1964) [ET: *The Theology of St. Luke* (Philadelphia: Fortress Press, 1982)].

  31. Cf. Feuillet, "Le chapitre X," 427.

  32. W. Marxsen also establishes a parallelism between Rev. and the outline of the Gospel of Luke. See *Einleitung in das Neue Testament: Eine Einführung in seine Probleme* (Gütersloh: Gerd Mohn, 1963) 231, cf. 190 [ET: *Introduction to the New Testament: An Approach to Its Problems* (Philadelphia: Fortress Press; Oxford: Blackwell, 1968)]. To the contrary, cf. P. Vielhauer, "Einleitung in das Neue Testament," *TRu* 31 (1966) 147.

  33. Conzelmann, *Die Mitte der Zeit,* 116–27.

  34. Cf. G. Harder, "Das eschatologische Geschichtsbild der sogenannten kleinen Apokalypse Markus 13," *TViat* 4 (1952) 71–107; cf. also F. Busch, *Zum Verständnis der synoptischen Eschatologie: Markus 13 neu untersucht* (Gütersloh: Gerd Mohn, 1938).

  35. E. Haenchen, *Der Weg Jesu* (Berlin, 1966) 455.

  36. K. Koch, "Spätisraelitisches Geschichtsdenken am Beispiel des Buches Daniel," *Historische Zeitschrift* 193/1 (1961) 30–31.

  37. Cf. the visions of the book of Daniel; *1 Enoch* 85—90, 93, and 91:12–17; *T. Levi* 16—18; *4 Esdras* 11, 2–3; *2 Apoc. Bar.* 53—71; 35—40.

38. D. Rössler, *Gesetz und Geschichte* (2d ed.; Neukirchen: Neukirchener Verlag, 1962) 54–77, esp. 68.

39. Charles, *APOT,* 2: 263–65.

40. W. Bousset, *Die jüdische Apokalyptik: Ihre religionsgeschichtliche Herkunft und ihre Bedeutung für das Neue Testament* (Berlin, 1903) 18.

41. Lohmeyer, "Die Offenbarung 1920–1934," 279.

42. Cf. the brief contrast between prophecy and apocalyptic by J. Moltmann, *Theologie der Hoffnung* (Munich: Chr. Kaiser, 1965) 120–21 [ET: *Theology of Hope* (New York: Harper & Row, 1967) 133–34]. Moltmann describes the relationship between cosmology and apocalyptic as "Vergeschichtlichung des Kosmos."

43. To the contrary, cf. D. S. Russell (*The Method and Message of Jewish Apocalyptic* [Philadelphia: Westminster Press; London: SCM Press, 1964] 127–39), who explains the pseudonymity as a "sense of contemporaneity."

44. Rössler, *Gesetz und Geschichte,* 55; cf. also W. Bousset, *Die Religion des Judentums im späthellenistischen Zeitalter* (HNT 21; 4th ed.; Tübingen: Mohr/Siebeck, 1966) 243.

45. Bousset, *Religion des Judentums.* For the conflict between theocracy and eschatology in the beginnings of the apocalyptic movement, cf. O. Plöger, *Theokratie und Eschatologie* (WMANT 2; 2d ed.; Neukirchen: Neukirchener Verlag, 1962) [ET: *Theology and Eschatology* (Richmond: John Knox Press, 1968)].

46. Hopkins, "Historical Perspective of Apocalypse, 1—11," 42.

47. What is decisive here is the *redactional reworking* of the tradition by Luke, as shown by Conzelmann (*Die Mitte der Zeit*) and not the historical origin of the tradition. For the latter, cf. C. H. Dodd, "The Fall of Jerusalem and the 'Abomination of Desolation,'" *JRS* 37 (1947) 48–54; P. Winter, "The Treatment of his Sources by the Third Evangelist in Luke XXI–XXIV," *ST* 8 (1954) 138–72; L. Gaston, "Sondergut und Markusstoff in Lk 21," *TZ* 16 (1960) 161–72.

48. Vielhauer, "Apostolisches, Apokalypsen," 439 [ET: 582–83]. Cf. also E. Schweizer, *Das Evangelium nach Markus* (NTD 1; Göttingen: Vandenhoeck & Ruprecht, 1967) 158 [ET: *The Good News According to Mark* (Richmond: John Knox Press, 1970)].

49. My translation differs here from RSV. For the translation of *hypomonē en Jēsou,* cf. BAGD, 847.

50. Feuillet, "Le chapitre X," 426–27.

51. A. Strobel, "Abfassung und Geschichtstheologie der Apokalypse nach Kp 17, 9–12," *NTS* 10 (1963–64) 433–45. Cf. Kümmel, *Introduction,* 329.

52. Strobel, "Abfassung und Geschichtstheologie," 437.

53. L. Brun, "Die römischen Kaiser in der Apokalypse," *ZNW* 26 (1927) 128ff. Rev. 17:10 ("He must remain only a little while") is explained by Brun with reference to the imminent expectation of Rev. He points out that because of his preference for series of sevens the seer must expect seven heads before the eighth. If the seer thinks that the time before the end is only short, then the seventh emperor can rule "only a little while." Brun refers to *4 Esdras* chaps. 11ff. as a support for this thesis, where the reign of the two side-wings, which is followed by the messianic kingdom, is also only for a short time.

54. Charles, *APOT,* 1: xcii.

55. C. H. Dodd (*The Apostolic Preaching and Its Developments* [London: Hodder & Stoughton, 1936] 87ff.) thinks that Rev. is a relapse into Jewish apocalypticism because of its exclusive emphasis on the future. In my opinion he overlooks the fact that

Rev. is distinctly Christian. Its understanding of present and future is christologically determined by its emphasis on the death and resurrection of Christ.

56. H. H. Rowley, *The Relevance of Apocalyptic* (3d ed.; London: Lutterworth Press, 1963) chap. 1.

57. J. Moltmann, "Probleme der neueren evangelischen Eschatologie," in *Verkündigung und Forschung* (Beihefte zu *EvT* 2; Munich: Chr. Kaiser, 1966) 115.

58. Lohmeyer, "Die Offenbarung 1920–1934," 285.

59. H. Schlier, "Zum Verständnis der Geschichte nach der Offenbarung Johannis," in *Zeit der Kirche* (3d ed.; Freiburg: Herder, 1962) 265.

60. Ibid.

61. Ibid., 262.

62. Halver, *Der Mythos im letzten Buch*, 148.

63. Lohmeyer, "Die Offenbarung 1920–1934," 286.

64. J. Behm, *Gott und die Geschichte: Das Geschichtsbild der Offenbarung* (Gütersloh: Gerd Mohn, 1925) 23.

65. Ibid., 22.

66. Lohmeyer, "Die Offenbarung 1920–1934," 62.

67. For Augustine's understanding of history, cf. E. Dinkler, "Augustine's Geschichtsauffassung," *Schweizer Monatschrife* 34 (1953) 514–26.

68. Lohmeyer, "Die Offenbarung 1920–1934," 193.

69. Ibid.

70. Ibid., 197.

71. Holtz, *Christologie der Apokalypse*, 217.

72. Ibid., 214.

73. Ibid., 22.

74. According to H. W. Kuhn (*Enderwartung und gegenwärtiges Heil. Untersuchungen zu den Gemeindeliedern von Qumran* [SUNT 4; Göttingen: Vandenhoeck & Ruprecht, 1966] 203–4), the community hymns of Qumran know of future and present eschatological statements. The statements of eschatological presence are based upon the salvific presence of God in the temple community of Qumran. This understanding of the presence of salvation in Qumran differs from the understanding of the primitive Christian communities insofar as the latter claim a christological foundation for their understanding of eschatological salvation.

75. Moltmann, "Probleme der neueren evangelischen Eschatologie," 103.

76. Holtz, *Christologie der Apokalypse*, 215.

77. F. Büchsel (*Die Christologie der Offenbarung Johannes* [Halle, 1907] 24) states: "In 7:14 it becomes clear that the gift of Jesus demands the personal activity of the faithful." Cf. Plöger, *Theokratie und Eschatologie*, 137.

78. Holtz understands the "exaltation of the community" as analogous to the exaltation of Christ. It is questionable, however, whether 5:10 and 1:6 can be interpreted as "Einsetzung zur Regentschaft über die Erde" (*Christologie der Apokalypse*, 48).

79. Halver (*Der Mythos im letzten Buch*, 137) proposes a middle position.

80. Cf. the commentaries and the synoptic survey by J. B. Bowman in "The Revelation to John."

81. The same is true of the imagery in Rev.: E. L. Schmidt ("Die Bildersprache in der Johannesapokalypse," *TZ* 3 [1947] 161–77) refers to the paradoxical character and the lack of perspicuity of the images. The images do not primarily present something, but

they express various thoughts "in-one-another" which are "next-to-another" in words.
M.-É. Boismard ("L'Apocalypse" in *Introduction à la Bible* [ed. A. Robert-A. Feuillet;
Tournai: Desclée, 1959] 714—16) stresses the conceptual and thematic determination of
the images.

83. The meaning of the preaching in Rev., like that of Jesus' preaching, "does not lie
in revealing apocalyptic secrets nor in giving the present a significance arising from a
divine reality beyond time, but it lies just in this, that in Jesus the Kingdom of God
came into being and in him it will be consummated. The promise of Jesus receives its
peculiar and reliable character through its fulfillment in himself." W. G. Kümmel,
Promise and Fulfillment (trans. D. M. Barton; STB 23; 3d ed.; London: SCM Press,
1957) 155.

83. Austin Farrer has also attempted in his commentary (*The Revelation of St. John
the Divine* [Oxford: At the Clarendon Press, 1964]) to indicate that the "short time"
before the end is decisive for an understanding of Rev. Whereas he had assumed in his
book (*A Rebirth of Images: The Making of St. John's Apocalypse* [Westminster, Md.:
Newman Press, 1949]) that the outline of Rev. corresponds twice to the Jewish festival
calendar, he now emphasizes that the form of Rev. corresponds to the schema of the
"Danielic half-week of tribulation" and the "eschatological discourse" of Mark 13. Farrer
maintains that the four series of septettes, which are "to be viewed as a half week of
(halved) weeks" (p. 9), are decisive for the formal structure of Rev. The sequence of Mark
13, however, is seen to be decisive for the thematic development of Rev. (p. 20). Therefore, Farrer divides the end time into three periods of time which follow one another:
The "day of waiting of the Saints" (chaps. 1—3; 4—7) is followed by the "day of the
usurpation of the anti-Christ" (chaps. 8—14), which in turn is followed by the "day of
Christ" (chaps. 15—22). This division of Rev., which is based on Mark 13, almost completely hides the formal structure of Rev., which is explicitly divided by means of the
three inaugural visions (1:9-20; chaps. 4—5; chap. 10), the four series of septettes, and
the eschatological section (21:1—22:5).

84. R. Bultmann, *Geschichte und Eschatologie* (2d ed.; Tübingen: Mohr/Siebeck,
1962) 36 [ET: *History and Eschatology: The Presence of Eternity* (New York: Harper &
Row, 1957)]. Cf. also E. B. Allo: "For us the Apocalypse is essentially an eschatological
book!" (*Apocalypse de Saint Jean* [3d ed.; Paris: J. Gabalda, 1963] lxiii). Those
addressed by the eschatological preaching are not, however, individuals, but a community.

85. Kümmel (*Introduction*, 327) states: "Then we must also say that the actual goal
of the prophetic-apocalyptic portrayal is not the course of the eschatological events, but
their significance for the church of his time ('kerygmatic picture of reality,' Goppelt)."

86. For the NT context of imminent expectation, cf. J. Rohr, *Die geheime Offen-
barung und die Zukunftserwartungen des Urchristentums* (Münster: Aschendorff, 1911).
In regard to the question whether Jesus or only the primitive Christian community knew
of an imminent expectation, cf. W. G. Kümmel, "Die Naherwartung in der
Verkündigung Jesu," in *Heilsgeschehen und Geschichte* (Marburg, 1965) 457-70; and
E. Käsemann, "The Beginning of Christian Theology," in *New Testament Questions of
Today* (Philadelphia: Fortress Press; London: SCM Press, 1969) 82-107 [=*ZTK* 57 (1960)
162-85].

87. E. Lohse, *Offenbarung des Johannes* (NTD 11; 8th ed.; Göttingen: Vandenhoeck
& Ruprecht, 1960) 42: "Der Tod der Zeugen wird hier mit einem Opfer verglichen (vgl.
Phil. 2:17; 2 Tim. 4:6 . . . . Während ihre Leiber in den Gräbern ruhen und auf den

Tag der Auferstehung warten, weilen die Seelen in einer Art Zwischenzustand bei Gott." It is questionable whether the thought of "a separation of body and soul after death" is present here.

88. Cf. A. Satake, *Die Gemeindeordnung in der Johannesapokalypse* (WMANT 21; Neukirchen: Neukirchener Verlag, 1966) 101-2. H. Strathmann ("martyrs," *TDNT* 4 [1967] 474-514) distinguishes between *syndouloi* (fellow slaves) and *adelphoi* (brothers) in 6:11.

89. The cries of the righteous serve in apocalyptic literature to indicate the end. Cf. Sir. 36:10; *1 Enoch* 47:1; 97:3-5; 99:3.

90. Cf. M. Kiddle and M. K. Ross, *The Revelation of St. John* (7th ed.; MNTC; London, 1963) xxxi.

91. The expression "those who dwell upon the earth" occurs in Rev. 3:10; 6:10; 8:13; 11:10; 13:8; 13:14ab; 17:8. A. Feuillet argues that this set expression refers in 11:10 to the Jewish persecutors of the church ("Essai d'interprétation," 183-200). However, there can be no question of a reference only to Jews in the other passages. The expression has a universal connotation and refers to all people hostile to the church.

92. A comparison with the *Apocalypse of Peter* indicates how restrained John is, in contrast to later Christian apocalyptic, in his description of the last judgment and the eschatological salvation. Cf. Hennecke-Schneemelcher, *Neutestamentliche Apokryphen,* 2: 475-83 [ET: 2: 663-83].

93. Rev. 6:12-17; 8:1; 11:15-19; 16:17-20; 14:6; 15:4.

94. G. Delling, "hēmera," *TDNT* 2: 19.

95. G. von Rad, *Theologie des Alten Testaments* (4th ed.; Munich: Chr. Kaiser, 1960) 2: 132 [ET: *Old Testament Theology* (New York: Harper & Row, 1965)]. His survey of texts shows that the prophets expect the day of Yahweh "to bring war in its train" (ET: 2: 123).

96. Bousset states (*Die Religion des Judentums,* 250): "Die Schilderungen der sogenannten messianischen Wehen sind ungemein zahlreich, aber im ganzen einförmig." Cf., e.g., Dan. 12:1; *1 Enoch* 99:4ff.; 10:1ff.; *(Jub.* 23) Mark 13; *4 Esdras* 4:51—5:13; 6:11-25; 9:1-3; 13:14-24; 1 Bar. 25; 27; 29; 48:31-41; 70; *Sib. Or.* 2:154ff.; *Apoc. Abr.* 30.

97. S. Brown, "The Hour of Trial (Rev. 3,10)," *JBL* 85 (1966) 308-14.

98. C. Müller, *Gottes Gerechtigkeit und Gottes Volk* (Göttingen: Vandenhoeck & Ruprecht, 1964) 61-62.

99. The demand for justice is behind the cry for vengeance. Cf. B. Weiss, *Briefe und Offenbarung Johannis* (Leipzig, 1904) 497.

100. H. Schlier, "thlipsis," *TDNT* 3 (1965) 146: "Hence the NT concept of *thlipsis* is not simply an adoption or development of the Jewish idea of eschatological suffering. We have here an understanding of the whole question of eschatology which has been newly disclosed in the concrete history of Jesus Christ."

101. Bultmann states (*Geschichte und Eschatologie,* 41): The continuity with Israel is not a historical continuity. "*The new people of God* has no real history, for it is the community of the end-time, an eschatological phenomenon" (ET: 36).

102. Charles, *APOT,* 2: 567.

103. E. Käsemann, "On the Subject of Primitive Christian Apocalyptic," in *New Testament Questions of Today,* esp. 123-24 [=*ZTK* 59 (1962) 257-84].

104. To the contrary, cf. G. Delling, *Das Zeitverständnis des Neuen Testaments* (Gütersloh: Gerd Mohn, 1940), 140. Cf. also T. Zahn, *Die Offenbarung Johannis* (Leipzig, 1926) 2: 414.

105. W. Bieder, "Die sieben Seligpreisungen in der Offenbarung des Johannes," *TZ* 10 (1954) 113–30.

106. Kümmel (*Promise and Fulfillment*, 20) states: "New Testament usage is therefore completely uniform as regards the temporal use of *eggys*: it denotes that an event will happen soon, by which it is meant or presumed that there will not be a long time to wait before it happens."

107. This imminent expectation could be called "constant expectation" ("Stetserwartung"—H. Schürmann). Cf. R. Schnackenburg, "Naherwartung," *LTK*, 7: 777–79.

108. Rev. 1:4, 8; 4:8; Schlatter, *Das Alte Testament*, 12–13.

109. Rev. 1:17; 2:8; 22:13. In the OT the "First and the Last" (Isa. 44:6 and 48:12) is a self-predication of Yahweh. However, the LXX did not apply the Greek notion to God. Cf. Holtz, *Christologie der Apokalypse*, 82.

110. Cf. F. Hahn, *Christologische Hoheitstitel* (2d ed.; Göttingen: Vandenhoeck & Ruprecht, 1964) 101–3 [ET: *The Titles of Jesus in Christology* (New York: World Pub. Co.; London: Lutterworth Press, 1969].

111. Moltmann, *Theologie der Hoffnung*, 277 [ET: 300–301].

112. Cf. M. Rissi, *Was ist und was geschehen soll danach* (ATANT 46; Zurich, 1965) 114–18.

113. Wars, earthquakes, and famines are, in Rev. as in Mark 13, parallel to the persecution of the Christians and to the preaching of the Gospel. However, in Luke the apocalyptic events take place only after the persecutions of the Christians. According to Mark and Rev. the apocalyptic events have already begun with the passion and resurrection of Jesus; only the last act is to take place. Cf. H. W. Bartsch, "Early Christian Eschatology in the Synoptic Gospels," *NTS* 11 (1965) 387–97.

114. The coming of the end is, as in the OT, dependent upon a condition to be fulfilled by persons. Cf. Bultmann, *Geschichte und Eschatologie*, 35 [ET: 29–31].

115. Translation differs from RSV.

116. The establishment of the kingdom of God, which Jewish apocalypticism hopes will take place in the eschatological future, is according to Rev. a reality already present upon the earth in the Christian community. The end does not effect a manifestation of God's kingdom, but an extension of the priestly-kingly community of salvation to the whole world.

117. According to O. Cullmann (*Königsherrschaft Christi und Kirche im Neuen Testament* [TS 10; 3d ed.; Zurich: Evangelischer Verlag, 1950] 12) the church is Christ's reign, which will be replaced by God's kingdom. However, John emphasizes in Rev. 1:6 and 5:10 that the community is a *basileia* for God.

118. R. Schnackenburg, *Gottes Herrschaft und Reich* (Freiburg: Herder, 1959) 235 [ET: *God's Rule and Kingdom* (New York: Herder & Herder, 1963)].

119. 4 *Esdras* 5:55 states: "Even as creation is already grown old, and is already past the strength of youth."

120. Cf. esp. G. Bornkamm, "Die Komposition der apokalyptischen Visionen in der Offenbarung Johannis," in *Studien zu Antike und Christentum* (2d ed.; Munich: Chr. Kaiser, 1963) 2: 204–22; Boismard, "L'Apocalypse," 635–63; and the thorough analysis of St. Giet, *L'Apocalypse*, 146–85.

121. Vielhauer, "Apostolisches, Apokalypsen," 440 (ET: 593).

122. Zahn (*Die Offenbarung des Johannes*, 1: 41) emphasizes that one cannot speak of "letters," since none of the messages has the form of a letter.

123. M. Hubert, "L'architecture des lettres aux sept Églises," *RB* 67 (1960) 349–53.

124. The *tade legei* ("[he] has this to say") corresponds to the prophetic "messenger formula." Cf. C. Westermann, *Grundformen prophetischer Rede* (2d ed.; Munich: Chr. Kaiser, 1964) 71ff. [ET: *Basic Forms of Prophetic Speech* (Philadelphia: Westminster Press, 1967)].

125. In the first three letters the accusation comes first (2:7; 2:14; 2:20); in the other letters it appears in another place (2:5b; 2:10a-c; 2:16; 2:25; 3:2–3; 3:11). Although the admonition is present in all the letters, the warning is lacking in the second and third letters. In the last four messages the phrase *ho nikōn* comes before the word of the Spirit.

126. J. Lindblom, *Die literarische Gattung der prophetischen Literatur: Eine literargeschichtliche Untersuchung zum Alten Testament* (Uppsala, 1924) 102.

127. R. H. Charles (*APOT,* 2: 144–45) and P. Gaechter ("The Original Sequence of Apocalypse 20—22," *TS* 10 [1949] 485–521) seek to correct the order of the verses. While Charles maintains that a literary redaction lies between John's outline and the edition of Rev., Gaechter argues that the lack of order is based on the author's faulty memory.

128. For a different division, cf. M. Rissi (*Die Zukunft der Welt,* 63 [ET: *The Future of the World* (London: SCM Press, 1970)]), who sees 22:1–5 as a description of Paradise. J. Comblin ("La liturgie de la nouvelle Jérusalem [Apoc. XXI, 1—XXII, 5]," *ETL* 29 [1953] 5–40) likewise divides the section into three parts: 21:1–8; 21:9–27; 22:1–5.

129. 2:7; 22:2; 2:11; 21:8; 2:17; 22:2; 2:26 transformed in 21:24; 3:5; 21:10; 22:4; 3:21; 22:5.

130. Lohmeyer, *Die Offenbarung des Johannes,* 169.

131. H. Zimmermann, "Christus und die Kirche in den Sendschreiben der Apokalypse," in *Unio Christianorum* (Paderborn: Schöningh, 1962) 184.

132. A. Nikolainen, "Der Kirchenbegriff in der Offenbarung des Johannes," *NTS* 3 (1963) 351–63.

133. Zimmermann, "Christus und die Kirche," 197.

134. Although Swete (*The Apocalypse,* xlii) has another division, he has worked out very correctly the basic principle: "The order of the Apocalypse is rather that of a series of visions arranging themselves under two great actions, of which the work of the Ascended Christ and the destinies of the Christian Church are the respective subjects."

135. E. W. Hengstenberg, *Die Offenbarung des hl. Johannes* (2d ed.; Berlin, 1861) 1: 333. However, Hengstenberg limits the "small scroll" to chap. 10:1–13.

136. For an understanding of the "scroll," cf. Holtz, *Christologie der Apokalypse,* 31–36.

137. H. P. Müller, "Die himmlische Ratsversammlung. Motivgeschichtliches zu Ap 5, 1–5," *ZNW* 54 (1963) 254–67.

138. Ibid., 255.

139. A. Loisy, *L'Apocalypse de Jean* (Paris, 1923) 298–99.

140. H. Conzelmann, "Geschichte und Eschaton nach Mark 13," *ZNW* 50 (1959) 218; cf. H. P. Müller, "Die Plagen der Apokalypse," *ZNW* 51 (1960) 268–79.

141. In regard to the division, cf. G. Harder, "Eschatologische Schemata in der Johannesapokalypse," *TViat* 9 (1963) 82.

142. Cf. Feuillet ("Le chapitre X," 420–23) who has the content of the "small scroll" begin only with chap. 12. Feuillet maintains that Rev. contains two main sections. The first has the destiny of Israel as its theme; the second treats the fate of the nations. However, for the author of Rev. Israel is identical with the church, since he no longer knows of the distinction between the Jewish-Christian and Pagan-Christian communities. My

interpretation is supported by J. Comblin (*Le Christ dans l'Apocalypse* [Theologie Biblique, Series 3/6; Tournai, 1965] 6 n. 1).

143. In regard to the whole chapter, cf. D. Haugg, *Die 2 Zeugen* (NTAbh 18; Münster: Aschendorff, 1936) 1–137. For a survey of the various interpretations, cf. J. Munck, *Petrus und Paulus in der Offenbarung Johannis* (Copenhagen, 1950) 7–16; Feuillet, "Essai d'interprétation," 183–200.

144. L. Cerfaux and J. Cambier *(L'Apocalypse de S. Jean lue aux chrétiens* [Lectio Divina 17; Paris, 1964] 94ff.) refer to the fact that the two kingly-priestly witnesses (11:4) are the antitypes of the two beasts of which the first represents political power, and the second, religious power.

145. Von Rad (*Theologie des Alten Testaments*, 2: 122 [ET: 112–13]) maintains that it was the task of the prophets to interpret the present, especially the political situation, from the viewpoint of faith.

146. Schlier ("Vom Antichrist," 111–12) explains: "The 'small scroll' contains the destiny of the Church."

147. O. Plöger, *Das Buch Daniel* (KAT 18; Gütersloh: Gerd Mohn, 1965) 118; A. Bentzen, *Daniel* (HAT 19; Tübingen: Mohr/Siebeck, 1952) 56–58.

148. A comparison with Luke 21:24 indicates that the author of Rev. has applied the saying about the fate of the historical Jerusalem to the church. Cf. Vos, *The Synoptic Traditions*, 121ff.

149. Cf. Rissi, *Was ist und was geschehen soll danach*, 69.

150. Schlier, "Vom Antichrist," 16–29.

151. The construction of this section (11:1—15:4) has been influenced not only by Daniel, but also by Zechariah 12 and 14. The elements of an eschatological attack of heathen hordes are completely present: Yahweh's bringing together of the nations, battle, and preservation of Zion.

152. J. Kroll (*Die christliche Hymnodie bis zu Clemens von Alexandria* [Darmstadt: Wissenschaftliche Buchgesellschaft, 1968] 17) maintains that these hymns are influenced by the Christian liturgy. Cf. also S. Läuchli, "Eine Gottesdienststruktur in der Johannesoffenbarung," *TZ* 16 (1960) 360–78; G. Delling, *Der Gottesdienst im Neuen Testament* (Göttingen: Vandenhoeck & Ruprecht, 1962) 52 [ET: *Worship in the New Testament* (Philadelphia: Westminster Press; London: Darton, Longman & Todd, 1962]; P. Prigent, *Apocalypse et liturgie* (Neuchatel: Delachaux et Niestlé, 1964). H. Bietenhard (*Die himmliche Welt im Urchristentum und Spätjudentum* [Tübingen: Mohr/Siebeck, 1950] 132) maintains to the contrary, and correctly, that all the hymns are constructed by the author and adjusted in Rev. to fit the situation of the divine action.

153. Rev. 17 and 18 belong to the visions of the bowls, since in 16:19 the judgment of Babylon has already taken place. Moreover, one of the seven angels who had seen the seven bowls shows the seer the image of the great harlot. Furthermore, Rev. 17—18 are oppositionally connected with Rev. 12—13: the woman clothed with the sun (12:1) is the antitype of the great harlot (17:1, 15); the woman in the desert (12:13, 14) is the antitype of the harlot in the desert (17:3). The emphasis in both chaps. falls on the persecution of the saints. Cf. "Die Komposition," 206–7. In addition, Rev. 17 stands in contrast to Rev. 21. It is not an accident that one of the angels with the bowls shows the seer the New Jerusalem. Verses 21:9 and 17:1, 2 agree to the word, but have different objects! The angel also names the New Jerusalem, the bride. Cf. K. L. Schmidt, "Jerusalem als Urbild und Abbild," *Eranos Jahrbuch* 18 (1950) 231.

154. The divine world-judgment of 20:11–15 falls out of the schema of Ezekiel which determines the construction of the visions in 19:11—22:5. Therefore the seer has intentionally placed it at the end of the description of the judgment. Cf. Harder, "Das eschatologische Geschichtsbild," 70–87, esp. 73; A. Vanhoye, "L'utilisation du livre Ezéchiel dans l'Apocalypse," *Bib* 43 (1962) 436–76.

155. For the literature, cf. H. Bietenhard, *Das tausendjährige Reich* (Zurich, 1955); J. W. Bailey, "The Temporary Messianic Reign in the Literature of Early Judaism," *JBL* 53 (1934) 170–87.

156. W. Metzger, "Das Zwischenreich," in *Auf dem Grunde der Apostel und Propheten* (Stuttgart, 1958) 112–13; J. Sickenberger ("Das tausendjährige Reich in der Apokalypse," in *Festschrift S. Merkle gewidmet* [Düsseldorf: Patmos-Verlag, 1921] 300–316) assumes to the contrary that the resurrected live in heaven. This same assumption is shared by J. H. Elliot (*The Elect and the Holy* [NovTSup 12; Leiden: E. J. Brill, 1966] 117): "[Apoc.] 20, 6 does speak of a celestial priesthood and reign but 1:6 and 5:10 do not."

157. P. S. Minear, "The Cosmology of the Apocalypse," *Current Issues in New Testament Interpretation* (ed. W. Klassen and G. F. Snyder; New York: Harper & Row, 1962) 23–37.

2
Redemption as Liberation
(Revelation 1:5-6 and 5:9-10)

Since redemption is central to Christianity, an adequate understanding of this subject is of prime importance. Christian theology, however, has been criticized for understanding redemption primarily as spiritual or as related to the invisible realm of human souls without reference to the external world.[1] If redemption were so understood, it would be limited to the spiritual life, and religion would have the function mainly of saving souls by bringing them into a spiritual community with God and Christ. I do not intend to discuss this spiritualistic and individualistic understanding of redemption, but rather to demonstrate that the author of the Rev., John,[2] did not share this view. Instead, he conceives of redemption and salvation[3] in political terms and in socio-economic categories.

John asserts that redemption involves liberation from bondage and slavery and that salvation gives new dignity to those who have been redeemed through the death of Jesus Christ. He expresses this new dignity through the titles *basileia* (kingdom) and *hiereis* (priests), which in antiquity designate the bearers of political power and sacral authority. The use of these two titles together is not surprising since in antiquity politics and religion were closely interrelated. Conceiving of redemption in political terms, the author asserts that final redemption and salvation are not now possible, but only when the state of dominion on earth is radically changed. Only when Satan and the concrete representation of demonic power, the Roman empire, no longer rule on earth is final salvation possible. Only when God and the Lamb reign on earth is salvation accomplished. Then a new, more humanized world shall be created by God where there shall no longer be weeping and mourning, hunger and thirst, pain and death.

A different interpretation of Rev. maintains that the eschatological end is only the manifestation of that which the church through redemption has already become. In my opinion, this interpretation is basically platonic and overlooks the eschatological reservation which John makes.[4] I hope to demonstrate in the following analysis of Rev. 1:5–6 and 5:9–10 that the author of Rev. conceives of redemption and salvation in political-social categories and that he underlines the significance of the eschatological reservation for the sake of preventing salvation from becoming an illusion.

A comparison of the way in which Christian redemption and salvation are formulated in the prescript of Rev. (1:5–6) with the way they are expressed in the "new song" (5:9–10) of the elders brings to the fore their differences while indicating at the same time certain similarities between these two passages.

To him who loves us
and has freed us from our sins by his blood
and made us a kingdom, priests to his God and Father.
(RSV)

tō agapōnti hēmas
kai lysanti hēmas ek tōn hamartiōn hēmōn en tō haimati autou
kai epoiēsen hēmas basileian hiereis to theō kai patri autou
Rev. 1:5–6

Worthy art thou to take the scroll
    and to open its seals,
for thou wast slain and by thy blood
    didst ransom [people] for God
from every tribe and tongue and
    people and nation,
and hast made them a kingdom and
    priests to our God,
and they shall reign on earth.
(RSV)

(axios ei labein to biblion kai anoixai tas sphragidas
    autou) hoti esphagēs
kai ēgorasas tō theō en tō haimati sou ek pasēs phylēs
    kai glossēs kai laou kai ethnous
kai epoiēsas autous tō theō hēmōn basileian kai hiereis
    kai basileusousin epi tēs gēs
(Rev. 5:9–10)

Both statements are phrased in hymnic-proclamatory style and have a significant position in the composition of the whole book.[5] Both have three parallel members, of which the first of each differs completely in wording. Rev. 1:5 speaks of the loving activity of Christ in the present; 5:9 refers back to the violent death of Christ. The second members also look similar and yet are different. Rev. 1:5 speaks of the setting free of the Christians from their sins by the blood of the Lamb; 5:9 speaks of the purchasing of persons from all humanity by the blood of Christ. The third members also differ in that the grammatically difficult construction *basileian hiereis* of the one is eased through *kai* and *tō theō* preceding *basileian* in the other. The main difference between the two, however, is the addition of the clause "and they shall reign on earth" (5:10b), which must be read in a future sense.[6] An analysis of both passages should investigate whether these differences represent, in each case, a distinct theological conception or a mere terminological rephrasing of the same theological conception.

THE PREDICATIVE STATEMENTS
ABOUT CHRIST'S ACTIONS
IN REVELATION 1:5-6.

E. Lohmeyer[7] has already observed that the prescript of Rev. is written in a definite hymnic and hieratic style. After the sender and the recipients are named in 1:4, the salutation follows. It promises peace and grace from God, from the seven spirits,[8] and from Jesus Christ. While God is characterized in a threefold way, Jesus Christ is characterized not only by three titles but also by three predicative statements. The salutation concludes with a doxology.[9] It is followed by a prophetic word in 1:7[10] and a word of God in 1:8[11] which refers back to the designations of God in 1:4 and so connects the end of the prescript with the beginning. Despite its hymnic-hieratic style, the prescript as a whole is nevertheless not taken over from an early Christian liturgy;[12] its content and vocabulary clearly refer to the content of Rev. and reveal characteristics of the language of the author.

The three honorary titles of Christ, the three predicative statements about his activity, and the doxology together form a unity of praise. Since the connection of the titles with the name "Jesus Christ" is grammatically incorrect[13] and the second title, "first-born of the dead," reflects traditional Christology, as is found in the hymn of Col. 1:18[14] and in the Pauline letters (Rom. 8:29 and 1 Cor. 15:20),[15] it could be possible that these titles were taken over by the author from tradition. But since the first and third titles reflect his theology, it is more probable that these titles only contain traditional material and were formed as a unit by the author himself.[16] These titles therefore do not represent an early Christian formula that refers to the death, resurrection, and exaltation of Christ.[17] Instead they express the author's own theological interest in emphasizing the relationship of Christ to his community. He is the eschatological witness upon whom the Christians can rely; he is the inaugurator and the representative of the new creation; finally he is the ruler[18] who has all kingship and power.

The three titles of Christ are followed by three predicative statements about the activity of Christ. The participial style,[19] the place of the participles at the beginning of every clause, the parallelism of the three members, the switch from the personal pronoun *hymin* (you) to *hēmas* (we),[20] and finally the doxology at the end of the unit give the impression that the whole unit is a hymnic formulation composed by the author or taken over from tradition. If the doxology were connected only by the author himself with the three predicative statements about the activity of Christ, then the three predicative statements could have originally formed a confessional formula which the author made into a hymn of praise.[21] John could have formed the whole unit (the titles, the predicative statements, and the doxology) into a hymn of praise in order to make the form parallel to the Pauline thanksgivings.[22] Since the whole prescript has been written in the form of the Pauline letter prescript, this assumption becomes even more probable.

If the aorist tense in the three predicative statements about the activity of Christ reflects early Christian language and traditional material, it must be asked to which tradition this material belongs. A form-critical investigation[23] would indicate that this material probably had its *Sitz im Leben* in the baptismal tradition. The first member of the statement in 1:5–6 has probably been altered by the author from the past to the present tense. The aorist of *agapaō* followed by the accusative is frequently found in early Christian pre-Pauline tradition (e.g. in Gal. 2:20,[24] 2 Thess. 2:16,[25] Eph. 1:5–6.; 2:4ff.; and 5:25ff.[26]). This tradition can be characterized as baptismal. As Rev. 3:9 indicates John knew this tradition in which the aorist of *agapaō* was used with the accusative. In contrast to the LXX text of Isa. 43:4, Rev. 3:9 does not place the verb *ēgapēsa* (I have loved) after the accusative, but rather before it as in the early Christian tradition.[27] Whereas the traditional formula spoke of the love of God or Christ in the past tense, in Rev. 3:9 and 1:5 the author emphasizes the loving activity of Christ in the present. Even though the present time is full of suffering and persecutions for Christians, Christ's love is now with them.

The second member of the formula in Rev. 1:5–6 refers to the setting free of the Christians from their own sins by the blood of Christ. The use of the term *haima* (blood)[28] in connection with forgiveness of sins[29] is found very early. It is not only present in the tradition of the word about the cup in the Lord's Supper,[30] but also in pre-Pauline formulas.[31] *Lysanti* ("to him who has freed"), which is preferable to the variant *lousanti*,[32] is used only here in the NT. It shares, however, its root with such expressions as *lytron, lytrousthai*, or *apolytrōsis*. These terms are used in connection with *haima* to denote "the redemption" (Rom. 3:24–26; Eph. 1:7; Heb. 9:12; 1 Pet. 1:19).[33] Whether they belong to the baptismal or to the eucharistic tradition is, however, a matter of debate.[34] The variant *lousanti* ("to him who has washed") could indicate that Rev. 1:5 was very early understood as referring to baptism. Through his blood Christ has set the baptized free from their own personal sins. Thus redemption is understood here in an anthropological sense as the liberation of the Christians from the evil actions and deeds of their past.

The third member of the formula in Rev. 1:6 speaks about the installation of the redeemed "to kingship, to priests for God." The grammatically difficult phrase *basileian hiereis*[35] (the abstract singular *basileian* is placed together with the concrete plural *hiereis*) probably refers to a textform of Exod. 19:6 which is not found in the LXX, but is in the version of Theodotion.[36] The verb *poiein*,[37] however, is neither in this Extext nor in the NT parallel text of 1 Pet. 2:9 where the LXX text of Exod. 19:6 has been taken over. Since the verb refers here to concrete persons who are given a new dignity, it should probably be understood in the sense of "investing" or "installing" someone. The usage of *poiein* in this sense is not found in classical Greek,[38] but in the LXX and in the NT, *Kai epoiēsen* is so used in Mark 3:14–19 where it refers to the institution of the twelve ("And *he appointed* twelve"),[39] and in Acts 2:36, where it refers to the investiture of Jesus as Lord and Messiah by God.[40] The closest parallel to Rev. 1:6 is, however, found in 1 Sam. 12:6; 1 Kings 12:31 and 13:33–34, where the aorist *epoiēsen* is also used in connection with the accusative of *hiereis*.[41] Both OT texts emphasize that in the Northern Kingdom every member of the nation could be installed by Jeroboam as a priest without having to come from the Levitical tribe. Thus Rev. 1:6 maintains that Christ installed the redeemed to kingship, to be priests for God, the Father. The use of the aorist and the reference to Exod. 19:6 (which is also found in 1 Pet. 2:9 in a passage full of baptismal allusions)[42] makes it probable that the third member of the statement about the activity of Christ belongs to a baptismal tradition.

In short, this analysis of Rev. 1:5–6 indicates that all three predicative statements about the activity of Christ represent formulary material which in all probability belonged to the early Christian baptismal tradition. The three predicative statements in their traditional form did not have the form of a hymn, as in the present context, but that of a confessional formula, which emphasized the loving activity of Christ at the beginning of Christian existence. This beginning is concretely explicated as the liberation of those who speak this formula from their own sins by the death of Christ, and as their investiture with the dignity and power of both kings and priests. By changing the first aorist to the present tense, the author stresses that Christ's love is now with those whom he redeemed and installed to kingship and to be priests for God, in spite of all persecutions and tribulations. Since in emphasizing the past this confessional formula views redemption and salvation as an already accomplished existing reality, it could lead to an enthusiastic misunderstanding, one which no longer takes seriously the fact that Christians are still living in time and history and cannot be secure about their salvation. The author's theological redaction in 5:9-10 reveals that he saw this danger of an enthusiastic misunderstanding of salvation because in taking over this baptismal formula he altered and expanded it in a significant way.

THE "NEW SONG" (REVELATION 5:9-10)

The "new song"[43] sung by the twenty-four elders affirms the worthiness (*axios*) of the Lamb to take over the lordship of the world. Thus it answers the central question of chap. 5, namely, "who is worthy to take the seven sealed scroll[44] and to break its seals" (5:2)? This question asks for the one who is able and worthy to be the eschatological regent of the world. After it is affirmed that no one in the whole world is worthy, the appearance of the powerful Lamb (*arnion*),[45] which was slain, is described. Here Christ, as in Paul, is both the crucified one and the Lord. In Rev. the Lord is portrayed by means of OT titles[46] as the expected messianic figure. The answer to the question why Christ is worthy is given explicitly in the consolation of the elder in 5:5 and in the "new song" in 5:9-10. 5:5 refers back to the promises to the victor in the so-called letters, especially to 3:21 where the absolute aorist tense of *nikaō* (to gain victory) is used together with royal imagery, emphasizing the participation of the victorious Christ in the lordship of God.[47] The reason given in Rev. 5:9-10 for the Lamb's worthiness to assume the eschatological reign over the world is threefold:

First, the Lamb is worthy because it was slain. The verb *sphazein* (to slaughter)[48] refers to the violent death of the Lamb and probably alludes to the slaughtering of the Paschal Lamb,[49] an image used early in the Christian tradition to interpret Christ's death, as 1 Cor. 5:7 (cf. 1 Pet. 1:18) indicates.[50] This image evokes the memory of Israel's exodus and liberation, which was considered in Judaism as a prototype for the final eschatological salvation.[51]

Second, the Lamb is worthy because it has purchased people for God from every tribe, tongue, people, and nation with his blood. The Lamb is pictured here as God's "purchasing agent." It has traveled throughout the whole world to purchase people for God. The price which it paid is its blood. This metaphoric language is used to emphasize the high value of the purchased ones as well as the universality of Christ's action. The verb *agorazein* (to purchase)[52] comes from business life and denotes commercial transaction as is also evident in Rev. 3:18 and 13:17. The image probably refers here to the slave-market since people are the objects of the purchase. However, it does not revert here to the sacral ransom of slaves, where the slave had to pay the price under the fiction that the god, in whose temple she or he deposited the money, purchased the slave from her or his human owner, since neither God nor the purchased are paying the price.[53] More probably, the reference is to the ransom of prisoners of war, who were deported to the countries of the victors and who could be ransomed by a "purchasing agent" of their own country.[54] Here the image refers again to the exodus tradition. As the blood of the Paschal Lamb was a sign for the liberation of Israel from the bondage and slavery of Egypt, so also is the death of Christ the cause for the liberation of the Christians from their universal bondage. This interpretation of *agorazein* is supported by Rev. 14:4, where it is said that the 144,000 on the Mount Zion are purchased from humankind (in v. 3 from the earth) as the first fruits (*aparchē*) for God and the Lamb. If *aparchē* is used here, as is usual in the NT, in the sense of the first whom others will follow,[55] then the 144,000 are the sign of the universal eschatological salvation of all people and nations.[56]

Third, the final reason for the worthiness of the Lamb is given in Rev. 5:10 which describes the positive goal of the Lamb's redemptive activity. As, according to Roman law, the freed prisoners of war were brought back home and reintegrated into their own nation, so here it is said that the purchased ones are "made for God to a kingdom[57] and to priests." The author, however, appears to be more interested in the *basileia* motif than in the priest motif,[58] as is evident from the emphasis given to the term *basileia* through the preceding dative *tō theō*, from the separation of the titles *basileia* and *hiereis* through *kai*, and especially from the addition of the phrase "and they shall reign on earth." Those who are ransomed for God are liberated "to be a kingdom for God and priests." They will exercise their kingship on earth in the eschatological future.

The "new song" of the elders thus depicts redemption and salvation in economic language and political imagery and understands it as an event analogous to the liberation of Israel from the slavery of Egypt. Insofar as John describes redemption and salvation in Rev. 5:9–10 in sociopolitical terms analogous to the liberation of Israel from Egypt, he has altered the anthropological understanding of redemption of the early Christian tradition as expressed in the baptismal formula of Rev.

1:5–6. Just as the exodus of Israel led to the constitution of Israel as a special nation and kingdom for Yahweh, so does the election of the Christians from humanity through the death of Christ lead to a new kingdom, whose members are priests. If they are victorious, they will exercise their kingship actively on earth in the eschatological future.

John's modification of the baptismal formula in Rev. 1:5–6 implies at the same time both an antagonistic-ethical and eschatological understanding of redemption. This antagonistic understanding is expressed throughout the book. The mythological figures of the dragon, the two beasts, and the great harlot Babylon symbolize in my opinion the Roman empire, the Roman Caesar and his cult, and finally the satanic powers behind these political realities.[59] As the inhabitants of the earth, the kings and merchants of the earth are now on the side of the Roman empire, so the new kingdom for God created by Christ through redemption is the realm and community where God is already on earth acknowledged as king. As the kingdom for God, the Christian community is understood in political terms as the alternative community to the Roman empire. However, despite their belonging to the kingdom for God through their baptism Christians still must decide whether to acknowledge the authority and power of the Roman Caesar or that of God and the Lamb. Only those who stand by this decision until death and do not take the sign of the beast shall reign on earth with the Messiah as the vision and blessing (*makarismos*) of the millennium promise.[60]

This antagonistic concept of Christian existence does not allow for a realized understanding of redemption and salvation, but demands an eschatological one. As long as the beast and Babylon have the power on earth it is an illusion and enthusiastic misunderstanding of the baptismal formula in Rev. 1:5–6 to understand it in the sense that those set free from their sins are already exercising their kingship. This enthusiastic understanding of salvation in early Christianity was connected with baptismal theology, as is evident in 1 Cor. 4:8; Rom. 5:17; 2 Tim. 2:11–12, Polycarp *Phil.* 5:2.[61] Over and against this enthusiastic understanding of salvation and its emphasis upon the present reign of the baptized, Paul, the writer of 2 Timothy, and Polycarp of Smyrna maintain the "eschatological reservation." In contrast to this eschatological understanding, gnostic writings (e.g., *The Gospel of Thomas*) spiritualize the notion of kingdom and kingship to the extent that it is no longer given in time and space, but only in experience.[62] To prevent such a spiritualized understanding of kingship and priesthood the author of Rev. stresses that in heaven Christ has assumed lordship over the world. Only when he establishes it on earth and only when the throne of God and the Lamb are found in the New Jerusalem on a new earth will those Christians who have remained faithful actively exercise their kingship and priesthood.

In conclusion, in Rev. 1:5–6 John quotes a traditional baptismal formula which stresses that by his blood Christ has freed the baptized from their sins, has installed them to kingship, and has made them priests for God. In the "new song" (Rev. 5:9–10), he modifies this anthropological understanding of redemption and salvation by expressing it in theological, sociopolitical language. He no longer speaks of redemption from personal sins, but of the ransom of slaves from the whole world. As Israel was freed from the slavery of Egypt and constituted as a kingdom of priests and a special nation through the covenant with Yahweh, so also are those who are purchased for God by the Lamb made a kingdom and priests. As such they are the anti-kingdom to the Roman empire. The author maintains the "eschatological reservation" against a spiritualistic-enthusiastic understanding of redemption and salvation. By underlining the eschatological aspect of salvation, he emphasizes the imperative that must follow the indicative of Christian existence. Only those who, like Christ, were faithful witnesses and have been victorious in the struggle with the Roman empire will have a part in the eschatological kingship and priesthood. Final redemption from the bondage of the nations and political powers, as well as final salvation expressed in kingship and priesthood, is only possible when God and Christ have assumed the power and kingship on a new earth, in a new world, where death no longer exists (Rev. 21:4). To pretend that redemption and salvation are already accomplished in baptism would therefore be an illusion. According to Rev. fully realized redemption and salvation presupposes not only the liberating and dignifying of individual persons, but also the creating of a new world.

NOTES

1. Cf. G. Scholem, "Toward an Understanding of the Messianic Idea in Judaism," in *The Messianic Idea in Judaism* (New York: Schocken Books, 1971) 1–36, 341, 343.

2. It is assumed here that John, the author of Rev., is *not* identical with the evangelist of the Fourth Gospel. For a discussion of the problem, cf. W. G. Kümmel, *Introduction to the New Testament* (14th ed.; Nashville: Abingdon Press, 1966) 327–29.

3. *Sotēria* ("salvation") is found in Rev. only in those hymnic formulas (7:10; 12:10; 19:1) that refer to the eschatological final salvation. In the soteriological hymn 12:10b–12 *sotēria* is used in parallel and is synonymous with *basileia tou theou*. "Redemption" and "salvation" are used in this chapter to refer to the salvific activity of Jesus Christ with regard to the community and to the final eschatological salvation.

4. Cf. J. Kallas, "The Apocalypse—An Apocalyptic Book?" *JBL* 86 (1967) 68–80, esp.

78. He maintains that Rev. represents a realized eschatology and is therefore platonic and not apocalyptic in character. A similar view had been proposed earlier by E. Lohmeyer, *Die Offenbarung des Johannes* (HNT 16; 2d ed.; Tübingen: Mohr/Siebeck, 1953) 193, 197. He holds such a realized eschatology with regard to the believers. Cf. also T. Holtz, *Die Christologie der Apokalypse des Johannes* (TU 85; Berlin: Akademie-Verlag, 1962) 214.

5. As a part of the prescript Rev. 1:5–6 is an introduction not only to the so-called letters but to the whole book, whereas 5:9–10 belongs to the introductory chapters to the apocalyptic section of the book.

6. The present tense *basileuousin* (Rev. 5:10) is attested by the best text witness A (Alexandrinus) and the Koine manuscripts. The future tense *basileusousin* ("they shall reign") is found in most of the manuscripts and accepted by the majority of the commentaries on Rev. However, A also has the present tense in Rev. 20:6, a text which refers quite clearly to the eschatological future. Therefore, the reading *basileuousin* is either a Hebraism connoting the future, or a mistake, or more probably a correction by the writer of A.

7. Lohmeyer, *Die Offenbarung des Johannes*, 10.

8. The seven spirits are also mentioned in Rev. 3:1; 4:5; 5:6. Cf. A. Skrinjar, "Les Sept Ésprits (Apoc. 1:4; 3:1; 4:5; 5:6)," *Bib* 16 (1935) 1–25, 113–40. The notion of the "seven spirits" is probably derived from the concept of the seven archangels. In Rev. they represent the spirit of God in its fullness and completeness or God's own action. Cf. E. Schweizer, "Die sieben Geister in der Apokalypse," *EvT* 11 NF 6 (1951/52) 502–12; idem, "pneuma," *TDNT* 6 (1968) 450. He stresses that this notion of the "seven spirits" is understandable only in the light of pre-Gnostic Jewish thinking.

9. *Kratos* (power) is used in connection with *doxa* (glory) in Rev. only in the parallel place of Rev. 5:13. But while Rev. 5:13 has four doxological expressions, Rev. 1:6 has only two such expressions as is also the case in 1 Pet. 4:11. This indicates that Rev. 1:6 represents a more traditional form than Rev. 5:13. Cf. R. Deichgräber, *Gotteshymnus und Christushymnus in der frühen Christenheit* (SUNT 5; Göttingen: Vandenhoeck & Ruprecht, 1967) 27–28. Moreover, it also indicates that the author of Rev. works with and alters his traditional material.

10. Cf. R. H. Charles (*A Critical and Exegetical Commentary on the Revelation of St. John* [ICC; New York: Charles Scribner's Sons, 1920] 1: 17–20) and my analysis (E. Schüssler Fiorenza, *Priester für Gott: Studien zum Herrschafts- und Priestermotiv in der Apokalypse* [(NTAbh NF 7; Münster: Aschendorff, 1972] 185–98).

11. The author repeats here the formula *ho ōn kai ho ēn kai ho erchomenos* ("who is and who was and who is to come") of Rev. 1:4 and inserts it between the titles *kyrios ho theos* ("the Lord God") and *pantokratōr* ("Almighty") which are used together seven times in Rev., namely in Rev. 1:8; 4:8; 11:17; 15:13; 16:7; 19:6; 21:22. The title *pantokratōr* is often used in the LXX but was known also in Palestinian traditions. Cf. Michaelis, "pantokratōr," *TDNT* 3 (1965) 914–15. In the NT the title is found in 2 Cor. 6:18. Cf. J. A. Fitzmyer, "Qumran and the Interpolated Paragraph in 2 Cor. 6:14—7:1," *CBQ* 23 (1961) 271–80; J. Gnilka, "2 Cor. 6:14—7:1 im Lichte der Qumranschriften und der Zwölf-Patriarchen-Testamente," in *Festschrift Josef Schmid* (Regensburg: Pustet, 1963) 86–99.

12. For a contrary opinion, cf. S. Läuchli, "Eine Gottesdienststruktur in der Johannesoffenbarung," *TZ* 16 (1960) 359–78, esp. 360ff.

13. The nominative form, according to Läuchli (ibid., 361) and Lohmeyer (*Die Offen-*

barung des Johannes, 10), is the main argument that the titles belong to a liturgical tradition. But the author of Rev. could have added the titles and placed them in the nominative form next to the genitive *Iēsou Christou* in a manner analogous to the form of the three titles for God in v. 4.

14. Col. 1:18 is part of an early Christian hymn found in Col. 1:15–20. Cf. E. Käsemann, "A Primitive Christian Baptismal Liturgy," in *Essays on New Testament Themes* (1949; trans. W. J. Montague; London: SCM Press, 1964; Philadelphia: Fortress Press, 1982) 149–68; J. H. Gabathuler, *Jesus Christus—Haupt der Kirche, Haupt der Welt* (Zurich-Stuttgart: Zwingli Verlag, 1966); N. Kehl, *Der Christushymnus im Kolosserbrief* (Stuttgart: Katholisches Bibelwerk, 1967); E. Schweizer, "Kolosser 1:15–20" (EKKNT Vorarbeiten 1; Neukirchen-Einsiedeln: Neukirchener und Benzinger Verlag, 1969) 7–31; R. Schnackenburg, "Die Aufnahme des Christushymnus durch den Verfasser des Kolosserbriefs," ibid., 33–50. For a survey, cf. J. T. Sanders, *The New Testament Christological Hymns: Their Historical Religious Background* (Cambridge: At the Univ. Press, 1971) 75–87.

15. Rom. 8:29: "first-born among many brethren" (RSV); 1 Cor. 15:20: "first fruits of those who have fallen asleep" (RSV). In 1 Cor. 15:20 Paul uses *aparchē* ("first fruits") instead of *prōtotokos* ("the first-born") in order to distinguish himself from the enthusiasts. Cf. H. Conzelmann, *Der erste Brief an die Korinther* (MeyerK 5; Göttingen: Vandenhoeck & Ruprecht, 1969) 316–17.

16. For a more thorough analysis, cf. Schüssler Fiorenza, *Priester für Gott*, 198–203, 237–62.

17. Cf., e.g., E. Lohse, *Die Offenbarung des Johannes* (NTD 11; 9th ed.; Göttingen: Vandenhoeck & Ruprecht, 1966) 15; A. Wikenhauser, *Die Offenbarung des Johannes* (RNT 9; 3d ed.; Regensburg: Pustet, 1959) 29; A. Farrer, *The Revelation of St. John the Divine* (Oxford: At The Clarendon Press, 1964) 62.

18. The title in Rev. 1:5, *ho archōn tōn basileōn tēs gēs* ("the ruler of kings of the earth"), expresses the messianic kingly dignity of Jesus Christ. However, it is discussed whether the genitive is an objective genitive, since the "kings of the earth" are in Rev. (with the exception of Rev. 21:24) always on the side of the beast and Satan, or whether it is a genitive which defines the relationship of the kings of the earth to the ruler Jesus Christ. In view of Rev. 1:6, 9 the expression could then be a designation of the true Christians as "kings of the earth" whose ruler is Christ. Cf. P. S. Minear (*I Saw a New Earth. An Introduction to the Visions of the Apocalypse* [Washington: Corpus Books, 1968] 14), who judges this as the "most likely meaning" of the title. The interpretation of "kings of the earth" as applying to Christians would correspond with the other two titles.

19. Cf. E. Norden, *Agnostos Theos: Untersuchungen zur Formgeschichte religiöser Rede* (Leipzig and Berlin, 1913; Darmstadt: Wissenschaftliche Buchgesellschaft, 1956) 351; J. Kroll, *Die christliche Hymnodik bis zu Klemens von Alexandria* (Braunsberg, 1921/22; 2d ed.; Darmstadt: Wissenschaftliche Buchgesellschaft, 1968).

20. Cf. G. Schille, *Frühchristliche Hymnen* (Berlin: Evangelische Verlagsanstalt, 1965) 18–20.

21. For the terminological distinction between confessional formula and hymn, cf. R. Deichgräber, *Gotteshymnus*, 107–17. According to Deichgräber, one of the main characteristics of the confessional formula in distinction to the hymn is that the community is mentioned.

22. Since the doxology in Rev. 1:5–6, as in Gal 1:5, takes the place of the Pauline

thanksgiving, it could be possible that the author connected the doxology with the confessional formula in Rev. 1:5b–6 in order to achieve a similar structure.

23. P. von der Osten-Sacken, "Christologie, Taufe, Homologie—Ein Beitrag zu Apok Joh 1:5f," *ZNW* 58 (1967) 255–56.

24. Cf. H. Schlier, *Der Brief an die Galater* (MeyerK 7; 12th Ed.; Göttingen: Vandenhoeck & Ruprecht, 1962) 99–103. He points out that Gal. 2:19–20 refers to the baptism event.

25. 2 Thess. 2:16 *ho agapēsas hēmas* ("who loved us") has a similar construction as Rev. 1:5b, where the aorist is followed by the accusative of the personal pronoun *we*. In 2 Thessalonians, however, the clause refers not to Christ but to God.

26. Cf. H. Schlier, *Der Brief an die Epheser* (4th ed.; Düsseldorf: Patmos-Verlag, 1963) 108. 255–56; J. Gnilka, *Der Epheserbrief* (HKNT 10/2; Freiburg: Herder, 1971) 117–18 and 2:4; H. Conzelmann, *Der Brief an die Epheser* (NTD 8; 10th ed.; Göttingen: Vandenhoeck & Ruprecht, 1965) 87, with reference to Eph. 5:2 and 5:25.

27. Isa. 43:4 (LXX) reads *kagō se ēgapēsa* ("and I have loved you"), whereas Rev. 3:9 reads *hoti egō ēgapēsa se* ("that I have loved you"). The aorist tense is not changed in Rev. 3:9 since the expression refers in its futuric context to the presence of the community.

28. The expression *haima Christou* ("the blood of Christ") is found in three contexts: (1) in connection with the redemption; (2) in connection with *rantismos* ("sprinkling" for atonement); and (3) in connection with *katharizein* and *hagiazein* ("to make clean" and "to make holy"). Cf. K. Wengst, "Christologische Formeln und Lieder des Urchristentums" (Diss.; Bonn Univ., 1967) 85–86. The expression is found in a baptismal context in Rom. 3:25; 5:9; Eph. 1:7; Heb. 9:14; 1 Pet. 1:18. It appears only once in the eucharistic tradition, namely in 1 Cor. 11:25.

29. Cf. G. Braumann, *Vorpaulinische christliche Taufverkündigung bei Paulus* (BWANT 82; Stuttgart: Kohlhammer, 1960) 38–42; R. Bultmann, *Theology of the New Testament* (trans. K. Grobel; New York: Charles Scribner's Sons, 1951) 1: 136–37.

30. The explicit connection between "blood" and "forgiveness of sins" is only made in Matt. 26:28. E. Schweizer (*The Lord's Supper According to the New Testament* [Philadelphia: Fortress Press, 1967] 10–11 n. 22) holds that the addition "for the forgiveness of sins" indicates how "theological realities already implicit in the sacrament were given explicit expression."

31. Cf. esp. Rom. 3:24–26 and perhaps 1 Cor. 1:30.

32. So Charles (*Revelation*, 1: 15) and W. Bousset (*Die Offenbarung des Johannes* [MeyerK 16; 6th ed.; Göttingen: Vandenhoeck & Ruprecht, 1906] 188) maintain that the reading *lousanti* ("to him who has washed") is possible because in their opinion the term expresses in later NT writings the notion of cleansing and washing. *Louō*, however, is used only here in Rev. 1:5 and in 1 Cor. 6:11 in an absolute form. All other parallels, which Bousset lists, do not have *louein* ("to wash") but *katharizein* ("to make clean").

33. Von der Osten-Sacken, "Christologie," 259–60.

34. This is discussed esp. in view of Rom. 3:24–26. Cf. O. Michel, *Der Brief an die Römer* (MeyerK 4; 12th ed.; Göttingen: Vandenhoeck & Ruprecht, 1963) 106; E. Käsemann, "Zum Verständnis von Röm 3:24–26," in *Exegetische Versuche und Besinnungen* (Göttingen: Vandenhoeck & Ruprecht, 1960) 1: 96–100.

35. Cf. my text-critical and exegetical discussion of the phrase: Schüssler Fiorenza, *Priester für Gott*, 70–72, 208–10, 227–35.

36. Ibid., 101–12.

37. Cf. H. Braun, "poieō," *TDNT* 6 (1968) 458–84. The verb is used in Rev. mainly in an antagonistic and eschatological sense.

38. Cf. V. Taylor, *The Gospel According to St. Mark* (2d ed.; New York: Macmillan Co., 1966) 230; J. Roloff, *Apostolat, Verkündigung, Kirche* (Gütersloh: Gerd Mohn, 1965) 145–46.

39. The clause *kai epoiēsen dōdeka* ("And he appointed twelve") in Mark 3: 14 does not render a Greek but a Semitic expression. K. G. Reploh, however (*Markus-Lehrer der Gemeinde* [SBM 9; Stuttgart: Katholisches Bibelwerk, 1969] 45) argues convincingly that v. 16 represents the more original text because it belongs to the list of names of the twelve, whereas Mark 3:14–15 displays the redactional activity of Mark.

40. H. Conzelmann, *Die Apostelgeschichte* (HNT 7; Tübingen: Mohr/Siebeck, 1963) 30. U. Wilckens, *Die Missionsreden der Apostelgeschichte* (WMANT 5; Neukirchen-Vluyn: Neukirchener Verlag, 1961) 72ff. Both argue that the formulation is typically Lucan in character. Cf., however, F. Hahn (*Christologische Hoheitstitel: Ihre Geschichte im frühen Christentum* [FRLANT 83; 2d ed.; Göttingen: Vandenhoeck & Ruprecht, 1964] 116 n. 1), who argues for the traditional character of the passage especially because of the usage of the verb *poiein*.

41. The closest parallel is 1 Kings 12:31 because it has the aorist form of *poiein* with the double accusative. Cf. A. Rahlfs, *Septuaginta*, 1: 665: *kai epoiēsen hiereis meros ti ek tou laou* ("and appointed priests from among some of the people").

42. Cf. E. Lohse, "Paränese und Kerygma im 1. Petrusbrief," *ZNW* 45 (1954) 68–69; J. N. D. Kelly, *A Commentary on the Epistles of Peter and Jude* (HNTC; New York: Harper & Row, 1969) 22–23, 65, 82.

43. This expression is often found in the Psalms (33:3; 96:1; 98:1; 114:9; 139:1). In Judaism it denotes the eschatological praise of the redeemed. Cf. Str-B, 3: 801–2. Similarly in Rev. *kainos* ("new") is the expression for eschatological salvation and perfection (2:17; 3:12; 21:1, 2, 5). Cf. J. Behm, "kainos," *TDNT* 3 (1965) 447–50; also R. H. Harrisville, "The Concept of Newness in the New Testament," *JBL* 74 (1955) 69–79, esp. 74–75.

44. Cf. my discussion of different interpretations: Schüssler Fiorenza, *Priester für Gott*, 174–276.

45. Cf. the discussion of the title by Holtz, *Die Christologie*, 35–50, 78–80; J. Comblin, *Le Christ dans l'Apocalypse* (Théologie biblique 3/6; Tournai: Desclee, 1965) 17–34.

46. The title "the lion of the tribe of Judah" refers back to Gen. 49:9–10, whereas the second title "the root of David," which is repeated in Rev. 22:16 (and also found in Rom. 15:12), alludes to Isa. 11:10. Both titles are known and interpreted in a messianic sense in Judaism (e.g., 4 Qpatr 3 and *4 Esdras* 12:31–32). Cf. I. T. Beckwith, *The Apocalypse of John* (1919; Grand Rapids: Baker Book House, 1967) 509.

47. Cf. the similarity between the structural parallels Father-Jesus and Jesus-Christians in Rev. 3:21 and Luke 22:28–30; Matt. 19:28. Note, however, that in Rev. the object of the reigning or judging is not mentioned. For a synoptic comparison, cf. L. A. Vos, *The Synoptic Traditions in the Apocalypse* (Kampen: J. H. Kok, 1965) 100–104.

48. O. Michel, "sphazō," *TDNT* (1971) 925–35.

49. Holtz, *Die Christologie*, 45.

50. Michel ("sphazō," 945 n. 42) notes to 1 Cor. 5:7: "In itself crucifixion as distinct from execution by the sword does not bear any close relation to slaughtering, so that

theological interpretation rather than historical event gives rise to the image of the slaughtered Lamb."

51. Cf. Str-B, 1: 85.

52. Cf. E. Pax, "Der Loskauf. Zur Geschichte eines neutestamentlichen Begriffs," *Anton* 37 (1962) 239-78.

53. Cf. A. Deissmann, *Licht vom Osten* (4th ed.; Tübingen: Mohr/Siebeck, 1923) 273ff. [ET: *Light from the Ancient East* (Grand Rapids: Baker Book House, 1965)].

54. W. Elert, "Redemptio ab hostibus," *TLZ* 72 (1947) 265-70.

55. Cf. Rom 16:15; 1 Cor. 16:15 (the first of the converts): 1 Cor. 15:20 (the first of the dead); Rom. 8:23 (the Spirit as the first gift); James 1:18 (first of the creatures).

56. This interpretation of Rev. 14:1-5 is dependent upon the understanding of "Mount Zion" in v. 1. An eschatological interpretation of these verses is supported by the observation that Mount Zion is regarded in apocalyptic literature as the place where the Messiah will appear (*4 Esdras* 13:25-50; *2 Apoc. Bar.* 40:1-2). The vision would then be a parallel to Rev. 20:4-6. For a discussion of the whole question, cf. A. Satake, *Die Gemeindeordnung in der Johannesapokalypse* (WMANT 21; Neukirchen-Vluyn: Neukirchener, 1966) 39-47. For a recent interpretation of the 144,000 as Christian ascetics, cf. C. H. Lindijar, "Die Jungfrau in der Offenbarung des Johannes," in *Studies in John: Festschrift J. N. Sevenster* (Leiden: E. J. Brill, 1970) 124-42.

57. The term *basileia* can mean "empire" or "sovereignty" in NT times. After the time of the Maccabees, however, it denotes more and more "world-empire," and is used without any definition or article as a term for the Roman empire. Cf. Str-B, 1: 183; H. Conzelmann, *An Outline of the Theology of the New Testament* (trans. J. Bowden; New York: Harper & Row, 1969) 108; F. C. Grant, "The Idea of the Kingdom of God in the New Testament," in *Sacral Kingship — La Regalita Sacra* (NumSup 4; Leiden: E. J. Brill, 1959) 437-46, esp. 440-41.

58. For an interpretation of the Sinai-tradition in Qumran which stresses the holy and priestly character of the eschatological community, cf. O. Betz, "The Eschatological Interpretation of the Sinai-Tradition in Qumran and in the New Testament," *RQ* 6 (1967/69) 89-107.

59. The majority of the commentaries on Rev. see in Rev. a concrete political conflict with the Roman empire expressed in mythological language (e.g., Swete, Charles, Loisy, Beckwith, Carrington, Wikenhauser, Caird, Visser, Kiddle-Ross). Similarly the Danielic vision of the four empires was recalled also in *Sib Or.* (5:214), *4 Esdras* (11:46), and *2 Apoc. Bar.* (40:3) with Rome as the fourth soon to be destroyed.

60. Cf. E. Schüssler Fiorenza, "Die tausendjährige Herrschaft der Auferstandenen (Apk 20, 4-6)," *BiLe* 13 (1972) 107-24. It is important to note that in Rev. 20:4-6 as well as in Rev. 22:5 (which refer to the active reign and kingship of the participants in the first resurrection) the substantive *basileia* is no longer used. Although the substantive *malkut* is still used in both the sense of active kingship and in the sense of a local kingdom, in Dan. 7:22-23, 1 QSb 5.21 and 1QM 19.8, the author of Rev. seems to distinguish clearly the active and the territorial-communal aspects when he uses only the verb to express the active reign of the eschatologically saved Christians.

61. Cf. J. M. Robinson, "Kerygma and History in the New Testament," in *Trajectories through Early Christianity* (Philadelphia: Fortress Press, 1971) 32-37.

62. B. F. Miller, "A Study of the Theme of 'Kingdom': The Gospel according to Thomas: Logion 18," *NovT* 9 (1967) 52.

PART TWO

REVELATION IN THE CONTEXT OF EARLY CHRISTIANITY IN ASIA MINOR

3

The Quest for the Johannine School:
The Book of Revelation and
The Fourth Gospel*

> The subject presents one of those questions in New Testament criticism
> in which mental bent, apart from the bias of prejudgment, is chiefly
> influential in determining the conclusions reached.[1]

This statement, with which I. T. Beckwith in 1919 introduced his discussion of the authorship of the Book of Rev., still proves true today. It can be applied equally to the question whether Rev. should be assigned to the same school or circle that was responsible for the Fourth Gospel and the Johannine epistles. Moreover, the judgment also pertains to the historical and theological interpretation of either Rev. or the Fourth Gospel. Mental bent and systematic presuppositions determine the various reconstructions of the history of the Johannine community as well as the theological interpretations of its literary works.

This chapter does not intend to reconstruct the history of the Johannine school or to explore the relationship of all the writings traditionally ascribed to "John," but to concentrate upon the relationship between Rev. and the Fourth Gospel. Such a comparison, however, must face the various methodological problems that result from the present state of scholarship. Even though studies of the Fourth Gospel, its historical setting, religious language, and theological perspective abound, scholars are far from agreement with respect to its crucial problems, for example its redactional process, historical-religious context, and basic theological tenets.[2] The same divergencies in interpretations can be found in the scholarly discussion of Rev.[3] Serious exegetical studies of this book are, however, much more rare, and popular—often bizarre—interpretations abound. Moreover, contemporary scholarship has studied Rev. not so much as an important work of the early Christian *Theologiegeschichte* (history of theology) but as a Jewish document with a slight Christian

*Seminar paper read at the 31st Meeting of the Society of New Testament Studies, August 1976. The research for this paper was supported by a NEH summer grant.

touch-up.[4] The scholarly discourse on Rev. still seems not only to reflect Luther's judgment that the book is not quite Christian, but also to mirror the prevalent scholarly prejudice against Jewish and early Christian apocalypticism.[5] Finally, a theological comparison of Rev. and the Fourth Gospel appears dependent upon the definition of the relationships among apocalypticism, wisdom theology, and Gnosticism as well as upon the exploration of their interaction within early Christian theology and tradition. Since these and other questions are far from being resolved, this chapter will have to raise more problems and issues than it is able to solve.

In order to specify the problems and to state the issues I shall first review the scholarly discussion of the authorship problem; secondly, analyze the function of the Johannine school hypothesis in contemporary scholarship; thirdly, discuss some linguistic and theological affinities cited as argument for the school hypothesis; and fourthly, attempt to locate the school-tradition of Rev. within the early Christianity of Asia Minor at the end of the first century C.E.

THE PROBLEM OF AUTHORSHIP

In reviewing the literature on the subject one has to agree with M. Kiddle:

> No subject of Biblical studies has provoked such elaborate and prolonged discussion among scholars as that of the authorship of the five books of the New Testament which are traditionally ascribed to "John." . . . And no discussion has been so bewildering, disappointing and unprofitable.[6]

The maze of conflicting arguments and the extent of scholarly confusion appear to stem from the contradiction between the external attestation of authorship by the ecclesiastical tradition and the internal literary and theological evidence of Rev. and the Fourth Gospel themselves.

Although neither Rev. nor the Fourth Gospel claims to be written by one and the same author, church tradition has ascribed both books to the authorship of John the apostle.[7] From the last quarter of the second century until the advent of modern critical scholarship the apostolic authorship of both books was widely held. The Tübingen school challenged this assumption by claiming that, because of their great difference in theology, the Book of Rev. and the Fourth Gospel cannot have been written by one and the same author. One and the same person could not have advocated the futuristic eschatology of Rev. and the realized eschatology of the Fourth Gospel. However, the problem regarding the same authorship for both works was not created by modern criticism.

Already in the third century Dionysius of Alexandria[8] had seen the problem and pointed out the stylistic and theological differences between the two writings. He concluded that Rev. and the Fourth Gospel could not have been written by the same author; he attributed the Fourth Gospel and 1 John to the authorship of the apostle John, but ascribed Rev. to "another John." Dionysius supported his argument for dual authorship with a reference to the two tombs at Ephesus which were reputed to be John's. Eusebius[9] also doubted whether the apostle John wrote Rev. and suggested that the presbyter John mentioned by Papias wrote the book. Thus some of the church fathers had already acknowledged the problem of the traditional assertion that one and the same author is responsible for Rev. and the Fourth Gospel. Moreover, they had already suggested the solutions which are still discussed in contemporary scholarship.

Since extensive discussions of the Johannine authorship question can be found in the general introductions and commentaries to Rev. or the Fourth Gospel, I shall here only summarize and classify the proposed solutions without debating too much the pro and con of individual arguments.[10]

First, scholars affirm the attestation of the patristic tradition that the Fourth Gospel and Rev. were written by John the apostle. Their main argument points to the difficulty of satisfactorily explaining how such an early and widely accepted church tradition could have been created so soon after the two books were written.

Second, only Rev. was written by the apostle John. The theology of wrath and the urgent messianic expectations of Rev. correspond to the characteristics of John the apostle, ascribed to him by other early Christian writings. The "son of thunder" (Mark 3:17) could easily have written the last book of the NT.

Third, Rev. is pseudepigraphical. This hypothesis can take a twofold line of reasoning: the book is claiming apostolic authorship because it was a heretical work, or it was written in honor of the apostle and therefore the author does not mention any name. In both instances the author merely followed apocalyptic and early Christian literary practice for which pseudonymity was a common literary device.

Fourth, not Rev. but the Fourth Gospel was written by John the apostle. This assumption was already put forward by Dionysius of Alexandria and seems to be supported by the internal witness of Rev. The author of Rev. does not claim to be an apostle, but refers to the twelve apostles as great figures of the past who have an eminent place in the New Jerusalem. He calls himself a servant, a brother of the Christians to whom he writes, a partner in their oppression, and a prophetic witness.

His authority is not derived from his apostleship but from the fact that, as a prophet, he received revelations from the resurrected Lord.

Fifth, neither Rev. nor the Fourth Gospel can claim apostolic authorship. Since at the time of their writing the apostle was long dead, both books owe their existence to the presbyter John who lived in Asia Minor and is mentioned by Papias. Other persons suggested are John Mark, Lazarus, or the Beloved Disciple.

Those scholars claiming that Rev. and the Fourth Gospel stem from the same author, be it the apostle, the presbyter, or someone else, must still account for the linguistic and theological differences of the two writings. Here again different solutions are proposed.

First, one way to explain the divergencies in style and theology is to point out the differences in scope and literary form of the two books. One is written as a "revelation" of the resurrected Lord presented in the form of apocalyptic visions; the other is a depiction of the life and words of Jesus in the form of a gospel.

Second, another way to explain the differences is to postulate a time interval between the origin of the two writings. The style and theology of the two books are different because the apostle or presbyter matured and got older. This explanation often assumes that Rev. expresses the youthful anger of the son of Zebedee, whereas the Fourth Gospel reflects the wisdom of the aged apostle.

Third, a favored way among exegetes to explain the theological differences between Rev. and the Fourth Gospel is to assume that the theology of the one work does not exclude but complements that of the other. This solution is aptly expressed by E. Lohmeyer who argues that the Fourth Gospel and Rev. develop the same timeless faith perspective that understands Christ as the "beginning and end" (Alpha and Omega). The Gospel does so with respect to the historical life of Jesus as a manifestation of his timeless being, whereas Rev. sees the eschatological future as a manifestation of his eternal life.[11]

Fourth, a last attempt to accept the same authorship for Rev. and the Fourth Gospel and at the same time to acknowledge the differences between the two works is to postulate that the apostle had two different secretaries or translators, one responsible for the editing of the Fourth Gospel and one accountable for Rev. This last proposal already comes close to the hypothesis that both writings owe their existence to a circle or school of disciples either of the apostle or of the presbyter.

THE JOHANNINE SCHOOL HYPOTHESIS[12]

The Johannine school hypothesis owes its existence to the authorship debate and serves clearly apologetic functions. Because of the theological differences between Rev. and the Fourth Gospel many scholars no longer postulate a common authorship of both books but claim that a circle of disciples or a school of the apostle or of the presbyter edited and promoted the Johannine writings. The school hypothesis thus replaces the personal continuity of authorship with the social continuity of a school or circle without relinquishing the claim to the authority of the apostle or presbyter John. The social continuity standing behind Rev. and the Fourth Gospel is thereby defined in basically two different ways. Some scholars use the category in a very loose sense as referring to a theological tradition, group, circle, or to Johannine Christianity as such. Others understand the term "school" in a more technical sense.

Because of affinities in language and theology between the Fourth Gospel and Rev. a first group of scholars postulates that the two writings were in some way related to each other through the medium of a social group of followers of the original authority standing behind them. The crystallization point is a common theological perspective which, even when changed and altered, still reflects the same tradition. O. Cullmann,[13] for instance, does not speak of a Johannine school but of a "circle" or special group within early Christianity that advocated a different type of tradition and theology than the Synoptic Gospels. He assumes the existence of such a circle in order to explain the redaction history and process of the Fourth Gospel and then attempts to situate the Johannine group in the history of early Christianity. He sees a definite interdependency between the Fourth Gospel, the Stephanus circle mentioned in Acts 6:1–2, and heterodox Judaism. Both the Fourth Gospel and the Hellenists of Acts are united in their rejection not only of the Jerusalem temple and cult but also of any localization of the divine presence in cultic institutions. Since the Epistle to the Hebrews and Rev. share this anticultic tendency Cullmann suggests that they might belong to the same circle as the Fourth Gospel and 1 John.[14] The authority standing behind the Fourth Gospel and the Johannine circle is the Beloved Disciple.

According to D. Moody Smith[15] Johannine Christianity was not a monolithic organizational or doctrinal unity. "Rather it is a community of common origin, language or rhetoric, and theological interests which includes, or has as its circumference, considerable theological diversity."[16] The Johannine circle as a whole probably did not think of itself as a school in the technical sense but exercised "certain pronounced scholastic functions and techniques." Since, according to him, Johannine Christianity represents a prophetic and spirit-inspired form of Christianity, Rev. appears to be the earliest work of the Johannine circle, followed by the Fourth Gospel and 1 John.

This vacillation of scholars in using the terms "school," "circle," "sect," "community," or "tradition" to describe the social continuity behind the Johannine writings indicates that the categories are imprecise and far from being clearly defined and delineated from each other. As B. H. Streeter has ironically stated: "The word 'school' is one of those vague, seductive expressions which it is so easy to accept as a substitute for clear thinking."[17] A second group of scholars has recognized the apologetic limitations of the school hypothesis as well as the exegetical fuzziness of the category. They have attempted to differentiate the expression "school" from that of "sect, circle, community or tradition," by insisting on the preoccupation of schools with studying, teaching, learning and writing.[18] For them the category "school" implies a strict literary interdependence and method. "Thus the Johannine school method is not what is usually meant by loose citations, or those more or less frequently quoted from memory. It is rather the opposite since the form of John's quotations is certainly the fruit of scholarly treatment of written OT texts."[19] The category "school" in this more narrow and technical sense is thus understood as describing a circle of pupils gathered around their teacher and authority. These pupils wrote or redacted the various Johannine writings at different times and to different degrees. Two examples of such a reconstruction of the Johannine school in which Rev. and the Fourth Gospel originated will suffice here.

The form of the Johannine school hypothesis proposed by C. K. Barrett[20] is widely influential today. According to Barrett, John, the son of Zebedee, migrated from Palestine to Asia Minor and settled in Ephesus where he composed apocalyptic works and gathered pupils around him. After his death one of his disciples incorporated the apocalyptic writings of the apostle into our present Book of Rev. Other pupil(s) authored the Johannine epistles, and another follower produced John 1—20. After the death of this disciple, who was the evangelist, a redactor edited chaps. 1—20 together with chap. 21 into the present form of our Fourth Gospel. Barrett's hypothesis accounts only for the direct literary continuity of Rev. to the head of the Johannine school, but not for that of the other Johannine writings.

Already at the turn of the century J. Weiss[21] had raised the question of how, in view of their theological differences, the Fourth Gospel and Rev. could have been sponsored by the same circle. Since the two writings appeared in a close temporal sequence (Rev. c. 95; Fourth Gospel c. 100-110), in the same region of Asia Minor (Ephesus), and have close linguistic affinities, one must explain how the same Christian group sponsored, if they did not create, the two writings. Even if one were to attribute the books to two different authors, one would still have to explain how their opposing theologies could have been accepted by the same early Christian circle. As a solution to the problem J. Weiss proposed the following hypothesis:

1. Before 70 C.E. the presbyter John wrote an apocalypse that had no concrete *zeitgeschichtlich* references, but repeated the apocalyptic words of Jesus.

2. Later he wrote the epistles against the false teaching of his opponents in which he saw the pronouncement of the coming of the antichrist fulfilled. In the epistles he still employed apocalyptic eschatology but he had already transcended it.

3. When the presbyter wrote down his memories of Jesus in the Gospel of the incarnated Logos, he had completely overcome apocalyptic eschatology. The messianic time was fulfilled in the life of Jesus.

4. At the occasion of the persecution of the community by Domitian a disciple redacted in his name the apocalypse written by John and focused it against Domitian and the imperial cult. The presbyter John was either too old to edit his previous work himself, or no longer agreed with it, or both.

5. After the death of the presbyter the Fourth Gospel was edited and chap. 21 was added. The same circle that sponsored Rev. in Weiss's opinion could have redacted the Gospel because in the meantime it was proven that the eschatological expectations of Rev. had not been fulfilled. Domitian was dead and the end had not yet come. The disciple whom Jesus loved and who was supposed to live until the Parousia had died. Realized eschatology, which was already in competition with apocalyptic eschatology when the final redaction of Rev. appeared, had won out.

As is the case with some scholars today, J. Weiss assumed that Rev. was the earliest work of the Johannine school. He argued, however, that the Johannine epistles present a middle ground between Rev. and the Fourth Gospel with respect to eschatology insofar as they still employ apocalyptic eschatological thinking but transcend it.

These examples of the Johannine school hypothesis elucidate that the categories "school," "circle," or "community" function to provide a personal, theological, or literary sociological continuity between Rev. and the Fourth Gospel. The crystallization figure of the Johannine school or circle can be identified as the apostle John, the presbyter John mentioned by Papias, the prophet John referred to in Rev., or the Beloved Disciple of the Fourth Gospel, who in turn can be understood as identical with the apostle or presbyter John. Other scholars combine the apostolic authorship hypothesis with that of the presbyter John's authorship and assume, for example, that the apostle wrote Rev. and the presbyter—who was a pupil of the apostle—wrote the Fourth Gospel and the Johannine epistles, or vice versa. What is important is that the school hypothesis is able to answer the authorship problem by preserving the authority of the apostle or presbyter John as standing behind all the Johannine writings without postulating the same authorship for them. The authorship can be partially ascribed to this authority as founder or head of the school or circle; it can be credited to one or more of his disciples who could have redacted and edited his writings or imitated his literary work and perpetuated his theological perspective in their own writings which were addressed to different problems and situations.

The hypothesis of the Johannine school or circle thus operates within the boundaries set by the problem and discussion of the Johannine authorship. It is determined by the ecclesiastical tradition which postulates the same author for Rev. and the Fourth Gospel. Because of this tradition exegetes a priori assume that in some way Rev. and the Fourth Gospel must belong to the same early Christian school, circle, or form of Christianity. The Johannine school—or circle—hypothesis is therefore often the presupposition of historical critical inquiry and not its result.

In conclusion, the Johannine school hypothesis appears to fulfill the following functions in contemporary exegetical scholarship.

First, it is able to do justice to the external evidence provided by church tradition. It can account for the tradition of apostolic authorship for both works, for the analysis of critics like Dionysius of Alexandria or the Tübingen school, and for the presbyter tradition of Papias and its modern revival.

Second, the school hypothesis claims to do justice to the internal evidence provided by the two writings. It not only explains the similarities and affinities in diction and theology but, at the same time, it also accounts for the divergencies and differences of the two books. The verbal, stylistic, and theological affinities provide the strongest argument for the assumption of a common tradition or school.

Third, the school hypothesis provides an exegetical-theological continuity between the Johannine writings. In elaborating "Johannine" theological concepts scholars are able to understand both writings in a complementary fashion. R. E. Brown, for instance, spells out this methodological principle resulting from the school hypothesis and consistently employs it in his commentary:

> Just as Acts is used along with the Gospel of Luke in a study of Lukan theology, so also must the other works of the Johannine school, Epistles and Revelation, be consulted before generalizing about the Johannine view of the church. . . . Now if John, I–III John and Revelation stem from differ-

ent writers within the Johannine school, it is to be expected that these writers would not agree on every point. Nevertheless quite often these other writings should help us fill in points in Johannine theology on which the Gospel has been silent.[22]

Yet before we can accept such a methodological principle, it has to be proven on exegetical grounds that Rev. and the Fourth Gospel are theologically in the same way interrelated as the Gospel of Luke and Acts are.

The following section of the chapter will therefore survey the linguistic and theological arguments which, according to scholars, speak for the place of Rev. in the Johannine school. In order to prove their case, scholars usually refer to the theological and linguistic affinities and similarities of the two writings. However, there exists no extensive independent exegetical study of the problem. It is usually discussed under the heading of "authorship" or in the context of the reconstruction of the Johannine school and theological traditions. Rather, the Johannine school discussion usually concentrates on the redactional development of the Fourth Gospel and its relationship to 1 John, while mentioning Rev. only in a peripheral way.

LINGUISTIC AND THEOLOGICAL
AFFINITIES OF REVELATION AND
THE FOURTH GOSPEL

Exegetes often use vocabulary studies to demonstrate a relationship between Rev. and the Fourth Gospel.[23] To my knowledge, however, there are few form-critical or theological-historical (*theologiegeschichtlich*) investigations which attempt to compare the two works and to relate them to each other.

The Fourth Gospel and Rev. have only the following eight words in common that are found nowhere else in the NT:

arnion (Lamb: twenty-nine times in Rev.; once in Fourth Gospel)
Ebraisti (in Hebrew: twice in Rev.; five times in Fourth Gospel)
exekentein (to pierce: once in Rev.; once in Fourth Gospel; both refer to Zech. 12:10)
kykleuein (to surround: once in Rev.; twice in Fourth Gospel)
opsis (face, countenance: once in Rev.; twice in Fourth Gospel)
porphyrous (purple: twice in Rev.; twice in Fourth Gospel)
phoinix (palm-tree: once in Rev.; once in Fourth Gospel)
skēnoun (to dwell, pitch tent: four times in Rev.; once in Fourth Gospel).

Since some of the eight words found only in Rev. and the Fourth Gospel could be derived from the OT text or general usage the linguistic distinctiveness (*Eigenart*) of both writings appears not to be too great.[24] Moreover, Rev. uses different expressions than the Fourth Gospel for the same words:

Lamb: *arnion* (Rev.)   *amnos* (Fourth Gospel)
Jerusalem: *Ierousalēm* (Rev.)   *Ierosolyma* (Fourth Gospel)
Liar: *pseudēs* (Rev.)   *pseustēs* (Fourth Gospel)
See: *idou* (Rev.)   *ide* (Fourth Gospel)

Furthermore, certain characteristic Johannine theological expressions and phrases[25] are not found at all in Rev.: *alētheia* (truth), *alethēs* (true), *zoē* (life), *aiōnios* (eternal), *menein en* (to continue in), *idios* (own), *skotia/skotos* (darkness), *pisteuein* (to have faith in). Three times *kosmos* (world) is used in Rev. but in a universalistic and not in the dualistic sense of the Fourth Gospel. The dualistic character of the *kosmos* is expressed in the Johannine literature, for instance, in the following opposites:[26]

agapan‖misein   (to love‖to hate)
zoē‖thanatos   (life‖death)
sōzesthai‖apollyein   (to save‖to lose)
tēn dikaiosynēn‖tēn hamartian poiein   (to do right‖to sin)
tēn alētheian poien‖pseudesthai   (to do the truth‖to lie)
ek tou theou‖ek tou diabolou einai   (to be from God‖to be from the devil)
ek tōn anō‖ek tōn katō einai   (to be from above‖to be from below)
en alētheia‖pseustēs einai   (to be truthful‖to be a liar)

On the other hand, key terms of Rev. are not found in the Fourth Gospel. Such terms are, for example: *pantokratōr* (Almighty), *basileis tēs gēs* (kings of the earth), *hypomonē* (consistent resistance), *thlipsis* (affliction), *thronos* (throne), *hagioi* (holy ones), *douloi* (slaves), *ekklēsia* (assembly), *mystērion* (mystery), *hē oikumenē* (the inhabited world), *adikein* (to injure, do wrong), *aparchē* (first-fruits), *prōtotokos* (firstborn).

If we compare the vocabulary[27] of Rev. with other NT writings the common linguistic characteristics of Rev. and the Fourth Gospel become even more qualified. Whereas Rev. and the Fourth Gospel have only eight words common to them alone, Rev. and Paul share thirty-three such words and Rev. and Luke have almost the same number in common. The closer affinity of Rev. to Pauline vocabulary comes even more to the fore when we compare those words which both authors use at least twice. Whereas Rev. and the Fourth Gospel share forty-six such words, Rev. and Paul have 157 in common. The same affinity of Rev. to

Pauline language can be observed in its use of small particles such as prepositions and conjunctions.

Exegetes are divided on how to judge the grammar of Rev. and the Fourth Gospel. Some claim that the two are very distinct, whereas others maintain that they share the same Aramaic or Hebraic imprint. H. B. Swete concludes his survey of the linguistic and grammatical arguments with the observation that the coincidences in language between the two works are remarkable, but that the general effect of style, vocabulary, and grammar is quite different in Rev. and the Fourth Gospel.[28] The stylistic and linguistic evidence appears thus to cut both ways and is far from being conclusive. Scholars, therefore, base their argument more strongly on the affinities in theological language and imagery.

The expressions most often cited as indications that Rev. and the Fourth Gospel belong to the same tradition and school are the christological titles "Lamb" (Rev. 28 times; John 1:29, 36), the "word" (Rev. 19:13; John 1:1, 14); the image of shepherding, and that of water for eternal life (Rev. 7:17; 21:6; 22:1, 17; John 4:14; 6:35; 7:37–8); the absence of a temple (Rev. 21:22; John 2:19, 21; 4:20–26) and the dwelling of God or Christ among people (Rev. 7:15; 21:3; John 1:14). Significantly, Rev. 1:17 and John 19:37b refer to Zech. 12:10 not in the LXX or Masoretic text-form but in that of the Theodotion text tradition.

Christological Titles

It is interesting to note that the two christological titles which Rev. and the Fourth Gospel have in common are found in texts which belong probably to the pre-evangelist stage of the Fourth Gospel.

The "Lamb" (arnion) is in Rev. a main title for Christ.[29] At no place has arnion the genitive tou theou. The derivation of the title from the Aramaic taljah which unites the Greek expressions arnion, pais tou theou (child of God), and hyios tou theou (Son of God) is therefore not very probable. It is, moreover, important to note that nowhere in Rev. does the author characterize Christ with features of the Suffering Servant of Isaiah 53,[30] but that he uses the doulos theou (slave of God) title for himself, for Moses, for Christians in general, or for the community's prophets. The derivation of the title from the conquering messianic Lamb of apocalyptic Judaism[31] is also doubtful since the title "Lamb" for the Messiah is not found in pre-Christian Judaism (T. Jos. 19:8 is a Christian interpolation).[32] Furthermore, it is not likely that the title recalls the lamb offered twice a day in the temple of Jerusalem (Exod. 29:38–46) or the lamb offered as a sin offering (Lev. 4:32), since the Lamb of Rev. has no sacrificial aspects or expiatory functions.[33]

The image of the "Lamb" in Rev. could be partially inspired by the

Paschal Lamb since it is sometimes found in connection with exodus typology (cf. Rev. 5:9–10; 15:3–4 and the plague visions). However, the kingly, messianic features of the Lamb are predominant. The Lamb of Rev. is the all-powerful and omniscient Davidic Messiah, who can therefore be called "Lord of Lords, and King of Kings" (17:14), a title which as a well-known ancient kingly predication had already been transferred to Yahweh. The basis for the exaltation of Christ and his enthronement as world-ruler was his death (cf. Rev. 5:9–10). The powerful Lamb of Rev. is marked forever by his death-wound (5:6: *to arnion to esphagmenon*). Just as the cross and resurrection of Jesus Christ are the decisive christological data in Paul's theology, so too does the image of the slain *(esphagmenon)* messianic Lamb dominate the Christology of Rev.[34] The earthly life of Jesus does not play any role in Rev.[35] The author stresses that Christ is "the first and the last, and the living one; I died and behold I am alive for evermore, and I have the keys of Death and Hades" (1:17–18). Some of the most important christological titles in Rev. are, therefore, mentioned already in the beginning: "the faithful witness, the firstborn of the dead" (cf. Col. 1:18), and "the ruler of the kings of the earth" (cf. 1:5).

The Fourth Gospel uses the title "Lamb" in a quite different way than Rev. The Fourth Gospel writes not only *amnos* instead of *arnion* but also has the attribute *tou theou* and the qualifying sentence "who takes away the world's sin" (John 1:29). The same emphasis on the expiatory functions of Christ is also found in 1 John (3:5; 1:7, 9; 2:1–2; 4:10).[36] Whereas the "Lamb" is the major christological image in Rev., the expression is found only twice in the Fourth Gospel, in a section which probably belongs to the pre-Johannine material and in its more original form is represented by John 1:36. According to R. Fortna,[37] the evangelist added the qualifying phrase in 1:29 to the messianic non-soteriological title of the source. However, the messianic understanding of the title in the pre-Johannine material becomes doubtful if there is no evidence that the expression was ever a messianic title in Judaism. Whereas the expiatory functions of the Lamb of God in the present context of the Gospel and its interpretation in the light of Isaiah 53 and the Paschal Lamb are accepted, the history of the development of the title remains obscure.

In order to explain the interconnection between the two similar titles in the Fourth Gospel and Rev., R. Schnackenburg suggests that it is possible that Rev. took up the expression "Lamb of God" (he does not specify to which Johannine level it belongs) and used in addition apocalyptic traditions to develop the figure of the Lamb as the eschatological conqueror and messianic ruler. "But the opposite process" according to him is "hardly possible—that the 'Lamb' (without further attribute) of Rev. explains the pregnant expression of John 1:29, 36."[38]

Yet in my opinion it is more probable that the characterization of Christ as the "Lamb" of the Fourth Gospel and Rev. developed independently from each other as the different expressions *ho amnos tou theou// to arnion* indicate. The two titles could represent an independent development of the early Christian understanding of Jesus as the Paschal Lamb (cf. 1 Cor. 5:7). (It is interesting to note in 1 Pet. 1:19 the expression "with the precious blood of Christ, like that of a lamb without blemish and spot" [RSV]. The characterization *amōmon* [spotless] for the eschatological followers of the Lamb in Rev. 14:5 recalls the expression of 1 Peter). This hypothesis would account for the messianic overtones of the expressions in the pre-Johannine material, since the exodus and Passover were understood in Judaism in a messianic sense. It would also explain why the author of Rev. does not apply the expiatory power of the blood of Christ, which he has taken over from pre-Pauline traditions,[39] to the Lamb (cf. 1:5–6; 5:9–10), since in Jewish thought the Paschal Lamb was generally not understood as a sacrifice.[40] If the slaughtered Lamb of Rev. alludes to the Paschal Lamb, the image of the Lamb evokes Israel's exodus and liberation from the bondage of Egypt as a *typos* for redemption and eschatological salvation.[41]

According to exegetes, the second christological title which speaks for a Johannine school tradition, is the *logos* title found in Rev. 19:13 and in the prologue of the Fourth Gospel (1:14). Beckwith states: "Without doubt the name is taken from the Johannine doctrine of the Logos, current in the home of the Apocalypse, and it is used in a sense different from that of the Fourth Gospel."[42] T. Holtz also concludes his discussion of the title with the assertion that the Logos title was a well-known and highly valued christological predicate in the communities of Rev. The author has taken over this Johannine title and adapted or transformed it in a Jewish Bible sense.[43]

Contrary to such opinions, in both books the title *logos* (Word) for Christ is not a major christological title, since it is used only once in each work. The *logos* title is found only in the prologue of the Fourth Gospel, and there without any attribute. The expression characterizes a preexistent figure, who as a divine being was "in the beginning" before the existence of creation. It is widely acknowledged that the title belonged to the logos hymn which was taken over by the evangelist from tradition. The origin, extent, and background of the hymn are very controversial.[44] It is clear, however, that the evangelist had no interest in developing the title, since it does not occur again in the main part of the Gospel. Therefore, it is questionable whether the *logos* title was such a well-known and

widespread christological title within Johannine Christianity as Beckwith and Holtz assume.

In Rev. the title also is used only once (19:13) but not in the absolute
form of the Fourth Gospel. Instead Rev. has *ho logos tou theou* ("The
Word of God"), a form which is often found in the OT. The description
of Christ in Rev. 19:11–16 employs names and characterizations that are
familiar from previous passages of the book. As the "faithful and true"
(cf. 3:14) Christ comes to judge in righteousness (cf. 19:2; 16:7; 15:3) and
to wage war (cf. 2:16). He has eyes like a "flame of fire" (1:4; 2:18) and
wears many diadems (cf. 12:3; 13:1). Whereas a blasphemous name is
inscribed upon the heads of the beast in chap., 13, Christ's name is completely secret (cf. 2:17). His bloodstained robe shows him as the glorious,
divine victor (cf. Isa. 63:1–2) and as such he is called "The Word of
God." This royal figure is accompanied by the armies of heaven; as a
weapon he has the "sword of his mouth" (cf. 1:16; 2:16); he rules the
nations (cf. 2:27) and executes the judgment (cf. 15:10; 16:10). The last
title given to the Parousia Christ is therefore: "King of Kings and Lord
of Lords" (cf. 17:14). This last title sums up all the descriptions and
names given to Christ in Rev. 19:11–16.

The title "Word of God" is thus only one of four given to the Parousia
Christ. The first name recalls Rev. 3:14 and stresses that "the faithful and
true witness" and the Parousia Christ are the same. The same adjectives
pistos kai alēthinos (faithful and true) also characterize the words of God
which announce the eschatological fulfillment in 21:5 (cf. 22:6). Christians can rely on the faithfulness and loyalty of Christ because he and
God will fulfill the prophetic words that they had laid down in Rev.
Thus another name of Christ is "The Word of God."[45] It is possible that
behind this name and the whole vision of Rev. 19:11–16 stands Wisd. of
Sol. 19:15, where the all-powerful Word of God is said to come down
from the royal throne in heaven as a warrior carrying the sharp sword to
rescue the Israelites from Egypt and to destroy their enemies. The same
Jewish (cf. *1 Enoch* 9:5) and Hellenistic tradition probably also stands
behind the poem about the "Word of God" in Heb. 4:12–13.[46]

In conclusion: the name "Word of God" does not imply the pre-
existence of the Parousia Christ but, together with the other names in
Rev. 19:11–16, emphasizes his messianic power as the fulfillment of the
words of prophecy. Consequently, the *logos* title in the Fourth Gospel
and in Rev. clearly has a different theological and traditional context.
Imagery and theology do not speak for a common origin of the two titles
in a common school or for a literary interdependence but clearly they
are derived from different traditions. Thus the christological titles *to
arnion* and *ho logos tou theou* do not speak for a common school behind

Rev. and the Fourth Gospel. Moreover, they indicate only a certain linguistic affinity to the pre-Johannine tradition but not to the evangelist or redactor stage of the gospel.

Eschatological Images and Metaphors

The images and metaphors of shepherd, the dwelling of God or Christ, the absence of the temple and the image of living water or water of life as eschatological gift are common to Rev. and the Fourth Gospel and are, therefore, often considered to be strikingly "Johannine."

Whereas the Fourth Gospel compares Christ with the shepherd (noun: *ho poimēn* 10:2, 11, 12, 14, 16; verb: *poimainein* in 21:16[47] with reference to Peter), Rev. uses solely the verb *(poimainein)*, which at least three out of four times in Rev. has the meaning "to rule or reign" (cf. 2:27; 12:5; 19:5). Since the verb "to shepherd" is, in Rev. 7:17, defined by its OT background (cf. Ps. 23:1–3; Isa. 40:11; Pss. Sol. 17:42 ff.), the metaphor is very different in the Fourth Gospel and in Rev.

According to Rev. the dwelling of God with human beings on the new earth in the New Jerusalem is *the* eschatological fulfillment (21:3; 7:17). Whereas in the interim time the dwelling of God is in heaven (cf. 15:5; 12:12; 13:6), eschatological salvation consists for Rev. in the presence of God on earth.[48] In distinction to Rev., the Fourth Gospel uses *skēnoun* (to pitch tent, dwell; John 1:14) only once with reference to the human life of the *logos*, and this reference is again found in the pre-Johannine tradition.[49]

O. Cullmann has suggested that the common understanding of the temple speaks for the fact that Rev. and the Fourth Gospel belong to the Johannine circle. Rev. uses the term in four different contexts: as the place of the true worshippers (11:1–2 probably traditional), as a metaphor for eschatological salvation (3:12; 7:15), as a reference to the temple in heaven during the end time (8:3 ff.; 11:14; 14:15, 17; 15:5, 6, 8; 16:1, 17) and once with reference to the New Jerusalem (21:22), which paradoxically states that in the New Jerusalem "there will be no temple because God and the Lamb are the temple." In line with his use of the temple image the author of Rev. also does not see in the interim time any liturgy on earth, but locates it only in heaven. This heavenly liturgy of praise is, in the eschatological future, replaced by the permanent worship of the priestly servants of God (22:3–5; cf. 7:15ff.). This understanding of the temple image and its function is very different from that of the Fourth Gospel,[50] according to which the body of Jesus replaces the temple (2:19, 21; cf. Mark 14:58‖, 15:29‖; Acts 6:14) and the worship in "spirit and truth" makes obsolete any temple worship (4:20–24). Whereas the temple understanding of the Fourth Gospel is formulated in view of the Jerusalem temple, the notion of Rev. is not influenced by this tradition of the Fourth Gospel.[51] Neither with respect to the expression *skēnoun* nor to that of the *naos* (temple) can it be said that the Fourth Gospel has christologized the eschatological images of Rev. which it understood in a presential realized way. The two books appear to follow quite different traditions.

The most striking common image of the Fourth Gospel and Rev. is that of the "living water" or the "water of life." Whereas the author of Rev. understands it as an image for eschatological salvation (7:17; 21:6; 22:1, 17), and has formulated the passages with reference to prophetic texts of the OT (cf. Isa. 40:10; 55:1; Ezek. 47:1–12; Zech. 14:8; 13:1; Jer. 2:13 calls God "a fountain of living water" [*pēgē hydatos zoēs*]) the Fourth Gospel clearly understands the metaphor in a christological sense (4:14; 6:35; 7:17–18). It is debated whether the evangelist draws from wisdom tradition (Wisd. of Sol. 9:5; Sir. 24:21; 51:24) and has developed the image with the help of gnostic and dualistic traditions[52] or whether he uses the same future-oriented prophetic traditions as the author of Rev. Therefore it is difficult to decide whether the two authors developed the image in dependence on a common school tradition which interpreted the same OT texts. The similarity in wording between Rev. 22:17, John 7:37, and *Didache* 10:6 (conditional sentence or participle [Rev. 22:17] followed by *erchesthō* [let him come]), as well as the possible eucharistic context of John 6:35, suggests much more that the image was taken over by Rev. and the Fourth Gospel from the eucharistic liturgy and does not represent the product of a common school tradition. The context of Rev. 22:17 would support this hypothesis.[53]

It appears, however, that the author of Rev. in 21:6 reinterprets in an eschatological sense what the invitation of 22:17 formulates in the present tense. In Rev. 21:6 he seems to draw together all the texts of Rev. that employ the image of the "living water." In addition to the image of the "water of life," 21:6 shares with Rev. 7:17 the expression *hē pēgē* (fountain) and with 22:17 *dorean* (without a price). Moreover, the form of "The Word of God" in Rev. 21:6 speaks for a common "Johannine school" background of the image, since the announcement is patterned after the form of the revelatory saying typical for the Fourth Gospel.[54] The self-presentation of the revealer (1) is followed by a conditional sentence or a conditional participle (2), which in turn is followed by a soteriological promise (3). (1) "I am the Alpha and the Omega, the beginning and the end. (2) To the thirsty, (3) I will give water without price from the foundation of the water of life" (RSV). The affinities in imagery and form between Rev. 21:6 and the Fourth Gospel could be an indication that the image of the "living water" is derived from a common school tradition. But, whereas in Rev. the speaker is God and the image refers to the eschatological fulfillment, in the Fourth Gospel the speaker is Christ and the image refers to the christological realization of the eschatological promise. Yet even if we cannot establish a common tradition for the image of the "living water," it may be possible that the author was familiar with the Johannine school tradition, as the form of the revelatory saying in Rev. 21:6 suggests. However, this possible familiarity with Johannine tradition does not necessarily imply that the author belonged to the Johannine school. The following verse (21:7) is a saying for the conqueror (*Überwinderspruch*) which shows traces of Pauline style (*kleronomein* ["to inherit"], *hyios* ["son"] instead of the Johannine *teknon* ["child"];[55] cf. 1 John 1:12; 3:1, 2; 5:2). It can formally be characterized as a "Sentence of Holy Law" similar to that found in Paul. Rev. 21:6–7 would thus indicate that the author could have been familiar with the Johannine as well as the Pauline school tradition without belonging to one of them.

In conclusion, the result of the preceding discussion raises the methodological question of whether it is possible to deduce from traces of literary and formal affinities in two works that their authors belong to the same social group. Is it not conceivable that an author could have access to various Christian traditions without belonging necessarily to a certain circle or school? This methodological question becomes the more important when we recall that according to Conzelmann, Ephesus was the center of the Pauline school. Whereas it is questionable whether we can locate the Johannine school in Asia Minor, Rev. clearly belongs to this region and could, therefore, have had access to the Pauline school tradition.

THE SCHOOL TRADITIONS AND
THE SCHOOL TRADITION OF REVELATION

Since one of the main tasks of a school is the transmission and reinterpretation of traditions, it is not enough to study the affinities in vocabulary between Rev. and the Fourth Gospel; we must further investigate whether both books transmit and interpret the same traditions.

OT and NT Traditions

Even though the Fourth Gospel uses and changes OT texts freely in order to make a theological statement, the evangelist nevertheless refers to the OT and draws attention to the quotation of OT texts through a great variety of formula quotations ("this was to fulfill the scripture").[56] In distinction to the Fourth Gospel, Rev. never refers to the OT as *graphē* (Scripture) and does not once introduce its OT material through a formula quotation. We only find one explicit reference to the OT: "They sing the song of Moses, the servant of God" (Rev. 15:3). Yet the song which follows is not connected in any literary way with the Song of Moses in Exodus 15 or Deuteronomy 32, but is an amalgamation of various OT themes. Thus Rev. does not even once strictly quote the OT. Moreover, the author of Rev. does not interpret the OT[57] but uses it in employing words, images, phrases, and OT patterns in order to make his own theological statement. "There is not a single instance in which the Christian prophet of the Apoc. has contented himself with a mere compilation or combination of Old Testament ideas. His handling of these materials is always original and independent."[58]

The author of Rev. takes over whole OT text sequences as patterns for his own visions and composition[59] but never refers to the OT as authoritative Scripture. This method of scriptural employment is, according to K. Stendahl, common to apocalyptic texts and rests on the conviction that "the prophetic spirit creates; it does not quote in order to teach or to argue."[60] The understanding and employment of the OT thus appears to link Rev. closer to early Christian apocalypticism than to the way the Fourth Gospel understands Scripture.

It is interesting to note, however, that, of all the NT writers, only the Fourth Gospel and Rev. refer to Zech. 12:10 and use the verb *exekentēsan* (they have pierced), which is not found in the LXX but in Theodotion. In John 19:37b the prophecy of Zech. 12:10 refers to the incident of the soldier piercing Jesus's side after his death (19:35). The Fourth Gospel explicitly states that this piercing of the side of Jesus was done so "that scripture might be fulfilled" and two scriptural quotations are introduced. The second quotation refers to Zech. 12:10: "They shall look on him whom they have pierced." The evangelist has probably taken over this quotation from a source but has understood it in the sense of the OT passage, since the mourning of Israel in Zech. 12:10–14 is an expression of the "spirit of compassion and supplication," which God pours out on the "inhabitants of Jerusalem" (12:10). Similarly, the evangelist understands the scriptural quotation as a salvation prophecy.[61]

The prophetic announcement of Christ in Rev. 1:7 is a conflation of Zech. 12:10 and Dan. 7:13. The text in Rev. refers not to the death of Jesus but to his Parousia. Thus it appears that the citation of Zech. 12:10 in the Fourth Gospel remains closer to the OT text than that in Rev. Moreover, the Rev. text shows great affinities with the saying of Matt. 24:30 in the "apocalyptic discourse."[62]

It is not necessary to decide here whether all three NT texts go back to a common original text and whether this one common non-Septuagintal text was already contained in a testimony-book.[63] It is clear that Rev. shares the OT text combination as well as its eschatological tenor with the Matthean form of the announcement in the Synoptic Apocalypse (Matthew 24; Mark 13; Luke 21). Whether or not the Rev. text presents the older form of this early Christian apocalyptic text is not clear. It is clear, however, that this use of the OT text conflation in an apocalyptic context gives more evidence for the familiarity of the author of Rev. with an early Christian "apocalyptic school" or tradition than with the "Johannine school."

This judgment can be substantiated when we attempt to isolate the allusions of various Rev. texts to other NT texts. As he does with respect to the OT traditions, the author does not quote texts known to us from the Gospels and early Christian Letters, but uses these texts in order to make his own statement.[64] He can thereby conflate texts or isolate one or more elements of a saying and integrate it into his own statement. The greatest affinities are found to the eschatological-apocalyptic traditions of the Gospels, especially the so-called Synoptic Apocalypse, to Q traditions and to the eschatological parable tradition.

Exegetes have long acknowledged that the first sevenfold series of the seals shows remarkable parallelisms to the Synoptic Apocalypse.[65] As we have already seen, the word of Christ in Rev. 1:7 is closely related to the announcement of the Parousia of the "Son of Man" in Matt. 24:30. Other allusions are the exhortation to watch (Mark 13:35, 37; Matt. 25:13) because Christ or the Parousia will come like a thief (Rev. 3:2–3; 16:5; cf. Matt. 24:42; Luke 12:39–40; especially close are Rev. 3:3b and Matt. 24:50; 12:8). The urgency of the watch-saying and the simile of the thief are also found in the Pauline tradition (1 Thess. 5:2–3; 2 Pet. 3:10). Paul, however, in distinction to Rev. and to the Synoptic passages, specifies that the thief comes "in the night." The proclamation of the gospel in Rev. 14:6 alludes to Mark 13:10 and Matt. 24:4, whereas the scene of the eschatological harvest in Rev. 14:14–20 refers to Mark 13:26–27 (and parallels) and to the eschatological parable of the Tares (Matt. 13:24–43). Interesting references to Luke's form of the apocalyptic discourse are Rev. 11:2b (Luke 21:24) as well as the announcement "the time is at hand" (Rev. 1:3b; 22:10), which Luke, however, ascribes to those who come in Christ's name and say: "The time is at hand" (Luke 21:8; 13:28). A similar emphasis on the *kairos* as end time and the nearness of the Lord is found in the Pauline tradition (Rom. 13:11; 1 Cor. 7:29; Phil. 4:5). The depiction of the beasts in Rev. 13, the antichrist (13:3, 7b, 8a, 11) and the pseudoprophet (13:11–18; cf. Rev. 16:13; 19:20; 20:10)

shows affinities with the characterization of the "false christs and prophets" of the apocalyptic discourse in Mark 13:22 (and parallels). In Rev.,
as in the Synoptic discourse, we have two related antagonistic figures
who deceive the people, if possible even the elect, by doing great signs.
A similar tradition is found in 2 Thess. 2:3–10 with respect to the "man
of lawlessness." Rev. 13:11, 13 also shows affinities with the tradition
about false prophets in Matt. 7:15.[66] A more careful study might show
many more affinities to the apocalyptic discourse of the Synoptics, but
the above-mentioned texts suffice to indicate that the author was familiar with this early Christian apocalyptic tradition. In view of this
familiarity with early Christian apocalyptic traditions, it is remarkable
that we do not find the "Son of man" title in Rev. (1:13 and 14:15 have
homoion [like]).[67]

Rev. 3:5c–8 refers to the eschatological Q traditions of Matt.
10:32 ‖ Luke 12:8 (see also 2 Tim. 2:11–12 for the parallel compound
"confessing and denying"). Rev. 3:21 promises to all Christians what
Luke 22:28–30 ‖ Matt. 19:28 promises to the twelve. Rev. 17:4b recalls
Matt. 23:25 ‖ Luke 11:39, and Rev. 18:24 has similarities with Matt.
23:25 ‖ Luke 11:50. An interesting combination of a saying from the Synoptic Apocalypse (Mark 13:29 ‖ Matt. 24:3) and one from Luke's special
material (Luke 12:35–39) is found in the announcement of Rev. 3:20
which links the expression "the standing of the Lord at the door" with
the eschatological feast and table fellowship and at the same time allego-
rizes the parable of Luke. That the expression "standing before the
door" is to be understood in an eschatological sense also becomes clear
when we compare the saying Rev. 3:20 with James 5:9. Moreover, an
allegorization of parable tradition can be found in Rev. 19:7–8 which
describes eschatological salvation with wedding imagery found in the
eschatological parables of Matthew (wedding feast Matt. 22:1–13, and
especially Matt. 25:1–13). The image of bridegroom and bride is evoked
in Mark 2:19 and John 3:29, a saying that is ascribed to John the Baptist.
Both Rev. 19:7–8 and the eschatological parables of Matthew place
emphasis on the blessing of the wedding guests. Consequently, the marriage imagery in Rev. appears to be closer to Synoptic traditions than to
the imagery of Paul. Finally, the author's familiarity not only with Pauline and Synoptic eschatological tradition but also with other forms of
early Christian apocalyptic materials is evidenced, for example, by the
promise of the "crown of life" in Rev. 2:10b, which is also present in
James 1:12 and in 2 Tim. 4:8.

The authors' roots in the early Christian eschatological tradition come
especially to the fore in the *Weckruf* (exhortation to watch) and the *Sie-*

gerspruch (the conqueror's saying) which are repeated in all of the letters to the seven churches of Asia Minor (chaps. 1—3). The exhortation in Rev. 1—3 ("she/he who has ears, let her/him hear") always has the same form (*ho echōn ous akousatō*).[68] This form is also found with slight deviations in the Synoptic tradition. The participial form of the "letters" (*Sendschreiben*) is similar to that in Matt. 11:15 and 13:9, 43, whereas the *ei tis* ("if any one") form of Rev. 13:9 comes closer to Mark 4:23 and 7:16. As the forms of Mark 4:9 or Luke 8:8b, 14:35 indicate, this basic form of the exhortation to watch (*Weckruf*) can be altered. In the Synoptic Gospels it is attached to the parable tradition as well as connected with eschatological discourse.[69] It is interesting to note that the function of Rev. 3:9 in its context is the same as that of Mark 13:14∥Matt. 24:15c in the Synoptic Apocalypse and has a parallel form in Mark 13:18.

The exhortation to watch is also found in *The Gospel of Thomas* (Logion 8, 63, 65, 69); in Logion 21 the two distinct Synoptic traditions, parable-motives and eschatological parenesis, are combined and connected with a *Weckruf.* Since the *Weckruf* does not have attestation in pre-Christian literature it probably originated in the eschatological announcements of early Christian prophecy. This *Sitz im Leben* is suggested also by the fact that the letters of Rev. continue the *Weckruf* with the attestation of the Spirit: "He or she who has an ear let him or her hear what the Spirit says to the churches."[70] The same prophetic understanding is also given in Rev. 14:13; 22:17; Acts 13:2; 1 Tim. 4:1 and Ignatius's *Phila.* 7.2. It is to be distinguished from the Paraclete understanding of the Fourth Gospel.[71]

The formal structure of the *Siegerspruch* ("to him or her who conquers") at the end of the seven letters, despite variations, is basically the same. The conditional participial clause is followed by the main clause in the future tense (3:21; cf. 2:26). This basic form corresponds to that of the "Sentences of Holy Law," which, according to E. Käsemann, were pronounced by early Christian prophets.[72] Outside of Rev., the verb is especially found in 1 John (2:13; 4:4; 5:4–5; John 16:33, which belongs with the whole of John 16 to the post-evangelist, redactional stage), and is therefore often characterized as "Johannine." However, the *Siegersprüche* reflect in content and form more the apocalyptic understanding of *nikaō* (to conquer; cf. *4 Esdras* 7:127–29: "But if he be victorious, he shall receive"). Whereas Rev. expresses with *ho nikōn* ("the one who conquers") a condition for the future salvation of Christians and uses the past tense of the verb only for Christ (cf. 5:5; 3:21), 1 John speaks of the Christian's victory, not as a condition still to be accomplished but as an

act which is already achieved.[73] In common with Jewish apocalyptic literature Rev. not only has the content but also the absolute form of *nikaō*
without the accusative object.[74]

The School Tradition of Revelation

The review of traditional materials in Rev. has shown that the author
uses early Christian prophetic-apocalyptic traditions and understands
the words of the book as prophetic *Geistrede* (speech of the Spirit).
However, the author does not quote but uses various OT and early Christian traditions in order to formulate his own statements. He employs
materials which, in content and form, belong to the OT prophetic-
apocalyptic (e.g., references to Daniel are most frequent) and early
Christian prophetic-apocalyptic traditions. This familiarity of the author
with prophetic-apocalyptic traditions and forms suggests that Rev. is the
work of a member of an early Christian prophetic-apocalyptic rather
than of the Johannine school. A detailed analysis of the theological
motives and traditional patterns of the book could substantiate this
hypothesis. Such an analysis would also show that the author develops
the materials and patterns found in the Synoptic Apocalypse in the
manner of a school tradition. H. Kraft's[75] recent commentary confirms
this hypothesis. Even though Kraft does not understand the origin of
Rev. in terms of a school, he nevertheless maintains that our present text
is the result of several revisions of a *Grundschrift* (original source-text)
which basically consisted of the sevenfold seal visions and climaxed in
the epiphany of God and the resurrection of the dead. The subsequent
revisions and expansions of this *Grundschrift* into the present form of
the book were occasioned by the attempts of the author to incorporate
the major eschatological themes known to him from Jewish and especially early Christian apocalypticism.

The author of Rev., however, was not only a transmitter of the early
Christian prophetic-apocalyptic school-traditions but appears to be the
head or leader of such a school. The *hymin* in Rev. 22:16 seems to indicate that the book is addressed to a special group of *Gemein-
depropheten.*[76] Their function may have been to teach and to guard the
words of his book (cf. 22:18f.). The position of the prophet-author of the
book is unique and he is not at all on the same level as the readers of
the book since he claims to be the *authoritative* mediator of divine revelation. Those who read, hear, and keep[77] the words of his prophecy are
therefore blessed (1:3; 22:7).

Although the author of Rev. was at home in an early Christian
prophetic-apocalyptic school, he nevertheless also had access to Pauline
and Johannine school traditions, as the traces of Pauline and Johannine

language in Rev. indicate. The author appears to have been more familiar with Pauline than Johannine school traditions because the book
shows more affinities with Pauline language, tradition, and form. That
the author understood himself in line with the Pauline tradition
becomes apparent in the form which he gave to his book.

K. Berger has attempted to show that the *Gattung* of the letter, tractate and apocalypse cannot be clearly distinguished. He argues that the
seven letters of Rev. are a good example of the *Gattung* "prophetic
letter."[78] But the difference in form between the seven letters and the
epistolary framework of Rev. indicates, in my opinion, that the author
understands his book not only as a prophetic letter in general, but also
specifically as a circular, authoritative pastoral letter and patterned it
after the already traditional Pauline letter form.

In conclusion. The author of Rev. is rooted in an early Christian
prophetic-apocalyptic school, but he also has access to Johannine as well
as Pauline traditions. Therefore, we must assume that, at the end of the
first century in Asia Minor, various Christian circles or schools lived side
by side within the Christian community, without necessarily being rival
Christian groups or separate institutions.[79] They may have shared
common Christian traditions without relinquishing their specific theological outlook. That different schools coexisted within the communities
becomes apparent in the polemic of Rev. against the adherents of the
teaching of Balaam at Pergamum (2:14) and against the prophet-teacher
whom the author calls Jezebel and her school of disciples (*ta tekna
autēs*)[80] at Thyatira (2:20). She and her followers were still active members of the community in which the author of Rev. appears also to have
had some followers (cf. 2:24–25). It is true that John wants to dissolve
this coexistence, but apparently he was not able to do so since his previous warnings were not successful. We can therefore assume that the
school of Jezebel was equal in influence to that of John but that John
discredits this school because he considers its theology and teaching to
be dangerous for the Christian community.[81]

If the assumption is correct that several schools and theological circles
coexisted and intersected in Asia Minor at the end of the first century
C.E., then we must ask anew the question of the relationship between
the Fourth Gospel and Rev. on a different level. We no longer need to
establish a direct literary interrelationship between both works but can
assume a dialectical exchange of theological thought between their
respective schools and traditions. For instance, it is clear that Rev. and
the Fourth Gospel represent opposite eschatological options. Yet we
cannot assume that the eschatology of the Fourth Gospel was developed
in direct confrontation with Rev. or vice versa, since the differences in

the eschatological language[82] and imagery of the Fourth Gospel and of Rev. do not indicate a direct literary dependency. However, it is possible that the eschatological option of the Johannine school developed or was modified in dialogue and in dialectic interaction with the early Christian prophetic-apocalyptic school tradition developed in Rev. as well.

NOTES

1. I. T. Beckwith, *The Apocalypse of John* (1919; Grand Rapids: Baker Book House, 1967) 354.

2. For a summary of the problems and literature, cf. R. Kysar, *The Fourth Evangelist and His Gospel: An Examination of Contemporary Scholarship* (Minneapolis: Augsburg Pub. House, 1975).

3. A. Feuillet, *L'Apocalypse. État de la question* (Studia Néotestamentica 3; Paris: Desclée de Brouwer, 1962); H. Kraft, "Zur Offenbarung des Johannes," *TRu* NF 38 (1973) 81–98; O. Böcher, *Die Johannesapokalypse* (Erträge der Forschung 41; Darmstadt: Wissenschaftliche Buchgesellschaft, 1975).

4. The Tübingen school (Baur, Köstler, Schwegler, B. Weiss, Hausrath, et al.) maintained that Rev. is a Judaistic counterpart to the universalism of Paul. The source-critical analyses of Vischer, Weyland, Holtzmann, Sabbatier, and J. Weiss have claimed that Rev. is a compilation from one or more Jewish sources. J. M. Ford, *The Revelation of John* (AB 38; New York: Doubleday & Co., 1975) claims that the book comes from the school of John the Baptist.

5. Cf. K. Koch, *The Rediscovery of Apocalyptic* (London: SCM Press, 1972).

6. M. Kiddle, *The Revelation of St. John* (MNTC; London: Hodder & Stoughton, 1940) xxxiii.

7. Justin *Dialogus cum Trypho* 81.4 (c. 160; conversion at Ephesus c. 135) claims that Rev. stems from the apostle John, but does not say anything about the author of the Fourth Gospel. Irenaeus (*Adv. Haer.* 2.22, 5; 4.21, 11; 5.26, 1) claims that both Rev. and the Fourth Gospel have as author John the Apostle.

8. Cf. Eusebius, *H.E.* 7.25.

9. Ibid., 3.25, 4; 3.39.

10. Cf. the review of the literature on the authorship problem in Feuillet, Kysar, and Böcher; the introductions of Kümmel or Wikenhauser; the introduction to the commentaries of, e.g., Bousset, Swete, Charles, Beckwith (*Apoc.*), or Barrett, Brown, and Schnackenburg (Fourth Gospel); and articles by, e.g., W. Heitmüller, "Zur Johannes-Tradition," *ZNW* 15 (1914) 189–209; J. Munch, "Presbyters and Disciples of the Lord," *HTR* 23 (1959) 223–43; E. Schwartz, "Johannes und Kerinthos," *ZNW* 15 (1914) 210–19; B. W. Bacon, "The Authoress of Revelation—A Conjecture," *HTR* 22 (1930) 235–50; P. Parker, "John the Son of Zebedee and the Fourth Gospel," *JBL* 81 (1962) 35–43; J. N. Sanders, "St. John on Patmos," *NTS* 9 (1962/63) 75–85. This listing of articles is neither complete nor representative but documents the possibilities of a constructive scholarly imagination.

11. E. Lohmeyer, *Die Offenbarung des Johannes* (HNT 16; 2d ed.; Tübingen: Mohr/Siebeck, 1963) 195.

12. For a review of research, see R. Culpepper, *The Johannine School* (SBLDS 26; Missoula, Mont.: Scholars Press, 1975) 1–38.

13. O. Cullmann, *Der johanneische Kreis: Zum Ursprung des Johannesevangeliums* (Tübingen: Mohr/Siebeck, 1975) [ET: *The Johannine Circle* (Philadelphia: Westminster Press; London: SCM Press, 1976)].

14. Cullman, *Der johanneische Kreis,* 57–60.

15. D. M. Smith, "Johannine Christianity: Some Reflections on Its Character and Delineation," *NTS* 21 (1975) 222–48.

16. D. M. Smith, *John* (Proclamation Commentaries; Philadelphia: Fortress Press, 1976) 69.

17. B. H. Streeter, *The Four Gospels: A Study of Origins* (London: Macmillan & Co., 1924) 459.

18. Cf. Culpepper, *The Johannine School,* 259.

19. K. Stendahl, *The School of St. Matthew and Its Use of the Old Testament* (2d ed.; Philadelphia: Fortress Press, 1968) 163.

20. C. K. Barrett, *The Gospel According to St. John* (London: SPCK, 1955) 113–14, cf. 52. R. E. Brown (*The Gospel According to St. John* [AB 29; Garden City, N.Y.: Doubleday & Co., 1966] cii) agrees with Barrett's assumption "that Revelation is the work that is most directly John's." Cf. also Smith (*John,* 85) for different arguments.

21. J. Weiss, *Die Offenbarung Johannes* (FRLANT 3; Göttingen: Vandenhoeck & Ruprecht, 1904) 146–64.

22. Brown, *John,* 1: cvii–cviii.

23. Cf. the reviews of the commentaries on Rev., e.g., H. B. Swete, *The Apocalypse of St. John* (1908; Grand Rapids: Wm. B. Eerdmans, 1951) clxxiv–clxxxvi; R. H. Charles, *A Critical and Exegetical Commentary on the Revelation of St. John* (ICC; Edinburgh: T. & T. Clark, 1920) xxix–xliv.

24. Cf. E. B. Allo, "L' Auteur de l'Apocalypse," *RB* 14 (1917) 321–75, esp. 335.

25. Cf. Brown (*John,* 1: 499–518, Appendix 1) on "Johannine Vocabulary," but with different conclusions.

26. Cf. G. Baumbach, "Gemeinde und Welt im Johannesevangelium," *Kairos* 14 (1972) 121–35, esp. 122.

27. Cf. Ch. Brütsch, *Die Offenbarung des Johannes* (2d ed.; Zurich: Zwingli Verlag, 1970) 3: 303–41, esp. 339–40. This work is based on R. Morgenthaler, *Statistik des neutestamentlichen Wortschatzes* (Zurich: Gotthelf Verlag, 1958).

28. Swete, *The Apocalypse,* cxxix.

29. Cf. the discussion of the title by T. Holtz (*Die Christologie der Apokalypse des Johannes* [TU 85; Berlin: Akademie-Verlag, 1962] 39–47) and the review by Böcher (*Die Johannesapokalypse,* 42–47).

30. Contra J. Comblin, *Le Christ dans l'Apocalypse* (Théologie Biblique 3/6; Paris: Desclée, 1965) 22–26.

31. Cf. C. H. Dodd, *The Interpretation of the Fourth Gospel* (Cambridge: At the Univ. Press, 1968) 230–38; C. K. Barrett, "The Lamb of God," *NTS* 1 (1954/55) 210–18.

32. Cf. J. Jeremias, "Das Lamm, das aus der Jungfrau hervorging (*T. Jos.* 19:8)," *ZNW* 57 (1966) 216–19; C. Burchard, "Das Lamm in der Waagschale," *ZNW* 57 (1966) 219–28. B. Murmelstein ("Das Lamm in Test. Jos. 19:8," *ZNW* [1967] 273–79) defends the authenticity of the Armenian version of *T. Jos.* 19:8.

33. The interpretation of the metaphor in Rev. 7:14 is difficult, since the agent is not the Lamb, but those who have come out of the great tribulation.

34. Cf. Holtz, *Die Christologie,* 212–13; M. Rissi, "The Kerygma of the Revelation to John," *Int* 22 (1968) 3–17, esp. 7–8.

35. That the birth of the divine child is mentioned in chap. 12 is due to the traditional material taken over by the author.

36. Cf. R. Schnackenburg, *Die Johannesbriefe* (HTKNT 13/2; 2d ed.; Frieburg: Herder, 1963).

37. R. Fortna, *The Gospel of Signs: A Reconstruction of the Narrative Source Underlying the Fourth Gospel* (SNTSMS 11; Cambridge: At the Univ. Press, 1970) 175, 182, 232–33.

38. R. Schnackenburg, *The Gospel According to St. John* (New York: Herder & Herder, 1968) 1: 300.

39. Cf. Rom. 3:24a–26 and 1 Cor. 10:6; 11:25. See E. Lohse, *Martyrer und Gottesknecht: Untersuchungen zur urchristlichen Verkündigung vom Sühnetod Jesu Christi* (FRLANT NF 46; 2d ed.; Göttingen: Vandenhoeck & Ruprecht, 1963) 138–41.

40. Brown, *John,* 1: 62. This speaks against the interpretation of Holtz (*Die Christologie,* 47) who stresses the expiatory character of the Lamb. Brown, however, attempts to deduce the expiatory character of the Paschal Lamb.

41. Cf. chap. 2 of this book, "Redemption as Liberation."

42. Beckwith, *The Apocalypse,* 732.

43. Holtz, *Die Christologie,* 176.

44. For a review of the literature, cf. H. Thyen, "Aus der Literatur zum Johannesevangelium," *TRu* NF 39 (1974) 1–69, 222–52.

45. It is interesting to note that the phrase *ho logos tou theou kai hē martyria Iēsou* unites the notions of *the word of God* and *the witness of Jesus.* The phrase probably was used in the community as an expression for Christian faith in general (Rev. 1:9; 6:9; 20:4; cf. also 12:17). Cf. Satake, *Die Gemeindeordnung,* 98–106. The author of Rev., however, uses this phrase to characterize the prophetic content of his book (1:2; 19:10). He stresses that the witness who guarantees the words of the book is Jesus Christ (22:20), whereas the Fourth Gospel emphasizes the guarantee of human eyewitnesses (cf. John 3:11; 19:35; 21:24).

46. Cf. O. Michel, *Der Brief an die Hebräer* (MeyerK 13; 6th ed.; Göttingen: Vandenhoeck & Ruprecht, 1966) 197.

47. It is interesting to note that John 21:16–17 has in common with Rev. 7:17 the expressions *poimainein* and *arnion.* However, the fourth evangelist says *boske ta arnia mou* ("feed my sheep") and *poimaine ta probata mou* ("shepherd my sheep"), which indicates that he did not have in mind the text of Rev. but the conventional image "of the shepherd and sheep for pastoral responsibility." Cf. B. Lindars, *The Gospel of John* (NCB; London: Oliphants, 1972) 635.

48. Cf. E. Lohse, *Die Offenbarung des Johannes* (NTD 2; 9th ed.; Göttingen: Vandenhoeck & Ruprecht, 1966) 104; H. Kuhaupt, *Der neue Himmel und die neue Erde* (Münster: Aschendorff, 1947) 157; M. Rissi, *Die Zukunft der Welt* (Basel: Friedrich Reinhardt, 1966) 63–69.

49. If the assumption of U. B. Müller (*Die Geschichte der Christologie in der Johanneischen Gemeinde* [SBS 77; Stuttgart: Katholisches Bibelwerk, 1975]) were correct that John 1:14, 16 is an independent hymn of praise and thanksgiving for the epiphany of the miracle worker Jesus, then we could assume that the author of Rev. was familiar only with this tradition and not with the whole prologue. Rev. 7:17 would then be another link to the *Semeia* (Signs) source.

50. For a more extensive discussion, cf. E. Schüssler Fiorenza, "Cultic Language in Qumran and in the New Testament," *CBQ* 38 (1976) 159–77.

51. The determination of the traditional patterns (*Vorlagen*) and the interpretation of Rev. 11:1–2 are much debated. In the present form the text stresses the protection of those who worship God (cf. Ezek. 29:6).

52. Cf. L. Goppelt, "hydōr," *TDNT* 8 (1972) 326; R. Bultmann, *The Gospel of John* (Philadelphia: Westminster Press; Oxford: Blackwell, 1971) 182ff.

53. Cf. the commentaries, e.g., Lohmeyer, *Die Offenbarung des Johannes,* 181–82; A. O. Prigent maintains such a liturgical context also for chap. 21; cf. "Une trace de liturgie Judéochrétienne dans le chapitre XXI de l'Apocalypse de Jean," *RSR* 60 (1972) 165–72.

54. E. Norden, *Agnostos Theos: Untersuchungen zur Formgeschichte religiöser Rede* (4th ed.; Darmstadt: Wissenschaftliche Buchgesellschaft, 1966) 186–87; R. Schnackenburg, *Das Johannesevangelium* (HTKNT 4; Freiburg: Herder, 1971) 2: 58 [ET: *The Gospel According to St. John* (New York: Seabury Press, 1980) 43–45].

55. Cf. Culpepper, *The Johannine School,* 272–73 and Appendix II; also Baumbach, "Gemeinde und Welt," 135.

56. Schnackenburg, *John,* 1: 38–39. See the review of E. D. Freed, *Old Testament Quotations in the Gospel of John* (Leiden: E. J. Brill, 1965) in Kysar's *The Fourth Evangelist,* 104–7; G. Reim, *Studien zum Alttestamentlichen Hintergrund des Johannesevangeliums* (Cambridge: At the Univ. Press, 1974).

57. Contra Comblin (*Le Christ*) and Kraft ("Zur Offenbarung des Johannes," 85).

58. Swete, *The Apocalypse,* cliv.

59. Cf. J. Cambier, "Les images de l'Ancien Testament dans l'Apocalypse de saint Jean," *NRT* 77 (1955) 113–22, esp. 116–17; G. Harder, "Eschatologische Schemata in der Johannes-Apokalypse," *TViat* 9 (1963) 70–87; H. P. Müller, "Die Plagen der Apokalypse," *ZNW* 51 (1960) 268–79.

60. Stendahl, *School of St. Matthew,* 159.

61. Cf. R. Schnackenburg, *Das Johannesevangelium* (Freiburg: Herder, 1975) 3: 343–45 [ET: *The Gospel According to St. John* (New York: Crossroad, 1982) 3: 292–94].

62. For a more detailed discussion, see my book *Priester für Gott: Studien zum Herrschafts- und Priestermotiv in der Apokalypse* (NTAbh 7; Münster: Aschendorff, 1972) 185–92.

63. Cf. B. Lindars, *New Testament Apologetic* (London: SCM Press, 1961) 122–27.

64. Cf. L. A. Vos (*The Synoptic Traditions in the Apocalypse* [Kampen: J. H. Kek, 1966] 218–19) for an index of passages.

65. Cf., e.g., A. Wikenhauser (*Der Sinn der Apokalypse des hl. Johannes* [Münster: Aschendorff, 1931] 5–16) and his commentary (*Die Offenbarung des Johannes* [RNT 9; 3d ed.; Regensburg: Pustet, 1959]) for the following division: Mark 13:7–13 corresponds to Rev. 5—6 (the beginning of the eschatological woes); Mark 13:14–23 corresponds to Rev. 12:1—14:10 (the great tribulation before the end); and Mark 13:24–27 corresponds to Rev. 19:11–21 (the Parousia). His division of Rev. does not, however, reflect the compositional elements of the surface structure. In chap. 6 of this book, "The Composition and Structure of Revelation," I attempt to delineate the formal structure of the book.

66. It would be interesting to explore the affinities between Revelation and Matthew more fully in the context of the discussion of early Christian prophecy (cf. the various articles of E. Schweizer on the milieu of the Matthean community).

67. This avoidance of the "Son of man" title in Rev. would have to be studied more

fully not only with respect to early Christian apocalyptic traditions but also in view of the function that the descent-ascent motif has in connection with the "Son of man" (cf. John 3:13) for the understanding of the Fourth Gospel and the Johannine group. Cf. W. A. Meeks, "The Man from Heaven in Johannine Sectarianism," *JBL* 91 (1972) 44–72.

68. Cf. M. Dibelius, "Wer Ohren hat zu hören, der höre," *TSK* 83 (1910) 461–71; F. Hahn, "Die Sendschreiben der Johannesapokalypse. Ein Beitrag zur Bestimmung prophetischer Redeformen," in *Tradition und Glaube; Festgabe für K. G. Kuhn* (Göttingen: Vandenhoeck & Ruprecht, 1972) 357–94, esp. 377–81.

69. Cf. Vos, *Synoptic Traditions*, 71–75.

70. U. B. Müller, *Prophetie und Predigt im Neuen Testament. Formgeschichtliche Untersuchungen zur urchristlichen Prophetie* (SNT 10; Gütersloh: Gerd Mohn, 1975) 51.

71. Contra Holtz (*Die Christologie*, 208ff.). It is interesting to note, however, that in the letters (*Sendschreiben*) the word of the Spirit is identical with the word of the resurrected Lord. Similarly, according to John 14:26, the function of the Paraclete is to teach the word of Jesus, but it is this which Jesus has spoken on earth. For the development of the Paraclete understanding, cf. U. B. Müller, "Die Parakletvorstellung im Johannesevangelium," *ZTK* 71 (1974) 31–77. At this point it becomes apparent that an understanding of the relationship between apocalyptic and gnostic revelations or "gospels" on the one hand and their interrelationship to the "canonical gospel" on the other hand is of crucial importance for a discussion of the relationship between Rev. and the Fourth Gospel.

72. E. Käsemann, "Sentences of Holy Law in the New Testament," in *New Testament Questions of Today* (Philadelphia: Fortress Press; London: SCM Press, 1969) 66–81. Cf. also L. Thompson, "Cult and Eschatology in the Apocalypse of John," *JR* 49 (1969) 330–50, esp. 347ff. For an extensive discussion of the prophetic form and self-understanding in Rev. and Paul, cf. Müller, *Prophetie und Predigt*, 109–75.

73. Schnackenburg (*Die Johannesbriefe*, 254 n. 3) points out that the Qumran community is also filled with the spirit of battle and the confidence of victory. According to him the difference between the Qumran and Johannine writings can be seen in the fact that at Qumran the eschatological victory is expected soon but is still to come, while according to the Johannine writings the victory is already achieved by Christ and is continuing in the community. Contrary to Schnackenburg this victory language does not achieve its full development in Rev. Rev. has a middle position between Qumran and 1 John: Christ has achieved the victory but the victory of Christians is still to come.

74. Cf. Hahn, "Die Sendschreiben," 385–86.

75. H. Kraft, *Die Offenbarung des Johannes* (HNT 61a; Tübingen: Mohr/Siebeck, 1974).

76. Cf. Satake, *Die Gemeindeordnung*, 46–86; A. T. Nikolainen, "Über die theologische Eigenart der Offenbarung des Johannes," *TLZ* 93 (1968) 161–70; D. Hill, "Prophecy and Prophets in the Revelation of St. John," *NTS* 18 (1971/72) 401–18, esp. 413. The hypothesis that Rev. is directed to a "school" or "circle" makes it comprehensible that the author could use such "coded" language and imagery and still could hope to be understood. Cf., e.g., C. Clemen ("Die Stellung der Offenbarung Johannis im ältesten Christentum," *ZNW* 26 [1927] 173–86) for the "conventicle" character of the book.

77. Both the Fourth Gospel and Rev. employ the verb *tērein* which in early Christian writings was understood in the sense of "keeping" or "guarding" a tradition (cf. Mark

7:9; Matt. 23:3; 28:20; Acts 10:5; 21:25; 1 Tim. 6:13–14). The Fourth Gospel uses the expression in the traditional sense in order to characterize the teachings of Jesus as a "holy tradition" *(logos)* given by the Father through Jesus (14:24) and received by the community (John 17:8, 14, 17). Cf. Culpepper, *The Johannine School,* 275. The author of Rev. might have been familiar with this technical vocabulary of tradition. He does not use it, however, to refer to early Christian traditions but to the words of his own book, which he thereby qualifies as the authoritative tradition of the resurrected Lord.

78. K. Berger, "Apostelbrief und apostolische Rede," *ZNW* 65 (1974) 190–271.

79. H. Koester, "GNOMAI DIAPHOROI. The Origin and Nature of Diversification in the History of Early Christianity," in *Trajectories through Early Christianity* (Philadelphia: Fortress Press, 1971) 141–57, esp. 143–57.

80. Cf. the similarity in wording in 2 John 1: *kai tois teknois autēs* ("and to her children"; cf. also vv. 4 and 13). It would be tempting to draw a line from the "Johannine school" to the "school of Jezebel" and to identify the "opponents" of Rev. with a segment of the "Johannine" school. For the possibility of such a hypothesis compare the following: E. Käsemann (*The Testament of Jesus* [Philadelphia: Fortress Press, 1968] 14ff.) links the theology of the Fourth Gospel with the enthusiastic tendencies found in the pre-Pauline, Pauline, and post-Pauline traditions. Culpepper (*The Johannine School,* 282–83) links the "false prophets" of 1 John with the conventicle reconstructed by Käsemann. In chap. 4 of this book, "Apocalyptic and Gnosis in Revelation and in Paul," I have attempted to point out the connections of the "opponents" in Rev. with the enthusiasts mentioned in 1 Corinthians and to compare the theology of Rev. with the Pauline theological reaction.

81. Cf. also Satake, *Die Gemeindeordnung,* 66.

82. "The last day" *(hē eschatē hēmera;* cf. John 6:39, 40, 44, 54; 11:24; 12:48) does not occur in Rev. If John 11:24 has a polemical point *(Spitze)* against the traditional early Christian eschatology, it is not directly formulated against the eschatology of the book. For the eschatological perspective of the Fourth Gospel, cf. Schnackenburg, *Johannesevangelium* 2: 530–44 [ET: 2: 426–37]; G. Fischer, *Die himmlischen Wohnungen: Untersuchungen zu Joh. 14, 2f.* (Eur. Hochschulschr. 23/38; Bern: H. Lang, 1975); and the review by Kysar in *The Fourth Evangelist,* 207–14.

4

Apocalyptic and Gnosis in
Revelation and in Paul

Biblical scholars generally hold that the author of Rev. used the apocalyptic genre to depict the religious and political struggles of the churches in Asia Minor at the end of the first century.[1] Although they agree in accepting this contemporary-historical *(zeitgeschichtlich)* understanding of Rev., they accentuate three different aspects: the literary genre, the religious-political situation, and the inner-ecclesial discussion. First, those emphasizing the apocalyptic genre classify the book, from a literary point of view, as Jewish apocalyptic literature, but from a theological point of view as belonging to Christian literature. The remarkably structured literary patterns, the hieratic language, the common stock of symbols and especially its visionary form, together with its Christian character make it "the central literary expression of Christian apocalyptic."[2] Second, the author of Rev. has written the book in time of tribulation and persecution in order to strengthen the faith, endurance, and hope of Christians in Asia Minor. Accordingly, Rev. reflects a politico-religious conflict with the Roman empire and a persecution of the church in Asia Minor under Domitian.[3] Third, the interpretation of Rev. from the point of view of the dispute of the author, John,[4] with his opponents, the Nicolaitans,[5] is less common. According to this interpretation the author polemicizes not only in the "letters" to the seven churches but also in the entire book against Gnostics.[6] He writes more in opposition to them than to the Roman state and emperor cult. The imagery of the book consequently is interpreted from the viewpoint of later gnostic mythology. I myself question whether the "anti-Roman" and "anti-Gnostic" interpretations are necessarily mutually exclusive. For we know from later writings of the church fathers, as W. H. C. Frend has pointed out,[7] that the Gnostics were able to adapt to the syncretistic Roman culture and religion, whereas the "Catholics," appealing to their Jewish heritage, refused to take part in idolatrous ceremonies and sacrifices, even when this meant persecution and death.

Another debated question is whether in the attempt to comfort persecuted Christians the author of Rev. uses Jewish thinking and apocalyptic language and imagery in order to express a genuinely Christian theology or whether he is still so completely immersed in Jewish apocalypticism that his Christian faith is incapable of transforming his Judaism and remains only at its surface.[8] Since the author writes to some of the churches in Asia Minor which Paul established or influenced, his theology is compared with the theology of the Pauline epistles and is judged deficient. W. Bauer may serve as an example of this type of theological judgment:

> The Apocalypse does not leave us with a particularly impressive idea of what sought to replace the Pauline gospel in the "ecclesiastically oriented" circles at Ephesus. Aside from Revelation's being a book of comfort and faith to threatened and persecuted Christians. . . . there remains for the most part a Jewish Christianity, presumably of Palestinian origin. This was undoubtedly better suited for the anti-gnostic struggle than was the Pauline proclamation, but in other respects it is hardly comparable.[9]

Concurring with the above-mentioned interpretations, Bauer assumes that the Book of Rev. is written in a situation of persecution, is directed against gnostic opponents within the churches, and expresses Jewish-Christian theology and thinking that correspond to the apocalyptic genre of the book. I question, however, whether Bauer's judgment concerning the comparison between the theology of Rev. and that of Paul is accurate or whether it has to be modified. My investigation, therefore, seeks to work out more clearly the following questions: first, who were the "opponents" of the author of Rev.; second, what was their place within early Christian theological development and thought; and finally, what was the theological answer or argument attempted by Rev.? This will perhaps enable us to see, on the one hand, John's qualities as a theologian in his own right and, on the other hand, his place within early Christian theology and thought.

JOHN'S OPPONENTS

The author of Rev. directly names his opponents in the messages (i.e., letters)[10] to the churches in Ephesus (2:1–7), Pergamum (2:12–17), and Thyatira (2:18–29). He praises the church of Ephesus for hating the works of the Nicolaitans, to whom the people "who call themselves apostles" (2:2) probably belong. These apostles appear to be itinerant missionaries.[11] However, the author of Rev. does not give the criteria for testing these migrant apostles, as do the *Didache* (11.8.16) and Hermas, *Mandates* (IX.11–15). Instead he praises the community for recognizing and rejecting them as false apostles. The teaching of the Nicolaitans, therefore, was probably brought into the community from the outside.

Twenty years later Ignatius also praises the church in Ephesus for rejecting "heretical" teachers who passed by on their way (Ignatius, *Eph.* 9:1;
cf. 6:2; 7:1; 8:1).[12]

The Nicolaitans are mentioned a second time in the message to the
church in Pergamum (2:15). But whereas the author of Rev. commended
the church of Ephesus for rejecting their works, he reproaches the church
of Pergamum for tolerating them. Moreover, those who hold the teaching of Balaam (2:14) are probably the same people as those who hold
the teaching of the Nicolaitans. This teaching, identified with that of
Balaam,[13] is explained theologically with reference to Num. 25:12 and
31:16 and is understood as advocating idolatrous activities and fornication. The phrase "to eat food sacrificed to idols" refers to food which
had already been consecrated to an idol as well as to participation in
pagan feasts.[14] Likewise *porneusai* (the practice of immorality) should be
understood in a literal sense as well as in a metaphorical sense, namely,
in reference to syncretistic tendencies and idolatry.[15]

Since in the message to Thyatira the prophet called Jezebel who
teaches within the community (2:20) is accused of teaching the same
vices, namely, eating meat offered to idols and practicing fornication,[16]
it is generally assumed that she and her friends and followers belong to
the same group as the Nicolaitans. But whereas the false apostles who
spread the teaching of the Nicolaitans in Ephesus were migrant missionaries, "Jezebel" and the adherents to the teaching of Balaam belong to
the communities of Thyatira and Pergamum. Thus the Nicolaitans seem
to be an integral part of these churches.[17]

As the characterization of their teaching indicates, the Nicolaitans are
a Christian libertine group within these churches of Asia Minor. It is
debated, however, whether they are "just secularized Gentile Christians
and nothing else"[18] preaching only a "practical error,"[19] or whether they
are already a gnostic (gnosticoid)[20] group with specific teachings, as they
are described by Irenaeus around 180 C.E.[21] The author of Rev. indicates
that they were not only concerned with moral praxis, but also with a certain *didache*[22] (2:14, 15, 20, 24). An example of their *didache* is mentioned in 2:24: "to know the deep things of Satan." Since the later
Gnostics, according to the church fathers, claimed to know *ta bathe* (the
depths of God)[23] it is hard to know whether or not the genitive "of
Satan" should be understood in a literal sense and taken to mean that
spiritual persons know the deep things and mysteries of Satan and therefore are able to take part in the immoral practices of their society without being overcome by them.[24] However, the author of Rev. could have
used the genitive also in an ironical sense, as he did in Rev. 2:9 and 3:9
with regard to the Jews. As the Jews claim to be the "synagogue of God,"
but according to John are in reality the "synagogue of Satan," so also

the probable claim of the Nicolaitans to know the deep mysteries of God is according to him knowledge not of divine but of demonic realities.[25] The spiritual person and true Gnostic, who possesses the gnosis of the true being of God or Satan, is through this gnosis freed from the world and its powers and therefore assured of final salvation. This gnostic freedom can be expressed in strict asceticism or great moral libertinism. According to the church fathers, the libertine direction of Gnosticism expressed its higher knowledge mainly in practicing immorality and in the eating of food sacrificed to idols.[26]

This understanding of freedom allowed the Gnostic to live in peaceful co-existence with the pagan society. Since loyalty to the Roman civil religion did not necessarily involve credal statements, but mainly required participation in certain cultic acts and ceremonies,[27] it was possible to conform to the pagan cult without giving up faith in the one true God and Jesus Christ. This was an important theological solution for Christians in Asia Minor, since eating at banquets meat which had been previously sacrificed to pagan gods or participating in the religious ceremonies of the trade guilds was necessary for social intercourse. It allowed a Christian citizen to take part actively in the social, commercial, and political life of society. In Asia Minor Ephesus was a great trading city, Thyatira had an unusually great number of trade guilds,[28] and Pergamum was the center of various pagan cults and one of the main places of the emperor cult.[29] The Nicolaitans probably had many followers in these cities because they advocated such a policy of adaptation by claiming that they knew the profundities of Satan and hence could not be overcome by him.

In summary, the Nicolaitans are, according to Rev., a Christian group within the churches of Asia Minor and have their adherents even among the itinerant missionaries and prophetic teachers of the community. They claim to have insight into the divine or, more probably, into the demonic. They probably express their freedom in libertine behavior, which allows them to become part of their syncretistic pagan society and to participate in the Roman civil religion. Since their teaching seems to have been the alternative to the author's own teaching, his sharp rejection of the Nicolaitans in the seven letters and his condemnation of the emperor cult in the main part of Rev. become understandable. The letters as well as the apocalyptic part are then directed against the same thinking and background.[30]

RELATION TO PAUL'S OPPONENTS
IN 1 CORINTHIANS

Whereas the Tübingen School regarded the Nicolaitans as Pauline in tendency,[31] scholars today consider them more as a Judaistic group. B.

M. Newman, for example, characterizes them as promoting "a 'heretical' gnostic Christianity of Jewish tint."[32] H. Koester also describes them with reference to Rev. 2:6, 16 as a "hostile Judaizing group" and places them in a line with the Judaizers mentioned in Galatians, Philippians, Colossians, and the letters of Ignatius. The Nicolaitans, therefore, should be distinguished from the opponents of Paul in 1 Corinthians. Koester apparently bases his conclusion, on the one hand, on the identification of those who claim to be true Jews (Rev. 2:9; 3:9) with the Nicolaitans and, on the other hand, on the assumption that the references to the OT figures, Balaam and Jezebel, indicate the self-understanding of the Nicolaitans and their involvement "in daring interpretation of Scripture" (cf. Rev. 2:14; also 2:20).[33] Since, however, the author of Rev. uses the OT as a source for his symbolic names, alludes to OT writings for his theological interpretations, and thus engages himself in "daring interpretation" and application of Scripture,[34] his attribution of the OT references to the teaching of the Nicolaitans and to the activity of the prophetess called Jezebel indicate more probably *his* interpretation and understanding of the Nicolaitans than their own self-understanding.

Moreover, it is a debated question whether those who call themselves Jews are actually Jews or whether, as Koester and Newman assume, they are Christians belonging to the group of the Nicolaitans. With regard to this question, it is important to observe the reference to the Jews[35] in the messages to the churches of Smyrna and Philadelphia. Both churches are praised for having endured persecutions by those who call themselves Jews and claim to be the synagogue of God but who are, according to Rev., the "synagogue of Satan." Whereas John praises these two churches for resisting the persecution of the so-called Jews, he does not criticize the other churches for giving in to persecution by the Nicolaitans, but for being invaded by them. Whereas some Jews endanger the churches by persecution from the outside, the Nicolaitans endanger them from within by means of "heretical" teachings. Therefore, the so-called Jews and the Nicolaitans should not be identified.

The Jews do not seem to represent a Christian group, but the Jewish citizenship of these cities. "The Jews were strong in Smyrna and had maintained in practice their position as a distinct people apart from the rest of the citizens."[36] An example of this bitter hostility of some Jews against Christians in Asia Minor can be seen in the decisive role that Jews in Smyrna played in the martyrdom of Polycarp.[37] Furthermore, the author of Rev. thinks that the churches of Smyrna and Philadelphia have to expect further difficulties and persecutions from the Jewish citizenship in the future (2:10–11). If the "Jews" and the "Nicolaitans" appear as two distinct parties, the categorization of the Nicolaitans as "Judaizers" proves to be largely unfounded. The Nicolaitans, then, probably do not belong to the Judaizing party attested in Galatians, Philippians, or Colossians.

Instead of identifying the "Jews" and Nicolaitans, I should like to suggest and elaborate some striking parallels that exist between the teaching and practice of the Nicolaitans and the problems posed by the so-called enthusiasts mentioned in 1 Corinthians.[38] In 1 Cor. 8:1—9:23 and 10:23—11:1 Paul discusses the Christian gnosis and freedom in regard to the eating of food sacrificed to idols and he raises the closely related questions of a possible participation in a pagan cult in 10:14–22. He maintains, however, that Christian freedom is limited by weakness and the need of other Christians. Paul's approach to this concrete question makes quite clear his stance in regard to "gnosis" and existence in the Spirit. Paul does not reject the claim to gnosis, but wants it modified and limited by *agapē* (love).[39] Quite different, however, is his reaction in regard to *porneia* (immorality; 1 Cor. 6:12–20), the parallel claim of freedom understood gnostically that is found in 1 Corinthians and Rev. Paul initially accepts as a generally valid maxim the claim of his opponents that "all things are lawful," but strictly rejects this claim to freedom when it is applied to the practice of immorality.[40] According to Paul, Christian freedom cannot be exercised against the conscience of the weaker Christian. For Paul, Christian existence is essentially bodily existence, not spiritual freedom from the body and the material world.

The similarity of the claims of the "opponents of Paul" in 1 Corinthians and those of the Nicolaitans in Rev. can also be seen in the reference of 1 Cor. 2:10a to *ta bathē tou theou* (the depths of God), which according to Paul only the *pneuma* (Spirit) of God, but not a human *pneuma*, can know (cf. Rom. 11:33).[41] Another parallel could be the claim of the "opponents" in Corinth to have gained resurrection already in baptism. This claim is a theologoumenon which we again find later in 2 Tim. 2:18 and Polycarp, Phil. 7:1; moreover, Hippolytus attributes this view to the Nicolaitans.[42] A further similarity could be the claim of Paul's "opponents," mentioned in 1 Cor. 4:8, that they have already become rich and kings, since the church of Laodicea is reproached because it claims to be "rich" (3:17). Since we know from Logion 2 of *The Gospel of Thomas*[43] that it was a gnostic belief to have already gained the lordship over the cosmos, it may be possible that the emphasis upon the kingship motif in Rev. should be seen in connection with this gnostic claim.

Although some of these parallels could be questioned or understood in a different way, their occurrence in connection with the surprising

combination of the problem of eating food sacrificed to idols and practicing immorality makes it probable that the Nicolaitans mentioned in
Rev. are not similar to the "Judaizers," but rather to the enthusiasts of
Corinth, or better yet, to the early Christian enthusiasts in general.
Those moving in this theological direction are said to have received ultimate perfection and salvation through baptism and "gnosis," to belong
already to the heavenly, spiritual world, and to be able to express this
spiritual freedom in eating meat sacrificed to idols and in committing
immoral acts.[44]

If Paul's "opponents" in Corinth and the Nicolaitans mentioned in
Rev. represent the same type of enthusiastic theology of freedom, then
it might prove fruitful to compare the theological answers given by Paul
and the theological reaction of the author of Rev. in order to see the
latter writer in perspective, and as a theologian in his own right.

PAUL AND JOHN

E. Käsemann has convincingly shown that Paul fought his battle
against the Corinthian enthusiasts under the banner of apocalyptic theology.[45] He has demonstrated this thesis in view of Paul's anthropology.
First, Paul did not take over the enthusiasts' realized eschatology by
which they affirmed that the Christian already participates in both the
cross and the resurrection of Christ. Rather, Paul stresses the eschatological dimension of Christian existence. He points out that Christians,
through baptism, take part only in the cross of the Lord and only in the
Spirit do they have the expectation and the hope for their own resurrection and the final salvation of the world. Second, Paul distinguishes
between the world as unredeemed and the church as redeemed creation,
as world in obedience to God. This does not mean, however, that the
church has already gained final perfection and salvation. The church still
has to strive for the future consummation of its salvation because it is
still exposed to the temptations and sufferings of the rest of the world
and still subjected to the power of death.

The apocalyptic question[46] as to whom the lordship over the world
belongs is still valid for the church as long as it has to live in this world.
This apocalyptic question is formulated by Paul in terms of the alternative between the lordship of Christ and the lordship of the ruling powers
of this cosmos. But, whereas Christ has overcome these powers and is
now exalted as cosmocrator, the same is not the case for the church and
Christians. The struggle is now reflected in the lives of Christians who
are called to freedom but are still, as those living in this world, in danger
of losing their share in the lordship of Christ and of falling victim again
to the cosmic powers. According to Paul, not in enthusiastic libertinism,

but only in the bodily obedience of Christians does the church prove itself as a new creation and make visible that Christ is the Lord of this world. Thus "The apocalyptic question 'To whom does the sovereignty of the world belong?' stands behind the Resurrection theology of the apostle, as behind his parenesis which centers round the call to obedience in the body."[47] With the help of apocalyptic theology Paul unmasks enthusiastic theology as an illusion with its emphasis on a realized eschatology that is expressed in a libertine spiritual self-understanding.

It is well known that in its content, as well as in its form, Rev. is a literary example of early Christian apocalyptic theology. It is less frequently observed, however, that the author did not primarily intend to write an apocalypse but an official letter to the churches in Asia Minor. Accordingly, he puts his apocalyptic visions and prophetic sayings within the framework of the already traditional Pauline letter form with an extended *praescriptio* and concluding admonitions and greetings.[48] Just as Paul emphasized towards his opponents in Corinth that he also had the authority of an apostle and the spiritual experience of a pneumatic, so also the author of Rev. stresses that his authority is prophetic authority and his message an authentic pneumatic message, since the *pneuma* articulates the messages given to the communities. Both writers also make little reference to Jesus of Nazareth. The center of their theologies is the resurrected and exalted Lord of the world. But whereas Paul sees Jesus Christ as the Lord mainly in cosmological terms,[49] the author of Rev. pictures Christ in political terms as the "King of kings" (19:16) and the powerful Lamb who alone is worthy to exercise lordship.[50] As Paul modified a cosmological theology by stressing the importance of the historical death of Jesus Christ on the cross,[51] so Rev. emphasizes that Christ's lordship over the world is rooted in his violent death (5:3–14). Against an enthusiastic, illusionary theology, which claims already to have a part in the heavenly world and kingship, both maintain that the resurrected Lord of the world had to suffer and to die in this earthly life. Paul must have been regarded by the enthusiasts in Corinth as reactionary, falling back into Judaistic thinking because of his eschatological emphasis and apocalyptic theology. Likewise the author of Rev. must have been and still is today judged as representing Judaism and a primitive Jewish-Christian theology[52] because of his apocalyptic Jewish language, which is marked by Hebrew Bible//Jewish diction, imagery, and thought.

However, it must be asked whether the author of Rev. represents and preserves only remnants of Jewish-Christian theology or whether he chooses it—as Paul did—as a means in his struggle against the Nicolaitans, who like Paul's opponents in Corinth represent a libertine-enthusiastic theology. The theological similarity between John and Paul would not necessarily imply a direct dependence of one upon the other. Rather it seems to be occasioned by the same type of theological background and dispute. Since John writes some years later to communities which had been influenced by Paul[53] and has himself a Jewish-Christian background, he could have been familiar with elements of Pauline theology. It cannot be ascertained, however, whether he was consciously influenced by them in writing his theological answer and in using apocalyptic language and thought in his argumentation against his opponents.

The following comparison between Paul's theology and that of Rev. is therefore not so much an attempt to assert or to assume the historical theological dependence of John on Paul, as it is an attempt to grasp the common theological elements and thought patterns of both in the midst of their historical-theological differences. The following two points will perhaps illustrate this structural comparison: The first concerns the importance of the "eschatological reservation" (*eschatologischer Vorbehalt*, i.e., futuristic eschatology) in the Book of Rev. for the understanding of Christian existence. The second concerns the manner in which the author of Rev. understands the relationship between the world and the church and its significance for Christian life.

First, whereas Paul counters a realized eschatology by insisting that Christians have not yet achieved their resurrection because the last enemy, death, still must be overcome,[54] John argues against a similar type of realized eschatology by affirming that Christians are indeed appointed to kingship and priesthood but are not yet taking part in the heavenly liturgy and are not exercising their kingship actively as long as they are not living on a New Earth and a New Heaven.[55] However, just as scholars have often overlooked the eschatological reservation[56] made by Paul against the enthusiastic understanding of salvation, so too they have often overlooked the eschatological reservation contained in the argumentation used by the author of Rev. An example of this neglect: although some scholars have comprehended the significance of futuristic eschatology in relation to the world, nevertheless they have attributed a realized eschatology to the church insofar as they have maintained that, for Rev., the church is in the present time already taking part in the heavenly liturgy.[57] Insofar as scholars have not taken into account that the "eschatological reservation" is made by Rev. also for the church, they have affirmed that the glorification and exaltation of the Christian community has already taken place[58] and that the eternity of the New Jerusalem is already present on earth in the church. Consequently, the eschatological end is understood as nothing more than a manifestation and disclosure of what has already been realized in redemption.[59] But this interpretation of Rev. is actually more similar to the self-understanding of the early Christian enthusiasts and gnosticizing elements than to the interpretation of Christian existence as explicated by Rev. Just as the enthusiasts, in making the transition from Christology to anthropology, claimed to be already resurrected with Christ in baptism, so too this interpretation of Rev. has maintained that the exaltation of Christians has already taken place in history analogously to Christ's exaltation.[60] Rev. 1:6 is claimed to be the basis of this interpretation because it states with reference to Exod. 19:6 that Christ has made Christians a kingdom (or kings) and that he has appointed[61] them to be priests for God. This statement is repeated almost word for word in the "new song" of Rev. 5:10.

This interpretaion, however, overlooks the fact that Rev. 1:6 represents a traditional formula[62] which could be understood in an eschatologically realized sense, especially when its *Sitz im Leben* was baptism. The "new song" of Rev. 5:9–10 composed by the author[63] attempts to modify this statement of Rev. 1:5–6 especially through the addition "and they shall reign on earth." The author emphasizes by this modification that Christians will actively exercise their kingship over the earth only in the eschatological future.[64] He makes the same "eschatological reservation" in a different form in the vision of the millennium with its concluding blessing (*makarismos*: 20:4–6). Moreover, the final clause at the end of the visionary part of the whole book emphasizes the same eschatological point when in Rev. 22:5 it is stated that those who have part in the New Jerusalem and new world "shall reign for ever and ever." Only those Christians who have part in the final salvation will actively exercise their eschatological kingship. Only those who are victorious and those who have overcome the great tribulation will be exalted to active kingship.[65]

The same is true in regard to the priesthood of the Christians. Those who have been freed from their sins and have been "made to [be] priests" will be the eschatological "high priests"[66] of the New Jerusalem, that is, if they ratify with their lives and behavior this gift received in baptism. Nowhere in Rev. does the author speak of a Christian liturgy or priestly liturgical service on earth. Christians, having been "made to [be] priests" in redemption, do not now exercise on earth any priestly functions but will exercise them only in the eschatological future. As long as eschatological salvation, which is represented for Rev. by the symbol of the throne[67] of God, is not yet present on earth, Christians are not in the immediate presence of God and the Lamb and therefore cannot directly take part in the heavenly liturgy. As Paul stressed with the "eschatological reservation" that the resurrection was in no way an anthropological but only a christological fact, so John emphasizes with his stress on the eschatological future that Christians are indeed appointed to kingship and priesthood in redemption but that only those who are victorious will be actively exercising their kingship and priesthood in the eschatological new world.

Second, the apocalyptic question "as to whom the lordship of the world belongs," which underlies Paul's eschatological and ecclesiological arguments as well as his admonitions and call to bodily obedience, is also central to the theology of Rev. not only with regard to its "eschatological reservation," but also with regard to its understanding of the relationship between the world and the church. However, Rev. focuses and formulates this question in political terms: "to whom does the lordship of the earth belong?"[68] Whereas Paul understood this apocalyptic question in terms of the alternative between the lordship of Christ over the world and that of the cosmic powers, the author of Rev. poses it in terms of the alternative between the kingship of God and Christ on the one hand and the dominion of the Roman emperor on the other hand. Therefore, Paul conceives of the church as redeemed creation, whereas Rev. sees the church rather as the "kingdom for God" in distinction to the Roman empire.[69] This political alternative is reflected in the life of the Christians who are appointed to kingship as partners in God's kingdom but are still in danger of losing their kingship and of becoming followers of the two beasts, which are, together with the great harlot Babylon (chap. 17),[70] a symbol of the Roman empire and state in Rev. The apocalyptic dualism between God and Satan is present on earth in the struggle between the Christian and the Roman civil religion and reign.

Whereas the Nicolaitans seem to have maintained that they "know the deep things of Satan" and are therefore no longer endangered by him, the author of Rev. stresses that Satan was thrown down to earth (12:9)[71] and thus is now the force and power behind the beast and his worship (*proskynēsis*). Rev. therefore distinguishes sharply between those who worship the beast and his power and those who worship God. Whereas the "eternal gospel" calls all to worship and to acknowledge God (14:7), in historical reality all who dwell on earth worship the beast and his image (13:8) and the whole earth follows the beast with wonder (13:3). All citizens have to accept the mark of the beast; otherwise they are no longer able to take part in the economic and social life of the earth (13:16–17). Only those whose names are found in the book of life of the slain Lamb (13:8) can resist this compulsion to idolatry. This means, however, that they must take upon themselves captivity and death (13:10)[72] because of their refusal to give the emperor honors which would symbolically ratify his claim for lordship over all humanity. This belief goes directly against the stance taken by gnostic groups, who had no scruples in engaging in trades and actions connected directly with pagan worship.[73] Whereas the Nicolaitans appear to have considered themselves as free to participate in idolatrous feasts because of their salvation in Christ, the author of Rev. emphasizes that salvation and Christian existence must be proved in the rejection of both idolatry and participation in the Roman civil religion. As Paul stressed against the enthusiasts in Corinth the limitedness of Christian freedom by love and the necessity of bodily obedience in everyday life, so also the author of Rev. emphasizes the demand for active resistance which results for him in tribulations, persecutions, captivity, and violent death. Whereas the dualistic gnostic world view functions to make clear that the true Gnostic definitely belongs on the side of God, light, truth, and salvation, the author of Rev. relies on apocalyptic dualism in order to emphasize that salvation is not a given and accomplished fact, a gift which can no longer be lost, but must be proved in Christian actions and life.[74] Only those who do not take part in the idolatry of the emperor cult and do not bend to the political power of Rome will be able to exercise their kingship and priesthood in the eschatological future.

CONCLUSION

By stressing that the gift of redemption must be proven (*Bewährung*) in the concrete religious-political situation of everyday life as well as by insisting that the "eschatological reservation" is still valid for Christians, the author of Rev. attempts to refute his opponents within the communities and to strengthen the faith and endurance of those same communities in the persecutions by the Roman state. He does this with the help of apocalyptic theology and mythological language. His theology proves itself to be a Christian theology in its own right and comparable to Paul's theological accomplishment. The question raised by H. D. Betz whether "later Jewish and Christian apocalypticism converge in a gnosticizing process" or whether "they resist it"[75] can therefore be answered for the theology of Rev. I have attempted to show that John, the author of Rev., like Paul, resisted "gnosticizing" tendencies with the help of an apocalyptic theology, whose elements were taken over from Jewish as well as from early Christian traditions. The *Sitz im Leben* for the development of a Christian apocalyptic theology appears to be, in the case of Rev., the discussion of and polemic against enthusiastic tendencies[76] within the communities of Asia Minor.

NOTES

1. W. G. Kümmel, *Introduction to the New Testament* (14th ed.; Nashville: Abingdon Press, 1966) 327–29. The earliest tradition for this date is found in Irenaeus, *Adv. Haer.* 5.30,3 [=Eusebius, *H.E.* 3.18]. Cf. also A. Strobel, "Abfassung und Geschichtstheologie der Apokalypse nach Kap. XVII. 9–12," *NTS* 10 (1962–63) 437–45.

2. W. A. Beardslee, *Literary Criticism of the New Testament* (Philadelphia: Fortress Press, 1970) 53–63, esp. 56; P. Vielhauer, "Apokalypsen und Verwandtes," in *Neutestamentliche Apokryphen* (ed. E. Hennecke-W. Schneemelcher; 3d ed.; Tübingen: Mohr/Siebeck, 1964), 2: 407–44 [ET: 581–642]. A. Farrer (*A Rebirth of Images* [Boston: Beacon Press, 1963] 262) stresses that the author's method is Gnostic.

3. The majority of the commentaries on Rev. hold this view (e.g., Swete, Charles, Loisy, Beckwith, Allo, Carrington, Wikenhauser, Bonsirven, Behm, Brütsch, Feret, Boismard, Lohse, Cerfaux-Cambier, Caird, Visser, Kiddle-Ross).

4. The name "John" is used here because the author so names himself in Rev. 1:1, 4, 9; 22:8, without adding any honorary title. Rev. is thus, in distinction to other apocalypses, not a pseudonymous book. The use of the name "John" does *not*, however, imply that the author of Rev. is identical with the author of John's Gospel and Letters or that he belongs to the same theological school.

5. A. von Harnack, "The Sect of the Nicolaitans and Nicolaus, the Deacon in Jerusalem," *JR* 3 (1923) 413–22; M. Goguel, "Les Nicolaites," *RHR* 115 (1937) 5–36; N. Brox, "Nikolaos und Nikolaiten," *VC* 19 (1965) 1–22. The question whether the Nicolaitans are named after the Nicolaus of Acts 6:5 is not important for our investigation. Harnack maintains that the Nicolaitans of Rev. and the second-century sect of the Nicolaitans are the same continuously existing gnostic sect.

6. G. A. van den Bergh von Eysinga, "Die in der Apokalypse bekämpfte Gnosis," *ZNW* 13 (1912) 293–305; B. M. Newman, *Rediscovering the Book of Revelation* (Valley Forge, Pa.: Judson Press, 1968). However, cf. P. Carrington (*The Meaning of the Revelation* [New York: Macmillan Co., 1931] 395–416 [Appendix II]), who considers the Nicolaitans as members of a primitive Hebrew Gnosticism, and attempts to combine this anti-gnostic polemic with the contemporary political interpretation of Rev. by ascribing these two different polemics to different times and sources (226–35).

7. W. H. C. Frend, "The Gnostic Sects and the Roman Empire," *JEH* 5 (1954) 25–37.

8. The Tübingen school (Baur, Köstlin, Schwegler, B. Weiss, Hausrath, et al.) maintained that Rev. is a Judaistic counterpart to the universalism of Paul. The source-critical analyses of Vischer, Weyland, Holtzmann, Sabbatier or J. Weiss have claimed that Rev. is a compilation from one or more Jewish sources. This is recently assumed again by U. B. Müller (*Messias und Menschensohn in der judischen Apokalypsen und in der Offenbarung des Johannes* [Gütersloh: Gerd Mohn, 1972] 157–216).

9. W. Bauer, *Orthodoxy and Heresy in Earliest Christianity* (Philadelphia: Fortress Press, 1971) 84.

10. T. Zahn (*Die Offenbarung des Johannes* [Leipzig: Deichert, 1924], 1, 41) empha-

sizes that one cannot speak of "letters," since none of the messages has the form of a letter. They seem to be constructed according to a certain literary scheme. Cf. M. Hubert, "L'architecture des lettres aux Sept Églises," *RB* 67 (1960) 349–53; see also K. Baltzer, *Das Bundesformular* (WMANT 4; 2d ed.; Neukirchen: Neukirchener Verlag, 1964) 168–69.

11. W. Bousset, *Die Offenbarung Johannis* (MeyerK 16; 6th ed.; Göttingen: Vandenhoeck & Ruprecht, 1906) 204, 206.

12. Bauer, *Orthodoxy and Heresy*, 83; R. M. Grant, *The Apostolic Fathers: Ignatius of Antioch* (New York: Thomas Nelson & Sons, 1966) 4: 38–40.

13. This identification of the Nicolaitans with the Balaamites is also based on the observation that both names are roughly etymological equivalents. See R. H. Charles, *A Critical and Exegetical Commentary on the Revelation of St. John* (ICC; Edinburgh: T. & T. Clark, 1920) 1: 52–53. A somewhat different translation is assumed by Farrer (*Revelation*, 74): "St. John produces a second play on the name: this 'victor of the people' (Nicolaos) is a Balaam (= 'master of the people')." However, such etymological derivations of the name are questionable. Cf. Harnack, "The Sect of the Nicolaitans," 413. He refers to Jude 11 and 8 where the false teachers are also compared with Balaam and accused of the same vices (p. 414).

14. Charles, *Revelation* 1: 63; A. T. Ehrhardt, "Social Problems in the Early Church," in *The Framework of the New Testament Stories* (Cambridge: Harvard Univ. Press, 1964) 276–90.

15. E. Lohmeyer, *Die Offenbarung des Johannes* (HNT 16; 2d ed.; Tübingen: Mohr/Siebeck, 1953) 31. See also G. B. Caird, *The Revelation of St. John the Divine* (HNTC; New York: Harper & Row, 1966) 39: "A good example for this is found in the story of Baal-peor, where the Israelites had intercourse with Moabite women; for the real offense in this action was that they were foreign women, who enticed them to eat meat which had been offered in sacrifice to pagan gods." It is important to see that we have a reference to Num. 25:1–18 also in 1 Cor. 10:8.

16. C. K. Barrett ("Things Sacrificed to Idols," *NTS* 11 [1964–65] 138–53) calls attention to the similarity in the "Apostolic Decree" (Acts 15:20, 29; 21:25). However, E. Haenchen (*Die Apostelgeschichte* [MeyerK 3; 5th ed.; Göttingen: Vandenhoeck & Ruprecht, 1965] 390 n. 2; ET: *The Acts of the Apostles* [Philadelphia: Westminster Press; Oxford: Blackwell, 1971] 449 n. 3) points out that Rev. 2:20–25 is not a reference to the "Apostolic Decree," but to Num. 25:1–18.

17. H. Zimmermann, "Christus und die Kirche in den Sendschreiben der Apokalypse," in *Unio Christianorum: Festschrift Jaeger* (Paderborn: Schöningh, 1962) 176–97, esp. 183–94; E. Lohse, *Die Offenbarung des Johannes* (NTD 11; 2d rev. ed.; Göttingen: Vandenhoeck & Ruprecht, 1966) 27–28.

18. Bousset, *Die Offenbarung*, 238.

19. I. T. Beckwith, *The Apocalypse of John* (1919; Grand Rapids: Baker Book House, 1967) 459.

20. For the terminology "pre-Christian gnosticism" or "gnosticoid" = "gnostisierend," see K. Rudolph, "Gnosis and Gnostizismus, ein Forschungsbericht, II," *TRu* 36 (1971) 1–61, esp. 21. The origin and definition of "Gnosis" and "Gnosticism" is very much disputed. See further the texts and discussions of the Colloquium of Messina in 1966, *Le origine dello gnosticismo* (ed. U. Bianchi; NumSup 12; Leiden: E. J. Brill, 1967). Scholars are also not in agreement on the question of whether there is evidence for a pre-Christian Gnosticism in the NT. The answer to this question depends

upon one's evaluation of the "opponents" in the Pauline letters, one's specification of the influences on the early Christian hymns, and the influences on the Pastoral letters or the Johannine literature. However, even someone as skeptical of the presence of gnostic elements in the NT as K. Beyschlag ("Zur Simon Magus Frage," *ZTK* 68 [1971] 395–426, esp. 426 n. 66) finds the earliest mention of early Christian Gnosis in Acts 20:29–30. Gnosis is therefore present in Christian circles within Ephesus between 80–100 C.E..

21. Irenaeus, *Adv. Haer.* 3.11,1; see also 1.26,3. Cf. G. Kretschmar, "Nikolaiten," *RGG,* 1486.

22. *Didachē* soon acquires in the dispute with gnostic groups a definite technical meaning (cf. 2 Tim. 4:2; Titus 1:9; Heb. 13:9; 2 John 9–10); see K.-H, Rengstorf, "didache," *TDNT* 2 (1964) 164 n. 5.

23. H. Schlier, "bathos," *TDNT* 1 (1964) 517–18; cf. van den Bergh van Eysinga, "Gnosis," 304.

24. W. Schmithals (*Die Gnosis in Korinth* [FRLANT 66; 2d ed.; Göttingen: Vandenhoeck & Ruprecht, 1965, 1966] 203; ET: *Gnosticism in Corinth* [Nashville: Abingdon Press, 1971]). For Rev., see Lohse, *Die Offenbarung,* 30.

25. A similar statement about Gnostics is found in Polycarp, *Phil.* 7:1–2: "And whoever perverts the sayings of the Lord and says there is neither resurrection nor judgment—such a one is the firstborn of Satan. Let us therefore forsake the variety of the crowd and their false teachings" [ET: M. H. Shepherd, "The Letter of Polycarp, Bishop of Smyrna, to the Philippians," in *Early Christian Fathers* (ed. C. C. Richardson; New York: Macmillan Co., 1970) 134]. See also N. A. Dahl, "Der Erstgeborene Satans und der Vater des Teufels (Polyk. 7:1 und Joh 8:44)," in *Apophoreta: Festschrift E. Haenchen* (BZNW 30; Berlin: Töpelmann, 1964) 72–84.

26. W. Schmithals, *Paul and the Gnostics* (Nashville: Abingdon Press, 1972) 108–9.

27. Frend, "The Gnostic Sects," 32: he mentions walking in a procession, sacrificing to the gods, swearing by the genius of the Caesar, or eating meat sacrificed to idols. Cf. also L. Koep, " 'Religio' und 'Ritus' als Problem des frühen Christentums," *Jahrbuch für Antike und Christentum* 5 (1962) 43–59, esp. 45.

28. W. M. Ramsay (*The Letters to the Seven Churches of Asia* [London: Hodder & Stoughton, 1904] 231 [Ephesus] and 350 [Thyatira]) states: "It may be regarded as certain that the importance of the trade-guilds in Thyatira made the Nicolaitans' doctrine very popular there."

29. The reference to "where Satan's throne is" in the letter to Pergamum has received different interpretations. See R. North, "Thronus Satanae Pergamenus," *VD* 28 (1950) 65–76. Most scholars assume that the text refers to the imperial cult, which had its center in Pergamum. The death of Antipas, however, was probably not owing to a general persecution, but a lynch law exercised by the citizens. Cf. Charles (*Revelation,* 1: 61): "Pergamum summed up in itself the intolerable offence and horror that such a cult, the observance of which was synonymous with loyalty to the Empire, provoked in the mind of our author."

30. Many exegetes (e.g., Völter, Vischer, Pfleiderer, Spitta, Wellhausen, Charles) consider the letters to be actual letters sent to the seven churches. The letters are according to them, therefore, not apocalyptic in character and were added only later to the book. However, it can be seen that the letters are composed as a part of the apocalyptic visions of Rev. not only in their formal structure and in the repetitions of the promises to the victor in chaps. 21—22, but also in the attempt of the author to make the letters a formal part of the inaugural vision of Christ by repeating the characteristics of Christ in the

beginning of the letters. Cf. also L. Poirier, "Les sept Églises ou le premier septénaire prophétique de l'Apocalypse" (Diss. 78; Washington, D.C.: Catholic University, 1943); U. Vanni, *La struttura letteraira dell' Apocalisse* (Aloisiana 8; Rome: Herder, 1971).

31. F. C. Baur, *Vorlesungen über neutestamentliche Theologie* (Leipzig: Fues, 1864) 207–30; G. Volkmar, *Kommentar zur Offenbarung Johannes* (Zurich: Drell, 1862) 80, 82–85; A. Hilgenfeld, "Die Christus-Leute in Korinth an die Nikolaiten," *Zeitschrift für Wissenschaftliche Theologie* 15 (1872) 220–26; E. Renan, *Saint Paul* (Paris: Michel-Levy, n.d.) 303–4.

32. Newman, *Rediscovering,* 30.

33. H. Koester, "GNOMAI DIAPHOROI: The Origin and Nature of Diversification in Early Christianity," in *Trajectories through Early Christianity* (Philadelphia: Fortress Press, 1971) 114–57, esp. 148–49.

34. A. Schlatter, *Das Alte Testament in der johanneischen Apokalypse* (BFCT 16; Gütersloh: Gerd Mohn, 1912); J. Cambier, "Les images de l'Ancien Testament dans l'Apocalypse de saint Jean," *NRT* 77 (1955) 113–22; E. Lohse, "Die alttestamentliche Sprache des Sehers Johannes," *ZNW* 52 (1961) 122–26.

35. For the author of Rev. "Jews" is still an honorary title in distinction to the Fourth Gospel where it is often used in a pejorative sense. Cf. Bousset, *Die Offenbarung,* 238.

36. Charles, *Revelation,* 1: 56; S. E. Johnson, "Early Christianity in Asia Minor," *JBL* 77 (1958) 14–15; E. Pax, "Jüdische und christliche Funde im Bereich der 'sieben Kirchen' der Apokalypse," *BiLe* 8 (1967) 264–79; J. A. Kraabel, "Judaism in Asia Minor" (Diss.; Harvard Univ., 1968).

37. *Martyrdom of Polycarp* 12.2; 13.2. Eusebius, *H.E.* 4.15, 26, 29. See Richardson's edition of *Early Christian Fathers,* 142.

38. See also H. B. Swete, *The Apocalypse of St. John* (1908; Grand Rapids: Wm. B. Eerdmans, 1951) 38, 154.

39. K. Niederwimmer, "Erkennen und Lieben," *KD* 11 (1965) 75–102; Barrett, "Things Sacrificed," 147–51; N. Johansson, "1 Cor. 13 and 1 Cor. 14," *NTS* 10 (1963–64) 383–92.

40. H. Conzelmann (*Der erste Brief an die Korinther* [MeyerK 5; Göttingen: Vandenhoeck & Ruprecht, 1969] 130–37; ET: *1 Corinthians* [Hermeneia; Philadelphia: Fortress Press, 1975] 108–13) presupposes, however, a Stoic prehistory. For the gnostic background, see Schmithals, *Die Gnosis in Korinth,* 217–30.

41. U. Wilckens (*Weisheit und Torheit* [BHT 26; Tübingen: Mohr/Siebeck, 1959] 82–83 n. 1) distinguishes between 1 Cor. 2:10 and Rom. 11:33. He maintains that 1 Cor. 2:10 reflects gnostic language and Rom. 11:3 reflects Jewish-apocalyptic terminology.

42. Hippolytus, *De resurrectione,* frag. 1; cf. Kretschmar, "Nikolaiten," 1486. For an early gnostic occurrence, see *De resurrectione (Epistula ad Rheginum), Codex Jung fo.XXIIr to fo.XXIIv* (ed. M. Maline, H. C. Puech, G. Quispel, and W. Till; Zurich-Stuttgart: Rascher, 1963) 43–50.

43. E. Haenchen, "Neutestamentliche und gnostische Evangelien," in *Christentum und Gnosis* (ed. W. Eltester; BZNW 37; Berlin: Töpelmann, 1969), 19–45, esp. 26–27. B. S. Miller ("A Study of the Theme of 'Kingdom' in the Gospel According to Thomas: Logion 18," *NovT* 9 [1967] 52–60) points out that the NT theme of kingdom is spiritualized in *The Gospel of Thomas* insofar as it is not located in time and space but in experience.

44. It cannot be ascertained for Rev. whether the gnostic libertinism of the Nicolaitans had as presupposition a redeemer myth. The same is the case for Paul. Cf. L. Schot-

troff, *Der Glaubende und die feindliche Welt* (WMANT 37; Neukirchen-Vluyn: Neukirchener Verlag, 1970) 224.

45. See E. Käsemann, "On the Subject of Primitive Christian Apocalyptic," in *New Testament Questions of Today* (Philadelphia: Fortress Press; London: SCM Press, 1969) 124–37, esp. 136–37 [=*ZTK* 59 (1962) 257–84].

46. For the religio-historical background of Käsemann's position, see P. Stuhlmacher, *Gerechtigkeit Gottes bei Paulus* (FRLANT 87; 2d rev. ed.; Göttingen: Vandenhoeck & Ruprecht, 1966); Ch. Müller, *Gottes Gerechtigkeit und Gottes Volk* (FRLANT 86; Göttingen: Vandenhoeck & Ruprecht, 1964).

47. E. Käsemann, "On the Subject of Primitive Christian Apocalyptic," 135–36. Contra Käsemann, see H. Conzelmann, "Paulus und die Weisheit," *NTS* 12 (1965–66) 231–44. J. Becker ("Erwägungen zur apokalyptischen Tradition in der paulinischen Theologie," *EvT* 11 [1970] 293–309) is also critical of Käsemann's emphasis upon apocalypticism, but concedes that the apocalyptic statements in Paul at least help to maintain the "Dialektik von Gegenwart und Zukunft in der glaubenden Gemeinde" (297). For the whole discussion, see E. Käsemann's answer to his critics, "Justification and Salvation History in the Epistle to the Romans," *Perspectives on Paul* (Philadelphia: Fortress Press, 1971) 76 nn. 27–28.

48. The salutation is similar to the more expanded form of Romans and Galatians. It also closes with a doxology, which is, however, in Rev. directed to Jesus Christ. The prescript corresponds to the epilogue: Rev. 1:1 to 22:6; 1:2b to 22:8; 1:3 to 22:7; 1:3b to 22:10b; 1:8 to 22:13. Elsewhere, I have attempted to demonstrate that Rev. has a certain correspondence between the prescript and the epilogue and between the messages to the churches and the visions of the New Jerusalem.

49. This is stressed in J. G. Gibbs, "Pauline Cosmic Christology and Ecological Crisis," *JBL* 90 (1971) 466–79. Käsemann contra Bultmann: "Anthropology is cosmology *in concreto.*" See E. Käsemann, "On Paul's Anthropology," in *Perspectives on Paul,* 1–31, esp. 27.

50. T. Holtz, *Die Christologie der Apokalypse des Johannes* (TU 85; Berlin: Akademie-Verlag, 1962) 27–54, 166–81.

51. H. Conzelmann, "Current Problems in Pauline Research," *Int* 22 (1968) 171–86; E. Schweizer, *Jesus* (Atlanta: John Knox Press, 1971) 91–106; Schottroff, *Der Glaubende,* 176–227.

52. C. H. Dodd (*The Apostolic Preaching and Its Developments* [London: Hodder & Stoughton, 1963] 40–41) states: "We are bound to judge that in its conception of the character of God and His attitude to man the book falls below the level, not only of the teaching of Jesus, but of the best parts of the Old Testament." R. Bultmann (*Theology of the New Testament* [New York: Charles Scribner's Sons, 1955] 2: 175) states that the "Christianity of Revelation has to be termed a weakly christianized Judaism."

53. We can no longer know why, for example, the churches of Colossae, Hierapolis, or Troas are not mentioned in Rev. For the question of the organization of the churches in Asia Minor, see Ramsay, *The Letters,* 171–96.

54. Cf. H. A. Wilcke, *Das Problem eines messianischen Zwischenreiches bei Paulus* (ATANT 51; Zurich: Zwingli, 1967) 100–104; Schottroff, *Der Glaubende,* 161–69.

55. For a more detailed argument, see my book, *Priester für Gott: Studien zum Herrschafts- und Priestermotiv in der Apokalypse* (NTAbh 7; Münster: Aschendorff, 1972).

56. For Rom. 6, see C. H. Tannehill, *Dying and Rising with Christ* (BZNW 32; Berlin:

Töpelmann, 1967) 7–14. Cf. also D. Georgi, *Die Gegner des Paulus im 2. Korintherbrief* (WMANT 11; Neukirchen-Vluyn: Neukirchener Verlag, 1964, p. 300 [Eng. trans. forthcoming, Philadelphia: Fortress Press, 1985]).

57. P. Seidensticker, *Lebendiges Opfer (Rom. 12:1)* (NTAbh 20/1–3; Münster: Aschendorff, 1954) 325; M. Kiddle and M. K. Ross, *The Revelation of St. John* (MNTC; 7th ed.; London: Hodder & Stoughton, 1967) 102–3; R. Deichgräber, *Gotteshymnus und Christushymnus in der frühen Christenheit* (SUNT 5; Göttingen: Vandenhoeck & Ruprecht, 1967) 47, 205.

58. Cf. A. Schlatter, *Die Theologie der Apostel* (2d ed.; Stuttgart: Calwer, 1922) 135.

59. Cf. Lohmeyer, *Die Offenbarung des Johannes,* 193; M. Rissi, *Die Zukunft der Welt* (Basel: Friedrich Reinhardt, 1966) 34; cf. also Holtz (*Die Christologie,* 191, 221) who, however, seeks to maintain the dialectic between the "already" and "not yet."

60. Holtz, *Die Christologie,* 50–52, esp. n. 1.

61. *Epoiēsen* is not found as a verb in Exod. 19:6. The clause is similar to 1 Kings 12:31, where *epoiēsen* is used with the double accusative and denotes the "appointment" of priests. For the translation and a more thorough discussion, see my book, *Priester für Gott,* 78–103, 222–26.

62. S. Läuchli, "Eine Gottesdienststruktur in der Johannesoffenbarung," *TZ* 16 (1960) 359–78; esp. 361–66; P. von der Osten-Sacken, "Christologie Taufe, Homologie," *ZNW* 58 (1967) 255–66; Schüssler Fiorenza, *Priester für Gott,* 203–36.

63. Schüssler Fiorenza, *Priester für Gott,* 263–90; K. P. Jörns (*Das hymnische Evangelium* [SNT 5; Gütersloh: Gerd Mohn, 1971] 49–52) demonstrates that the hymns in Rev. do not reflect the hymns of the liturgy of the early church but are compositions of the author for the context of the book.

64. The future tense *basileusousin* ("they shall reign") is attested by most of the manuscripts and accepted by the majority of the commentaries, but the present tense is found only in Codex Alexandrinus and the Koine text. Since A also reads the present tense in Rev. 20:6 (a place which speaks quite clearly about the eschatological future), the present tense is either a Hebraism connoting the future, or the variant in A is a mistake or a deliberate correction by a later writer at a time when the millennium already was identified with the time of the church.

65. Cf. the promises to the victorious in the seven letters, especially Rev. 2:27–28; 3:21; and 21:7. This emphasis upon the kingship motif in connection with the eschatological reward for the victor has to be seen against the enthusiastic gnosticizing background.

66. The title is not used directly but is probably implied in Rev. 22:3–5 in the characterization of those Christians who have part in the New Jerusalem. See Schüssler Fiorenza, *Priester für Gott,* 386–88; 414–16.

67. Cf. O. Schmitz, "thronos," *TDNT* 3 (1965) 165–66. It is important to notice, however, that in contradistinction to apocalyptic or gnostic writings Rev. does not describe several heavens or a journey or ascension through such heavens.

68. Cf. also M. Rissi, "The Kerygma of the Revelation of John," *Int* 22 (1968) 3–17, esp. 10: "John is not interested in any cosmological speculation, for the 'cosmos' in his view is the world of man (11:15)." Striking, however, is the emphasis of Rev. upon God as creator (Rev. 4) and *pantokratōr* (Almighty). This emphasis could be made against a gnosticizing belief in a demiurge.

69. L. Brun, "Die römischen Kaiser in der Apokalypse," *ZNW* 26 (1937) 128–51; R. Schütz, *Die Offenbarung des Johannes und Kaiser Domitian* (FRLANT 32; Göttingen:

Vandenhoeck & Ruprecht, 1933); Beckwith, *The Apocalypse,* 198–207; P. Touilleux, *L' Apocalypse et les cultes de Domitien et de Cybèle* (Paris: Geuthner, 1935); K. Gross, "Domitian," *RAC* 4: 95; E. Stauffer, *Christ and the Caesars* (Philadelphia: Westminster Press; London: SCM Press, 1955); L. Koep, "Antikes Kaisertum und Christusbekenntnis im Widerspruch," *Jahrbuch für Antike und Christentum* 4 (1961) 58–76, esp. 68–70.

70. K. G. Kuhn, "Babylon," *TDNT* 1 (1964) 514–17, esp. 516 n. 16. See also 1 Pet. 5:13 and the commentaries.

71. *Drakōn* can also be translated "serpent." Therefore, G. A. van den Bergh van Eysinga, B. M. Newman, and P. Carrington have seen here a reference to the gnostic serpent doctrine of the Ophites. If this is the case, then Rev. attacks this belief by identifying the serpent with the opponent of God, Christ, and Christians, namely, with Satan.

72. For this understanding of Rev. 13:10, see J. Schmid, "Zur Textkritik der Apokalypse," *ZNW* 43 (1950) 112–25.

73. Frend, "The Gnostic Sects," 32.

74. Cf. Rev. 20:4–6, which is not to be understood only as a special reward for the martyrs. All Christians who have resisted the imperial cult will participate in the messianic kingdom and kingship as well as in eschatological priesthood. Cf. K. H. Marshall, "Martyrdom and the Parousia in the Revelation of John," *SE* 4 (1968) 333–39.

75. H. D. Betz, "On the Problem of the Religio-Historical Understanding of Apocalypticism," *JTC* 6 (1969) 135–56, esp. 155.

76. For a similar but more generalized view, see A. Sand, "Zur Frage nach dem 'Sitz im Leben' der apokalyptischen Texte des Neuen Testaments," *NTS* 18 (1972) 167–77. For the opposite thesis, see R. M. Grant, *Gnosticism and Early Christianity* (rev. ed.; New York: Harper & Row, Torchbooks, 1966) 38. According to Grant, the origin of gnosis is connected with the collapse of Jewish apocalyptic hope after 70 C.E.

5
Apokalypsis and Propheteia:
Revelation in the Context of
Early Christian Prophecy

In recent years scholars have paid renewed attention to the phenomenon and institution of early Christian prophecy.[1] Not only have form-critical and tradition-historical studies attempted to recover genuine prophetic expressions within the NT texts, but history of religions and redactional-theological analyses have also sought to delineate the historical impact and theological significance of early Christian prophecy. Far from being conclusive these studies have highlighted the illusive character of early Christian prophecy. Scholarly investigations are severely limited not only by the sparcity of sources of early Christian as well as contemporary Jewish and Greco-Roman prophecy, but also by the theological presuppositions and theoretical models used for the historical reconstruction of these sources. Theologically, scholars have tended to insist on the word- and kerygma-character of early Christian prophecy, while theoretically employing the Pauline understanding of prophecy to construct the model of genuine early Christian prophecy. Methodologically, scholars have formulated a fairly comprehensive definition of prophecy[2] as a yardstick for early Christian texts that speak of prophecy.

Since the Book of Rev. explicitly claims to be a work of early Christian prophecy, one would expect that scholars would study the book as a primary source of early Christian prophecy. Yet for the most part this is not the case. Rigid differentiations between Jewish (Old Testament) and early Christian prophecy, between apocalypticism and prophecy, and between prophecy as kerygmatic event and as visionary-ecstatic expression prevent the analysis of Rev. as a source for the historical reconstruction of early Christian prophecy in Asia Minor at the end of the first century C.E. The question as to whether Rev. is a genuine work of early Christian prophecy is dismissed too quickly because of the assumption that—as an apocalyptic, visionary account—Rev. cannot be at the same time a literary expression of early Christian prophecy. Moreover, the "Jewish" character of the book leads to its classification with OT prophecy or Jewish apocalypticism. Therefore, even the most recent commentaries on Rev. do not situate the work in the context of early Christian prophecy[3] but only discuss it with reference to Jewish apocalyptic literature. This refusal to accept John's *apokalypsis Iēsou Christou* (revelation of Jesus Christ) as a paradigm of early Christian prophecy is summed up in the following statement:

> there is no word or passage in the New Testament which can, in my opinion, be classified beyond doubt or question as prophetic utterance. The one possible exception is the content of the book of Revelation and especially the letters of Rev. 2—3: but the words of John, and indeed his experience . . . are so remarkably unlike those of other New Testament speakers or writers and so strikingly like those of the Old Testament prophets that one may be justified in regarding him as unique: at the very least it is unwise to regard him as typical of New Testament prophets.[4]

Although scholars may differ in the exegesis of specific passages in Rev., they do not doubt that the book speaks about prophets and prophecy. Not exegetical analysis but the overall interpretation and evaluation of the exegetical-historical information is a matter of dispute. Those scholars who acknowledge Rev. as a work of Christian prophecy attribute it to the primitive church in Palestine or Syria because of its Jewish-apocalyptic character. Even though the final redaction of Rev. addresses Christian communities living in an originally Pauline missionary area, the relationship of Rev. to the post-Pauline or other Christian traditions of Asia Minor is virtually not discussed. Yet our information about NT and early Christian prophecy for the most part comes from this area.

Therefore, I will here raise the question of whether the historical theological claim of Rev. as a prophetic expression of early Christianity in Asia Minor is justified. However, before this question can be fruitfully explored, one must discuss whether or not the author of Rev. may be grouped among the Christian prophets and whether his book is a genuine expression of early Christian prophecy. In the first section, I will discuss whether John is to be grouped with the OT prophets and understood as similar to the Teacher of Righteousness at Qumran. In the second section I will raise the question of whether the sharp distinction between early Christian prophecy as reflected in the Pauline letters and prophecy in Rev. can be maintained. Finally in the last section I will attempt to develop a model of interpretation that can understand Rev. in the context of early Christian prophecy in Asia Minor at the end of the first century C.E. This model will challenge the exclusive alternatives "prophetic or apocalyptic, OT or early Christian prophecy, Paul or Revelation, Palestine or Asia Minor" underlying scholarly evaluations and constructive models for early Christian prophecy.

REVELATION'S AFFINITY
TO OLD TESTAMENT PROPHECY

In his various contributions David Hill[5] has insisted that John is very much like the prophets of the OT because his work is concerned with salvation history and the interpretation of the OT. Like the classical prophets and in particular the Teacher of Righteousness at Qumran, John claims an authority which sets him apart from Christian prophets and places him above the Christian community. In order to evaluate this thesis, its theological presuppositions and exegetical postulates must be examined.

First, it is claimed that John's self-understanding and authority is not that of an early Christian prophet but is rather like that of the classical prophets. His affinity with the OT prophets is evident in John's use of Scripture. The allusions to OT texts, especially to those of the classical prophets, intend "to show that the history of the church unfolds in conformity with the witness of Scripture."[6] Therefore, Hill agrees with A. Feuillet[7] that Rev. represents a "re-reading" (*une relecture*) of the OT in the light of the Christ event. This understanding of Rev. as a Christian interpretation of the OT is also shared by H. Kraft.[8]

One must ask, however, whether or not the author of Rev. was really interested in adding an "inspired volume" to the traditional prophetic corpus and in proving that the "OT prophecies are fulfilled in the events in which he and his fellow Christians are involved." Against such a hypothesis, it should be noted that the author of Rev. does not once introduce his OT materials with a "formula quotation" (cf. John 19:24: "This was to fulfil the scripture") nor does he correctly quote them. In the whole Book of Rev. we find only one explicit reference to the OT. In Rev. 15:3 it is stated: "They sing the song of Moses, the servant of God." Yet the song which follows is not connected in any literary way with the song of Moses in Exodus 15 or Deuteronomy 32, but is an amalgamation of various OT themes. Therefore Rev. does not even once quote the OT. John uses OT texts as he uses Jewish apocalyptic, pagan mythological, or early Christian materials in an allusive "anthological" way. He does not interpret the OT but uses its words, images, phrases, and patterns as a language arsenal in order to make his own theological statement or express his own prophetic vision. He adapts or borrows whole OT text sequences as patterns for his own original compositions but never refers to the OT as authoritative Scripture. Although Hill acknowledges that Rev. refers to the OT prophetic books "allusively" and "not by direct citation," he nevertheless likens the use of Scripture in Rev. to the scriptural exposition in Acts. However, he neglects to note that in Acts 13:14–43 the OT is employed quite explicitly.

His conclusions—that, although a prophet of the "NT era," John should be understood as similar to the Teacher of Righteousness at Qumran—must also be questioned. While the Teacher of Righteousness had the authority to give a "definitive elucidation of the revelation given to Moses and to the words of the prophets (1QpHab 7, 4–5)," Rev. does not claim the same authority for John. A comparison between the two very similar passages 1QpHab 7, 4–5 and Rev. 10:7 elucidates this. According to 1QpHab 7, 4–5 God has revealed to the prophet Habakkuk the eschatological events but not the end of time; God has made known however to the Teacher of Righteousness "all the mysteries of the words of his servants, the prophets." The parallel passage 1QpHab 2, 5–10 also stresses that God appointed the Teacher of Righteousness so that he could interpret all the words of the prophets who have announced the events of the last days. Thus the prophetic activity of the Teacher of Righteousness consists in the knowledge and interpretation of the mysteries of God proclaimed by the classical prophets.[9]

Rev. does not attribute to John the same prophetic authority. John's task is not exposition and interpretation of the OT prophets but prophetic proclamation about many peoples, kings, and nations. At the sound of the seventh trumpet, "the mystery of God as he announced to his servants the prophets" will be fulfilled (Rev. 10:7). Rev. does not distinguish either between John and the prophets or between the OT and early Christian prophets. The observation that the use of Scripture in Rev. resembles that of Qumran is correct. Not only does Rev. share this use of Scripture, however, with Qumran but also with other apocalyptic writings.

> This "anthological" style is not focused on Scripture itself. Once again Scripture is only a language. And indeed in any given part of the broad framework, the apocalyptic teaching cloaked in this "anthological" style is structured by events of the contemporay history of the author.[10]

Therefore, the use of the OT in Rev. links it to Jewish apocalyptic and early Christian prophecy. The author of Rev. is not bent on the exposition and explication of the OT as authoritative Scripture. It is not the OT prophets, but his own historical-theological situation, which is the locus of revelation. Yet it is precisely in using the OT in such an apocalyptic "anthological" fashion that Rev. proves to be a genuine expression of early Christian prophecy. According to K. Stendahl the apocalyptic style rests on the conviction that "the prophetic spirit creates; it does not quote in order to teach or argue."[11]

Early Christian prophecy, then, must be distinguished from early Christian homily and exegesis.[12] Whereas early Christian homily focuses on the interpretation and exposition of Scripture and tradition, early Christian prophecy announces judgment or salvation. While the homily is the interpretation of the divine word in Scripture, prophecy claims to be the revelation and authority of the *Kyrios* (Lord). John's use of the OT, therefore, characterizes Rev. not as an exposition of classical prophecy but as a genuine early Christian prophetic-apocalyptic writing. As the "words of prophecy," Rev. does not aim at didactic instruction but at prophetic proclamation and uses, among other literary sources, the classical prophets. The allusions of Rev. to the OT are an indication that Rev. shares in the style and conviction of apocalyptic literature.

Second, Hill nevertheless maintains that Rev. is not apocalyptic in character. Although John takes over the "apparatus of apocalyptic," the book is not an apocalyptic work but is similar to OT prophecy. It is the idea of salvation history (*Heilsgeschichte*) that underlies its view of history rather than apocalyptic pessimism which views the present time as evil and corrupt. Whereas prophetic vocation interprets history as salvation history, the apocalyptic perspective is interested "only in the last generation and the events immediately preceding the end."[13] Although Hill concedes that it is almost impossible to distinguish adequately between apocalypticism and prophecy, he accepts G. von Rad's[14] delineation and definition of the two phenomena. According to von Rad the apocalyptists were not concerned with God's action in history, whereas the prophets understood history and their own time as the locus of God's revelation and action. According to this distinction Rev. is clearly an expression of prophecy insofar as the author speaks to his own time and community. Nevertheless, according to this distinction, Rev. is also an expression of apocalypticism since the author is interested in history only as the last time before the end. It seems doubtful, therefore, that this distinction which von Rad formulated with respect to classical prophecy and Jewish apocalypticism can also be used to differentiate between early Christian prophecy and apocalypticism, especially since in NT times Jewish apocalyptic writers understood themselves as prophets.

I have shown elsewhere that the main concern of Rev. is not salvation history but eschatology.[15] History is completely submerged in eschatology and receives its significance from the imminent end. In line with Jewish apocalyptic literature John characterizes his own situation and history as unjust and evil, a time of powerlessness and persecution. He does not merely use the style and language of Jewish apocalypticism but also shares the apocalyptic mood and pessimistic evaluation of the present world and history. Nevertheless in distinction to Jewish apocalypticism John does not explain the tribulations and sufferings of the present time with reference to the fact that time and world have become old and are reaching their end (*4 Esdras* 5:55), but rather with reference to the fact that the Christians are redeemed from the nations. Yet, it is not so much John's conviction that God intervenes on behalf of God's people in history as proclaimed by the OT prophets, but rather his belief that the end time has been inaugurated in the death and resurrection of Jesus Christ, that constitutes the heart and inspiration of his prophecy. It is not his conception of salvation history but his Christology that enables John to discard pseudonymity, *ex eventu* prophecy (prophecy from the event), and surveys of world history. John's authority as a prophet is derived precisely from his apocalyptically conceived Christology. It is Jesus Christ, the first-born of the dead,[16] from whom the author receives the "words of prophecy" announcing the imminent end of history and tribulation. The understanding of prophecy in Rev. is apocalyptic insofar as it is bound to the imminent return of the resurrected Lord who now speaks to the Christian community through the prophets. Its theological impact derives from the apocalyptic conviction of living in the last times and of the impending eschatological salvation in the very near future.

This apocalyptic-prophetic conviction of Rev. is expressed not only in the content but also in the formal structure of the book. The literary structure and visionary accounts of Rev. do not follow a chronological but a topical order.[17] Since Rev. does not progress in historical-successive fashion but reveals in ever-new images and visions the present time of the community as the eschatological end time, it is impossible to reconstruct a historical-chronological development of events. The prophetic visions and auditions of Rev. are not predictions of future events nor are they calculations of the end time. Eschatological vision and apocalyptic prophecy have the function of strengthening and consoling the Christian community as it experiences persecution and suffering for its witness to God's and Christ's power and kingship in this world.

Third, the scholarly alternative—either prophetic or apocalyptic, as derived from the discussion of Jewish apocalyptic origins—should not be applied to Rev. As the "words of prophecy" the book is rooted in early Christian apocalyptic experience and conviction. Apocalyptic language and imagery are not just "wrapping" (*Einkleidung*) so to speak but they are constitutive for the theological perspective and self-understanding of Rev. as early Christian prophecy.

Nevertheless the exclusive alternative formulation "either [OT] prophetic or apocalyptic" continues to muddle scholarly discussions of Rev. In his influential article on prophecy and prophets, G. Friedrich claims that Rev. marks the transition from early Christian prophecy to apocalyptic. The view of prophecy in Rev. is radically different from that of the Pauline letters which express the "authentic" understanding of early Christian prophecy. Whereas parenesis is central for early Christian prophecy in the Pauline literature, predictions are the center of the prophetic-apocalyptic work of John.

> The many visions and auditions make him more of an apocalyptic seer than a primitive Christian prophet. The prophet is very different in Paul. He certainly receives revelations but he is not characterized by visions and auditions which transport him out of the world. His chief mark is the Word which God had given him to proclaim. The prophet in the Pauline congregations is not the seer but the recipient and the preacher of the Word.[18]

P. Vielhauer's somewhat ambivalent treatment and evaluation of Rev. also maintains a definite separation between apocalyptists and prophets.

> As far as their vocation is concerned, the prophets were not apocalyptists but charismatic leaders of the churches, and the seer John did not compose the Apocalypse in his capacity as prophet—for the other prophets mentioned by him wrote no such books—but at the direct command of the exalted Lord, and that means with authentic prophetic consciousness.[19]

Vielhauer, however, does not elaborate how John could have written Rev. "with authentic prophetic consciousness" but not in "his capacity as a prophet." Such contradictory statements seem to be due to the widely accepted scholarly assumption that the early Christian prophets could not have been seers and apocalyptists even though the seer John claims to be an early Christian prophet and his work is the only extensive extant source of early Christian prophecy.

D. Hill takes over Vielhauer's characterization of Rev. Although he concludes his analysis of early Christian prophecy with the statement that we cannot identify any early Christian utterance with certainty as a prophetic utterance, he nevertheless maintains that the words of Rev. are "remarkably unlike those of other New Testament speakers or writers." In distinction to the author of Rev. the prophets in the Pauline churches were community prophets and did not believe themselves "called to add any inspired volume to the prophetic corpus." Because of his interest in proving that John was unlike any other early Christian prophet, he accepts the foregone conclusion that the early Christian prophets were not apocalyptic seers but community prophets and, as such, did not write prophetic books.[20]

One should note that our extant sources on early Christian prophecy do not provide sufficient information to settle this question with certainty. The assumption of form-critics that prophetic expressions must always be short oracular utterances and that *Schriftlichkeit* (the state of being "written down") is the hallmark dividing prophecy from apocalyptic cannot be substantiated. We know that contemporary Jewish apocalyptic writers understood themselves and their works in terms of prophecy.[21] At the time of the NT the works of the classical prophets had long been written down and had become Scripture. Because classical Hebrew prophecy was known as "literary prophecy," the writers of apocalyptic works could understand their activity and authority as a continuation of that of the classical prophets. Literary activity constitutes only a difference in degree but does not destroy the prophetic character of apocalyptic works.[22]

The claim of Rev. to be early Christian prophecy, then, must be taken seriously. Its main objective is not the reinterpretation of the Hebrew Scriptures nor the calculation of the end time events, but the prophetic communication of the revelation (i.e., *apokalypsis Iēsou Christou*) to the seven communities in Asia Minor. The book's goal is not instruction in OT classical, Jewish apocalyptic, or early Christian traditions but prophetic proclamation and parenesis. Rev., therefore, should not be misunderstood as an only slightly Christianized form of Jewish apocalyptic theology[23] but must be valued as a genuine expression of early Christian prophecy whose basic experience and self-understanding is apocalyptic. If this is the case then we must understand Rev. in the context of early Christian theology and community.

REVELATION AND
EARLY CHRISTIAN PROPHECY

Those who acknowledge Rev. as early Christian apocalyptic prophecy tend to regard it as an alien element in the theological context of Asia Minor. The *Sitz im Leben* of Rev. is a Jewish-Christian conventicle whose traditions are those of the primitive Christian community of Jerusalem or of Palestine-Syria. Therefore, Rev. does not reflect the theology and community structures of Christian churches in Asia Minor at the end of the first century C.E.

According to A. Satake[24] the Christian community understood the community prophets within the framework of Jewish apocalyptic traditions. Like the sages of Jewish apocalypticism they transmit and interpret the Hebrew Bible traditions. Whereas the existence of the community prophets is due to Jewish apocalypticism, the self-understanding of John is clearly determined by the revelation of the resurrected Lord. In that case, the communities of Rev. can be characterized as a "Jewish-Christian conventicle" whose traditions and prophecy are rooted in Jewish apocalypticism and whose structures preserve the primitive Christian community order of the church in Palestine.

Satake's review of the Christian community order found in Acts,

Colossians, Ephesians, 1 Peter, the pastoral epistles, Ignatius of Antioch, the Johannine epistles, and in the letter of Polycarp concludes that one cannot speak of *the* Christian community order in Asia Minor. Yet, despite the variety in the forms of church leadership, none of these writings reflects a church order similar to that of Rev. where the community prophets appear to be the only official leaders of the churches. Although the church structure of the Johannine epistles shows affinities to that of Rev., it is nevertheless different insofar as the Johannine epistles do not mention prophets as leaders of the communities.

Such a charismatic leadership of prophets was present, however, in the primitive church of Palestine. Acts mentions prophets active in the church of Jerusalem and in the Jewish-Hellenistic community of Antioch in Syria. The Logia source Q and the pre-Matthean tradition also indicate the leadership of prophets in the primitive Palestinian or Syrian church. Thus Satake conjectures that Jewish Christians who left Palestine after the destruction of Jerusalem and the Jewish War introduced their prophetic church order in Asia Minor by founding their own Christian communities. But Satake's study does not discuss the leadership of prophets known from the Pauline letters nor does it explore the relationship of the Jewish-Christian communities of Rev. to those of the Pauline mission. On the other hand, U. Müller's[25] study of the problem correctly points out against Satake's thesis that the origin and continuation of such a Jewish-Christian conventicle is difficult to imagine in the traditionally Pauline missionary area of Asia Minor. Hence, Müller stands the thesis of Satake on its head when he claims that John and his prophetic circle rather than the communities represent a primitive Palestinian theology and community order.[26]

This conclusion is based on the assumption that community prophecy (*Gemeindeprophetie*) no longer existed in the churches of Asia Minor. It is clear that Müller understands the references in Rev. to prophets not as references to Christian prophets within the communities of Asia Minor but to all prophets who mediate eschatological revelation. The author himself was an itinerant prophet and not a prophetic community leader in Asia Minor. His understanding of the function of the prophets points to a *Sitz im Leben* in the primitive community of Palestine or Syria, reflected for example in Matthew or the *Didache,* that is rooted in primitive Christian apocalyptic expectations of the imminent end.

Together with Bauer[27] and Satake, Müller concludes that the prophetic apocalyptic theology of Rev. is an alien element in the theology and community order of Asia Minor at the end of the first century C.E. According to Acts, the pastoral epistles, and especially Ignatius, the Asian church already knew institutionalized ecclesial offices and no longer could tolerate a charismatic, prophetic church leadership. The author of Rev., however, differs from the theology of the Asian churches not just in his prophetic understanding of church leadership but also in his eschatology that is steeped in OT apocalyptic traditions and stresses the imminent Parousia of the Lord. John reactivates primitive Christian apocalyptic expectations in order to counter either "realized eschatology" or the growing acceptance of the delay of the return of Christ. Therefore John introduces the early Christian apocalyptic "Son of man" (*hyios tou anthrōpou*) Christology that was alien to Christian theology in Asia Minor.

Although Müller's attempt to take seriously the claim of Rev. to Christian prophecy and to situate the book within the theological context of early Christian development is rather persuasive, its methodological assumptions and conclusions are open to question.

First, it is questionable whether the letters of Ignatius provide a descriptive and historically accurate account of the actual situation in the churches of Asia Minor at the turn of the first century C.E. Since John and Ignatius wrote with only a short interval between each other,[28] both cannot reflect the same church order. Ignatius's emphasis on the authority of the bishops, presbyters, and deacons does not square with the fact that Rev. fails to mention any church leaders except the prophets. Since Ignatius does not mention any prophets within the communities of Asia Minor it can safely be assumed that in his time prophetic community leadership must have been abandoned or must have never existed within the Christian communities of Asia Minor that are addressed by Ignatius and Rev. Müller, therefore, maintains that the author of Rev. and his prophetic followers were not community but itinerant prophets whereas Satake claims that the churches of Rev. are, as Jewish-Christian conventicles, not identical with those whom Ignatius addresses. Both scholars fail to question the presupposition that Ignatius reflects the actual church order of the churches in Asia Minor.

Although this historical assumption is shared by many scholars, it must be questioned because it does not take seriously the tendency and literary-historical function of the Ignatian letters. First, it fails to take into account that Ignatius might reflect a Syrian-Palestinian church order and not the actual situation in Asia Minor, while Rev. claims to be at home in the Christian communities of Asia Minor. Second, the assumption fails to take serious account of the polemical character of Ignatius's[29] (or the pastoral epistles') emphasis on a nonprophetic church order. Such a polemic emphasis seems to have become necessary not because the authority of the bishop or presbyter was unchallenged but exactly because it was not accepted without question. The letters indicate that some communities celebrated the Eucharist and conducted their communal life without paying too much attention to the bishop.

Although early Christian prophets are not mentioned and prophecy seems to be limited to OT prophecy, we find at least one indication that Ignatius attempts to claim prophetic activity and power for the bishop. In the letter to the Philadelphians he asserts that he spoke as a prophet in Philadelphia.

> When I was with you I cried out, I spoke with a loud voice, God's own voice: "Pay attention to the bishop and the presbytery and deacons." . . . The Spirit made proclamation, saying this: "Do nothing apart from the bishop."[30]

Since some members of the community in Philadelphia seem to have suspected this prophetic announcement was a fraud, Ignatius insists that he did not receive his information about the divisions in the community from any human being but from the Spirit. It is interesting to note that Ignatius's prophetic proclamation is, in its form, very similar to the stereotypical formula concluding the seven messages in Rev.:[31] Whoever has ears to hear, let them hear what "the Spirit says to the churches." The same formal elements are also found in the eschatological announcement in Rev. 14:13b: "Blessed indeed, says the Spirit." Ignatius thus claims prophetic inspiration and prophetic form for his central theological emphasis on the authority of the bishop. He, the bishop, speaks as a prophet. Such a claim to prophecy would not have been necessary if, in the Asian churches, the office and function of the bishop already had replaced those of the prophet. The opposite seems to be the case. Only because prophets and prophecy had great authority in the Asian churches was it necessary to legitimate the authority of the bishops as the unifying center of the community explicitly with a "word of prophecy."

Thus Ignatius's polemic arguments indicate that monarchical episcopacy only gradually captured and replaced the office of the prophet and the authority of prophecy within the churches of Asia Minor. The last stage in the composition of the *Didache* (15:1–2)[32] reflects the same transition from dependence on the prophets to the leadership of bishops and deacons who perform "the task of the prophets." The community is admonished not to disregard or to ignore them since they have the same honorable standing as the prophets and teachers. But, such an appeal becomes necessary only if the community tends not to acknowledge the authority of the bishops and deacons as equal to that of the prophets. The fact that Rev. does not mention local officers of the communities and speaks only of prophetic ecclesial leadership could be a sign that the author and the communities to whom he writes tend to disregard and ignore these officers as unimportant. This would explain why Ignatius has to claim the authority of God for his demand to respect and obey the bishop.

Second, crucial for Müller's modification of Satake's interpretation is his sharp distinction between itinerant and community prophets. As itinerant prophets John and his prophetic circle do not reflect the actual situation within the Asian communities. Yet, this widespread distinction between itinerant prophets and community prophets cannot be sustained.[33] Neither the *Didache* nor Rev. itself supports this distinction.

The *Didache* knows of itinerant prophets and apostles who are supposed to stay only one day within the community. Like Rev. the *Didache* does not clearly distinguish between prophets and apostles but seems to understand their function as very similar to that of the teachers. "Implicitly at least the 'apostles' are identified with the prophets through the unexpected use of 'false prophet' (not 'false apostle') in 11:5–6."[34] As in Rev. so in the *Didache* the itinerant prophet speaks "in the spirit" (*en pneumati*). The *Didache*, however, is quite clear that the itinerant prophet has the option of settling down within the community and of becoming a prophet of the community. If this happens then the community is responsible for the prophet's financial support and must give such a prophet the "first fruit" offering that was due to the Jewish high priest. Only if no prophet lives in their midst must the community give the first fruits to the poor (13:1–7).

Rev. also knows of itinerant apostles and speaks of a community prophet who had gathered disciples around her.[35] Like the community addressed by the *Didache*, the church in Asia Minor has the right to test the itinerant apostles and prophets. The community of Ephesus is commended for rejecting those itinerant teachers who call themselves apostles. Since the community is also praised for hating the Nicolaitans we can assume that the itinerant apostles belong to the prophetic circle of the Nicolaitans. The polemics of Rev. against the adherents of the teachings of "Balaam" at Pergamum (2:14) and against the prophet teacher at Thyatira who is labeled Jezebel indicate that the Nicolaitans were active in several of the communities to whom Rev. is addressed. Both in Pergamum and in Thyatira they are still members of the community. Although we do not know much about the Nicolaitans, it is obvious that they are a rival prophetic group since Nicolaus is mentioned among the seven Hellenists of Acts, of whom at least four were considered to be prophets by the tradition.

The expression "her children" (*ta tekna autēs;* 2:23) characterizes Jezebel as the head of a prophetic "school," "circle," or "house church."[36] The expression "child of someone" must be distinguished from the expression "children of God" that denotes all Christians. Being a "child of someone" means to belong to someone's fellowship or to be a disciple of someone. Thus Paul calls the Corinthians, the Galatians, and Onesimus his "children" because they are his converts. In a similar fashion the followers of the prophets are their "children." The prophetess Jezebel and her disciples were still an active part of the community at Thyatira in which John also seems to have had at least some potential followers (2:24–25). John stresses that he has made attempts to win her over to his own theology but without any success. Therefore we can assume that in Thyatira the prophetic circle of Jezebel rivaled the influence of John who discredits this group because he considers its teachings to be false and dangerous for the Christian community. The influence combatted by John is not that of the local bishop but that of a rival prophetic group.

Analysis of the texts about the prophetic circle of the Nicolaitans indicates that the scholarly alternatives "either itinerant or community prophets" or "either apostles or prophets" is not substantiated and should be abandoned. Moreover, it indicates that Rev. is not addressing the problem of episcopal church order but rather the rivalry between different prophetic circles since at least two different prophetic circles coexisted within the communities of Asia Minor to whom Rev. is addressed. Therefore, it is unlikely that the "angels" to whom the seven messages are written are the local bishops or elders of these churches,[37] especially since Rev. does not mention bishops elsewhere. Müller's[38] suggestion that John addresses the seven messages to "angels" because he does not want to mention the official local leaders of the churches also lacks any textual support.

That the seven messages are sent to "angels" has formal as well as contentual reasons. From a formal-structural point of view the seven messages or letters are integral elements of the inaugural vision so that Rev. 1:12—3:22 form a literary unit. As heavenly visionary writings they are addressed to "angels" who are clearly representative of the whole community. Within the literary framework of the vision the recipients of the words of prophecy are visionary figures, while otherwise the words of prophecy are directly addressed to the churches. Hence, the puzzle that the resurrected Lord speaks through a human person to heavenly beings is probably due to the framework of the literary vision.

Such a formal literary interpretation of the problem becomes even more plausible when we consider the great affinity of the apocalyptic angelic interpreter (*angelus interpres*) to the Christian prophet. Rev. 19:10 and 22:9[39] insist that the angelic interpreter does not stand above the Christian prophets but is a "fellow servant" of John and his prophetic followers. The "angels" of the communities have the same function as the Christian prophets, namely to make known the testimony of Jesus (*martyria Iēsou*) to the Asian communities. Therefore the angelic interpreter is not only a "fellow servant" of the Christian prophets but also a "fellow servant" with all those in the communities "who keep the words of this book" (22:9c). Since the function of the seven angels is the same as that of John and of the other prophets, namely to communicate the prophetic message of the resurrected Lord, the seven angels seem to be the visionary counterparts of the prophets in the communities. Such a suggestion is supported by 22:16—"I, Jesus, have sent my angel to you [*hymin*] with this testimony for the churches"—where clearly a circle of prophets is named as the recipient of the prophecy for the churches. Thus John seems to be the leader of a group of prophets who, like Jezebel, are members of the seven communities to whom Rev. is written.

Such a hypothesis does justice to Hill's observation that John has an exceptional position among the other prophets. This exceptional position seems to be similar to that of Paul who also understood his call as analogous to that of the OT prophets. This hypothesis also does justice to the insight of Satake that Rev. must have been addressed to a small group since its language and imagery would not have been accessible to all the members of the Asian churches. Finally, it takes into account Müller's insight that Rev. is steeped in Jewish apocalyptic traditions without having to separate the prophetic circle of John from the seven communities. Therefore, it is necessary to explore how the Jewish apocalyptic theology of Rev. relates to the theological situation of the Christian community in Asia Minor at the end of the first century C.E.

THE PROPHECY OF JOHN IN THE
THEOLOGICAL CONTEXT OF
ASIA MINOR

Satake and Müller have argued not only that the stress in Rev. on prophetic leadership does not square with the episcopal-presbyteral church order of Asia Minor but also that the theology of Rev. was alien to the Christian churches of the post-Pauline tradition. Because of its OT, Jewish apocalyptic language and traditions, Rev. is widely regarded as an only "slightly christianized Judaism." Therefore, it is also important to question whether the book could have been understood by Christians of Asia Minor at the end of the first century C.E.

Because of its Jewish apocalyptic character Rev. is usually understood to be a product of Jewish-Palestinian Christianity. As a result, scholars explore all the possible Jewish apocalyptic traditions but pay scant attention to its interrelation with early Christian theology. Studies comparing Pauline and post-Pauline theology are almost completely lacking.

Because of its traditional ascription to the apostle John, Rev. is, at the most, discussed in its relationship to the Johannine writings and thought to belong to the "Johannine school."[40] Scholars have not sufficiently explored its affinity to Pauline and post-Pauline theology and especially its connection with early Christian prophecy mentioned in the Pauline literature, although the final redaction of the book clearly addresses communities living in an area where Pauline and post-Pauline writings are at home. Hence, the following remarks raising the question of the relationship of Rev. to the theological understanding of the Pauline and post-Pauline tradition must remain tentative and suggestive.

First, Müller is quite correct in maintaining that Rev. is steeped in early Christian apocalyptic traditions and that its announcement of the imminent return of the Lord should be understood in the context of early Christian apocalyptic prophecy. One should note, however, that the origin and basis of John's imminent eschatological expectation does not prove that it is a fairly foreign element for the local churches in Asia Minor.[41] On the one hand, he himself concedes that such an imminent expectation, provoked by the historical situation of persecution and suffering, is also found in 1 Peter. On the other hand, he overlooks the fact that 1 Pet. 4:7, 17 reflect a parenetic pattern that is found not only in Rev. but also in the Pauline and post-Pauline as well as in other late NT writings.[42] This parenetic pattern is, therefore, not limited to a single geographical area or church but is widespread. Its carriers were probably early Christian prophets who had already mediated Jewish apocalyptic traditions to Paul. It is likely, then, that the communities of Asia Minor would have known this prophetic-apocalyptic pattern and have been familiar with its already formulaic imminent expectation.

Müller argues that the communities were not familiar with apocalyptic near-expectation because their eschatological zeal had died down and they, like Colossians and Ephesians, emphasized the "already" of eschatological salvation. He thus seems to assume that such an emphasis on realized eschatology was completely shared by the communities of Asia Minor. It is more likely, however, that the prophetic circle of the Nicolaitans and not the churches advocated such a realized eschatological interpretation, and that Rev. was written to counter their eschatological emphasis. I have shown elsewhere that the author of Rev. attempts to correct the realized eschatological implications of the baptismal tradition with his emphasis on imminent judgment and salvation and his call for endurance and steadfast resistance. Thus the stress in Rev. on futuristic-apocalyptic eschatology functions in a way similar to Paul's "eschatological reservation"[43] or the stress on apocalyptic eschatology in the post-Pauline tradition.

Müller's main argument for the Palestinian provenance of the theology in Rev. is the use of the "Son of man" (*hyios tou anthrōpou*) title.[44] But one must question whether it is correct to assume that the author intended to introduce into Asia Minor the *hyios tou anthrōpou* Christology which is not found in the Pauline tradition and was avoided by Luke. It seems, rather, that John also evades the titular meaning. He does not use this christological title as a title but qualifies it in apocalyptic fashion, although the title must have been known to him from the Synoptic tradition. That the apocalyptic qualification of the title in 1:13 and 14:14 with *homoion* (like) is not just stylistic but theologically intended becomes evident when we consider 1:7 and 3:5c. An analysis of 1:7 shows that Rev. shares its OT text combination as well as its eschatological tenor with the Matthean form of the Parousia announcement in the Synoptic Apocalypse.[45] It is thus likely that John deliberately omitted the *hyios tou anthrōpou* title because it was not familiar to the Christians in Asia Minor. Moreover, Rev. 3:5c seems to know the eschatological Q tradition (Luke 12:8‖Matt. 10:32) but does not refer to the "offspring of humanity," although the original text would have provided this title. The analysis of the text seems thus to indicate that Rev. omits or qualifies the *hyios tou anthrōpou* title because this traditional christological title was not familiar to its audience.

Positively, it must be pointed out that the Christology of Rev. is structurally very similar to that of the Pauline and post-Pauline tradition. Like Paul Rev. does not speak of the life of Jesus but stresses the death and resurrection. In particular, the Lamb-Christology of Rev. develops an early Christian tradition found in Paul and post-Pauline Christianity (cf. 1 Cor. 5:7; 1 Pet. 1:18–19).[46] Moreover, several of the christological titles, especially of the messages, are at home in the Pauline and post-Pauline traditions.[47] The same is true for the expressions of redemption found in the key passages Rev. 1:5–6 and 5:9–10.[48] Although the structural similarity in their Christology does not prove that Rev. is dependent on Pauline and post-Pauline traditions, it nevertheless indicates that the theology of Rev. is not foreign to the communities of Asia Minor but has some affinities with them. It is therefore methodologically unjustified to ascribe one type of eschatology to these communities but another to Rev. A better model would provide the hypothesis that two rival eschatological-prophetic directions, namely those of the Nicolaitans and John, compete for theological acceptance and attention in these communities.

Second, such an interpretation of Rev. is also able to shed new light on the prophetic claim and formal execution of the work by the author. Recent research on prophecy in early Christianity has challenged the traditional distinction between community prophecy whose representative is Paul and apocalyptic prophecy whose representative is John. Instead, scholars have come to recognize that early Christian prophecy belongs to the context of early Christian apocalyptic.[49] Early Christian prophecy is expressed in apocalyptic form and early Christian apocalyptic is carried on by early Christian prophets. Early Christian prophecy is an ecstatic experience "in the Spirit" (*en pneumati*) and the revelation of divine mysteries. Paul's characterization of prophecy already reflects early Christian apocalyptic theology which he has received through early Christian prophets. Thus Rev. as "the words of prophecy" shares the content and function of early Christian apocalyptic prophecy. Paul and John share the same prophetic-apocalyptic traditions also found in the Synoptic or Johannine traditions. J. Baumgarten[50] mentions as thematic complexes of pre-Pauline and Pauline apocalyptic prophecy: expectation of the Parousia and the last judgment, resurrection and eternal life, exaltation and translation, angelology and demonology, cosmos and new creation, enthusiasm and imminent expectation. It is apparent that all these thematic unities and topics constitute the content of Rev. as well. Moreover, not only the content of Rev. but also its prophetic functions are similar to early Christian prophecy as found in Paul. While J. Panagopoulos[51] enumerates five functions of the prophetic word (eschatological, addressing a specific concrete situation, revelatory word of the resurrected Lord, paraclesis of the church, and multidimensional in form), E. Cothenet[52] speaks of three main functions: "prophetic-apocalyptic, exhortatory-prophetic (paraclesis)," and "benedictory-prophetic." Without question Rev. shares these functions of early Christian prophecy: it is an apocalyptic-eschatological revelation of Jesus Christ; its main purpose is exhortation and strengthening of the communities; it is to be read in the communal worship assembly; and finally it is not individual but communal prophecy.

Formally, the author of Rev. seems consciously to imitate the form of the Pauline letter and thus indirectly to claim the authority of Paul for his work of prophecy. The prescript (1:4–6) has a fully developed and stylized form which is very similar to that of Galatians.[53] The opening salutation with the peace greeting especially resembles the Pauline pattern. The concluding greeting in 22:21 again imitates that of the Pauline letters. K. Berger[54] has pointed out that the genre (*Gattung*) of the letter, tractate, and apocalypse cannot be clearly differentiated. He argues that the seven messages of Rev. are a good example of the genre "prophetic letter." Thus it is important to recognize the great difference in form between the seven letters and the epistolary framework of Rev. This difference in form emphasizes that John understands his prophecy not only as a prophetic letter in general but explicitly characterizes it as a circular, authoritative apostolic letter which is patterned after the already traditional Pauline letter form. The observation that apocalyptic elements are often found in the prescript, proemium, and final greetings[55] of the genuine Pauline letters becomes significant here.

Third, not only the Pauline letter form but also the title *apokalypsis Iēsou Christou* ("The Revelation of Jesus Christ") suggests that John understands his prophetic claim as akin to that of Paul. Since, on the one hand, the noun *apokalypsis* (revelation) appears only here in Rev. whereas the verb *apokalyptein* (to reveal) is competely missing, and, on the other hand, the full name of *Iēsous Christos* occurs only in 1:1, 2, 5 in connection with *martyria* (testimony) or *martys* (witness) it is clear that the expression *apokalypsis Iēsou Christou* is deliberately chosen as a headline. Although the author seems to prefer the terms *martyria/martyrein* (testimony/to testify) when expressing his own understanding of Christian prophecy and revelation, nevertheless he does not entitle his work *martyria* but *apokalypsis Iēsou Christou*. The significance of this choice is often overlooked because Rev. is usually seen as the paradigm of apocalyptic literature and therefore the title is taken for granted. However, we have no evidence that the title *apokalypsis* had already become a technical term for characterizing a certain type of revelatory literature. Therefore, it is doubtful that the author chose this title in order to qualify his prophecy as an apocalyptic document.

The terms *apokalypsis/apokalyptein* are rare in the OT, occur only seldom in the Gospels, and appear outside the Gospels exclusively in the Pauline and deutero-Pauline literature.[56] The Pauline provenance of *apokalypsis* is underlined by the fact that the full title *apokalypsis Iēsou Christou* occurs only in the Pauline and post-Pauline tradition. Whereas 1 Cor. 1:7, 2 Thess. 1:7 and 1 Pet. 1:7, 13 (cf. 4:13) point to the revelation of Jesus Christ in the Parousia, Gal. 1:12, 16 speaks of the appearance of Christ in a vision to Paul. Gal. 1:12 restates 1:1 in insisting that Paul received the gospel not through human intermediaries but through a revelation of Jesus Christ, who is "the present Christ and whose presence is identical with the content of the Pauline gospel."[57] Gal. 1:15–16 describes Paul's vocation by analogy to the call of the OT prophet and in specifically Christian terms. Paul's claim that his calling took the form of a revelation of Jesus Christ points to a visionary experience. H. D. Betz is correct in claiming that Paul did not distinguish so sharply as modern exegetes do between verbal and visionary revelation or between external (1 Cor. 9:1; 15:8) and internal (v. 16: "in me") revelatory experience.[58] The appearance of Jesus Christ in a vision is synonymous with the revelation of the gospel to Paul. Paul refers also in Gal. 2:2 and especially in 2 Cor. 12:1, 7[59] to his visionary and ecstatic experiences. Yet, whereas in

2 Cor. 12:7 *apokalypsis* characterizes the ecstatic, visionary experience which has unutterable character, in 1 Cor. 14:6 it is classified together with knowledge, prophecy, and teaching as intelligible speaking which must complement the speaking in tongues. Thus *apokalypsis* denotes a visionary, ecstatic experience similar to prophecy.

It therefore seems probable that John deliberately chose the title *apokalypsis Iēsou Christou* in order to characterize his own experience as a Christian prophetic experience similar to the call-experience of Paul. Hence, the headline as well as the prescript of Rev. indicate some familiarity with Paul's letter to the Galatians. Like the Christian prophets in 1 Corinthians, John receives his revelation "in the Spirit." This revelation is an experience of Jesus Christ who is now present and speaks to the Christian community through the prophet. Thus the range of meaning of *apokalypsis* in the Pauline and post-Pauline tradition correctly circumscribes the content of Rev.

In conclusion, I have attempted to argue that Rev. must be understood as a literary product of early Christian prophecy. As such it must be situated within the theological context of Asia Minor which was greatly determined by Pauline and post-Pauline theology. Neither John's theological self-understanding nor the church order reflected in Rev. contradicts such an assumption.

Rev. not only shares many language affinities with the Pauline and post-Pauline literature but also claims Pauline literary form and an authority similar to that of the apostle. This might be the reason why John never gives himself the title "prophet" but calls himself "slave" (*doulos*).[60] In choosing this title John characterizes his authority as similar not only to that of the OT prophets but also to that of Paul. And yet, it is significant that John only alludes to Pauline style and authority but does not explicitly claim the name of Paul for his work as the writers of the Pauline school have done. John writes his book in his own name and claims his own prophetic authority, because prophecy and prophetic leadership were still highly respected in the churches of Asia Minor at the turn of the first century C.E. It is not the episcopacy or presbyterate, but a rival prophetic "school" or "circle," which is competing with John and his followers for acceptance and influence in the churches.

In arguing for Pauline allusions and imitation, however, I do not want to maintain that the "school" of John is commensurate with the Pauline "school" which Conzelmann[61] posits as existing in Ephesus. I only want to stress that John was familiar with the Pauline tradition and at home in the communities of Asia Minor. Since Rev. also reflects Synoptic apocalyptic traditions and is familiar with some "Johannine" materials, it cannot be claimed for the Pauline "school." Instead it transmits apocalyptic early Christian traditions and suggests the existence of a prophetic-apocalyptic "school" or "circles." Early Christian prophetic groups seem to have interpreted and expanded Christian apocalyptic-eschatological traditions and materials. Since Paul already had access to such apocalyptic-eschatological traditions handed down through early Christian prophets, we are justified in assuming a historical continuum running from pre-Pauline prophetic-apocalyptic circles to the Book of Rev., Papias, and the Montanist movement in Asia Minor.[62]

NOTES

1. Cf. esp. the contributions in *Prophetic Vocation in the New Testament and Today* (NovTSup 45; Leiden: E. J. Brill, 1977); the introductory discussions in G. Dautzenberg, *Urchristliche Prophetie: Ihre Erforschung, ihre Voraussetzungen im Judentum, und ihre Struktur im ersten Korintherbrief* (BWANT 104; Stuttgart, 1975) 15–41; U. B. Müller, *Prophetie und Predigt im Neuen Testament* (SNT 10; Gütersloh: Gerd Mohn, 1975) 11–19; E. Cothenet, "Prophetisme dans le NT," *DBSup* 8 (1972) cols. 1222–1337; J. Reiling, *Hermas and Christian Prophecy* (NovTSup 37; Leiden: E. J. Brill, 1973); E. E. Ellis, s.v. "Prophecy in the Early Church," IDBSup; and the discussion of the SBL seminar group on early Christian prophecy; cf. the *1973/1974 SBL Seminar Papers*.

2. Cf. the working definition of "prophet" within the Hellenistic world discussed by the SBL seminar. See M. E. Boring, "What Are We Looking For?" in *1973 SBL Seminar Papers* (Missoula, Mont.: Scholars Press, 1973) 2: 142–54 and the review of this discussion by Boring, "The Apocalypse as Christian Prophecy," in *1974 SBL Seminar Papers* (Missoula, Mont.: Scholars Press, 1974) 2: 43–62, esp. n. 5.

3. An exception is the popular commentary of G. R. Beasley-Murray, *The Book of Revelation* (rev. ed.; London: Marshall, Morgan & Scott, 1978) 19–29. F. Rousseau (*L'Apocalypse et le milieu prophétique du NT* [Montreal: Bellarmin, 1971] 130–46) is more concerned with the structure and redactional history of Rev. and therefore discusses the book only in very general terms in the context of early Christian prophecy. O. Böcher (*Die Johannesapokalypse* [Darmstadt: Wissenschaftliche Buchgesellschaft, 1975]) does not mention prophet/prophecy or the position of Rev. in the context of early Christian theology as a special concern of scholarly discussion.

4. D. Hill, "Christian Prophets as Teachers or Instructors in the Church," in *Prophetic Vocation,* 108–30, esp. 130.

5. Ibid., 119–22; idem, "Prophecy and Prophets in the Revelation of St. John," *NTS* 18 (1971–1972) 401–18; idem, "On the Evidence of the Creative Role of Christian Prophets," *NTS* 20 (1973–1974) 262–74, esp. 269–70.

6. Hill, "Prophecy and Prophets," 417.

7. A. Feuillet, *L'Apocalypse: État de la question* (Paris: Desclée, 1963) 65.

8. H. Kraft, "Zur Offenbarung des Johannes," *TRu* NF 38 (1973) 81–98, esp. 85.

9. Cf. the translation, G. Vermes (*The Dead Sea Scrolls in English* [Harmondsworth: Pelican, 1968; Baltimore: Penguin Books, 1976] 236–39) and the discussion by Dautzenberg (*Urchristliche Prophetie,* 62ff.) for the literature.

10. D. Patte, *Early Jewish Hermeneutic in Palestine* (SBLDS 22; Missoula, Mont.: Scholars Press, 1975) 172.

11. K. Stendahl, *The School of St. Matthew and Its Use of the Old Testament* (2d ed.; Philadelphia: Fortress Press, 1968) 159.

12. For this distinction, cf. Müller, *Prophetie und Predigt,* 237–39.

13. Hill, "Prophecy and Prophets," 405.

14. Cf. G. von Rad, *Theology of the Old Testament* (New York: Harper & Row; London: Oliver & Boyd, 1965) 2: 303ff.; cf. also W. R. Murdock, "History and Revelation in Jewish Apocalypticism," *Int* 21 (1967) 167–87.

15. See chap. 1, "History and Eschatology in Revelation," in this book.

16. Rev. 1:5; cf. also Col. 1:18b; 1 Cor. 15:20. In the inaugural vision Christ is characterized as the one "who died and is alive" and who has the "keys of Death and Hades" (Rev. 1:18; cf. 2:8). For the importance of resurrection-faith for the development of early Christian apocalyptic, cf. my article, "The Phenomenon of Early Christian Apocalyptic: Some Reflections on Method," in *Apocalypticism in the Mediterranean World and the Near East* (Tübingen: Mohr/Siebeck, 1983) 295–316.

17. Cf. chap. 1, "History and Eschatology in Revelation," and chap. 6, "The Composition and Structure of Revelation," in this book.

18. G. Friedrich, "prophētes," *TDNT* 6 (1968) 851.

19. P. Vielhauer, "Introduction," in *New Testament Apocrypha* (ed. E. Hennecke–W. Schneemelcher; Philadelphia: Westminster Press, 1965) 2: 607.

20. Hill, "Prophecy and Prophets," 415ff.

21. *4 Esdras* 12:42 stresses: "For of all the prophets thou alone art left to us, as a cluster out of the vintage, as a lamp in a dark place, as a haven of safety for a ship in storm." In 14:22 the prophet Ezra prays: "If, then, I have found favor before thee, send unto me the Holy Spirit that I may write all that happened in the world since the beginnings." And Ezra is told: "And when thou shalt have finished some things thou shalt publish, and some thou shalt deliver in secret to the wise. Tomorrow at this hour thou shalt begin to write" (14:26). For the translation, see R. H. Charles, *APOT,* 2: 615–22. Similar injunctions to write are also found in *Jub.* 32:21–26; *1 Enoch* 81:5–7.

22. Cf. G. Tucker, "Prophetic Speech," *Int.* 32 (1978) 31–45, esp. 32–33: The prophetic book represents "the final stage in the development of the tradition and a quite distinct genre of literature with certain typical features." Cf. also his "Prophetic Superscriptions and the Growth of a Canon," in *Canon and Authority: Essays in Old Testament Religion and Theology* (ed. G. W. Coats and B. O. Long; Philadelphia: Fortress Press, 1977) 56–70. The same is pointed out by K. Berger, "Apostelbrief und apostolische Rede. Zum Formular frühchristlicher Briefe," *ZNW* 65 (1974) 190–231, esp. 213. *Schriftlichkeit* is thus a common characteristic of the prophetic letters, the apocalypses, and the apostolic letters, underlining their revelatory character.

23. Cf. R. Bultmann, *Theology of the New Testament* (New York: Charles Scribner's Sons, 1965) 2: 175; C. H. Dodd, *The Apostolic Preaching and Its Development* (2d ed.; London: Hodder & Stoughton, 1944) 40–41.

24. A. Satake, *Die Gemeindeordnung in der Johannesapokalypse* (WMANT 21; Neukirchen: Neukirchener Verlag, 1966).

25. U. B. Müller, *Zur frühchristlichen Theologiegeschichte. Judenchristentum und Paulinismus in Kleinasien an der Wende vom ersten zum zweiten Jahrhundert n. Chr.* (Gütersloh: Gerd Mohn, 1976).

26. Ibid., 31.

27. W. Bauer (*Orthodoxy and Heresy in Earliest Christianity* [Philadelphia: Fortress Press, 1971] 84) states: "The Apocalypse does not leave us with a particularly impressive

idea of what sought to replace the Pauline gospel in the 'ecclesiastically oriented' circles at Ephesus. Aside from Revelation's being a book of comfort and faith to threatened and persecuted Christians . . . there remains for the most part a Jewish Christianity, presumably of Palestinian origin."

28. Cf. H. Kraft (*Die Offenbarung des Johannes* [HNT 16a; Tübingen: Mohr/Siebeck, 1974] 87–94) for a discussion of the community situation reflected in the seven messages of Rev. and in the letters of Ignatius.

29. Such an approach to Ignatius is developed in W. Schoedel's paper, "Ignatius of Antioch and a Social Description of Early Christianity," which he prepared for the AAR/SBL Social World of Early Christianity group.

30. Ignatius, *Phil.* 7.1–2; cf. R. M. Grant, *The Apostolic Fathers. Ignatius of Antioch* (New York: Thomas Nelson & Sons, 1966) 4: 104–5. Cf. also J. L. Ash, Jr. ("The Decline of Ecstatic Prophecy in the Early Church," *TS* 37 [1976] 227–52, esp. 234–35), who points out that Polycarp as well as Melito of Sardis—both venerated bishops—were considered to have been prophets. He shows that in Asia Minor Justin Martyr, Irenaeus, and Montanism had great appreciation for the charisma of prophecy.

31. Cf. T. Holtz, *Die Christologie der Apokalypse des Johannes* (TU 85; Berlin, 1962) 208–11; F. Hahn, "Die Sendschreiben der Johannesapokalypse," in *Tradition und Glaube: Festschrift für K. G. Kuhn* (Göttingen: Vandenhoeck & Ruprecht, 1972) 380–81; Müller, *Prophetie und Predigt*, 48–56. A direct utterance of the prophetic Spirit is also mentioned in Rev. 22:17; Acts 13:2; 21:11; 1 Tim. 4:1; Hermas, *Mandate* 11.5,6,8; and Montanism. For a review of these passages, cf. H. Weinel, *Die Wirkungen des Geistes und der Geister im nachapostolischen Zeitalter bis auf Irenäus* (Freiburg: Mohr/Siebeck, 1899) 83–96.

32. Cf. R. A. Kraft, *The Apostolic Fathers: The Didache and Barnabas* (New York: Thomas Nelson & Sons, 1965) 3: 64; J. P. Audet, *La Didache. Instructions des apôtres* (EBib; Paris: J. Gabalda, 1958) 200–206.

33. For this distinction, cf. especially A. von Harnack, *Die Lehre der zwölf Apostel, nebst Untersuchungen zur ältesten Geschichte der Kirchenverfassung und des Kirchenrechts* (TU 2/1–2; Leipzig: J. C. Hinrichs, 1884) 93–158.

34. Kraft, *Apostolic Fathers*, 170–71.

35. For a discussion of Jezebel and the Nicolaitans, see chap. 4 of this book, "Apocalyptic and Gnosis in Revelation and in Paul."

36. For a discussion of the "school" concept, cf. chap. 3 of this book, "The Quest for the Johannine School." R. E. Brown (*The Community of the Beloved Disciple* [New York: Paulist Press, 1979]) seems to have accepted my suggestion that at the end of the first century various Christian schools or circles lived side by side within the Christian community in Asia Minor; but he develops this idea for the Johannine communities in terms of "house churches" rather than "schools" (pp. 98–103). The relationship of the prophetic "schools" or circles of Jezebel and John to the "house churches" of the Johannine epistles and the "Paraclete" advocates needs to be explored.

37. Cf. J. Sickenberger, "Die Deutung der Engel der sieben apokalyptischen Gemeinden," *RQ* 35 (1927) 135–49; Satake, *Gemeindeordnung*, 150–55. Kraft (*Offenbarung*, 50–52) thinks of actual messengers who would bring the letters from Patmos to the communities.

38. Müller, *Theologiegeschichte*, 34.

39. Cf. my book *Priester für Gott. Studien zum Herrschafts- und Priesterbegriff in der Apokalypse* (NTAbh 7; Münster: Aschendorff, 1972) 238–48; F. F. Bruce, "The

Spirit in the Apocalypse," in *Christ and the Spirit in the New Testament: Essays in Honour of C. F. D. Moule* (ed. B. Lindars and S. S. Smalley; Cambridge: At the Univ. Press, 1973) 333–44; J. Massyngberde Ford, "For the Testimony of Jesus in the Spirit of Prophecy," *ITQ* 42 (1975) 284–91. However, an association with Pentecost seems to be unlikely here.

40. See chap. 3 of this book, "The Quest for the Johannine School," for the arguments.

41. Müller, *Theologiegeschichte*, 40.

42. Cf. 1 Thess. 5:1; Phil. 4:4–6; Rom. 13:11–14; Heb. 10:23–31; James 5:7–11; 1 John 2:18–19; Rev. 22:12; and also *Barnabas* 4:9; 21:3; Ignatius, *Eph.* 11:1; *2 Clement* 12:1; 16:3. L. Goppelt, *Erster Petrusbrief* (MeyerK 12/1; Göttingen: Vandenhoeck & Ruprecht, 1978) 281–82.

43. Cf. E. Käsemann, "On the Subject of Primitive Christian Apocalyptic," in *New Testament Questions of Today* (Philadelphia: Fortress Press; London: SCM Press, 1969) 108–37; E. Schüssler Fiorenza, s.v. "Eschatology of the NT," IDBSup.

44. Müller, *Theologiegeschichte*, 44.

45. For a detailed discussion, cf. my book *Priester für Gott*, 185–92; for John's familiarity with Synoptic traditions, cf. L. A. Vos, *The Synoptic Traditions in the Apocalypse* (Kampen: J. H. Kok, 1965).

46. Cf. Müller, *Theologiegeschichte*, 46, and Holtz, *Die Christologie*, 44–47.

47. See Hahn, "Die Sendschreiben," 367ff.

48. Cf. chap. 2 of this book, "Redemption as Liberation."

49. Cf. H. A. Guy, *New Testament Prophecy: Its Origin and Significance* (London: Macmillan & Co., 1947) 104–12; H. Kraft, "Die altkirchliche Prophetie und die Entstehung des Montanismus," *TZ* 11 (1955) 249–71; idem, "Vom Ende der urchristlichen Prophetie," in *Prophetic Vocation*, 162–85.

50. J. Baumgarten, *Paulus und die Apokalyptik: Die Auslegung apokalyptischer Überlieferungen in den echten Paulusbriefen* (WMANT 44; Neukirchen: Neukirchener Verlag, 1975).

51. J. Panagopoulos, "Die urchristliche Prophetie: Ihr Charakter und ihre Funktion," in *Prophetic Vocation*, 1–32.

52. E. Cothenet, "Prophetisme et ministère d'après le Nouveau Testament," *La Maison-Dieu* 107 (1971) 29–50, esp. 40–44.

53. Cf. my book, *Priester für Gott*, 168–73.

54. Berger, "Apostelbrief," 190–231.

55. Baumgarten, *Paulus und die Apokalyptik*, 232.

56. *Apokalypsis:* Rom 2:5; 8:19; 16:25; 1 Cor. 1:7; 14:6; 14:26; 2 Cor. 12:1, 7; Gal. 1:12; 2:2; Eph. 1:17; 3:3; 2 Thess. 1:7; 1 Pet. 1:7, 13; 4:13. *Apokalyptein:* Rom. 1:17, 18; 8:18; 1 Cor. 2:10; 3:13; 14:30; Gal. 1:16; 3:23; Eph. 3:5; 2 Thess. 2:3, 6, 8; 1 Pet. 1:5, 12; 5:1.

57. H. D. Betz, *Galatians* (Hermeneia; Philadelphia: Fortress Press, 1979) 71.

58. Ibid., 69–72.

59. Cf. A. T. Lincoln, "Paul the Visionary: The Setting and the Significance of the Rapture to Paradise in II Corinthians XII. 1–10," *NTS* 25 (1978–1979) 204–20, and H. Saake, "Paulus als Ekstatiker. Pneumatologische Beobachtungen zu 2 Kor xii 1–10," *NovT* 15 (1973) 153–60. Rev. 10:3–4 seems to come close to 2 Cor. 12:4, especially since the *arrhēta rhēmata* ("things that cannot be told") practically are synonymous with *mysteria*.

60. Cf. also James 1:1; 2 Pet. 1:1; Jude 1:1.

61. Cf. H. Conzelmann, "Paulus und die Weisheit," *NTS* 12 (1965–1966) 231–44. Conzelmann conjectures that the "school of Paul" has received and elaborated on traditional Jewish wisdom traditions.

62. H. Koester ("*GNOMAI DIAPHOROI:* The Origin and Nature of Diversification in the History of Early Christianity," in *Trajectories through Early Christianity,* ed. J. M. Robinson and H. Koester [Philadelphia: Fortress Press, 1971] 154–55) envisions four rival Christian groups active at the turn of the first century in Ephesus. These groups included the originally Pauline church (Ephesus; Luke/Acts), a Jewish Christian "school" dedicated to the interpretation of the OT (Cerinthus), a heretical sect (the Nicolaitans), and finally the Jewish-Christian conventicle of Rev. However, Koester does not discuss the relationship of Rev. to the "continuous line running from the apocalyptic trend in Paul's church at Thessalonica (2 Thessalonians) to the rise of Montanism."

PART THREE

LITERARY VISION AND COMPOSITION

6

The Composition and Structure
of Revelation

The unitary composition of Rev. does not result from a final redactor's arbitrary compilation but from the author's theological conception and literary composition. An interpretation of Rev., therefore, must not only highlight the theological themes and intentions of the author but also show how he embodied his theology in a unique fusion of content and form.

An analysis of the specific form-content configuration (*Gestalt*) of Rev. should focus on how theology and form are interrelated as well as on the tradition-history of each. Against the old dichotomy of content and form, the New Criticism maintains that the form is not a container for the content but the patterning and arrangement of it. If one changes the order of a text one changes its meaning.[1] However, one has to see the difference between a work of literature and the NT writings. Whereas a work of art is considered as a system or structure of signs serving a specific esthetic purpose, the NT literature is not written with such a goal. Since the NT books are theological and historical writings, one must not only analyze the literary patterns and structure of a writing but also their relation to its theological perspective and historical setting.

An analysis of the total form-content configuration of Rev. therefore must employ not only the methods of form- and tradition-criticism, redaction criticism, compositional analysis, and genre-criticism but also structuralist and structural or architectural analysis. Since my studies of Rev.[2] have generally concentrated on its theological perspective and interests, I have approached the question of its composition and structure primarily with a concern to detect the peculiar theological interests and arguments of the author. This chapter presupposes these studies but shifts our attention to the formal organization and structural composition of Rev.

First, I will discuss the attempts to define the structure and plan of Rev. from a source-critical and tradition-critical point of view. Second,

I will discuss the component types or forms and the complex literary type or genre of Rev. Third, I will attempt to analyze the compositional techniques of the author, to discern the plan and structure of Rev. as a whole, and to underscore how the structure and theological perspective, the form and content, are fused into a unique configuration of the total arrangement of Rev.

SOURCE-CRITICAL AND
TRADITION-CRITICAL INTERPRETATION

The Book of Rev. makes quite a different impression when it is heard than when it is analyzed. The hearer of the text is impressed by its rhythmic and archaic language, by the repetition of sounds and words, and by the wealth of colors, voices, symbols, and image associations.

Quite a different reaction takes place in analyzing the book and in interpreting its images, language, content, and theology. The text presents repetitions, doublets, and artificial constructions. The logical flow of thought and the temporal sequence of the visions appear to be interrupted and disturbed, the sense of time and development confused, and the images and symbols often arbitrary and multivalent. Traditional exegesis which rejects the historical-critical approach has attempted to explain the doublets, inconsistencies, and repetitions of the text either as due to the faulty memory of the author who wrote the book in lengthy intervals or has postulated that the author died and an incompetent student has edited the whole work with more or less understanding.

Revelation: A Compilation of Sources

Source-critical analyses attempt to order the narrative in such a way that it represents a logical, linear, and unified theological system. They single out and separate those elements which either destroy the logical or temporal sequence and contradict the main symbols, or do not agree with what is perceived as the central Christian theological statement of the book.

Many scholars, particularly in the nineteenth century, detected a certain lack of cohesion and consecutive development, and perceived certain theological statements and symbols as unchristian or subchristian in character. They consequently proposed different source-critical solutions to the problem.[3] The various compilation theories maintain that the present text of Rev. lacks an inner cohesiveness and a conscious order because it consists of a number of Jewish and/or Christian sources which were more or less skillfully combined by one or more redactors. Rev. consequently manifests the same editorial process as other Jewish apocalypses revised or edited by Christian writers.

E. Vischer,[4] for example, assumed that Rev. was originally a Jewish apocalypse written in Hebrew or Aramaic and then later translated into Greek and revised theologically by a Christian redactor. Independently of Vischer, Weyland presented a similar solution postulating that a Christian in 130–140 C.E. compiled and edited two Jewish sources written around 69 and 81 C.E. respectively. J. Weiss,[5] on the other hand, contended that the basic source of Rev. was a Christian apocalypse (late 60s C.E.) which was combined with a Jewish apocalypse (ca. 70 C.E.) by the final editor in the time of Domitian. This theory can be modified when a number of Jewish and Christian sources are thought to have been compiled by a redactor or when one presupposes that the redaction of Rev. went through several stages and revisions. Those who contend that the basis of our present text is Jewish or that it stems from very early Christian sources usually attribute Rev. 1—3 and the epistolary framework to the final Christian redactor.

J. M. Ford's commentary[6] revives the compilation theory of the last century. Like Weyland she assumes two Jewish apocalypses and one later Christian redaction. The first document consists of chaps. 4—11 and is attributed to the circle of John the Baptist because it reflects the expectation of "He that Cometh." In its oral form this source should be assigned to the time of John the Baptist and therefore mirrors a time prior to Jesus' public ministry. The second apocalypse includes chaps. 12—22 and was written in the mid or late 60s C.E. It represents the theological viewpoint of those disciples who predicted the fall of Jerusalem and ascribed this catastrophe to the unorthodox behavior of their contemporaries. The final redactor of Rev. added chaps. 1—3 and 22:16a, 20b, 21. He was a Jewish-Christian disciple of John the Baptist. This peculiar form of the compilation theory, however, does not sufficiently establish the different Jewish apocalyptic sources on linguistic and theological grounds. It neglects the considerable linguistic evidence which compelled older commentators[7] and most recent investigators[8] of the language of Rev. to discard the source-theories and to maintain the compositional unity of Rev. The unitary character of the language and symbol system of Rev. argues against such an arbitrary dissection of the text.

Revelation: Composed of Traditional Patterns

The revision theory (*Überarbeitungshypothese*) presupposes a primary Jewish or Christian original source-text (*Grundschrift*) that was complete in itself but was reworked through successive revisions and editions into the present text. C. Weizsäcker, for example, considers Rev. as the work of one author who had structured it into three interconnected septets.[9] Into this framework he later inserted several visions derived from various sources. We are able to isolate these later insertions because they do not have any close connection with the original seven-series nor do they fit into the present plan and structure of Rev. D. Völter expands this hypothesis insofar as he maintains that our present form and text of Rev. underwent several revisions in five different periods. His criteria for distinguishing these revisions and periods are: contradictions, lack of consecutiveness and sequence, and distinct Jewish or Christian theological images and thought. Hence, his reconstruction attempts to restore the logical and historical sequence of the visions and to reconcile conceptual differences and theological contradictions.

The fragmentary theory (*Fragmententheorie*)[10] does not seek to disassemble the text and to reorder it according to logical or theological principles, but accounts for its doublets and discrepancies by assuming that the author used various oral and written traditions for the composition of his work. An investigation of various textual unities shows that the author often follows a certain tradition, but that he alters the traditional pattern whenever necessary to make his own theological point.

A good example is the inaugural vision (Rev. 1:12–20) where we are able to see the way in which the author uses Daniel 10 as his pattern (*Vorlage*). The author alters this traditional text with features from Daniel 7 ("Son of man"; description of hair) and from Ezekiel (characterization of voice). Moreover, he expands the scene with an "I am" revelatory saying and with the interpretation of the seven golden lampstands and stars. Underlying Rev. 5 is the pattern of the heavenly assembly of the gods.[11] The three septets of the eschatological plagues are also traditional. They resemble the Egyptian plagues of the Book of Exodus which in turn follow an ancient pattern of magical action.[12]

G. Harder[13] has analyzed Rev. and found the following additional traditional patterns: the pattern of Ezekiel[14] is found in 19:11—22:5 and probably resembles the ancient pattern of the Divine Warrior;[15] the motif of the divine judgment from the book of life and the book of deeds is given in 20:11–15, and the pattern of the two cities is presented in chaps. 17—18 and in 21:2, 9–27. Other traditional patterns that occur are the pattern of the world cataclysm (6:1—7:17) and that of the exodus plagues (8:1—11:14; 15:5—19:10). The motif of the wine-press of God, combining Isa. 63:3 and Joel 4:13, is found in Rev. 14:9–20 and 19:13. Elements of the prophetic pattern (of Elijah) are given in 10:1—11:14, and mythological elements in 12:1—14:5 and 19:11–20. Even though one might disagree with some of the definitions of G. Harder, his analysis proves that the author of the book used traditional patterns and materials for its composition.

Yet the fragmentary theory insists that the author has so thoroughly incorporated his traditional patterns and sources that Rev. now mirrors for the main part his own language, theological vision, and literary composition. The tradition-historical understanding of Rev., therefore, can account for the linguistic and symbolic unity of the book as well as for its discrepant features and materials which do not quite fit into their present context.

In his recent commentary H. Kraft combines features of the revision theory with those of the fragmentary theory. He postulates successive revisions of an original source-text (*Grundschrift*) by the same author and the incorporation of various early Christian traditions in order to account for the linguistic unity as well as for the inconsistencies of the theological and formal composition of Rev. The author's foundational document consisted of the visions of the seven seals. In adding the trumpet and bowl septets to the first septet the author changed the character of the seal-visions, which originally announced the woes of the end time, to a series of divine punishments. Since the author was familiar with other standard early Christian end time expectations, (e.g., the appearance of the eschatological prophet, the great persecution, the election and protection of the righteous, and the final eschatological salvation and paradise), he incorporated these and other traditional eschatological *topoi* through additions and insertions into the three plague septets. The incorporation of the *topoi* of the great eschatological persecution and temptation into the plan of the book imprinted on it a dualistic character. The final redactor added the seven messages to the churches, expanded the inaugural vision, and gave the whole an epistolary framework. Kraft offers no conclusion on whether the author of Rev. wrote the seven messages or whether a final redactor added them. Yet he asserts in his introduction "that the final redactor of Rev. was an artist who composed the book."[16]

Kraft's analysis confirms my thesis that Rev. is not chronologically ordered but theologically-thematically conceived.[17] The growth of Rev. is occasioned by the attempt of the author to incorporate the main eschatological *topoi* and expectations known to him from Jewish and especially early Christian apocalypticism. The final author is a skillful artist who incorporated the various theological themes and traditions in such a way that he achieved a unitary composition and an optimal configuration of form and content. Kraft underlines the importance of isolating traditions and reconstructing patterns (*Vorlagen*) in order to highlight the specific artistic and theological achievements of the author.

Kraft does not sufficiently perceive, however, the unitary composition of Rev., but equates structural elements of the composition with sources or stages of development. He neglects thereby the lesson which structural analysis has driven home that the total configuration (*Gestalt*) and composition of a work cannot be derived from its sources or traditions but only from the formal expression and theological intention of the author. This intention is not something that lies behind the text, but it manifests itself in the form-content configuration of a work.

COMPONENT FORMS AND THE COMPLEX TYPE OR LITERARY GENRE OF REVELATION

As NT form criticism studies primarily the smallest units but not the whole work, redaction criticism attempts to elucidate the nature and extent of the author's activity in collecting, arranging, and editing traditional materials. Composition criticism[18] broadens the analyses of redaction criticism by concentrating on the author's activity in molding traditional patterns and newly created materials into a new and unique form of expression. Composition critical analysis shows that small units or component literary types change their formal characteristics and function differently when they are incorporated into the new framework of a complex literary type[19] or genre (*Gattung*). It is therefore important to analyze the smallest units and larger patterns of a work as well as to determine the complex literary type or macro-genre into which they are incorporated.

Literary Forms or Component Types of Revelation

A form-critical review and classification can highlight the richness of expression and formal construction of Rev. The hymnic[20] sections of Rev. are composed mostly in an antiphonal form (4:9–11; 5:9–12; 7:10–12; 11:15b, 17–18; 16:5b–6, 7b; 19:1b, 2, 3, 4b; 19:5b, 6b–8a). The hymnic sections incorporate the following traditional forms: the *trisagion* ("Holy, Holy, Holy"; 4:8c), doxology (1:6; 4:9; 5:13b–14; 7:12); *axios* acclamation ("worthy art thou"; 4:11; 5:9b–10, 12), the thanksgiving formula (11:17–18); the responsory or choral *amēn* and *hallelujah;* the "judgment doxology" (16:5–7); the homage to the beast (13:4); the injunction to rejoice (12:12a; 18:20); the woe oracle (12:12b); the hymn of acclamation (12:10b–12; 15:3b–4); the proclamation of God as king (11:17; 19:6); and the proclamation of God's victory (7:10; 12:10; 19:1). Other forms are the cries of vindication (6:10) and of despair (6:16), the lament or dirge (18:1–24), and the curse (22:18–20).

The prophetic character of Rev. is expressed in the prophetic announcement (e.g., 1:7; 14:9), the words and promises of God (e.g., 1:8; 16:5; 21:5–8), the prophetic injunctions or commands, the seven blessings (1:1; 14:3; 16:15; 19:9; 20:6; 22:7, 14), the lists of virtues or vices

(9:20–21; 13:4–8; 14:4–5; 21:8, 27; 22:7, 14) and in the direct interpretations of the visions by an angel or the author (e.g., 1:20; 7:13–17; 13:18; 14:4–5; 17:7–18; 19:8b). We find the prophetic form of the inaugural or commissioning vision (1:12–20; chaps. 4—5; 10:1—11:2) as well as that of the prophetic messenger speech (e.g., chaps. 2—3). This form-critical summary does not pretend to be exhaustive. It does, however, show that the author employed traditional forms and patterns which ought to be studied more carefully.

The author not only employs small formal units but also organizes his materials in more complex forms and patterns. An analysis of the first septet shows that he has composed each of the seven letters as a prophetic letter, which follows a definite pattern consisting of the following five sections:[21] The introduction combines the address and the command to write. Then follows the prophetic messenger formula *tade legei* ("he has this to say"; 2:1, 8, 12, 18; 3:1, 7, 14), which is combined with the characterizations of Christ taken over from the inaugural vision. The third section is the most elaborate. It is introduced with an "I know" sentence (2:2, 9, 13, 19; 3:2, 8, 15) and closes with an exhortation. This section can include some or all of the following elements: a description of the situation ("I know that"), censure ("But I have this against you"), call to repentance, a revelatory saying introduced with "see," an announcement of the Lord's coming and an exhortation. The fourth section of the prophetic letter consists of the call to hear the message (2:7, 11, 17, 29; 3:6, 13, 22) and it has the same form in all the letters: "She or he who has an ear let him or her hear what the Spirit says to the churches." This injunction[22] emphasizes the fact that the eschatological exhortations and promises are directed to all the churches. The last section of the prophetic letter consists in the eschatological promise which, despite varying contents, has the same form (*tō nikōnti,* participle of *nikaō* [to conquer], with the main verb in the future tense).

The constant elements of the prophetic letter are: the address, the command to write, the messenger formula, the call to hear, and the promise to the victorious; however, the individual elements of the "I know" section (*oida*) can vary. In spite of this uniformity in structure the seven prophetic letters are not monotonous. Four of them contain praise and censure (1,3,4,5); two communities receive only praise (2,6) and Laodicea only censure (7).

The Complex Literary Genre of Revelation

At first glance it appears easy to say which literary genre (*Gattung*) or complex type the author had in mind in composing his work. Obviously the total form-content configuration of Rev. is not that of a theological handbook, a sermon on eschatological topics, or a theological compendium. The author clearly indicates that he intends to write a public pastoral letter to seven churches in Asia Minor and that he understands this letter as the "words of prophecy."[23]

Nevertheless, Rev. does not read like a letter or homily. It is difficult to identify which complex literary type the author had in mind in writing the book. Did he intend to create a liturgy or a drama, a cosmic myth, a prophetic book, or an apocalypse? Or did he use all of these genres to fill out the epistolary framework which reflects his true literary intention?

1. The hymnic language, liturgical symbols, and cultic settings of Rev. have suggested to some that the author intended to write the book in the form of a liturgy. Exegetes have suggested several concrete liturgical structures as models for Rev. Some think that it follows the sequence of the Jerusalem temple liturgy or the Jewish calendar of feasts. Others consider Christian worship as constitutive for the structure of Rev. They suggest that the author used a eucharistic liturgy or a Christian initiation ritual as the basis for his composition. M. H. Shepherd's proposal combines both suggestions and argues that the paschal liturgy gave to the author the model for the structure of his book.[24] Yet even a superficial comparison of a ritual book with Rev. indicates that all these proposals force a liturgical pattern on the text. Therefore most exegetes stress the liturgical setting and forms within Rev.,[25] but concede that liturgical symbols and forms are structural component forms of the book and are combined with other component types and forms in the composition of Rev.

The liturgical interpretation is often linked with the understanding of Rev. as a drama, since in Greek tragedy the roots of drama and cult are closely interconnected. Interpreters have not merely acknowledged the dramatic character of the book but have maintained that Rev. is patterned after the Greek drama, since it has *dramatis personae,* stage props, chorus, a plot, and a tragic-comic ending. F. Palmer[26] considers Rev. a drama of five acts and three scenes, whereas Bowman[27] maintains that seven acts with seven scenes constitute the book. E. Stauffer,[28] on the other hand, proposes that the outline of Rev. and its plot is patterned after the stages and scenes of the imperial games which were celebrated in Ephesus. The most compelling argument for the influence of Greek dramatic forms on the composition of Rev. is the use of choruses by the author. Recent studies of the hymnic materials in Rev. have convincingly demonstrated that the hymns comment on and complement the visions and auditions of the book. Thus they function in the same way as the chorus in the Greek drama, preparing and commenting upon the dramatic movements of the plot.

Even though Rev. contains dramatic elements, it is nonetheless evident that it is not written in the dialogue form of a drama just as it does not represent a liturgical formulary. Liturgical and dramatic elements are component-types of the book but they do not constitute its complex literary type.

2. The Book of Rev. clearly employs the language of myth.[29] Its mythic world view divides the universe into heaven, earth, and underworld inhabited by angels and demons. The book speaks of great portents in heaven, of sacred books, and of seven stars. Furthermore, its animal figures speak and act. The book contains elements of traditional mythologies, for example, the birth of the divine child, the sacred marriage, the divine city (*polis*), the divine warrior, and the battle between Michael and the primeval snake. The author employs sacred numbers and figures, which have an affinity to the astral myths of late antiquity.

The number seven, for example, was already an integrated element in Jewish beliefs (e.g., apocalypticism) and was the number of divine perfection and holiness. In Rev. it characterizes not only the churches, their angels, and the spirits of God but also functions as a basic structural component in the composition of the book. The four septets—the letters, the seals, the trumpets, and the bowls—decisively structure Rev. It has therefore been argued that the whole plan and composition of Rev. is patterned after the number seven.[30] Some reconstruct seven series of seven, whereas others recognize only five or six series of seven. The difficulty of such reconstructions, however, lies in their failure to explain why the author clearly marked four series of seven but did not mark the others, even though the existing septets prove that he was quite capable of doing so.

J. Gager has recently attempted to apply a structuralist understanding and analysis of myth to the composition of Rev. He maintains that not only does the pattern of seven determine the structure of the book, but also that the binary structure of myth is decisive. The patterns of seven and two "meet to create a 'machine' for transcending time."[31] In his proposal the sections and patterns of Rev. are all pressed into the binary structure of victory/hope (4:1—5:14; 7:1—8:4; 10:1–11; 11:15–19; 14:1–7; 15:2–8; 19:1–16; 21:1—22:5) and oppression/despair (6:1–17; 8:5—9:21; 11:2–14; 12:1–17; 13:1–18; 14:8—15:1; 16:1–20; 17:1–18; 19:17—20:15).

Gager's division clearly omits the inaugural vision and the seven letters. Moreover, it obscures the structural impact of the four septets and appears to divide the text in a topical rather than a formal manner. Finally, it must be questioned whether the main goal of the author in composing the book was "to make possible an experience of millennial bliss as living reality" or "to experience the future as present." The opposite appears to be the case. The author does not encourage the con-

sistent resistance (*hypomonē*) of Christians by eliminating the difference
in time between the present and the eschatological future. Instead, he
stresses that Christians do not yet actively exercise their kingship.
Eschatological salvation is near but not yet present. Like the prophets of
Israel, he encourages the churches by interpreting their situation and
task in the light of the eschatological future. He speaks of future salvation for the sake of exhortation.

3. Exegetes still question whether the author intended his work to be
a prophecy or an apocalypse.[32] He understands himself as a Christian
prophet[33] and intends his work to be a "word of prophecy." Moreover,
he employs most of the traditional prophetic forms. Rev. contains
prophetic vision reports and messenger speeches, prophetic oracles and
symbolic actions, announcements of judgment and proclamations of salvation. Prophetic summonses, warnings, threats and exhortations, technical legal language as well as hymns of praise, woe oracles, and laments
or dirges are found in the book. The author not only uses prophetic
forms but also patterns whole sections after OT prophetic books. Yet,
since we also find prophetic forms in apocalyptic literature, it becomes
apparent how difficult it is, on formal grounds, to distinguish prophetic
and apocalyptic literature.

Since Rev. gave the whole literary genre of apocalyptic literature its
name, it is usually assumed that the book represents this literary type.
However, until more careful form-critical and composition-critical analyses are made it will be hard to determine which component types are
essential for the complex literary type "apocalypse" in distinction to that
of prophecy. The symbolism and mythical images, the codified language
and outlooks in the future, the form of visions and auditions, the angelic
interpreter, the cosmic stage setting and the eschatological orientation
doubtlessly characterize Rev. as an apocalyptic book. Nevertheless,
essential component elements such as pseudonymity, secrecy, historical
periodization, journeys through the heavenly worlds, or lists of revealed
things are conspicuously absent in Rev.[34]

An either/or solution, that is, that Revelation is either a prophetic or
an apocalyptic book, appears to be misconstrued for two reasons. The
first is that Jewish apocalypticism integrates the prophetic-historical and
the mythopoeic-cultic perspective and forms. According to P. D.
Hanson,[35] apocalyptic eschatology has as its "parents" prophecy and the
mythopoeic world view. Whereas prophecy understands divine activity
as involving a movement from promise to fulfillment and has as its primary sphere the changing flux of history, the mythopoeic world view.
recounts a cosmic divine drama which is merely reflected in earthly
events. Where prophecy aims to translate Yahweh's plans and commands

into the politico-historical realm, the mythopoeic view offers an escape from historical realities either by reenacting the cosmic activities of the gods in ritual celebrations or by fleeing into the heavenly realm of timeless vision. Jewish apocalypticism did not eliminate time and history as the ritual pattern as ancient myth did. Instead it remained bound to the prophetic scheme of promise and fulfillment. History is not reduced, graphically speaking, to a circular movement reenacting again and again the actions of the gods, but takes the form of a linear development according to a divine plan toward a promised goal.

It is hard to define the peculiar literary genre of apocalyptic literature since it utilizes all the traditional forms of liturgy, myth, and prophecy, and transforms them into new literary forms. An example of such a transformation is the fusion of the mythopoeic pattern of the Divine Warrior with that of the prophetic oracle in the hybrid form of the salvation-judgment oracle.[36] The element of judgment[37] appears to gain greater importance in the development of apocalyptic-eschatological patterns than the element of the Divine Warrior which is more and more incorporated into the judicial pattern. Language and elements of the combat-myth pattern are without doubt found in Rev., and it is very probable that the last section of the book, 19:11—22:9, follows this pattern. Yet the author appears to have known this pattern through the mediation of OT prophetic books. In Rev. the language and pattern of divine warfare appears to be subordinated to the judicial language and patterns of prophetic judgment.[38]

The second reason why Rev. cannot be called exclusively prophetic or apocalyptic is that one of the characteristics of early Christian apocalypticism is the combination of apocalyptic vision and exhortation for the sake of prophetic interpretation. An analysis of the Synoptic Apocalypse (e.g., Mark 13) shows the alternation between parenetic and apocalyptic sections.[39] Tradition-historical studies have shown, moreover, that an originally apocalyptic-eschatological "midrash"[40] was gradually expanded to address the situation and needs of the Christian community. Though in Judaism apocalypticism is the "successor" of prophecy, the early Christians conceived of themselves as a prophetic community. Early Christian prophecy utilized apocalyptic patterns and language to admonish and to interpret the situation of the community.[41]

In Rev. apocalyptic imagery and patterns also serve prophetic admonition and interpretation. The author begins his book with exhortation and interpretation of the Christian situation in the form of a prophetic vision (1:9—3:22) and ends it with visionary promise and exhortation (19:11—22:9). The central chapters (10—14) are explicitly characterized as prophetic interpretation of the Christian community's situation.

Like all of the OT prophetic books, Rev. begins with an introduction.[42] This introduction is similar to that of Amos 1:1–2 insofar as it combines the literary genre of the superscription (Rev. 1:1–3)[43] with a motto (1:7–8)[44] characterizing both the content and tone of the book. Inserted between the traditional prophetic form of introduction is the prescript similar to that of the Pauline[45] letters (1:4–6). The introduction (1:1–8) thus characterizes the whole book as a book of prophecy functioning as an apostolic open letter and address to the communities of Asia Minor.

It is therefore not accidental that Rev. as a whole has the form of the early Christian apostolic letter and that the apocalyptic visions, symbols and patterns are set in an epistolary framework.[46] The author does not underscore the authority of his work by means of pseudonymity, secrecy, and fictional timetables. He understands it rather as a work of Christian prophecy. The apocalyptic language and imagery of the book serve prophetic interpretation. The author has used dramatic, liturgical, mythopoeic, prophetic, and Christian language and patterns to formulate his own literary account of early Christian prophecy. If the epistolary framework of Rev. is not an accidental, secondary addition but expresses the author's intention to write a work of Christian prophecy, then any analysis and delineation of the structure and plan of Rev. has to take into account the author's intention in choosing this literary type for the book.

COMPOSITION AND STRUCTURE
OF REVELATION

In order to understand the particular form-content configuration (*Gestalt*) of Rev. as a work of early Christian prophecy, we must attempt to rediscover not only the techniques of composition and the means of integrating various traditional patterns and forms into the literary movement of the book, but also the architectonic designs controlling the arrangement of the materials and the organization of the whole book.

Techniques of Composition

Even though the author works with traditional forms and materials, Rev. as a whole does not make an encyclopedic impression because the author does not preserve his traditions and sources unchanged but revises, alters, and adapts them to their present context. This technique of composition can best be seen in his use of OT materials to which he alludes but which he never reproduces in quotations. He often fuses various OT texts to make his own statement or to create a new symbolic expression.[47]

Another means of achieving a unitary impression is the author's use of a common stock of symbols and images. In Rev. the individual vision does not have its own exclusive set of symbols which is found nowhere else in the other visions of the book. The main symbols and images are distributed over the whole book (e.g., the image of the throne or the symbol "white"). The author, moreover, underlines the unitary character of the work through image clusters and symbol associations. For instance, the image of the throne[48] has to be seen in connection with other expressions and symbols of kingship in order to grasp its full impact. Or the notion of the "eschatological war" is intensified and enhanced by a variety of terminology and symbols of war.[49]

Further techniques of composition are preannouncements (e.g., the promises to the victor are repeated in chaps. 21—22 and the announcement of the final judgment in 14:6–20 is developed in chaps. 17—20); cross-references (e.g., the characterization of Christ in the inaugural vision reoccur in chaps. 2—3, and the characterizations of the figure as someone like a "son of humanity" is also found in 14:14, and features of the figure in 1:12–20 reoccur in 19:11–16; a more detailed investigation could highlight many more such cross-references); and contrasts (e.g., the beast is a contrast figure to the Lamb and the great harlot is a contrast image to the woman in chap. 12 as well as to the bride of the Lamb, the New Jerusalem).

A primary means chosen by the author to achieve an interwoven texture and unitary composition is the use of numbers and numerical structures. The basic numerical structuring elements are the two commissioning book visions and the four septets (the seven letters and the three septets of the eschatological plagues). These plague septets are in turn structured into groupings of four and three. By integrating the plague septets into the narrative structure, the author combines a cyclic form of repetition with the end-oriented movement of the whole book. Since the three plague septets do not simply repeat each other but evolve from and expand each other, they are open cycles. The narrative movement of the seven-sealed scroll is therefore best diagrammed as a conical spiral moving from the vision of the Lamb's enthronement as the eschatological ruler to that of the Parousia, Christ's coming.

The forward movement of the narrative is also interrupted through the interludes. They are visions or hymns of eschatological protection and salvation (e.g., 7:1–17; 11:15–19; 12:10; 14:1–5; 15:2–4; 19:1–9; 20:4–6). Insofar as the author interrupts the patterns of continuous narrative and cyclic repetition through the insertion of these anticipatory visions and auditions, he expresses in his composition the relationship between present reality and eschatological future. The hymns and acclamations

serve as a commentary on the apocalyptic action of Rev. Their contribution to its structure is interpretation and comment. Thus they function
in a manner similar to the chorus in the Greek tragedy which com-
mented and explained the actions of the principals in the drama.

Very important for the composition and structure of Rev. is the technique of intercalation[50] of texts which makes a diagramming of the successive sections of Rev. almost impossible. The author employs the
method of intercalation in the following way: he narrates two formal
units or two episodes (A and A') that essentially belong together.
Between these two formal units or episodes he intercalates another form
or scene (B) and thus requires the reader to see the combined text as a
whole. For instance, in structuring the introduction to the whole book
the author intercalates the following formal units: superscription (A),
prescript (B), and motto (A'). An example of the intercalation of content
units is the introduction to the trumpet septet. After the appearance of
the seven angels with the seven trumpets in 8:2 (A), there follows a
heavenly liturgy 8:3–5 (B) and then the plagues begin at 8:6 (A').

The combination of an interlude and the method of intercalation
often results in a double intercalation. The author appears to have used
this combination in tying the main sections of the book together. For
example: 10:1—11:14 is clearly marked as an interlude inserted into the
septet of the trumpets (8:6—9:21 A; 10:1—11:14 B; 11:15—19 A'). At the
same time 10:1—11:14 serves in the author's mind as an introduction to
the following section, chaps. 12—14, since it refers to the same time
period as well as to the prophetic Christians' persecution by the beast.
The vision of the small prophetic scroll is thus held together by the pattern A (10:1—11:14)—B (11:15-19)—A' (chaps. 12—14) and is tied to the
trumpet septet of the seven-sealed scroll through the same pattern. By
the same method of intercalation it is tied at the other end to the bowl
septet. The introduction to the bowl septet (15:1-8) is patterned analogously to that of the trumpet septet: appearance of the seven angels 15:1
(A), heavenly liturgy 15:5-8 (B), and execution of the plagues in 16:1–21
(A'). In this sequence 15:2–4 is an interlude and at the same time
represents an intercalation (chap. 14 A; 15:1 B; 15:2–4 A'). The vision of
the small prophetic scroll thus reaches a climax in 15:2–4 which at the
same time ties it to the bowl septet of the seven-sealed scroll.

Another example of double intercalation is the position of the Babylon visions (Rev. 17:1—19:10). The remark in 16:19 and the introduction
in 17:1 characterize these Babylon visions as an appended interlude to
the bowl septet. Yet C. H. Giblin[51] has convincingly pointed out that
the Babylon visions are part of the ABA' pattern in 17:1—22:9, since the
author intercalates the Parousia and judgment section 19:11—21:8 (B)
between the Babylon visions 17:1—19:10 (A) and the New Jerusalem

visions 21:9—22:9 (A'). Thus the technique of intercalation links Rev. 17:1—19:10 with the last part of the book in such a way that it is difficult to decide whether the visions of Babylon belong to the bowl septet or to the final section of Rev.

The recognition of the method of intercalation has far-reaching consequences for the understanding of the composition and structure of Rev. The method of intercalation presents one of the greatest obstacles to the correct understanding of Rev. Since exegetes are trained to divide a text into sections which follow each other in a logical linear fashion, we usually search for the markers which divide Rev. into different sections. The following phrases have been suggested as marking off the sections of Rev.:[52] "in the spirit" (1:10; 4:2; 17:3; 22:6), "that must shortly come to pass" (1:1; 1:19; 4:1; 22:6), "lightnings, voices and thunder" (4:5; 8:5; 11:19; 16:18), and the "doxology" (4:8-11; 5:8-14; 7:9-12; 11:15; 15:3-4; 19:1-8). However, these "dividing marks" do not occupy such a clear position in the outline of Rev. that the author could have intended to indicate the structure of his work with them. The author does not divide the text into separate sections or parts, but joins units together by interweaving them with each other through the method of intercalation. It is therefore more crucial to discern the joints of the structure which interlace the different parts than to discover "dividing marks."

The passage most generally used for dividing the book is Rev. 1:19.[53] It is often conjectured that in this text the author divides the book into two parts. The expression "the things that are" refers to the first part 1:9—3:22, whereas "the things that are to come hereafter" designates the main apocalyptic part 4:1—22:5. Yet, it is questionable whether this division of Rev. does justice to the author's intention since it separates parenesis and apocalyptic vision. Moreover, the position of the statement in its present context indicates that it refers not to the whole book but to the following letters which speak about what is now and what will be in the future. In addition, it must be pointed out that the author places the letter-septet on one level with the so-called apocalyptic visions, since he makes the letters clearly a part of the inaugural vision. Finally, through the seven pattern, he has linked 1:9—3:22 to the following seven cycles. The opening remark in 4:1 links this vision to the preceding message visions as well.[54] Since the "first trumpet voice" (4:2) is clearly the same as the "voice like a trumpet" (1:10, 12), the speaker in the two visions is the same. Moreover 3:21b points to the following throne vision of chaps. 4—5. As the seventh element of the preceding seven-series opens up a new series of visions in the plague septets of the book,[55] so the seventh element of the letter vision opens up a new series of visions. It is therefore inappropriate to separate the letter septet from the following visions of the book.

The Structure and Architectonic Pattern of Revelation

Of all the structural patterns and the compositional techniques employed in Rev., the following three appear to be most decisive for the structuring of the book.

1. The pattern of seven.
2. The two scroll visions and the christological inaugural visions in 1:12–20 and 19:11–16.
3. The method of intercalation and interlocking, of "joining."

The combination of all three compositional techniques results in the following outline of Rev. which consists of four major parts:

I. The inaugural vision and the letter septet (1:9—3:22);
II. The seven sealed scroll (4:1—9:21; 11:15–19; 15:1, 5—16:21; 17:1 —19:10);
III. The small prophetic scroll (10:1—15:4);
IV. The visions of judgment and salvation (19:11—22:9).

The outline which I proposed in chap. 1, "History and Eschatology in Revelation,"[56] differs from the present proposal insofar as the earlier article assumes that the Babylon visions form their own separate section (17:1—20:15) with those of judgment. Such a division however does not take sufficiently into account the structural and theological importance of the vision 19:11–16 (cf. 19:11 and 4:1; 19:11–16 and 1:12–20). It also overlooks the fact that the author links the Babylon visions to the septet of the bowls. It also does not recognize the intercalation 17:1—22:9.

A structuralist analysis of the actantial level[57] of the four main parts of Rev. supports the proposed outline for the surface structure. The actantial model is presented graphically in the following figure of the six actants:

Ordainer (OR) ——————————— Object (O) ——————————→ Recipient (R)

Helper (H) ——————————————→ Subject (S) ←——————— Opponent (Op)

Actants should not be confused with the actors of the manifestations but they are structural elements which have been obtained by reducing an infinite set of variables (the various personages and actions of the narrative) to a limited number of structural elements (actantial roles or spheres of action). Rev. as a whole can be projected onto the model in the following way:

God (OR) ——————— Judgment/Salvation (O) ——————————→ Community Cosmos (R)

Angel Seer (H) ——————————→ Christ (S) ←——————— Antidivine powers (Op)

Parts 1:9—3:22; 4:1—19:10 and 19:11—22:9 repeat this actantial scheme of the whole of Rev. Section III (10:1—15:4) of Rev., however, represents a different model:

God (Or) ——————— Eschatological War (O) ————————► Community Humankind (R)

Beasts, Babylon, Kings (H)——► Dragon (S) ◄——— Christ, Michael, Christians (Op)

This structuralist analysis of the actantial level of Rev. thus confirms the central position of the small prophetic scroll for the surface structure. Moreover, the seven letter visions do not form a separate unconnected part of Rev. but belong integrally to the book. Finally, the analysis of the actantial level confirms the conclusion that the prophetic-apocalyptic judgment/salvation pattern is basic for Rev.

In my analysis of the complex type (*Gattung*) of Rev. I have maintained that this prophetic-apocalyptic pattern is integrated into that of the prophetic-apostolic letter. If the epistolary framework defines the complex literary type of Rev., then the pattern of inclusion or symmetry has to be shown as the architectonic pattern of the whole work. That this is the case is indicated by the author's preference for the ABA' pattern and the technique of intercalation. Since the two scroll visions and the three septets are decisive for the pattern of Rev. 4:1—19:10, this central unit of the book clearly exhibits the pattern ABA'. The letter septet, moreover, corresponds with the last section, 19:11—22:9. The introductory vision of this section 19:11-16 clearly resembles the inaugural vision and the seven letters (19:12; cf. 1:14 and 2:17; 19:15; cf. 2:27 and especially the sword symbol in 19:15; cf. 1:16; 2:12). Moreover, the promises of the letters to the victorious one recur in 19:11—22:9. The first unit and the last unit of Rev. are thus related to each other as promise and fulfillment. The surface structure of Rev. can then be outlined in the following way:

A   1:1–8
B   1:9—3:22
C   4:1—9:21; 11:15–19
D   10:1—15:4
C'   15:1, 5—19:10
B'   19:11—22:9
A'   22:10—22:21

This concentric ABCDC'B'A' pattern of Rev. shows that the whole book is patterned after the epistolary framework which represents an inclusion. Insofar as the center of the pattern is the prophetic scroll, the structure of the book underscores that the main function of Rev. is the prophetic interpretation of the situation of the community. The structuralist analysis of the actantial level is thus congruent with the architectural analysis of the book.

In order to defend this reconstruction of the structure of Rev. against the accusation that it represents just one more subjectivist enterprise in the analysis of the plan of Rev., we must apply to it the internal and external control which architectural critics[58] have worked out. In the preceding section it was shown, as space allowed, that this symmetric pattern controls not only the whole genre of the book but also the arrangement of smaller and larger units. It also became apparent that the pattern is located, not in the tradition, but in the compositional activity of the author. Moreover, the pattern is a widely employed pattern in the literature of antiquity.[59] It is especially interesting to note the affinity of the structure of Rev. with that of Greek drama. According to the compositional rules of tragedy, the climax falls near the center of the action, and the denouement comes near the end. The narrative poetry of republican Rome follows the same compositional rules.[60] Students of the literature of Israel and Judaism have found the same structural pattern.[61] The pattern is also present in the visual art of the time. Two examples appear to be especially interesting for the understanding of Rev. Two Roman coins of 35–36 C.E. bear images of the temples of Divus Augustus and Apollo. These temple images exhibit the balanced structure ABCDC'B'A'.[62] Even more significant with respect to Rev. is the fact that the golden candelabra which appears on the arch of Titus in Rome consists of a centerpiece paralleled on either side by three pieces and thus exhibits the pattern ABCDC'B'A'.[63] Internal and external evidences thus support our reconstruction of the architectonic pattern of Rev.

In conclusion, the epistolary framework of Rev. represents not an artificial and unimportant setting for the apocalyptic-mythopoeic vision, but provides—together with the prophetic-apocalyptic judgment/salvation genre—the macro-form or complex type of Rev. (ABCDC'B'A'). The author derives the authority of his work not from pseudonymity and fictional timetables, but from patterning it after the authoritative Pauline letter form. He structures his apocalyptic visions after the traditional Christian apocalyptic pattern which emphasizes the element of exhortation. The basic movement of the narrative represents the prophetic movement from promise to fulfillment. This linear movement is partly deflected through the cyclic form of the three plague septets. Yet these septets are broken cycles since they represent a forward movement to greater fulfillment. The center of the book is the prophetic interpretation of the political and religious situation of the community (10:1— 15:4). The structuralist and architectonic analysis of Rev. confirms the assumption that the author intended to write a work of prophecy in the form of the apostolic letter. Moreover, it underlines the dramatic character of Rev. In choosing the concentric pattern ABCDC'B'A' the author makes the small scroll of prophecy in Rev. 10:1—15:4 the climactic center of the action. The author has fused his materials, patterns, and theological perspective into the unique form-content configuration (*Gestalt*) of Rev.

NOTES

1. Cf. R. Wellek and A. Warren, *Theory of Literature* (3d ed.; New York: Harcourt, Brace, Jovanovich, 1956); N. Frye, *Anatomy of Criticism* (Princeton, N.J.: Princeton Univ. Press, 1973); G. Schiwy, *Der französische Strukturalismus: Mode, Methode, Ideologie* (Hamburg: Rowolt, 1969); *The Structuralists: From Marx to Lévi-Strauss* (ed. R. T. DeGeorge and F. M. DeGeorge; New York: Doubleday & Co., 1972); S. Wittig, "The Historical Development of Structuralism," *Soundings* 58 (1975) 145–66; E. Watkins, "Criticism and Method: Hirsch, Frye, Barthes," ibid., 257–80.

2. E. Schüssler Fiorenza, "Gericht und Heil. Zum theologischen Verständnis der Apokalypse," in *Gestalt und Anspruch des Neuen Testaments* (ed. J. Schreiner; Würzburg: Echter, 1969) 330–47; idem, "Die tausend-jährige Herrschaft der Auferstandenen (Apk 20:4–6)," *BiLe* 13 (1972) 107–24; idem, *Priester für Gott: Studien zum Herrschafts- und Priestermotiv in der Apokalypse* (NTAbh 7; Münster: Aschendorff, 1972); idem, "Religion und Politik in der Offenbarung des Johannes," in *Exegetische Randbemerkungen: Schülerfestschrift R. Schnackenburg* (Würzburg: Echter, 1974); idem, *The Apocalypse* (Chicago: Franciscan Herald Press, 1976).

3. For a review, cf. R. H. Charles, *Studies in the Apocalypse* (2d ed.; Edinburgh: T. & T. Clark, 1915) 185–90.

4. Vischer, on the other hand, assumed two sources (*Apoc. of John Mark*, 60 C.E. and *Apoc. of Cerinthus*, 70 C.E.) and two redactions, one in Trajan's and one in Hadrian's time.

5. In assuming an original Christian source-text (*Urschrift;* 1:4—3:22), Weiss follows F. Spitta. He had ascribed the seven letters to an original apocalypse (*Urapokalypse*=U), which was written soon after 60. In addition to it the Christian redactor (in the time of Trajan) had two Jewish sources, the trumpet-source J¹ (time of Caligula) and the bowl-source J² (time of Pompeius).

6. J. M. Ford, *The Revelation of John* (AB 38; New York: Doubleday & Co., Anchor Books, 1975). Weyland had also postulated two Jewish sources (א written under Titus and ב written under Nero) and a Christian redactor.

7. Cf. the commentaries of Swete, Bousset, Zahn, and Beckwith.

8. Cf. A. Lancelotti, *Sintassi ebraica nel greco dell' Apocalisse. I: Use delle forme verbali* (Collectio Assiniensis 1; Assisi, 1964); U. Vanni, *La Struttura Letteraria dell' Apocalisse* (Aloisiana; Rome: Herder, 1971); G. Mussies, *The Morphology of Koine Greek as Used in the Apocalypse of John* (NovTSup 27; Leiden: E. J. Brill, 1971).

9. F. Spitta assumed that the three septets represent different sources, while Weizsäcker observed that the three septets form a harmonious structure which was interrupted by the insertion of various other text-units (e.g., chaps. 7; 10—13; 17).

10. Cf. esp. W. Bousset, *Die Offenbarung Johannis* (MeyerK 16; 6th ed.; Göttingen: Vandenhoeck & Ruprecht, 1906) 101ff.

11. H. P. Müller, "Formgeschichtliche Untersuchungen zu Apc 4f" (Diss.; Heidelberg University, 1962) Appendix II and III; idem, "Die himmlische Ratsversammlung. Motivgeschichtliches zu Apk 5, 1–5," *ZNW* 54 (1963) 254–67.

12. H. P. Müller, "Die Plagen der Apokalypse. Eine formgeschichtliche Untersuchung," *ZNW* 51 (1960) 268–79.

13. G. Harder, "Eschatologische Schemata in der Johannes-Apokalypse," *TViat* 9 (1963) 70–87.

14. A. Vanhoye, "L'utilisation du livre d'Échéchiel dans l'Apocalypse," *Bib* 43 (1963) 436–76; Schüssler Fiorenza, "Die tausendjährige Herrschaft," 116–18.

15. Cf. A. Yarbro Collins, *The Combat Myth in the Book of Revelation* (HDR 9; Missoula, Mont.: Scholars Press, 1976).

16. H. Kraft, *Die Offenbarung des Johannes* (HNT 16a; Tübingen: Mohr/Siebeck, 1974) 17.

17. See chap. 1 of this book, "History and Eschatology in Revelation." The three main theological themes are the prophetic interpretation of the present situation of the community, the imminent expectation, and the establishment of the rule of God and Christ over the world in judgment.

18. For the distinction between redaction- and composition-criticism, cf. N. Perrin, *What is Redaction Criticism?* (Philadelphia: Fortress Press, 1970) 1–2 and 65–66. Cf. also D. Patte, *What is Structural Exegesis?* (Philadelphia: Fortress Press, 1976).

19. For the categories, cf. K. Koch, *The Growth of the Biblical Tradition* (New York: Charles Scribner's Sons, 1969) 23–24. For an explanation of *Gestalt* theory in literary criticism, cf. E. Güttgemanns, *Offene Fragen zur Formgeschichte des Evangeliums* (Munich: Chr. Kaiser, 1970) 184–88 [ET: *Candid Questions Concerning Gospel Form Criticism* (PTMS 26; Pittsburgh: Pickwick Press, 1979)].

20. G. Delling, "Zum gottesdienstlichen Stil der Johannesapokalypse," *NovT* 3 (1959) 107–37, 121ff.; R. Deichgräber, *Gotteshymnus und Christushymnus in der frühen Christenheit* (SUNT 5; Göttingen: Vandenhoeck & Ruprecht, 1967) 44–59; K. P. Jörns, *Das hymnische Evangelium* (SNT 5; Gütersloh: Gerd Mohn, 1971).

21. F. Hahn, "Die Sendschreiben in der Johannesapokalypse. Ein Beitrag zur Bestimmung prophetischer Redeformen," in *Tradition und Glaube: Festgabe für K. G. Kuhn* (Göttingen: Vandenhoeck & Ruprecht, 1972) 357–94.

22. A variation of the call "to hear" is found in Rev. 13:9. In the Synoptic tradition this injunction is connected with the parable tradition and the apocalyptic tradition. The call underlines the fact that the exhortations and promises of the letters are directed to all the churches.

23. Rev. 1:4–6 is a prescript in a fully developed and stylized form. In the salutation proper the sender and the recipients are mentioned (4a); the opening blessing follows (4b–5a); and a doxology concludes the prescript (5b–6). The concluding greeting is 22:21.

24. M. H. Shepherd, *The Paschal Liturgy and the Apocalypse* (Richmond: John Knox Press, 1960) 83. For a discussion of the question and literature, cf. Jörns, *Das hymnische Evangelium*, 180–84.

25. Cf. J. Leipoldt, *Der Gottesdienst der ältesten Kirche* (Leipzig: Dorffling & Francke, 1937) 47–48; L. Thompson, "Cult and Eschatology in the Apocalypse of John," *JR* 49 (1969) 330–50.

26. F. Palmer, *The Drama of the Apocalypse* (New York, 1903); R. R. Brewer, "The Influence of Greek Drama on the Apocalypse of John," *ATR* 18 (1936) 74–92.

27. J. B. Bowman, "The Revelation of John. Its Dramatic Structure and Message," *Int* 9 (1955) 436–53.

28. E. Stauffer, *Christ and the Caesars* (Philadelphia: Westminster Press; London: SCM Press, 1955).

29. R. Halver, *Der Mythos im letzten Buch der Bibel* (Hamburg: Reich, 1964); B. Reicke, "Die jüdische Apokalyptik und die Johanneische Tiervision," *RSR* 60 (1972) 173–92; P. Carrington, "Astral Mythology in the Revelation," *ATR* 13 (1931) 289–305.

30. Cf. Bowman, "The Revelation," chart, and esp. E. Lohmeyer, *Die Offenbarung des Johannes* (HNT 16; 2d ed.; Tübingen: Mohr/Siebeck, 1953).

31. J. G. Gager, *Kingdom and Community* (Englewood Cliffs, N.J.: Prentice-Hall, 1975) 52.

32. For the wider context of this discussion, cf. P. von der Osten-Sacken, *Die Apokalyptik in ihrem Verhältnis zur Prophetie und Weisheit* (Munich: Chr. Kaiser, 1969); J. Kallas, "The Apocalypse—an Apocalyptic Book?" *JBL* 86 (1967) 69–80.

33. Cf. D. Hill, "Prophecy and Prophets in the Revelation of St. John," *NTS* 18 (1971/72) 401–18; E. Boring, "The Apocalypse as Christian Prophecy: A Discussion of the Issues Raised by the Book of Revelation for the Study of Early Christian Prophecy," *1974 SBL Seminar Papers* (Missoula, Mont.: Scholars Press, 1974) 2: 43–57.

34. For the difficult problem of the component literary types and the complex literary type or macro-genre "apocalypse," cf. J. M. Schmidt, *Die jüdische Apokalyptik: Die Geschichte ihrer Erforschung von den Anfängen bis zu den Textfunden von Qumran* (Neukirchen: Neukirchener Verlag, 1969) 316–17.

35. P. D. Hanson, *The Dawn of Apocalyptic* (Philadelphia: Fortress Press, 1975) 402–3.

36. Ibid., 106ff.

37. Cf. L. Hartmann, *Prophecy Interpreted* (Lund: C. W. K. Gleerup, 1966) 23–54; G. W. E. Nickelsburg, *Resurrection, Immortality and Eternal Life in Intertestamental Judaism* (HTS 26; Cambridge: Harvard Univ. Press, 1972) 174.

38. Various students of F. M. Cross, Jr. have attempted to show that the Divine Warrior pattern is basic for apocalyptic literature as well as for Rev. Cf. esp. P. D. Hanson, R. J. Clifford, J. J. Collins; for Rev., see A. Yarbro Collins, *The Combat Myth in the Book of Revelation*. Yet in Rev. the "war" language seems to be a part of the prophetic judgment language.

39. Mark 13:5b–6 (parenetic = p); 13:7–8 (apocalyptic = a); 13:9–13 (p); 13:14–20 (a); 13:21–23 (p); 13:24–27 (a).

40. Cf. Hartmann, *Prophecy*, 235–42.

41. U. B. Müller, *Prophetie und Predigt im Neuen Testament* (SNT 10: Gütersloh: Gerd Mohn, 1975) 19–46.

42. Cf. G. M. Tucker, *Form Criticism of the Old Testament* (Philadelphia: Fortress Press, 1971) 72–73.

43. For my discussion of apostolic authorship, cf. chap. 3 of this book, "The Quest for the Johannine School."

44. See my book *Priester für Gott*, 180–98, for a detailed analysis.

45. Kraft (*Die Offenbarung*, 28–29) points out that the author not only used the Pauline epistolary form but also characterizes the letters as a "catholic" or ecumenic letter collection because there are seven of them.

46. For the interrelationship of the genres "apostolic letter" and "prophetic or apocalyptic book," cf. K. Berger, "Apostelbrief und apostolische Rede," *ZNW* 65 (1974) 190–231.

47. This method often results in bizarre non-symbolic (*unbildlich*) images: cf. Rev. 5:5 where the Lamb is called "lion of the tribe of Judah" and "the root of David" (Gen. 49:9, 10; Isa. 11:1, 10). Cf. J. Cambier, "Les images de l'Ancien Testament dans l'Apocalypse de saint Jean," *NRT* 77 (1955) 113–22.

48. The symbol of the throne occurs throughout Rev. 1:4; 2:13; 3:21; 6:16; 7:9, 10, 11, 15, 17; 8:3; 11:16; 12:5; 13:2 (beast); 14:3; 16:10 (beast); 16:17; 19:4, 5; 20:4 (heavenly court); 20:11, 12; 21:5; 22:1, 3.

49. Basic for an understanding of the "war" language in Rev. is the understanding that Christ has already won the victory (5:5) but that Christians still are subject to the "war" which the beast wages and are still in danger of succumbing to it.

50. This method was already pointed out by R. J. Loenertz (*The Apocalypse of Saint John* [New York and London: Sheed & Ward, 1948] xviii–xix). For Mark, cf. J. R. Donahue, *Are You the Christ?* (SBLDS 10; Missoula, Mont.: Scholars Press, 1973).

51. C. H. Giblin, "Structural and Thematic Correlations in the Theology of Revelation 16—22," *Bib* 55 (1974) 487–504.

52. Cf. Vanni, *La Struttura*, 105–67.

53. The argument is not convincing that the command "write what you see" (cf. 1:11) does not refer to the letters, because they are not visions (cf. Kraft, *Die Offenbarung*, 43, 48).

54. P. S. Minear, *I Saw a New Earth* (Washington, D.C.: Corpus Books, 1968) 66–67.

55. Cf. Vanni, *La Struttura*, 120–30; Loenertz, *The Apocalypse*, xv.

56. Cf. Giblin, "Structural and Thematic," for the arguments that 17:1—19:10 belong closely together with 19:11–21. It is therefore impossible to decide with certainty to which "section" the unit 17:1—19:10 belongs. It is best understood as a unit.

57. The actantial model was designed by A. J. Greimas (*Sémantique structurale* [Paris: Larousse, 1966] 180) for mythical narratives. See also his "Eléments pour une théorie de l'interprétation du récit mythique," *Communications* 8 (1966) 28–59. Dan O. Via, *Kerygma and Comedy in the New Testament* (Philadelphia: Fortress Press, 1975) 131–32.

58. Cf. C. H. Talbert, *Literary Patterns, Theological Themes and the Genre of Luke-Acts* (SBLMS 20; Missoula, Mont.: Scholars Press, 1974) 8–9.

59. I am grateful to J. R. Donahue for having brought to my attention the work of G. E. Duckworth (*Structural Patterns and Proportions in Vergil's Aeneid* [Ann Arbor: Univ. of Michigan Press, 1962]); J. L. Myres (*Herodotus: Father of History* [Oxford: At the Clarendon Press, 1953]) shows that Herodotus employs the pedimental mode of composition (e.g., ABCB'A').

60. Cf. L. Richardson, *Poetical Theory in Republican Rome* (New Haven, Conn.: Yale Univ. Press, 1944) 19–20.

61. Cf., e.g., R. Pesch, "Zur konzentrischen Struktur von Jona 1," *Bib* 47 (1966) 577–81. A. Vanhoye (*La structure littéraire de l'Épître aux Hébreux*) [Paris and Brussels, 1963] 59, 22, 259) characterizes the structure of Hebrews as "concentric symmetry."

62. L. Richard, "The Temples of Apollo and Divus Augustus on Roman Coins," *Essays and Studies Presented to William Ridgeway* (ed. E. C. Quiggin; Cambridge: At the Univ. Press, 1913) 198–212.

63. It is possible that the author of Rev. has this golden lampstand in mind in 11:4 and 1:12–13, 20.

7
Visionary Rhetoric and
Social-Political Situation

> Our visions, stories and utopias
> are not only aesthetic:
> they engage us.
>
> Amos Wilder

In his summary of the overall outline and analysis of the Apocalypse, W. Bousset stresses that Rev. 14:1–5 was not taken over from a source but that it is formulated as "contrast-image" by the author. But he concludes: "It is not quite clear what the author means by this scene."[1] This exegetical helplessness before the passage is confirmed by I. T. Beckwith (1919) and repeated by R. H. Mounce (1977): "Verses 1–5 are often referred to as in some respects the most enigmatic in the book."[2] Such an exegetical conundrum is surprising because this passage (14:1–5) has a clearly marked composition and structure: It consists of

1. *Vision:* 14:1 describes the 144,000 with the Lamb on Mount Zion,
2. *Audition:* 14:2–3 announce the voice from heaven and the choral song before the throne of God which none could learn except the 144,000 and
3. *Explanation:* 14:4–5 identify the 144,000 with a four-fold characterization: they are virgins, followers of the Lamb, a first fruit, and blameless.

The literary context of this segment is also clear: the 144,000 around the Lamb on Mount Zion are the anti-image of the beast and its followers which were depicted in the preceding chapter (Rev. 13). The tableau is followed by three angelic proclamations to the whole world; the first angel proclaims the gospel of God's judgment and justice to all the world. These "glad tidings" consist especially in the "fall of Babylon," as the second angel underlines (14:8). The third angel threatens those who worship the beast with eternal punishment (14:9–11). The whole section of proclamation is concluded with two sayings addressed to

Christians: 14:12 is a comment of the seer with respect to the *hypomonē* ("consistent resistance") of the saints while the blessing (*makarismos*) in 14:13 is pronounced by a voice from heaven. It refers to those who "die in the Lord," a traditional Christian expression.

While one might quibble over the translation of certain expressions in the angelic warnings or in the description of the two beasts and their mark or stamp (*charagma*), the overall interpretation of the context is not contested. The *zeitgeschichtlich* interpretation (history contemporary to the author) of the beast and its cult agent as referring to Rome is widely accepted, although exegetes might differ on whether the "beast" refers to Nero or Domitian. Although today we have widespread agreement on the 144,000 as the anti-image to the followers of the beast, commentators do not come to the same conclusions as to their identity. Some of the following identifications are suggested. The 144,000 are understood as Jewish Christians, elect and "saved" Christians, Christian ascetic males, the eschatologically saved and protected "holy rest" of Israel, the "perfect" victims and sacrifice, the high priestly followers of the Lamb, the military army of the Lamb gathering on Zion for the messianic battle, those who have followed the Lamb into death, or those who follow the Lamb in heaven.[3]

For each of these interpretations (and others could probably be added) some contextual or tradition-historical argument can be adduced. The possibility of interpretational variance would increase even more if we would hold a church- or world-historical rather than an eschatological *zeitgeschichtlich* interpretation, or if we would see the visions of the book as predictions of events in our times and as promises to readers of today rather than to those in the first century. Finally, a "timeless" interpretation would add a different kind of variance insofar as it sees in the 144,000 symbols of "timeless truth" about discipleship, victory, or sacrifice; structuralist charting of opposites or types in turn could endow such a synchronic interpretation with apparent scientific exactitude. No wonder many exegetes and Christians throughout the centuries have relinquished an understanding of the book in despair while others have found it to be a source not only of spiritual but also artistic inspiration.

Rather than add one more "definite" interpretation of the 144,000 followers of the Lamb on Mount Zion, I would like to explore some of the conditions and possibilities for interpreting the language of Rev. in general and of this passage in particular. I will do so in order to complement my analysis of the composition, form, and macro-structure,[4] as well as the prophetic-apocalyptic setting of Rev.,[5] with an analysis of its rhetorical language and symbolic universe. I have selected Rev. 14:1–5 as an example to show how the rhetorical language of a text must be explored so that its symbolic-poetic images make "sense" within its overall context and it has "meaning" and the power of "persuasion" in its own particular historical-social situation.

I will therefore argue that Rev. must be understood as a poetic-rhetorical construction of an alternative symbolic universe that "fits" its historical-rhetorical situation. An adequate interpretation of Rev. 14:1–5, therefore, must first explore the poetic-evocative character of its language and symbols; second assess its rhetorical dynamics in a "proportional" reading of its symbols to elucidate their particular interrelations and the author's persuasive goals; and third show why the construction of the symbolic universe of Rev. is a "fitting" response to its historical-rhetorical situation. It has become clear by now that I understand symbolic actions not to be just linguistic-semantic but also always social-communicative. They need to be analyzed as text as well as subtext in terms of their historical-social "world": as subtext insofar as history is not accessible to us except in textual reconstructions although history itself is not a text. In other words, we are never able to read a text without explicitly or implicitly reconstructing its historical subtext within the process of our reading.[6]

THE MYTHOPOEIC LANGUAGE
OF REVELATION

In 1972 N. Perrin insisted that literary criticism "has to include consideration of the ways in which literary types and forms of language function, and a consideration of the response they evoke from the reader or hearer."[7] He argues that Jesus' preaching of the kingdom of God (*basileia tou theou*) has been misunderstood as apocalyptic conception because its symbolic language character has been overlooked. In his understanding of symbol N. Perrin follows P. Wheelwright's distinction between steno- and tensive symbol.[8] Whereas a steno-symbol always bears only a one-to-one relationship and is mostly used in scientific discourse, the tensive symbol can evoke a whole range of meanings and can never be exhausted or adequately expressed by one referent.

According to N. Perrin, Jewish as well as early Christian apocalyptic symbols are generally steno-symbols whereby each symbol has a one-to-one meaning relationship with the persons and events depicted or predicted. This is also the case when authors no longer refer to persons or events of the past but express their hope and vision for the future. Apocalyptic language is a secret code or sign-system depicting events that can be equated with historical persons or theological themes. Insofar as Perrin classifies apocalyptic symbols as steno-symbols or "signs" which must be decoded into a one-to-one meaning, he perpetuates the dichotomy between apocalyptic language and eschatological content or essence that has plagued scholarship in the past two hundred years.

The notion that the "essence" of theological meaning can be distilled from apocalyptic language reflects two rather prevalent but nevertheless inadequate assumptions in biblical interpretation: on the one hand the assumption that we are able to separate linguistic form and theological content and on the other hand the claim that imaginative symbolic language can be reduced to abstract philosophical language and conceptuality.[9] As early as 1779 J. G. Herder had poked fun at such an attempt:

> It [Rev.] carries, like everything else, its destiny along with itself. . . . The book consists of symbols; and philosophers cannot endure symbols. The truth must exhibit itself pure, naked, abstract, in a philosophical way. . . . No question is asked whether the symbols are pregnant with meaning, true, clear, efficient, intelligible, or whether there is in the whole book nothing but symbols. It is enough that there are symbols. We can make nothing out of symbols. At the best they are mere descriptions of the truth and we wish for demonstrations. Deductions, theorems, syllogisms we love. . . . Nature herself attempers different minds in various ways. She gives to one more of the power of abstraction, to another more of the power of synthesis; seldom are both found in company. In our academic education, there are unspeakably more teachers of that than of this. One is formed more for abstraction than for inspection; more for analysis than for pure comprehension, experience, and action. . . . Full of his systems of learning, of prejudices, and polemic hypotheses, let him indeed read anything in it, but let him not venture to condemn. . . . To the dumb one does not speak. The painter does not perform his work for the blind.[10]

The American scholar M. Stuart, who in 1845 published an excerpt from Herder's book *Maran Atha* as an appendix to his two-volume commentary on the Apocalypse, also underlined the aesthetic character of the work. He develops the following three hermeneutical principles: (1) The Apocalypse is a book of poetry; (2) it has to be understood in terms of Oriental poetry and therefore requires the same principles of interpretation as the parables of Jesus; and (3) generic and not specific and individual representations are to be sought in the book before us. Therefore in discussing Rev. 14:1–5 he points to the "episode" character of this passage but insists that "all which is intended by the symbols there exhibited, is merely to indicate the certainty of victory."[11]

This tendency to reduce the particular historical symbolic universe and literary expression of Rev. to the "generic" has prevailed among scholars who have advocated a literary analysis of Rev. in the most recent past. P. Minear has most consistently pursued a literary-critical analysis of its mythopoeic language and symbols. He objects to an understanding of Rev. as a system of signs in need of decoding, of symbols as equations with historical events and persons, and of images forecasting definite incidents and happenings.

He argues, for instance, against an interpretation of Rev. 17—18 that understands these chapters as anti-Roman polemics. To "equate Babylon with Rome would be literalism and historicism of the worst sort. The figure Babylon can convey the prophetic message and mentality without such an explicit association. We do not first require an exact knowledge of his immediate circumstances to grasp his message."[12] According to Minear the symbol Babylon as well as "the prophetic master-image of warfare between the rival kings points to realities of a primordial and eschatological order";[13] it points to the archetypal conflict of the demonic and the divine. "The invisible struggle among transcendent powers is for the prophet himself a fully contemporaneous reality, yet the struggle itself could not be compressed within the bounds of specific circumstances."[14]

In a similar fashion J. Ellul asserts that those exegetes who understand Babylon as the symbol of Rome and the "seven kings" as Roman emperors confuse the symbolic language of Rev. with a secret code. According to him, "Babylon is not the symbol of Rome, it is Rome, a historical reality which is transformed into a more polymorphous reality of which Babylon traditionally has been the expression. Rome is an actualized symbol, the historical presence of a permanent complex and multiple phenomenon . . . it is the historical actualization of the Power."[15] According to him Rome is the historical representation not just of ultimate Power but also of "the City" as the construction of all human culture and all civilization. It stands for all cities, those of the past and of the present. E. Lohmeyer and H. Schlier had already argued in a similar fashion.[16]

While Minear stresses that the historical references to Rome enhance our understanding of the underlying mythological, archetypal reality Babylon, Ellul maintains that the historical reality Rome is the representation of *the* ultimate Power and City. It seems that for both scholars the concrete historical reality and conditions of Roman power and rule along with its oppressive consequences for Christians in Asia Minor have become the symbolic manifestations of ultimate, transhistorical realities and archetypes. This interpretation, however, overlooks the fact that not Rome but the image of Babylon is the symbolic representation in Rev. To understand the symbolic representation not in historical but in archetypal or philosophical terms does not avoid its interpretation as "representation" of something which the interpreter is able to name. Archetypal, ontological interpretation reduces symbolic language to essential substance but does not explore its evocative powers in a given historical situation.

Rather than explore and highlight "the disposition of the work for openness," essentialist interpreters assume it is like "an apricot with a hard and definite meaning at its core."[17] To understand Rev. as a poetic work and its symbolic universe and language as an asset rather than as a "scholarly confusion," it becomes necessary for interpreters to acknowledge the ambiguity, openness, and indeterminacy of all literature. Nevertheless, an intellectually rigorous and historically careful reading of Rev. can show that

> this indeterminacy of meaning has nothing in common with the conception that poetic language has no *particular* meaning, but is valuable only as a stimulus of feeling. Indeterminacy sees the language of poetry and fiction as at least as precise as ordinary language, but as having a different function—that of opening up rather than limiting meanings. The indeterminacy is not on the surface; we know exactly what (the writer) did and even why he [sic] did it. What is open are the full implications, the values, and the various incidents. The 'confusion' . . . is at 'the deep level where it is required' . . . because a literary experience is by nature open [emphasis and parentheses added].[18]

In order to explore the whole range of the symbols in Rev. 14:1–5— take, for instance, the symbol of Mount Zion, which in N. Perrin's terms is a symbol of ancestral vitality—it would be necessary to develop a lexicon of the imagery in Rev. with respect to its sources and its idioms together with a history of its traditions and interpretations as well as their influence or effective history. Although G. Herder had already demanded such a lexicon, it is still a desideratum of scholarship today.

The "range" of meaning that the symbol of "Mount Zion" evokes becomes obvious in the commentaries. Reference is made to the historical Mount Zion, its use as a short form for Jerusalem, to the heavenly Jerusalem, to eschatological expectations that the Messiah will appear on Mount Zion for eschatological warfare, as well as to the promise that the "holy rest" of the people of God will be gathered and protected there. But attempts to show that the author means the heavenly and not the historical or the eschatological and not the heavenly temple-berg are inconclusive.[19] Moreover, attempts to show that the seer is influenced here by a definite prophetic[20] or apocalyptic text expectation[21] are also inconclusive. Yet this indeterminacy could become a plus if we would understand apocalyptic language as poetic language, that is, as opening up rather than limiting, as evoking rather than defining meanings. Only then would we be able to perceive the strength of the image with all its possible overtones of meanings for the writer as well as for the audience.

THE RHETORICAL STRATEGY
OF REVELATION

If Rev. is not to be likened to an "apricot with a hard core" but more to an "onion" consisting of layers and layers of meaning, then the question arises, how are we able to say that it is an "onion" and not a heap of apple peels? In other words, how can we delineate the "particular" meaning of Rev. without ending up in total confusion and without accepting every abstruse interpretation that is proposed for the book's often bizarre symbols? Is the book "open" to any interpretation, or does its "particularity" require that a proposed "meaning" must make "sense" with regard to the overall structure of the book as well as with respect to its "function" within a particular historical situation?

These questions can be further explored if we consider Rev. not just as a symbolic-poetic work but also as a work of visionary rhetoric. While the poetic work seeks to create or organize imaginative experience, the rhetorical seeks to "persuade" or "motivate" people "to act right."[22] Poetry works by representation and is fulfilled in creation while rhetoric seeks to teach and instigate; poetry invites imaginative participation while rhetoric instigates a change of attitudes and motivations. Or in the words of A. Wilder: "Our visions, stories, and utopias are not only aesthetic: they engage us."[23]

Since participation and persuasion, imagination and change are not exclusive of each other, poetic and rhetorical elements can be successfully intertwined in a single work. Speaker, audience, subject matter, and "rhetorical situation" are constitutive for any rhetoric utterance. In these terms Rev. is a poetic-rhetorical work. It seeks to persuade and motivate by constructing a "symbolic universe" that invites imaginative participation. The strength of its persuasion for action lies not in the theological reasoning or historical argument of Rev. but in the "evocative" power of its symbols as well as in its hortatory, imaginative, emotional language, and dramatic movement, which engage the hearer (reader) by eliciting reactions, emotions, convictions, and identifications.

In writing down "the words of prophecy" to be read in the worship assembly of the community, John seeks to motivate and encourage Christians in Asia Minor who have experienced harassment and persecution. John does not do so simply by writing a letter of exhortation but by creating a new "plausibility structure" and "symbolic universe" within the framework of a prophetic pastoral letter. Apocalyptic vision and explicit parenesis have the same function. They provide the vision of an "alternative world" in order to encourage Christians and to enhance their staying power in the face of persecution and possible execution.

Rather than "essentialize" the individual image, therefore, we must trace its position within the overall form-content configuration (*Gestalt*) of Rev. and see its relationships to other images and within the "strategic" positions of the composition. Images are not simply patterns or ornaments but they are "about something." Only a "proportional" analysis of its images can determine what they are about within the structure of the work by determining the phase of action in which they are invoked. Such an analysis of symbolic relations must highlight the hortatory or persuasive functions of the multivalent images and symbols in producing cooperative or non-cooperative attitudes and actions.

Whereas the poetic image can employ a full range of meaning and often contains a complex bundle of meanings which can be contradictory if they are reduced to their ideational equivalents, rhetorical symbols are related to each other within the structure of a work in terms of the ideas, values, or goals of the author, which must be at least partially shared with the audience.[24] In interpreting Rev. as a rhetorical work we must therefore look first for the strategic position and textual relations of the symbols and images within the overall dramatic movement of the book. Second, we must pay attention to the explicit rhetorical "markers" that seek to "channel" the audience's understandings, emotions, and identifications in such a way that it is persuaded and moved to the desired action.

First, since I have elsewhere analyzed the overall compositional movement of Rev., I will presuppose this analysis here in order to indicate how Rev. 14:1–5 makes "sense" within the overall dramatic action. According to my interpretation, this segment belongs to the central section of Rev. 10:1—15:5, which, in ever-new episodal images interprets the present situation of the community on earth in its confrontation with Rome's power and cult.[25] An "episode" is thereby understood as a "brief unit of action" that is integral but distinguishable from the continuous narrative. If we assume that the "narrative" line of Rev. is indicated by the four septets then this segment is similar in function to the first septet of the messages and it is the center around which the septet of plagues is grouped.

The vision of the 144,000 with the divine name on their foreheads is clearly an antithetical vision to those of the dragon and the two beasts. It continues the motif of the measuring of the temple, the two witnesses, and the woman with the child, while anticipating the vision of the victors who sing the song of Moses and the Lamb (15:2–4). It is also interlinked with other heavenly-earthly-eschatological visions of redemption

and salvation: on the one hand, it recalls the exaltation and enthronement of the Lamb in chap. 5, the "sealing" of the 144,000 elect of the
tribes of Israel as well as the eschatological great multitudinous company
of the Lamb in chap. 7; on the other hand it points forward to the victory
of the Lamb and those with him in 17:14, to the vision and audition of
the "sacred marriage of the Lamb" in 19:10, to the Messianic millennial
reign in 20:4–6, and to the "liturgical" service of those with the divine
name on their heads in the New Jerusalem (22:3–5). It also alludes to
the promise to the victor in 3:12 and the new "Zion"/Jerusalem in
21:1—22:5.

At the same time the vision of the 144,000 followers of the Lamb is
the anti-vision of the "Lamb-like" beast and its followers who have taken
the beast's name on their right hands and foreheads (chap. 13), as well
as the antipode to the gathering of the anti-divine forces at Har
Magedon (16:17). It is a "warning" to those who are in the process of
losing their share in the New Jerusalem. Similarly the audition refers the
audience back to the heavenly liturgies of 5:11–12; 7:11–12; 11:15–19;
12:10–12 and points forward to the song of the eschatological victors in
15:2–4 and 19:1–5. Its antidotes are the worship of the dragon and the
blasphemies of the beast from the sea (13:4–6; 16:11,21) as well as the
lament of the kings, merchants, and seafarers over Babylon (18:9–20).

These auditions have the same function of commenting on the dramatic action and of guiding the perception of the audience which the
choir had in the classical drama. By juxtaposing visions and auditions
of salvation with those of the anti-divine powers, the seer seeks to persuade and motivate his audience to make their decision for salvation and
for the world of God in the face of the destructive power represented by
the beasts and Babylon as the symbols of Rome. This function is underlined by the explanatory remark that closes the vision and audition in
v. 3: it underlines this eschatological tension of decision by stressing
that only the 144,000 are able to "learn" the "new song" which
the heavenly choir sings. They are those who are bought free, "separated
out," or liberated from the earth (*apo* implies their separation from
the earth).[26]

Second, the strategic function of the vision and audition of 14:1–3 is
underlined by its explicit interpretation in vv. 4–5, by the following séc-
tion with three angelic proclamations to all of humanity of vv. 6–11, and
by the special words of blessing to the Christians in vv. 12–13. They function as rhetorical markers that appeal to the active decision of the
audience and make sure that the multivalent images and symbols are
understood in a certain way. They must be understood in the context of
the explanatory remarks of chap. 13 and the proclamation of 14:6–13.

This interpretation of Rev. 14:1–5 understands those who are bought free from the earth as *parthenoi* (male virgins), as the followers of the Lamb, and as spotless first fruits. The present status of the eschatologically redeemed is a consequence and outcome of their behavior in the past. The first and last part of the interpretation stress the cultic purity of the 144,000 who are characterized in this vision as high priests, because they have the name of God and the Lamb on their foreheads. The middle section of the interpretation elaborates their "being with the Lamb" as following the Lamb.

This interpretation given by the author is grammatically difficult because the text leaves open whether they were or are followers of the Lamb. If the statement is parallel to the other two in structure, then the verb *ēsan* (they were) should be inserted. This, however, makes the grammatical reading of the sentence difficult. As the sentence stands now the reader can add the past and the present tense simultaneously: they have been and still are followers of the Lamb.[27] Whereas the beast from the abyss will "go" (*hypagei*) to destruction (17:18), the Lamb leads to eschatological salvation (cf. 7:17). Yet we are also reminded of the oracular pronouncement in 13:10: if anyone is to be taken captive, into captivity she or he goes (*hypagei*). Following the Lamb in the past included going to captivity, while now on the eschatological Zion it means salvation and fullness of life.

Whereas the statement that the 144,000 are first fruits and spotless because in their mouth was found no lie, is clear in the context of the book, the explanation that they are *parthenoi* (for they have not soiled or defiled themselves with women) is most difficult. Part of the difficulty, however, results from the mistaken assumption of exegetes that they must take this statement literally,[28] when they usually do not take either *agorazein* (to purchase), Mount Zion, *hypagein* (to go), *aparchē* (first fruits), or *amōmoi* (spotless) in a literalist sense but interpret them within the language context of the book. To assume that either the heavenly or the eschatological followers of the Lamb are a class of exclusively male ascetics[29] seems to be unfounded in the overall context of the book.

The expression *parthenoi* probably points, within the present scene, to the cultic purity of the Lamb's followers as well as to their representation of the "bride of the Lamb," the New Jerusalem, which is qualified as "holy" in 21:9–11. The anti-image to the holiness of the bride arrayed in white linen is that of Babylon who corrupts the nations with oppressive power.[30] The mention of "women" could also allude to the prophetess in Thyatira called Jezebel, who in John's view "seduces"

Christians to idolatry and accommodation to pagan society. This possibility is enhanced but not proven if we consider that the expression "in their mouth was found no lie" not only refers to the list of vices which excludes people from the New Jerusalem (21:7; 22:15) but also to those people who claim to be Jews but lie (3:9) and to the second beast, the false prophet (16:13; 19:20; 20:10).

Thus, the interpretation of the vision and audition is not given in less symbolic language and cannot be reduced to a one-to-one meaning. Its function is to underline the agency of the 144,000. While the vision and audition highlight the election of those who are with the Lamb on Mount Zion, an accurate interpretation stresses that their actions and lives are the preconditions for such eschatological salvation. It thus has the same rhetorical function as the angelic proclamation, which calls all of humanity—of which the 144,000 are the first fruits—to the worship of God, announces the fall of Babylon in whose abominations the 144,000 *parthenoi* did not share, and threatens with eternal punishment the worshipers of the beast who take its sign, while those who have the name of God on their foreheads are promised participation in the liturgy of heaven in the future.

Here, at this opposition between the worship of God and that of the beasts, the *hypomonē*, that is, the "consistent resistance" or "staying power" of the saints, who keep the word of God and the faith of Jesus, come to the fore. The macarism at the end of this section sums up its overall rhetorical message and thus forms a transition to the judgment visions in 14:14–20. "Blessed [*makarismos*] are the dead," according to a word of the Spirit, who have died "in the Lord," that is, as Christians. Like the souls under the heavenly altar in 6:9–11 they can rest from their labors because their deeds or what they have become in their actions follow them.

In conclusion, the vision and audition of Rev. 14:1–3 function within the context of the book to highlight the election as well as the eschatological salvation of the 144,000, while the attached interpretation (vv. 4–5) underlines that their life-practice is the condition for eschatological salvation. The tableau functions at the same time as anti-image to that of the beast and its followers as well as to the glory of Babylon. Thus the whole section 14:1–5 in its wider context underlines the fundamental decision that the audience faces: either to worship the anti-divine powers embodied by Rome and to become "followers" of the beast (cf. 13:2–4) or to worship God and to become "companions" of the Lamb on Mount Zion. This decision jeopardizes either their lives and fortunes here and now or their future lives and share in the New Jerusalem, Mount Zion.

The images of eschatological salvation and the heavenly world of God seek to mobilize the readers' emotions, to attract and persuade them to make the right decision here and now and to live accordingly in this life. At the same time these passages seek to alienate their allegiances and affects from the present symbols of Roman power by ascribing to it images of degradation, ugliness, ultimate failure, and defeat. With ever new images and symbols of redemption and salvation the visionary rhetoric of Rev. 10:1—15:4 seeks to persuade the audience to decide for the worship of God and against that of the beast, which is shown as doomed to failure and destruction. The Book of Rev. not only seeks to convince Christians that this is the right decision but also seeks to provoke them to stake their lives on it.

THE RHETORICAL SITUATION
OF REVELATION

My elaboration of the rhetorical strategy of Rev. has already indicated the kind of rhetorical situation which has generated it. It now remains to elaborate why its particular rhetorical response to the social-political and religious situation of the churches in Asia Minor is a "fitting" response. In other words, the social-historical-political parameters which are the ultimate horizon of Rev. as of any other cultural artifact must be (re)constructed, in the words of F. R. Jameson, so

> as to constitute not merely a scene or background, not an inert context alone but rather a structured and determinate situation, such that the text can be grasped as an active response to it. . . . The text's meaning then, in the larger sense of *Bedeutung* will be the meaningfulness of a gesture that we read back from the situation to which it is precisely a response.[31]

What is the rhetorical situation to which the particular world of vision of Rev. can be perceived as an active response? In addressing this question it must be kept in mind that it is the rhetorical situation that calls forth a particular rhetorical response and not vice versa.

A rhetorical situation is characterized by exigency and urgency. An exigency which cannot be modified through the rhetorical act is not rhetorical. Thus the controlling exigency of the situation specifies the mode of discourse to be chosen and the change to be effected. In other words, any rhetorical discourse obtains its rhetorical character from the exigency and urgency of the situation that generates it. And yet the rhetorical situation is not only marked by urgency but also constituted by two types of constraints: those which affect the audience's decision or action and those which are limitations imposed on the author.[32]

The exigency of the rhetorical situation of Rev. is best characterized by the letter of Pliny to the emperor Trajan:

> In the meanwhile the method I have observed towards those who have been denounced to me as Christians is this: I interrogated them whether they were Christians; if they confessed it I repeated the question twice again adding the threat of capital punishment; if they still persevered, I ordered them to be executed. . . . Those who denied they were, or had ever been Christians, who repeated after me an invocation to the Gods, and offered adoration with wine and frankincense to your image, which I had ordered to be brought for that purpose, together with those of the Gods, and who finally cursed Christ—none of which acts it is said, those who are really Christians can be forced into performing,—these I thought it proper to discharge. Others who were named by that informer, at first confessed themselves Christians and then denied it. . . . They all worshipped your statue and the images of the Gods and cursed Christ.[33]

Pliny states here in plain words what Rev. tells us in images and symbols, especially in chap. 13. Yet Rev. adds another aspect when it stresses that those who do not have the mark of the beast are not able to buy or to sell.[34] Not only threat to life, imprisonment, and execution but also economic deprivation and destitution are to be suffered by those who refuse to take the mark of the beast, that is, to be identified as its followers. Although exegetes are not quite able to explain the mark of the beast and its number,[35] its economic significance is plain. In other words the beast not only threatens the followers of the Lamb with death, but also makes it impossible for them to have enough to live.

Under the Flavians, especially Domitian, the imperial cult was strongly promoted in the Roman provinces. Domitian demanded that the populace acclaim him as "Lord and God" and participate in his worship. The majority of the cities[36] to which the prophetic messages of Rev. are addressed were dedicated to the promotion of the emperor cult. Ephesus was the seat of the proconsul and competed with Pergamum for primacy. Like Smyrna it was a center of the emperor cult, had a great theater, and was famous for its gladiatorial games. Pergamum was the official center of the imperial cult. Already in 29 B.C.E. the city had received permission to build a temple to the "divine Augustus and the goddess Roma," which is probably referred to in Rev. 3:13 by the expression "the throne of Satan." In Thyatira the emperor was worshipped as Apollo incarnate and as the son of Zeus. In 26 C.E. Sardis competed with ten other Asian cities for the right of building a temple in honor of the emperor but lost out to Smyrna. Laodicea was the wealthiest city of Phrygia and had especially prospered under the Flavians.

The Asiarchs, the high priests of the Asian Koinon (assembly), presided over the imperial cult. One high priest was probably elected annually from one of the Asian cities to the most prestigious office a wealthy citizen could aspire to. "These priests wore unusually ornate crowns adorned with miniature busts of the imperial family."[37] In such an environment Christians were bound to experience increasing conflicts with the imperial cult, especially since they claimed Jesus Christ and not the Roman emperor as "their Lord and God." Rev. knows of harassment and persecutions of individual Christians in various localities. It anticipates an increase of persecutions and sufferings for the near future, not least because of the increasing totalitarianism of the reign of Domitian.

This experience of harassment, persecution, and hostility challenged Christians' faith in Christ as Lord. Their experience of hunger, deprivation, pestilence, and war undermined their belief in God's good creation and providence. Christians experienced painfully that their situation in no way substantiated their faith conviction that they already participated in Christ's kingship and power.[38] This tension between theological conviction and experienced reality must have provoked difficult theological questions that seemed to have been addressed differently by leading prophets in the churches of Asia Minor. The Book of Rev. implicitly informs us of such a theological dilemma by arguing against rival Christian apostles and prophets and by indicting the Jewish community as a "synagogue of Satan." In a situation where the leader does not control the production of symbols or where there are competing voices, she or he must defend their message over and against heresies and extend its range of consensual validations.[39] These are the rhetorical constraints on the audience that intensify the exigency of the political situation of Rev.

First, the political situation was aggravated and the necessity to make a decision became more pressing because Jewish Christians like John could less and less claim Jewish political privileges for themselves. Jews had the privilege of practicing their religion in any part of the empire and were exempted from military service and the imperial cult. Under the Flavians, however, their situation had become more precarious. Vespasian ordered that all Jews and proselytes had to pay a special tax to the Romans in place of the tax formerly paid to the Jerusalem temple. Domitian[40] enforced the tax and singled out for payment especially the proselytes and God-fearers who were not Jews by birth. Moreover, Judaism was regarded with suspicion because of its strange customs and refusal to participate in the civil religion of its political environment. After the destruction of Jerusalem and the temple the self-interest of Jewish communities in Asia Minor demanded that they get rid of any potential political "trouble-makers" and "messianic elements" in their midst, and Christians certainly seemed to be among them.[41]

The messages to the churches of Smyrna and Philadelphia reflect this conflict. John's identification of the synagogue as a congregation of Satan should not be misread as anti-Judaism since he has great appreciation for the faith and the symbols of "true Judaism." But apparently true Judaism for him is messianic apocalypticism. As a Jewish Christian John is well aware that the established Jewish communities of Asia Minor could not tolerate the deviance of Christians who seem also to have been poor and powerless in Smyrna and Philadelphia and to have experienced slander from their Jewish communities.[42]

Second, not only among Jews but also among Christians there was a tendency to adapt and acquiesce to the political powers. John bitterly polemicizes against rival Christian prophets in Ephesus, Pergamum, and Thyatira. Ephesus is praised for rejecting "the false apostles" and for its hatred of the works of the Nicolaitans, whereas Pergamum is severely criticized for tolerating those who hold the teachings of Balaam. The community in Thyatira in turn is censured for accepting the influence and teaching of a woman prophet and her school.[43] It is likely that all three code names "Nicolaitans, Balaam, and Jezebel" characterize the same group of Christian prophets who allowed eating food sacrificed to idols and accepted compromise with the emperor cult. This theological stance had great political, economic, and professional advantages for Christians in Asia Minor, for the meat sacrificed to idols was served at meetings of trade guilds and business associations as well as private receptions.[44]

This alternative prophetic position thus proposed a theological compromise that allowed Christian citizens to participate actively in the commercial, political, and social life of their cities. They probably justified their stance with reference to Paul (Rom. 13:1–7). Like Timothy, they might have urged their congregations to make supplications, prayers and intercessions for kings and those in "high places" in order to be able to lead a "quiet and peaceable life, godly and respectful in every way" (1 Tim. 2:2–3). Like 1 Peter[45] they could have admonished: "Fear God. Honor the emperor" (2:17). Since "honoring the image of the emperor" did not demand credal adherence but was a civil-political gesture, some might have argued it was possible to do so without compromising one's faith.

Moreover, to oppose the imperial cult and to refuse participation in socio-religious affairs would mean to take the religious claims of the imperial religion at face value. The religious claims of the emperor and state, on the one hand and the claims of God and Christ on the other hand are not in conflict because both claims belong to a radically different order as is maintained, for example, in John 18:36–38. Jesus Christ's claim to kingship and power is not of a political nature but pertains to the spiritual-religious life of the church, since Christians are taken out of this world and by virtue of their baptism already share in the kingly power of their Lord. No one, not even Satan, can harm the elect for they have insight into the very depth and mystery of the demonic and divine.[46]

In responding to this theological challenge John, like Paul before him, stresses that behind idols stands the demonic power of Satan, the ultimate adversary. No compromise with the imperial cult is possible because God and Christ are the true rulers of the world. John's theological response is rooted in a different social-political experience. He himself seems to have experienced suffering and exile,[47] while the two communities that deserve Christ's praise and receive no censure are obviously poor and without power. Those communities that receive censure are rich, complacent, and do not experience any harassment.[48]

It seems, therefore, that John advocates an uncompromising theological stance toward the imperial religion because, for him and his followers, the dehumanizing powers of Rome and its vassals have become so destructive and oppressive that a compromise with them would mean an affirmation of "those who destroy the earth" (11:18). Therefore Rev. stresses "Christ is alive, although he was killed." Those who will resist the powers of death determining their life will share in the power and glory of Christ. To those who are poor, harassed, and persecuted the promises to the "victor" pledge the essentials of life for the eschatological future: food, clothing, home, citizenship, security, honor, power, glory.[49]

To achieve acceptance for his alternative prophetic stance, however, John did not claim exceptional personal status and authority. He consistently calls himself *doulos* (slave) rather than *prophētēs* (prophet) and places himself emphatically on the same level with the audience (1:9). He also does not write a pseudonymous book appropriating the authority of one of the great prophets or apostles of the past for his message. Neither does he appeal to any church leaders or offices known in the communities of Asia Minor.[50] He does rely on legitimization, but it derives not from human authority but from Christ himself. Like the prophets of old he proclaims: "Thus says the Lord" (as in *tade legei*). Like the apocalyptic seers he creates a symbolic universe that is mythological insofar as it represents a conception of reality that points to the ongoing determination of the world by sacred forces.

A strategic legitimating function of symbolic universe for individual as well as communal life according to P. Berger and T. Luckmann is the "location" of death. It enables individuals to go on living and to anticipate their own deaths with the terror of death sufficiently mitigated.

"Symbolic universe shelters the individual from ultimate terror."[51] The same is true for its social significance: it is a sheltering canopy over institutions and legitimates the political order by reference to a cosmic order of justice and power. With respect to the future it establishes a "common frame of reference" bestowing meaning on the suffering of the community and on individual death. The empirical community is transported to a cosmic plane and made majestically independent of the vicissitudes of individual existence.

Such world construction in myth is primarily occasioned by conflicting definitions of reality which are aggravated if only one party has the power to enforce its own interpretation of reality. This was the case as we have seen in the rhetorical situation of Rev. In constructing a symbolic universe John attempts to maintain the superiority of his prophetic view of reality and of God as well as to help individual Christians face the terror of death. Since the exigency of the situation is defined not just in terms of Roman power but represents political power in cultic terms, the symbolic universe of Rev. needed to appeal to common traditional cultic symbols in order to be competitive. Yet such an appeal was not possible since Christians had no cult, no temples, no priests, no sacrifices.[52] Since John rejects all pagan cultic activity as idolatry and seeks to alienate his audience from the magnificent symbols and cultic drama of the emperor cult, he could not, as Ignatius did, appeal to the symbols and images of the mystery cults. "You are all taking part in a religious procession carrying along with you your God, shrine, Christ, and your holy objects, and decked out from tip to toes in the commandments of Jesus Christ"(Ignatius, *Eph.* 9:2).

Although the open and multivalent images of Rev. have many overtones derived from Greco-Roman society and religion, the dominant tenor of its symbolic language is the cult of Israel. The symbols of temple, priest, sacrifice, garments, headdress, hymns, altar, incense and cultic purity are all derived from Jewish religion. In taking over these traditional Jewish symbols John makes a plea to Jews and Jewish Christians who "own" the tradition to accept him and his vision. At the same time it must be observed that Rev. never uses cultic symbolic language to describe Christian worship and communities. The cultic-religious symbolic language of Israel serves as a "language" to construct the heavenly world and the future where no cultic mediation is necessary anymore.[53] By employing traditional Jewish cultic symbols John seeks not only to alienate his audience from pagan mysteries and the emperor cult, but also to project essential stability, collective coherence, and eternal bliss in order to overcome their experienced alienation.[54]

I have argued that the symbolic universe and action of Rev. is a "fitting" response to its rhetorical situation. It remains to show how the dramatic action of the overall composition fulfills this rhetorical function. According to K. Burke[55] the mythic or ritual structure which follows the form of a cathartic journey moves the audience from alienation through purification to redemption. The first part, which is considered a *viaticum*, is "the way in." It states the primary conditions in terms of which the journey is to be localized or specified in time. This function is fulfilled by the first section, the seven messages of Rev. (1:9—3:21).

The next part within the journey metaphor is the definite "pushing off from shore" and the certainty "of being underway." On a particular journey one can be underway for varying periods of time. Chapters 4—9 culminating in the seventh trumpet take the audience "on the way" of the journey which opened up with the death, resurrection, and exaltation of Christ.

Eventually, according to Burke, one has to arrive at the "withinness of withinness." Here one arrives at knowledge and perception of the tensions (e.g., pollution, psychosis, civil disorder, class conflicts), that is, at the exigency of the rhetorical situation that is symbolized and explored. Chapters 10—14 and 15:2-4 represent structurally this "withinness of withinness" of the symbolic drama of Rev.

From this point on "we are returning" and shall go back to the starting point, but with a "difference" which is constituted by an emotional or intellectual "splitting," a "separating out" which happens in Rev. 15:1—19:10. The last part of the dramatic action completes the journey and the separating-out process. The journey is complete "when the passion (persecution and suffering) has been transformed into an assertion." The book closes with such a "final separating out" and an assertion in 19:11—22:5. Language cannot remove or correct "the brute realities" of the social-political exigency and of religious "tensions," but it can help us to control their destructive effects. In taking his audience on the dramatic-cathartic journey of Rev., John seeks to "move" them to control their fear and to sustain their vision.

Finally, a theological interpretation of the NT has to assess the impact of John's world of vision and dramatic symbolic action on the contemporary reader and audience. W. C. Booth has argued for a revived ethical and political criticism that would "appraise the quality of the response invited by the whole work. What will it do with or to us if we surrender our imaginations to its path?"[56] Critics of Rev. have pointed out that the book preaches vengeance and revenge but not the love of the Sermon on the Mount.[57] It is therefore sub-Christian, the Judas of the NT. I myself in turn have argued that the book is written "with a jail-house" perspective, asking for the realization of God's justice and power. It therefore can only be understood by those "who hunger and thirst for justice."[58]

This dispute can be clarified through the concept of "rhetorical situation" that I have tried to develop here. If the "rhetorical situation" generates a "fitting" response, then Rev. cannot be understood when its "rhetorical situation" no longer "persists." Wherever it persists, however, the book will continue to evoke the same response sought by its author. In other words, wherever a social-political-religious "tension" generated by oppression and persecution persists or re-occurs, the dramatic action of Rev. will have the same cathartic effects it had in its original situation.[59]

Wherever a totally different "rhetorical situation" exists, however, the book no longer elicits a "fitting" response. What I am arguing here is that we should not reduce "the reader" to a timeless, ideal reader because in so doing we essentialize and dehistoricize the book. Rather than pose an abstract reader, we must detect and articulate our own presuppositions, emotions, and reactions to the work in an explicit way, as well as sort out what kind of quality of response becomes dominant in our own reading.

What will Rev. do to us if we surrender our imagination to its dramatic action? For example, the symbols for Rev. for both the oppressive and eschatologically redemptive communities are female because cities were personified as women. Moreover, Rev. symbolizes idolatry in the prophetic and cultic language of Israel as "whoring" or as "defilement with women." In our present rhetorical situation where we have become conscious of androcentric language and its socializing function we can detect a quite different rhetorical function and impact of these symbols. They no longer seek to persuade all Christians to persistent resistance and loyal faithfulness unto death, but they appeal to quite different emotions. Rev. engages the imagination of the contemporary reader to perceive women in terms of good or evil, pure or impure, heavenly or destructive, helpless or powerful, bride or temptress, wife or whore. Rather than instill "hunger and thirst for justice," the symbolic action of Rev. therefore can perpetuate prejudice and injustice if it is not "translated" into a contemporary "rhetorical situation" to which it can be a "fitting" rhetorical response.

NOTES

1. W. Bousset, *Die Offenbarung Johannes* (MeyerK 16; 6th ed.; Göttingen: Vandenhoeck & Ruprecht, 1906) 146.

2. R. H. Mounce, *The Book of Revelation* (Grand Rapids: Wm. B. Eerdmans, 1977) 266; see also I. T. Beckwith, *The Apocalypse of John* (1919; Grand Rapids: Baker Book House, 1967) 653.

3. For a recent review of literature, cf. O. Böcher, *Die Johannesapokalypse* (Erträge

der Forschung 41; Darmstadt: Wissenschaftliche Buchgesellschaft, 1975) 56–63. W. Weicht's "Die dem Lamm folgen: Eine Untersuchung der Auslegungen von Offb. 14, 1–5 in den letzten 80 Jahren" (Diss.: Pont. Univ. Gregorianae, Rome, 1969) was not available to me.

4. See chap. 1 of this book on "History and Eschatology in Revelation," and chap. 6 on "Composition and Structure of Revelation."

5. See chap. 3 of this book on "The Quest for the Johannine School," and chap. 5 on "Apokalypsis and Propheteia."

6. For the distinction between text and subtext, cf. F. R. Jameson, "The Symbolic Inference; or Kenneth Burke and Ideological Analysis," in *Representing Kenneth Burke* (ed. H. White and M. Brose; Baltimore: Johns Hopkins Univ. Press, 1982) 68–91.

7. N. Perrin, "Eschatology and Hermeneutics," *JBL* 93 (1974) 1–15, esp. 10.

8. Cf. P. Wheelwright, *Metaphor and Reality* (6th ed.; Bloomington, Ind.: Univ. of Indiana Press, 1975). See also N. Perrin, *Jesus and the Language of the Kingdom* (Philadelphia: Fortress Press, 1976) 21–32.

9. See my article, "The Phenomenon of Early Christian Apocalyptic: Some Reflections on Method," in *Apocalypticism in the Mediterranean World and the Near East* (ed. D. Hellholm; Tübingen: Mohr/Siebeck, 1983) 295–316, for a discussion of this problem.

10. M. Stuart, *Commentary on the Apocalypse* (2 vols.; New York: Van Nostrand & Terrett, 1845) 2: 502–3.

11. Ibid., 1: 202.

12. P. S. Minear, *I Saw a New Earth. A Complete New Study and Translation of the Book of Revelation* (Washington, D.C.: Corpus Books, 1968) 246.

13. Ibid., 233.

14. Ibid., 246.

15. J. Ellul, *Apocalypse. The Book of Revelation* (New York: Seabury Press, 1977), 189.

16. E. Lohmeyer, *Die Offenbarung des Johannes* (2d ed.; Tübingen: Mohr/Siebeck, 1953); H. Schlier, "Zum Verständnis der Geschichte nach der Offenbarung des Johannes," in *Die Zeit der Kirche* (Freiburg: Herder, 1958) 265–74; "Jesus Christus und die Geschichte nach der Offenbarung des Johannes," in *Besinnung auf das Neue Testament* (Freiburg: Herder, 1964) 358–75.

17. Cf. R. Barthes, *Critique et Vérité* (Paris: Éditions de Seuil, 1966), 50, and P. Rosenthal, "Deciphering S/Z," *College English* 37 (1965) 133.

18. W. Heyman, "Indeterminacy in Literary Criticism," *Soundings* 59 (1976) 352.

19. The "indeterminacy" of meaning is given in the text: On the one hand Mount Zion is clearly distinguished from "heaven," for while the voice comes "from heaven" the 144,000 stand on Mount Zion. Nevertheless, the issue is not clear-cut, since the 144,000 are also characterized as "following the Lamb" who stands before the throne of God in "heaven" (cf. Rev. 5) or shares God's throne in the New Jerusalem.

20. Cf. 2 Kings 19:20–34; Isa. 11:9–12; 23; 24; 25:7–10; Zeph. 3:13; Mic. 4:6–8; or Joel 2:32.

21. Cf., e.g., *4 Esdras* 13:25–50; *2 Apoc. Bar.* 40:1–2 or *4 Esdras* 2:42–47.

22. See K. Burke, *The Philosophy of Literary Form: Studies in Symbolic Action* (New York: Vintage Books, 1956); idem, *A Grammar of Motives and a Rhetoric of Motives* (Cleveland: Meridian Books, 1962). For an elaboration and discussion of Burke's work, see esp. W. H. Rueckert, *Kenneth Burke and the Drama of Human Relations* (Berkeley and Los Angeles: Univ. of California Press, 1982) and H. D. Duncan, *Communication and Social Order* (New York: Bedminster Press, 1962).

23. A. Wilder, *Theopoetic: Theology and Religious Imagination* (Philadelphia: Fortress Press, 1976) 79. I presented this paper in a much shorter and less developed form at the SBL annual meeting in 1980, and I would like to thank Professor A. Wilder for his very helpful response to the earlier form.

24. See H. D. Duncan, *Language and Literature in Society* (Chicago: Univ. of Chicago Press, 1953) 109–10.

25. See my book *Invitation to the Book of Revelation* (Garden City, N.Y.: Doubleday & Co., 1981) 107–50. For different understandings of this section, see the review of L. Lambrecht, "A Structuration of Revelation 4, 1—22, 5," in *L'Apocalypse johannique et l'Apocalyptique dans le Nouveau Testament* (BETL 53; Louvain: The Univ. Press, 1980) 77–104.

26. Rev. 5:9 which speaks about the redemption of Christians uses *agorazein* with *ek*. See chap. 2 of this book, "Redemption as Liberation."

27. D. Guthrie, "The Lamb in the Structure of the Book of Revelation," *Vox Evangelica* 12 (1981) 64–71.

28. For a review of interpretations given to this difficult passage, see C. H. Lindijer, "Die Jungfrauen in der Offenbarung des Johannes XIV 4," in *Studies in John: Festschrift J. N. Sevenster* (NovTSup 24; Leiden: E. J. Brill, 1970) 124–42.

29. A. Yarbro Collins (*The Apocalypse* [NTM 22; Wilmington, Del.: Michael Glazier, 1979] 100) suggests that the approval of celibacy in Rev. might have been inspired by the Israelite traditions of holy war and priesthood. John's exclusively male terminology is therefore explainable since only men were warriors and priests in Israel.

30. Rather than to see *parthenoi* in the context of the symbolic action in Rev., Lindijer seeks to connect the word with all the other passages in the NT, contemporary Jewish, and early Christian writings which speak about virgins/virginity/celibacy.

31. Jameson, "The Symbolic Inference," 83.

32. See esp. L. F. Bitzer, "The Rhetorical Situation," in *Rhetoric: A Tradition in Transition* (ed. W. R. Fisher, East Lansing, Mich.: Michigan State Univ. Press, 1974) 247–60.

33. *Letters* X.96. Pliny the Younger, *Letters* (Loeb Classical Library; Cambridge: Harvard Univ. Press, 1969) 2: 401–2.

34. Cf. also A. Yarbro Collins, "The Political Perspective of the Revelation to John," *JBL* 96 (1966) 252–54.

35. For a review, see Böcher, *Die Johannesapokalypse*, 84–87; B. Reicke, "Die jüdische Apokalyptik und die johanneische Tiervision," *RSR* 60 (1972) 189–91; W. G. Baines, "The Number of the Beast in Revelation 13:18," *HeyJ* 16 (1975) 195–96.

36. See W. M. Ramsay, *The Letters to the Seven Churches of Asia* (New York: A. C. Armstrong & Son, 1904); E. Yamauchi, *The Archeology of New Testament Cities in Western Asia Minor* (Grand Rapids: Baker Book House, 1980); C. J. Hemer, "Unto the Angels of the Churches," *BH* 11 (1975) 4–27, 56–83, 110–35, 164–90.

37. Yamauchi, *The Archeology*, 110.

38. For the elaboration of this traditional Christian self-understanding, see my work in *Priester für Gott. Studien zum Herrschafts- und Priestmotiv in der Apokalypse* (NTAbh 7; Münster: Aschendorff, 1972) 168–290.

39. Cf. Duncan (*Language and Literature*, 87) stresses the "persuasive functions of symbols in the production of cooperative and non-cooperative attitudes."

40. E. M. Smallwood, "Domitian's Attitude Towards the Jews and Judaism," *Classical Philology* 51 (1956) 1–13; P. Keresztes, "The Jews, the Christians, and Emperor Domitian," *VC* 27 (1973) 1–28.

41. See M. Hengel, "Messianische Hoffnung und politischer 'Radikalismus' in der

'jüdisch-hellenistischen Diaspora,'" in *Apocalypticism in the Mediterranean World,* 655–86. For the "muted and fragmentary form" of apocalyptic elements in rabbinic literature, cf. A. J. Saldarini, "The Uses of Apocalyptic in the Mishna and Tosepta," *CBQ* 39 (1977) 396–409.

42. It is debated whether the author has Jewish or Jewish-Christian communities in mind. H. Kraft (*Die Offenbarung des Johannes* [HNT 16a; Tübingen: Mohr/Siebeck, 1974] 61) thinks of a Jewish-Christian group which seeks to avoid persecution by calling themselves "Jews." This is not stated in the text, however.

43. For a discussion of Jezebel and the Nicolaitans, see chap. 4 of this book, "Apocalyptic and Gnosis." Today, however, I would be more hesitant to characterize this group as "gnosticizing."

44. See also Mounce, *The Book of Revelation,* 102–4.

45. See, however, N. Brox, *Der erste Petrusbrief* (EKKNT 21; Neukirchen-Vluyn: Neukirchener Verlag, 1979) 116–17. He argues that v. 17 is traditional and not formulated by the author of 1 Peter. Yet the statement fits well in the overall context of the household-code *(Haustafel)* admonitions as D. Balch (*Let Wives Be Submissive: The Domestic Code in 1 Peter* [SBLMS 26; Chico, Calif.: Scholars Press, 1981]) has elaborated.

46. See chap. 4 of this book, "Apocalyptic and Gnosis."

47. For such an understanding, see Ramsay, *The Letters to the Seven Churches,* 82–92. Kraft argues, however, that John went to Patmos in order to have a revelatory experience (*Die Offenbarung des Johannes,* 40–41). His argument is not convincing.

48. The communities in Smyrna and Philadelphia were powerless and poor. These two communities receive only praise.

49. See also D. Georgi, "Die Visionen vom himmlischen Jerusalem," in *Kirche: Festschrift für G. Bornkamm zum 75, Geburtstag* (ed. D. Lührmann and G. Strecker; Tübingen: Mohr/Siebeck, 1980) 351–72.

50. See chap. 5 of this book, "Apokalypsis and Propheteia." See also D. E. Aune, "The Social Matrix of the Apocalypse of John," *BR* 36 (1981) 16–32. Aune, however, misrepresents my proposal.

51. P. L. Berger and T. Luckmann, *The Social Construction of Reality: A Treatise in the Sociology of Knowledge* (Garden City, N.Y.: Doubleday & Co., Anchor Books, 1967) 102.

52. See my "Cultic Language in Qumran and in the New Testament," *CBQ* 38 (1976) 159–77.

53. See my book, *Priester für Gott,* 397–416.

54. For the stabilizing effect of ritual and cult, see M. Douglas, *Natural Symbols* (New York: Vintage Books, 1973) and the review of her work by R. Isenberg and D. E. Owen, "Bodies, Natural and Contrived: The Work of Mary Douglas," *RelSRev* 3 (1977) 1–16.

55. K. Burke, "Othello: An Essay to Illustrate a Method," *Hudson Review* 4 (1951) 165–203; cf. Rueckert, *Kenneth Burke,* 208–26.

56. W. C. Booth, "Freedom of Interpretation: Baktin and the Challenge of Feminist Criticism," *Critical Inquiry* 9 (1982) 45–76, esp. 59.

57. See esp. A. Yarbro Collins, "Revelation 18: Taunt-Song or Dirge," in *L'Apocalypse johannique et l'Apocalyptic dans le Nouveau Testament* (ed. J. Lambrecht; BETL 53; Louvain: The Univ. Press, 1980) 204.

58. See esp. my *Invitation to the Book of Revelation* for a perspective on my interpretation.

59. This explains why the political left as well as the political right can appeal to the book. It is therefore important in preaching and teaching to elaborate the original "rhetorical situation" of Rev. Since it does not address a democratic and highly technologized society, the book would be misunderstood if it were seen, e.g., as advocating political quietism and resignation in the face of the possible nuclear devastation of the world.

Epilogue

THE RHETORICALITY OF APOCALYPSE AND
THE POLITICS OF INTERPRETATION[1]

With the closure of one and the arrival of the next millennium,[2] interest in apocalyptic in general and in the Apocalypse of John or the Book of Revelation in particular is bound to increase. This new edition of my work seeks to contribute to the millennial discourse at the turn of the century. However, to do so means to participate in a hegemonic Christian discourse which is oblivious to the different periodizations of time and history found in other cultures and religions. Hence it is especially important to underscore the rhetorical-political dimensions of this millennial discourse, which has been shaped significantly by the visionary rhetoric of the Book of Revelation.

The essays collected in this new edition[3] examine Revelation's visionary rhetoric in various ways. They span three decades of scholarship on Revelation.[4] During this period a paradigm shift took place in biblical studies in general and Apocalypse studies in particular. This shift entails a displacement of the hegemony of literalist-positivist, historical- and literary- (i.e., source criticism) "scientific" method, and essentialist, universalist, or salvation historical interpretations. This hegemony has been replaced by multiple approaches and multihued hermeneutical-theological perspectives. To elucidate the shift from a "scientific-positivist"[5] to a rhetorical-political paradigm I will focus on a feminist hermeneutical debate in the study of Revelation that is of methodological significance to biblical studies in general. The disagreements between different readings of Revelation, I argue, can be adjudicated only in a rhetorical-political paradigm of inquiry and not in a "literalist" scientific one.

In a first step I will therefore sketch the basic tenets of such a rhetorical-political paradigm of interpretation.[6] With the theoretical frame in place, in a second step I will return to the feminist controversy concerning how to read the gendered polysemic language of Revelation and explore its ramifications with regard to a particular text. The feminist debate over the misogynism of Revelation and the theoretical issues and assumptions undergirding this debate can serve to explore the methodological issues that surface in a rhetorical paradigm of interpretation.

THE RHETORICALITY[7] OF REVELATION
AND ITS INTERPRETATION

The essays of this volume reflect 30 years of scholarly discussion and research on the last book of the Christian Testament.[8] The first essay (chapter 1) was published in 1968 when I was still a doctoral student. A different form of the last one (Epilogue) was prepared for the 1997 SBL seminar on Reading the Apocalypse, which under the leadership of David Barr has over the years provided a receptive forum for the discussion of my work.[9] These essays utilize different methods of analysis in order to make sense not only of the book's multivalent language and mythic imagery but also of the multifarious scholarly attempts to understand it. Together they have pioneered a rhetorical paradigm shift in Apocalypse research[10] and contributed to its taking hold in other areas of Christian Testament studies.

Toward a Political-Rhetorical Paradigm[11]
As historical-critical studies, form and redaction criticism, the methods that I employed in my early work,[12] already implicitly use a literary-rhetorical analysis insofar as they look for the forms and arguments of a writing as well as for its *"Sitz im Leben,"* i.e., the generative rhetorical situation of literary forms and texts. However, since they are critical studies indebted to the Enlightenment, they also share in the Enlightenment's "scientific" ethos, which negates rhetorical argument and obscures the power relations that constitute it.[13] While some of the methodological issues raised first in these essays have become commonplace in Apocalypse research, others are still disputed. For instance, the structuralist notion of apocalyptic genre, which was in vogue when this collection was first published,[14] has given way to the more pragmatic-rhetorical understanding of the literary form of apocalypses. Too, my contention that the epistolary frame is crucial for the understanding of Revelation as a prophetic-apocalyptic book is now widely accepted in one form or another.[15] Moreover, the essentialist, transhistorical, and universalist hermeneutical approach that was predominant in midcentury has widely been replaced by a careful focus on particular historical, literary, and ideological features of Revelation, although generalizing statements in the fashion of a liberal universalizing humanism are still sometimes at work.

Furthermore, the salvation historical interpretation, which interprets chapters 4–11 as referring either to the history of Israel or to the time of the Jewish Christian community and chapter 12–22 as referring either to that of church and humanity or to that of the universal church in the end-time, is generally abandoned today. Yet this dualistic division of the book into two discrete parts is still championed widely, albeit with different hermeneutical underpinnings. Thus my proposal for a concentric, conic-spiraling composition of Revelation has been generally recognized but it has not been able to dislodge the dual structure approach. Yet, in a rhetorical paradigm of interpretation, one does not need to claim that only one structuration is correct and all the others are wrong. While having to decide for one definite overall structuration in order to be able to interpret the book, one nevertheless can appreciate the rich multiplicity of outlines, all of which shed new light on the book's different aspects.

To give another example: Already in 1973 I had argued that the polemics against the Nicolaitans, the followers of "Jezebel" and of "Baalam," must be understood as integral to the overall polemics of the book.[16] But whereas I have maintained that this intramural polemics is based on a different attitude toward accommodation with Roman imperial power, more recently scholars have utilized this argument in order to bolster the "perceived crisis"[17] or "no crisis at all"[18] reading of the rhetorical-historical situation that Revelation addresses. In a recent article Harry O. Maier, for instance, elaborates this intramural argument in sectarian[19] terms:

> Consequently chapter 17 recasts in the role of the harlot the rhetorically named Jezebel of Rev 2:20, whose colorful Hebrew Bible career includes the charge of harlotry. . . . In this parodic, fantastic cast of characters, the alleged idolaters of Rev 2:14-15, 20-22 thus unsuspectingly encounter themselves not only sharing the character of the one drunk on the blood of its model citizens—namely, the Christian community to whom they would appeal by their alleged false prophecy—but also excluded from the heavenly city. The similarity of depiction functions rhetorically to persuade John's wavering audience to resist his opponents' teaching.[20]

While I have read John's polemics against his prophetic rivals as attempting to persuade the audience to follow John's politics of consistent resistance and thus as crucial for the persuasive power of Revelation's argument against the Roman empire, other scholars have tended to make this intramural, sectarian argument the primary rationale for John's polemics against his internal opponents. Rather than speaking to a situation of oppression, powerlessness, and destruction, John's sole concern allegedly is to prove that he and not the prophet called "Jezebel" is the true prophet and leader of the community.[21] At stake here is a political reading which such a politics of interpretation displaces with a sectarian parochial one.[22]

Feminist scholars of Revelation also have taken up my argument but have made John's polemics against "Jezebel" the predominant hermeneutical key for the whole book. They have argued that Revelation is a misogynist tract, which advocates the dehumanization of wo/men[23] and eradicates them from its community because the only actual historical wo/man mentioned is vilified. Tina Pippin's work,[24] which is an original and creative attempt to reread the Book of Revelation in and through the unmasking of its gender codes, has greatly contributed to such a reading of Revelation. Hence, the growing consensus among feminist scholars regarding the feminine figures of Revelation is best summarized in Pippin's own words:

> Females in the Apocalypse are few but noticeable, and their future is prophesied. The prophetess Jezebel and her unrepentant followers will be thrown upon a bed and will die (2:22-23). The Whore of Babylon is dethroned and made desolate and totally destroyed, as the ceremonial lines proclaim: "Fallen, fallen is Babylon, the great."(18:2). Even the Woman Clothed with the Sun is "banished" for protection and safekeeping to the wilderness. . . . The female becomes the absent cause—the cause of both evil and good—but nonetheless is erased from the text. The bride image (the New Jerusalem) alone is left standing, but only briefly; she is replaced by the imagery of the city. . . . I want to show that all females in the Apocalypse are victims; they are objects of desire and violence because they are all stereotyped archetypal images of the female. . . .[25]

At another place she sums up her reading of Rev. 17–18: "Having studied the evils of Roman imperial policy in the colonies, I found the violent destruction of Rome very cathartic. But when I looked in the face of Rome, I saw a *woman*."[26]

Contrary to such a naturalized reading simply in terms of gender, I have argued that the androcentrism of Revelation is conventional. Without question the rhetoric of Revelation is determined by its masculine language. The question is whether such gendered language functions as exclusive of wo/men or as inclusive generic language. If one reads the androcentric language of Revelation as exclusive, one comes for instance to the conclusion that there are no wo/men sharing in the New Jerusalem.[27] If one reads the language of Revelation as conventional, generic language in an inclusive way, one can comprehend the rhetoric of the book as shaping the desire of both wo/men and men but not of all wo/men and men.

In other words, any gender analysis that does not reflect on the constructedness and inflection of gender in and through relations of domination is in danger of becoming apolitical. Like any other text, Revelation needs to be analyzed critically as to its rhetorical strategies and the power relations it inscribes. Rather than, for instance, evaluating Revelation's symbolic depiction of Babylon and its destruction simply in terms of gender, one must explore what kind of different effects identification with the image of Babylon, the Great City, would have had if the hearer or reader were, for example, a Roman slave or a Jewish freeborn wo/man in the first century.

If one reads Revelation as an argument that depends on its rhetorical-historical situation, one can investigate and critically assess its power of persuasion. Rather than focus on "woman" in Revelation, one must explore its politics of meaning in order to adjudicate whether the discourses of Revelation are misogynist. To do so one needs to investigate whether and how much the rhetoric of Revelation shares in the hegemonic discourses of domination and dehumanization. If one situates the adjudication of the meaning of Revelation not on the level of text but on the level of interpretation, one can perceive the differences in the interpretation of Revelation as epistemological differences. An ethics of interpretation accordingly has the task of critically reflecting on the theoretical frameworks or "lenses" and their implications for understanding Revelation's rhetoric. Hence, before I take up the feminist hermeneutical debate in more detail, I need first to clarify what I mean by a rhetorics and ethics of inquiry.

Toward a Rhetorics and Ethics of Inquiry

By asserting that a given interpretation of the text represents an objective, value-free, disinterested "scientific" reading, "scientific" exegesis claims to be able to comprehend the definitive meaning intended by the author and to overcome its own perspectival understandings. Admittedly, exegetical commentary is not free from rhetorical argument, but such argument must be restricted to showing how competing interpretations have misread the text as well as to establishing a single and true meaning. Yet "scientific" exegesis not only enables the correct understanding of Revelation and its historical contexts, but also closures its multivalent meanings. It does not acknowledge and reflect upon the fact that it interacts with the text from a particular sociopolitical and religious-theological location. Consequently, it remains oblivious to the fact that it engages not just in hermeneutical but also in rhetorical practices.

A rhetorics of inquiry asserts to the contrary that in the act of interpretation one does not just understand and comprehend texts and symbols (hermeneutics) but also produces new meanings by interacting with them and the audience one seeks to persuade. As

Lorraine Code puts it, rhetorical "discourse becomes a poiesis, a way of representing experience, reality, that remakes and alters it in the process."[28] Biblical scholarship as a rhetorical or communicative practice must show how biblical texts and their contemporary interpretations are political and religious discursive practices. Authorial aims, point of view, narrative strategies, persuasive means, and authorial closure, as well as audience perceptions and constructions, are rhetorical practices that have determined not only the production of Revelation but also its subsequent interpretations.[29]

Such an understanding of rhetoric/rhetorical as a persuasive, communicative practice of interpretation that involves interests, values, and visions must be carefully distinguished from its popular use. Popular parlance often labels those statements as "rhetoric/rhetorical" which it believes to be "mere talk," stylistic figure, or deceptive propaganda, as a clever form of speech that is not true and honest but rather lacks any substance. Rhetoric is often misunderstood as "mere" rhetoric, as stylistic ornament, technical device, or linguistic manipulation, as discourse utilizing irrational, emotional devices that are contrary to critical thinking and reasoning. When I use the terms *rhetoric, rhetoricity, rhetorical,* I do not use them in this colloquial sense.

I also do not conceive of rhetorical analysis as just one more mode of literary or structural analysis. Rather I understand it as a means for analyzing how Revelation and its interpretations participate in creating or sustaining oppressive or liberating theo-ethical values and sociopolitical practices. In distinction to formalist, structuralist, or aesthetic literary approaches, a critical rhetorics insists that context is as important as text. What we see depends on where we stand. One's social location or rhetorical context is decisive for how one sees the world, constructs reality, or interprets biblical texts. Biblical scholarship that continues to subscribe to a value-neutral epistemology covertly advocates an apolitical reading of canonical texts and does not take responsibility for its political assumptions and interests.

Once biblical scholarship begins to acknowledge its own social locations and interests, whether of race, gender, nation, or class, scholars will be held accountable as to why they privilege one particular interpretation over other possible readings. Competing interpretations of Revelation are not simply either right or wrong; rather, they constitute different ways of reading and constructing sociohistorical and theo-ethical meanings. Not detached value-neutrality but an explicit articulation of one's rhetorical strategies, interested perspectives, ethical criteria, theoretical frameworks, religious presuppositions, and sociopolitical locations for critical public discussion are appropriate in a rhetorical paradigm of biblical scholarship.

Hence, a rhetorics[30] of inquiry cannot limit itself to analyzing the text of Revelation but must attend to the argumentative discourses of contemporary scholarship and their theoretical presuppositions, social locations, investigative methods, and sociopolitical functions. In distinction from aesthetic, structuralist, and psychological literary criticism, which works with a "deeper" archetypal meaning of gender and conceptualizes a rhetorical-political analysis in universalizing terms, rhetorical criticism stresses the importance of a speech context and sociohistorical matrix for understanding the persuasive force of the various arguments of scholars.

> Treating each other's claims as arguments rather than findings, scholars no longer need implausible doctrines of objectivism to defend their contributions to knowledge. At a practical level, to stress rhetoric is to discount claims to neutrality. . . . Detailed attention to rhetoric can reveal underlying issues and better ways to consider them responsibly. It also fosters more effective thinking, speaking and acting by . . . students and by audiences outside the academy.[31]

Feminist epistemological studies have greatly contributed to the revival of such a cross-disciplinary rhetorics of inquiry.[32] Nevertheless, their pioneering contributions are almost never recognized. For instance, in a most recent discussion in a 1997 SBL Seminar paper on "The Rhetorics of Revelation," Robert Royalty does not mention once that I have for a long time advocated and developed a rhetorical approach to Revelation.[33] This neglect of feminist epistemological work becomes understandable when one considers the negative "feminine" gendering of both rhetoric and religion in the anti-rhetorical discourses of philosophy and science.[34] Like wo/men, religion and rhetoric figure as the excluded or idealized "other" in modern Western discourses. Like wo/men, both religion and rhetoric are reduced to emotion and passion, to style devoid of substance by the modern rationalist tradition. They are identified with custom, fiction, or colorful ornament, likened to opium and pie in the sky, or associated with trickery and treachery.[35] Throughout the centuries, wo/men not only were excluded from public speaking and academic institutions, but "woman" also became a rhetorical figure of exclusion and subordination that has the function of containing not only religious but also rhetorical discourses and their unruly sociopolitical possibilities.

Not only religion and theology but also rhetoric has been coded as "feminine other" in contrast to the masculine "hard" sciences. Coded as feminine, theology and rhetoric have been banished by the Enlightenment university to the margins of intellectual activity and public discourses. This marginalization and suppression of rhetoric has been achieved in part through its feminization. According to a well-known maxim, "facts are masculine, and words are feminine." Like wo/men, rhetoric is said to be about ornamentation and seduction. Rhetoric has been called "the harlot of the arts" who needs to be kept in place and under surveillance so that it will not corrupt the chaste mind of masculine science and inflict upon its adherents relativistic opinion in place of the certainty of scientific or religious truth.

Like the proverbial "bad girl," rhetoric is said to play loose with scientific truth and objective fact, and like the virtuous wife, "good rhetoric" has been confined to departments of preaching in theological schools.[36] Thus metaphor, trope, and manner of speaking have been gendered in the anti-rhetorical Western tradition and likened to the treacherousness of wo/men. False eloquence reminds one of the garrulousness and endless gossiping of wo/men, whereas decorum demands that an orator not speak with the small and shrill voice of a woman.[37] However, it must not be overlooked that this gendered discourse on rhetorics and religion does not speak about actual wo/men but about feminine metaphorization.

Biblical criticism, as I have argued elsewhere,[38] has also remained in the captivity of empiricist-positivist science for far too long insofar as it has until now spent much of its energy applying to and reinscribing into Christian Testament texts ancient rhetorical categories, disciplinary technologies, esthetic stylistics, and the scattered prescriptions of oratorical handbooks in antiquity.[39] Hence one could ask the following rhetorical question also of biblical studies in general and those on Revelation in particular:

> When respectable academics come to rhetoric's abode, have they really abandoned their old faith in the mythical value-freedom of academic discourse? Or do they entertain a hope of transforming rhetoric into a practice that pious ex-positivists can embrace in good conscience, while they continue to devalue the passions and logic of the political (and religious) economy?[40]

The resistance of biblical studies to a rhetorics of inquiry becomes even more intelligible when one considers that beginning with Plato and Aristotle not only logic but also rhetoric had strong links with political conservatism and has legitimated relations of domination.[41] Although Aristotle developed an elaborate theory of rhetoric,[42] he kept it in place as an imperfect system, subordinate to science and reason in which freeborn wo/men had only a partial and slave wo/men had no share at all.

Although they differ in their politics of inquiry, most of the recent studies of Revelation recognize the symbolic-rhetorical character of Revelation's language and imagery. Nevertheless, they do not always affirm the paradigm shift from a "scientific," descriptive, reflective, representational, and propositional understanding of Revelation's language to a constructive, evocative and rhetorical one as most appropriate for understanding the book's symbolic universe. To reduce a critical rhetorical-political approach to "social functionalism," as Leonard Thompson does,[43] is a gross misreading of this paradigm shift. In a rhetorical understanding, language is not a straitjacket into which our thoughts must be forced nor is it a naturalized, closed, gendered linguistic system. Rather, it is a medium that is shaped by its sociopolitical contexts and that changes in different sociopolitical locations.[44]

A rhetorical criticism recognizes that grammatically androcentric language can function either as "natural," as gender specific, or as generic inclusive language. I have proposed the following four socio-linguistic assumptions as crucially important for a rhetorical-political understanding of the rhetoricity of Revelation.[45]

1. Language and knowledge of the world are rhetorical. That is, they are articulated in specific situations, by particular people, for a certain audience and with certain interests in mind. This is the reason that a critical rhetorics and ethics of inquiry must pursue a hermeneutics of suspicion with regard to biblical texts understood as rhetorical texts, their persuasive narrative worlds, and their ideological functions for inculcating the Western kyriarchal order. Such a hermeneutics of suspicion is an interpretive activity through which thinking "escapes the power of the linguistic even while it is itself linguistically constituted."[46]

2. Grammatically androcentric/kyriocentric language is not simply reflective or descriptive of reality but, as an ideological production, it is also regulative. A hermeneutics of suspicion insists that practices of understanding the "world," such as speaking, writing, reading, or reasoning, are never outside of language or outside of time and history; that is, they are never transcendentally located outside of the "world." Hence a rhetorics of inquiry focuses on the ambiguity and instability of grammatically gendered language and text and works with a theory of language that does not assume linguistic determinism. It understands language as a convention or tool that enables writers and readers to negotiate linguistic tensions and inscribed ambiguities and thereby to create meaning in specific contexts and socio-political locations.

3. Language is not just polysemic, performative, and constructive-poetic: it is political. Language shapes and is shaped by precon-

structed notions of kyriarchal reality or of how the world "really" is. For that reason, a critical intratextual analysis of the language and rhetoric of texts does not suffice. It must be complemented by a critical systemic analysis of sociopolitical and religious structures of domination and exclusion. Consequently, a hermeneutics of suspicion is called for that interrogates not only how the text but also how the reader is linguistically constituted. It does not reduce text or reader to an ahistorical core, to the "truth" or to "human nature," but seeks to understand them as produced in or against the interest of kyriarchal relations of domination; that is, it understands them sociopolitically.

4. Taking up my rhetorical and political emphasis as crucial for understanding Revelation's grammatically incorrect, bizarre, and extraordinary anti-language,[47] Allen Dwight Callahan has called for a "nonrepresentational criticism" in Apocalypse studies that is indebted to postcolonial theories and practices.[48] Utilizing postcolonial criticism, he has shown that the language of the oppressor can be subversively used by those disenfranchised to construct an alternate symbolic universe and understanding of the world. For instance, for the Rastafarians, a prophetic messianic sect of Jamaica, biblical language functions, as Theophus Smith has pointed out, "iconically to configure and reconfigure Jamaican history and ongoing experience."[49] According to Callahan, the Rastafarians do not use the language of the King James Bible typologically or allegorically but as a "nonrepresentational glossary of reality" and "counter-hegemonic lexicon."[50]

In short, a rhetorics of inquiry understands the persuasive power of Revelation's anti-imperial discourse in terms of rhetorical convention, compositional arrangement, social location, and the speaker-audience relationship. It analyzes Revelation as a moment of rhetorical exchange and cultural-religious argumentation between John and his audience, a moment that is determined by their common sociopolitical and cultural-religious situation. Thus it pays special attention to the constraints placed on Revelation's rhetorical discourse by its socio-cultural-religious location and rhetorical situation.

Consequently a rhetorics and ethics of inquiry must first of all critically analyze whether proposed interpretations do justice to the text's rhetoric. It must critically ask, for instance, whether interpretations of Revelation reinscribe the kyriarchal sex/gender system or whether they interrupt its ideological strategies. Such a rhetorics of inquiry concurs with postmodern discourse analysis in that all texts, interpretations, and historical reconstructions are relative and perspectival. If what one sees depends on where one stands, social-ideological loca-

tion and rhetorical context are as decisive as text for how one reconstructs historical reality or interprets biblical texts. The sociopolitical locations and interests of interpreters determine all knowledge
production on Revelation.

By understanding different interpretations as discursive arguments that construct reality and are shaped by it, one can place into
the center of attention their politics of interpretation and develop
an ethics of reading. In the following I will return to the feminist
debate on how to read the androcentric/kyriocentric gendered language of Revelation and engage the rhetorics of inquiry for exploring its implications for research on Revelation. However, it must not
be overlooked that the debate on how to read the gendered language of Revelation is part of a broader feminist discussion on the
basic categories of analysis. Whereas white Western feminist scholars
have stressed gender as a basic category of analysis, feminist subaltern and postcolonial studies have argued that gender is one of various multiplicative, interactive ideological categories of oppression
that determine wo/men's identity. In other words what "wo/man"
or "gender" means is differently constructed depending on one's
positioning within kyriarchal power relations.[51]

READING THE RHETORICAL POLITICS
(REV. 17–18)

I return to the feminist discussion of and disagreement about the
misogynism of Revelation in order to stage a rhetorical debate on
the politics of interpretation and the theoretical frames of meaning[52] produced by different reading paradigms. In so doing I do not
seek to prove that my own interpretation is the superior one. Rather
I want to elucidate that all interpretations are perspectival and
determined by their sociohistorical location. Although it is not usually admitted because of the scientistic ethos of the academy, one
always must choose a perspective and standpoint from where to
read, if one wants to make sense out of the polyvalence of the text.
Hence it becomes important to reflect critically and assess the
hermeneutical ramifications of such a choice.

Moreover I want to explore and investigate this rhetorical
debate not just on exegetical or feminist grounds but also in
terms of the methodological issues raised by a rhetorics of inquiry.
I am not interested here in an apologetic defense of Revelation
that denies the powerful negative impact of the book's androcentric, or better, kyriocentric,[53] i.e., lord/ master/ father/ husband,
i.e. elite-male-centered, language and symbolic universe.[54]
Rather, I want to point out that the interpretation of Revelation

depends on the theoretical lenses and methodological approaches employed.

In short, I refer to this feminist debate in order to argue that the Book of Revelation cannot be adequately understood through an analysis simply in terms of gender because gender is always constructed and inflected by relations of domination. This does not mean that it is not important to study the "conventional" gendered metaphors and language of the book. I do not want to argue that they have not and do not produce misogynist readings, because they have done so and continue to do so. Instead I want to stress that one must avoid absolutizing and universalizing gender as basic category of analysis. Hence one must look carefully at both Revelation's and one's own frames of meaning and their understanding of language "as a reality-generating system."[55]

Reading Gender in Revelation

In her contribution to the *Women's Bible Commentary* Susan Garrett has elaborated the significance of reading Revelation in terms of gender:

> Each of these symbols reflects the male-centered view of the first century: women are caricatured as virgins, whores or mothers. . . . The stereotyped feminine images in the book do not represent the full spectrum of authentic womanhood, either in John's day or in our own. . . . Exploring the cultural roots of John's metaphoric language about women will enable us to understand what he was trying to say at those points, but the dehumanizing way in which he phrased his message will remain deeply troubling.[56]

This statement clearly indicates that Garrett does not differentiate between actual wo/men and the feminine as trope or metaphor. She equates wo/men as persons with the stereotyped feminine images of Revelation. Tina Pippin also seems to remain within the boundaries of the naturalizing sex/gender system when she identifies Revelation's female-feminine symbols and images—such as mother, whore, and bride—with "real women." She repeatedly states that she wants to focus on "real women," in order to uncover the misogyny of the text. However, she then goes on to read the female images of the Apocalypse as feminine archetypes[57]:

> I want to focus on the clearly identified women in the text who are destroyed and on the general "apocalypse of women" brought about in the utopian vision of the New Jerusalem. By the "apocalypse of women" I mean the misogyny and disenfranchisement

that are at the root of gender relations, accompanied by (het-
ero)sexism and racism along with violence, poverty, disempower-
ment and fear. . . . The text of the Apocalypse, with its female
archetypes of good and evil, virgin and whore is an account of a
political and religious and also gender crisis of the end of the first
century C.E.[58]

My objection to such an approach is not directed against a deconstructive reading that brings to the fore the gender inscriptions of
the text. Rather my objection is and has been that such a deconstructive reading does not go far enough since it employs an archetypal approach that reinscribes and naturalizes the andro/kyriocen-
tric feminine representations of the text as a self-evident and
self-contained totality. By establishing a one-to-one relationship
between female/feminine language and symbol on the one hand
and actual wo/men on the other, a gender reading does not destabilize but rather literalizes the gender inscriptions of Revelation.

Although, for instance, Garrett recognizes the "mixed" character
of the image of Babylon, which refers to a city, she nevertheless
insists that it is the image of a wo/man rather than the feminine
image of the empire. Similarly Tina Pippin goes on to read Rev.
17–18 in a universalizing fashion as referring to a wo/man, although
she recognizes the class markers of the feminine figure of Babylon.[59]
Such a literalization and naturalization of the book's gendered language cannot comprehend the vacillation and ambiguity of a text
that slips and slides between feminine and urban characterization,
between masculine and beastly symbolization, between images of
war and justice, violence and salvation, defeat and hope, ethical
struggle and divine predestination. It is this ambiguity and slippage
inscribed in the text, I would suggest, that "reveals" an unresolved
political-religious crisis at the end of the first century.

To reify such textual ambiguities into a closed system of antagonistic dualisms reinscribes linguistic-religious gender determinism.
It does not allow for ambiguity and change in meaning but only for
an "either/or" dualistic alternative. By naturalizing and reifying the
text, it ends up in the same place as a literalist religious, historical,
or linguistic positivism does. Overinterpreting the text in gender
terms negates the possibility of readers' ethical decision and resistance insofar as it does not leave a rhetorical space for wo/men who
desire to read Revelation "otherwise." Though a gender reading of
Revelation seeks to interrupt the gender ideologies inscribed in the
book, it is in danger of naturalizing and reinscribing them in feminist terms. Although this interpretive approach delights in the postmodern language of multiplicity, surplus of meaning, and play of

desire, it does not allow for a *different feminist* reading of Revelation's symbolic world.

By contrast, a critical rhetorical multisystemic interpretation of the gendered language of Revelation in terms of sociopolitical and cultural-linguistic systems of domination, that is, in terms of Roman imperialism, I argue, is able to avoid an archetypal gender reading that reinscribes the dualistic sex/gender system. Such an approach insists that the "female" personifications of mother, virgin, or whore in Revelation must be problematized not only in terms of gender but also in terms of the systemic structures of race, class, and imperialist oppression.

A systemic analysis of domination can show that the Western gender discourse does not produce and negotiate just *androcentric* but *kyriocentric*, i.e., master/ lord/ father/ husband—*elite-male-centered* relations of domination, not only between wo/men and men but also between wo/men and wo/men. For instance, the image of the whore in Rev. 17–18 does not speak about a female person or refer to actual historical wo/men. Rather Revelation deploys it as figure of speech in order to characterize the idolatrous[60] imperial power of Rome. Such a reading, I submit, is able to destabilize the Western construction of gender by pointing out that it functions as a politics of meaning that does not speak about actual wo/men but inculcates the kyriarchal gender ideology of femininity, i.e., that of the "white lady."

Differing from a complex systemic feminist analysis, reading *as a woman* or reading simply in terms of gender reinscribes cultural femininity by naturalizing Revelation's symbolic figurative language. It perpetuates the Western sex/gender system according to which wo/men and men are essentially different and in which masculine and feminine represent antagonistic or complementary archetypes of being human. In so doing, its reading of Revelation reifies and stabilizes sociocultural gender constructs as natural, essential, or "universal." At the same time *reading as a woman* unifies and naturalizes gender identity by obfuscating or denying that the subjectivity of wo/men readers is traversed by multiple structures of oppression. Yet, for Tina Pippin's reading of Revelation, gender remains the overarching lens of interpretation:

> The ideology of gender in the text is a neglected area in studies on the Apocalypse, so a focus on gender and misogyny is partially justified by the history of the neglect of these topics. But in this reading for gender I am promoting a western, white feminist reading and hermeneutic. Gender oppression has to be linked with other forms of oppression that women experience.

> Since I am not third world or living in poverty or in the midst of war, my voice is limited. In my gender analysis of the Apocalypse I cannot claim to speak for any women readers of this text except myself. The majority of women suffer multiple oppressions—sexism, racism, ableism, classism, ageism, heterosexism, colonialism. I am not listing these oppressions just to be "politically correct." Rather, I am called by women of color to face my own role in their multiple oppressions and our mutual enslavement.[61]

This "confessional" statement at once assumes and elides responsibility for its construction of white elite wo/men's agency and identity as universal. It unwittingly reinscribes the privileged position of the white educated elite woman by privatizing and individualizing its own theoretical "reading *as a woman*." Thereby it mystifies the fact that it produces its reading of Revelation from the cultural position of "the white lady" and that it does so for readers who are differently positioned in the kyriarchal systems of oppression. Without question, every feminist voice is limited and cannot speak *for* wo/men, but insofar as we "speak" we always speak *to* and seek to communicate *with* others.

A Critical-Systemic Reading of Rev. 17–18

I have problematized and critically explored here the hermeneutical underpinnings of the reinscription of the sex/gender system that is at stake in a one-dimensional gender reading *as a woman* in order to point to a different reading of Revelation in general and Rev. 17–18 in particular. A rhetorical political feminist reading utilizing the lens of the multiplicative structures of domination engendered by Roman imperialism[62] points to four areas of ideological struggle over the meaning of gender in Revelation:

1. Although Babylon is figured as an elite woman, the rhetorical-symbolic discourse of Revelation clearly understands it as an imperial city and not as an actual woman. Just as the figure of "beast" does not connote "animal" or that of the "ten horns" an animal's "bony outgrowth," neither does "harlot" in the rhetorics of Revelation connote "wo/man." The rhetorical markers in the text again and again refer the reader to a certain "city" and not to an actual wo/man.

Whereas in chapter 17 Babylon is seen primarily as a feminine figure (17:1-7, 9,15-16) and secondarily as a city (17:5, 18), in chapter 18 Babylon is primarily characterized as a city (18:2, 4, 10, 16, 18-19, 21) and only three times as a "woman" (18:3, 7, 16). This reversal in emphasis indicates that the rhetorical argument shifts from feminine figuration to that of city. The author's explanatory identification of "the woman" vision as that of the "the great city which has dominion over the kings of the earth" in 17:18 serves as a rhetorical directive telling the audience that they should understand this image in terms of imperial Rome. [63] In any case, at no time does Rev. 17–18 refer to an individual wo/man but only to a feminine figuration. [64]

The narrative sequence concerning Babylon in 17:1—19:10 may be compared to a triptych with three panels. After a general introductory headline in 17:1-2, the first panel (17:3-18) describes and interprets the world capital, Babylon. The second panel (18:1-24) [65] differs stylistically insofar as the destruction of the great city is not described but only reflected in the dirges of the kings, merchants, and ship owners. The legal claim of the persecuted victims against Babylon is now granted. The powerful capital of the world is destroyed not just because it has persecuted Christians but also because it has unlawfully killed many other people. Rev. 18:24 must therefore be understood as the hermeneutical key to the whole Babylon series of judgments. That the question of justice is at the heart of Revelation's politics of meaning is also underscored by the third panel (19:9-10) which presents a heavenly liturgy praising the justice of G*d's [66] judgments and announcing the marriage feast of the Lamb. [67]

This whole narrative rhetoric ratifies Rev. 14:8, the announcement of imperial Babylon/Rome's judgment, which the second angel proclaims in traditional prophetic language (cf. Isa. 24:19; Jer. 51:7f; Deut. 4:27). The expression "Babylon the great" recurs in Rev. 16:19; 17:5; and 18:2, 10, 21. Most exegetes hold that in the context of Revelation Babylon is a prophetic name for Rome, since Rome was understood in Jewish (Esd. 3:1-2, 28-31; Apoc. Bar. 10:1-3; 11:1; 67:7; Sib. Or. 5:143, 159) and early Christian literature of the time as "Babylon." Both Babylon and Rome shared in the dubious distinction of having destroyed Jerusalem and the temple. However, Babylon must not be reduced to a simple code or steno-symbol for Rome since John uses the name Babylon in order to evoke a whole range of scriptural-theological-political meanings. [68]

For its image of the imperial city as "whore" Revelation not only utilizes the conventional metaphor of woman for a city or country— which is still in vogue today—but also relies on the prophetic language of the Hebrew Bible that indicts Jerusalem and the people of Israel for idolatry, metaphorically likened to "prostitution," [69] a figure of speech which was by then conventional language and would have been understood by the hearers/readers of Revelation as such. Just as, for example, the image of the Lamb refers to an actual historical person, Jesus, and not to an actual sheep-animal, so the label of prostitute refers to an actual imperial city and not to a sexually lewd female. In short, the vision of Babylon the great does not tell us anything about the author's understanding of actual wo/men.

2. Whereas a feminist analysis solely in terms of gender identifies Revelation's references to *porneia/porneuein* as expressions of sexual desire, a complex-rhetorical-political analysis argues that the sexual metaphor of "whoring" or "practicing immorality" is a *conventional metaphor* connoting idolatry. Revelation's gendered language of economic-political realities, I have argued, needs to be scrutinized both for its ideological-misogynist evocation and its religious exclusivist bias. Since the "harlot" trope is taken over from the classical prophets who also spoke of nations and cities as prostitutes and harlots (Nah. 3:4: Nineveh; Isa. 23: Tyre and Sidon; Isa. 1:21; Hos. 1–4; Jer. 3:6-10; Ezek. 16; 25:5-21: Jerusalem and Israel), this trope must be problematized as engendering an ideological tradition that has been and is activated against wo/men in the interest of a misogynist politics.

The controverted question remains as to whether Revelation wants to activate this tradition for misogynist ends or whether it intends its use as an argument against idolatry. The language of prostitution and immorality signifies in the classical prophets unfaithfulness to Israel's G*d, which was enacted in foreign alliances and the worship of other Gods. It is not femininity and sexual morality, I contend, but the politics of power that is central for the argument of Revelation. As Adela Yarbro Collins has pointed out:

> Like Nineveh, Rome has seduced many nations into alliance because of its overwhelming and attractive power. Like those of Tyre, its commercial enterprises are widespread, enriching some and making the poverty of others harder to bear. Idolatry is a factor here as well, although the image has shifted. Rather than depicting the people of G*d as a prostitute who has lusted after male gods . . . instead of remaining faithful to Yahweh, Revelation presents the foreign god as female, as a prostitute who seduces the inhabitants of the earth.[70]

Instead of exploring the politics of meaning that comes to the fore in this specific rhetorical accentuation of Revelation, Collins's interpretation resorts to the archetypal theory of Carl Gustav Jung and Erich Neumann. While she finds no evidence of sexual desire in the depiction of Babylon/Rome, she sees in it the depiction of the "Terrible Mother":

> Her character as a prostitute symbolizes the seductive and charming power of the Great Mother's lure toward self-dissolution in the unconscious sea of participation, of non-individuation. . . . The beast upon which she rides is her phallic consort,

showing her power over the animal world of fertility. . . . The
Terrible Mother must be appeased by blood and needs to be
soaked with and nourished by blood in order to be fruitful.[71]

Such an archetypal gender reading depoliticizes Revelation's
imperial language and imagery in order to make sense out of the
feminine figuration of Rome as prostitute. This Jungian perspective
finds in the depiction of Rome as the Great Mother "a struggle of
Christian faith as a religion of individuation to free itself" from
Greco-Roman "participation mystique."

If one reads the sexually charged language of Revelation not in
psychological but in political terms, however, one can understand it
as conventionally coded feminine language for a city. Hence one is
able to explore its significance for Revelation's political critique of
imperialism. "The wine of its fornication" from which the "dwellers
of the earth have become drunk" stems from the intercourse of
Babylon with the "kings of the earth," by which "the wealth of its
wantonness" has enriched the merchants of the earth.[72] Not sex but
power, wealth, and murder are the ingredients of Babylon/Rome's
"fornication." The conventional use of "practicing immorality" as
signifying idolatry is here redefined as political "intercourse" that
negotiates wealth, power, and violent death.

Whereas the merchant ship owners, kings, and all the nations of
the earth were "drunk" with Babylon's wantonness, i.e., their sharing in its power and wealth, Babylon is drunk with "the blood of the
witnesses of Jesus" (17:6) and that of "prophets, and of saints, and of
all who have been slain on earth" (18:24). If one reads the problematic statement "these who have not defiled themselves with
wo/men" (Rev. 14: 4)[73] in light of the rhetorics of Rev. 17–18, then
it becomes clear that Revelation's use of conventional Hebrew Bible
language[74] does not refer to sexual intercourse with actual wo/men.

3. If one reconstructs the rhetorical situation of Revelation as one
of debate and struggle over right action, one can recognize John's
voice as one voice but not as the only or the most authoritative one
in this debate. Rev. 2:20 refers to a wo/man prophet whom John calls
Jezebel after the Phoenician queen Jezebel, for teaching Christ's servants to "practice immorality and to eat food sacrificed to idols."
Read against the grain, Revelation tells us that one of the renowned
leaders of the churches in Asia Minor was a wo/man who could
claim the official title "prophet." Such a reading is possible because,
unlike in Rev. 17–18, the text refers here to an actual wo/man.

Since John further claims that like Jezebel the Balaamites and
Nicolaitans, whom he also vilifies with Hebrew Bible invectives, are
teaching the "sons of Israel" that they might eat food sacrificed to

idols and practice immorality" (2:14-15), it is obvious that Revelation's "othering" and vilifying invectives are hurled against *both* wo/men and men.[75] Insofar as John uses the same expressions "practicing immorality or fornication" to refer to the followers of "Jezebel" and to those of "Balaam," he does not vilify her alone. He does not accuse her of moral depravity because she is a "woman" but because he disagrees with her theological stance. John does not argue against the wo/man prophet "Jezebel" because she usurped prophetic office and leadership *as a woman,* but because he did not agree with her teachings. It seems that their difference is not just doctrinal but political-cultural. It is rooted in a quite different experience and evaluation of Roman power and influence in Asia Minor.

This is the only time when Revelation refers to an actual wo/man in sexually coded language. To read this reference in an essentialist manner as directed against wo/men qua women is seriously to misread it. Instead, a rhetorical-political reading can understand this sexually coded reference to a wo/man prophet as the tip of the iceberg or as a symptom for what has been submerged of wo/men's historical reality through Revelation's grammatically masculine language and vituperative polemics. Read against the grain, this reference to "Jezebel" indicates that wo/men not only were members of the communities of Asia Minor but also had leadership in them. Their presence in the audience of Revelation could be one of the reasons why the book uses female figures as central images in its politics of meaning. Against such a political-rhetorical interpretation, which I have proposed here, a reading just in terms of gender would insist that grammatically masculine language must be read as gender-specific, having a one-to-one relation of meaning, and hence the audience of Revelation must be seen as male. However, this argument does not interrupt but reinscribes the kyriocentric androcentrism produced by grammatically masculine language, which marginalizes and eliminates historical wo/men from our cultural and religious records.

4. Finally, a dualistic reading of Revelation just in terms of gender is also in danger of reinscribing the widespread cultural-religious dichotomy between the "good" and the "bad woman." Barbara Rossing's dissertation has convincingly shown that the author of Revelation was familiar with the feminine coding of the dualistic cultural pattern of ethical choice found in Greco-Roman and in Jewish wisdom literature.[76] However, it must not be overlooked that this ethical dualism symbolized by two feminine figures is embedded in a tripartite symbolism. A binary reading of Revelation's female representations as "good and bad woman" does not appreciate that

the author introduces and relates to each other three, and not just two, powerful feminine figures—Babylon, the Whore, and New Jerusalem, the Bride. Revelation does not work with a simple either/or dualism but dialectically[77] mediates this ethical dualism by inserting as a third figure, the birthing Wo/man (not the Mother) of chapter 12.[78] They symbolize in a dialectical fashion the Powerful Queen of Heaven, the Powerful Queen of Earth, and the Powerful Queen of the New Heaven and New Earth. Such a three-part structure also can be observed in Rev. 17–18 and in that of chapter 12, as well as in that of the New Jerusalem segment.[79]

Chapter 12 takes the form of an inclusion. Between the great portent of the glorious wo/man and the powerful dragon (12:1-6), on the one hand, and the vision of the dragon's persecution of the wo/man (12:13-17) on the other, John inserts the vision about war in heaven waged by the dragon (12:7-12). He first draws the audience's attention to the glorious sign in heaven, but at the end of each section he shifts the focus again toward the earth. The whole vision appears to be a mythological elaboration of the *eschatological war* motif already sounded in 11:7.

The myth of the Queen of Heaven with the divine child was—as Adela Yarbro Collins has shown[80]—internationally known at the time of John. Variations appear in Babylonia, Egypt, Greece, Asia Minor, and especially in the texts about astral religion. Elements of this myth are the Goddess and the divine child, the great red dragon and his enmity to mother and child, and the motif of the protection of mother and child. Revelation 12 also incorporates these elements. As in other versions of the myth, the dragon seeks the child not yet born in order to devour and kill it. The dragon therefore pursues the pregnant wo/man for the child she carries. In other forms of the myth, the wo/man is either carried away to give birth in a protected place, or she gives birth in a miraculous way and escapes the onslaught of the dragon together with the newborn. In Revelation 12 the child is exalted to heaven while the wo/man is carried to the desert for the sake of her own protection.[81]

Some features of this international myth appear also in the Roman imperial cult. A coin of Pergamum, for example, shows the goddess Roma with the divine emperor. In the cities of Asia Minor, Roma, the Queen of Heaven, was worshipped as the Mother of the Gods.[82] Her oldest temple stood in Smyrna. Her imperial child was celebrated as the "world's savior," incarnation of the Sun-God Apollo. John probably intends such an allusion to the imperial cult[83] and the Goddess Roma insofar as he pictures the wo/man clothed with the sun as the anti-image of Babylon, the symbol of the world-power of his day and its allies (chapters 17–18).

Revelation reinterprets this international ancient myth in terms of Jewish expectations. Its emphasis on the travail of the wo/man does not derive from the ancient pagan myth but takes inspiration from the Hebrew Bible's image of Israel-Zion in messianic times. The vision of the wo/man in labor pains alludes to Israel-Zion seen as a pregnant wo/man awaiting the delivery of the messianic age in Isa. 26:16-27; 54:1; 66:7-9 (cf. also Mic. 4:9-10).[84] With the symbolic language of Isaiah and this ancient pagan myth, Revelation invokes the image of the messianic child being born accompanied by the birth-pangs of the messianic woes.

While the "wo/man clothed with the sun" is clearly a female figure, as Rossing has elaborated, the New Jerusalem, like Babylon, is strongly characterized as a cosmic city. If a dualistic contrast is intended it is the *political contrast* between the capital of the world of oppression and the capital of the world of G*d, in which tears, hunger, and death—the characteristics of the world of injustice—have passed away. It is not a contrast between two types of wo/men.

The "first" heaven and earth now belong to the past. The antagonistic dualism between the reign of G*d and Christ in heaven and that of Babylon, the Dragon, and his allies on earth and in the underworld no longer exists. The "new heaven and earth" stand in continuity with the former heaven and earth, but they form a qualitatively new and unified world. This new reality is characterized by G*d's presence among the peoples of G*d. The vision of the New Jerusalem, arrayed like a bride in the splendor of the "righteous deeds of the saints,"[85] makes symbolically present G*d's eschatological salvation and reign, which entails that heaven will move down to earth.[86]

The last series of visions in 21:9—22:9 magnificently elaborate in visionary symbolization the eschatological salvation announced in 21:1-8. This series is structurally designed to form the third panel in the triptych 17:1—22:9, insofar as, like the Babylon visions, it is introduced by one of the seven bowl angels (21:9 cf. 17:1) and concludes with a dialogue between the angel and the seer (22:6-9 cf. 19:9-10). In contrast to 17:1, where John is carried into the wilderness, in 21:10 he is carried to a great mountain where one of the bowl angels shows him the "bride, the wife of the lamb,"[87] (21:9) a contrast image to the "great harlot," Babylon/Rome (17:1). Just as Babylon is arrayed in scarlet and purple, adorned with gold, jewels, and pearls (17:4, 16-17), so the New Jerusalem sparkles with precious jewels and pearls (21:18-21). It radiates from the glory of G*d like a most rare precious gem, like jasper, clear as crystal (21:11). Nothing "unclean" and no abomination scars the beauty of the New Jerusalem (21:27; 22:3a) in contrast to the gaudy appearance of Babylon, who is called "the mother of abominations" (17:5). Just as Babylon has a "name on its forehead" (17:5), so the citizens of the New Jerusalem have "G*d's name on their foreheads" (22:4). Their names are written in the "Lamb's book of life" (21:27) in contrast to Babylon's followers, whose names are "not written in the book of life" (17:8).

The "kings of the earth," who not only are vassals of Babylon/Rome but also destroy it (17:15-18), bring their glory to the New Jerusalem (21:24). Thus Revelation depicts the eternal glory of the New Jerusalem as the dwelling place of G*d (21:10—22:5) by contrasting it with Babylon's doom as the dwelling place of demons (18:1-3, 9-19). Through these rhetorical parallels John draws the picture of the New Jerusalem as the alternative image of the Great City Babylon/Rome. He contrasts the splendor and power of the Roman empire with that of the empire of G*d and Christ in order to encourage readers to resist the murderous power of Rome. Read in rhetorical-political terms, Revelation speaks not of gender and sex but of power used either for destruction or for well-being.

CONCLUSION

In the beginning of this essay I stressed that a rhetorics of inquiry does not only have the task of adjudicating on exegetical-textual grounds which interpretations are right and which are wrong. Rather, its task is to assess ethically and politically what kind of reality and vision such texts and interpretations generate. Moreover, it must clarify the underlying methodological assumptions and interpretative lenses used in certain readings and assess their implications for shaping the symbolic/moral universe of texts and interpreters.

I have tried to show, therefore, that a reading of Revelation in terms of a dualistic gender framework inscribes or reinscribes the Western sex/gender system,[88] whereas a rhetorical-political reading is able to underscore the sociopolitical-religious power of Roman imperialism that affects wo/men differently. I have argued further that a rhetorical-political analysis that reads Revelation in terms of the structures of oppression inscribed in the text is more appropriate for a historical-postcolonial reading, whereas a gender reading is more apt to underscore the Western sex-gender frame and misogynist assumptions of biblical texts and their readings.

As I pointed out almost 15 years ago,[89] when reading Revelation, contemporary "audiences" always interpret the text in terms of the sex-gender system and they are bound to activate unconsciously the most prominent reading paradigm in Western culture. Hence, the work of feminists who uncover and demystify the gender code of Revelation is crucially important as long as it does not "naturalize" this dualistic code. As I have argued throughout this essay, a reading approach that single-mindedly focuses on gender and identifies gender constructs with actual women is in danger of revalorizing the symbolic sex-gender system of the text in modern Western terms, although seeking to deconstruct it. Hence a reading in terms of gender must remain embedded in a sociopolitical-religious rhetorics and ethics of inquiry that can adjudicate which texts and interpretations use androcentric language as conventional generic language but reinscribe misogynism and the language of hate if they are not read against the grain.

A reading of Revelation in terms of the multiplicative structures of oppression I have argued here, can correct a dualistic-androcentric feminist lens and help Western readers to read "against the grain" of their own cultural religious assumptions or prejudices as well as against those of the grammatically and symbolically kyriocentric text. A feminist rhetorical-political reading of Revelation utilizes gender as one but not as the sole lens. It does not naturalize and reify the text in terms of the dualistic kyriocentric Western sex-gender system. Instead it points out that gender is an ideological construct that is produced by and in turn legitimates and "naturalizes" relations of domination. Hence the constructedness of gender in texts and interpretations can come only to the fore when the structures of domination become the focus of feminist readings.

Julia Esquivel's poem "Thanksgiving Day" expresses poetically the politics of interpretation that animates a reading strategy critical of all forms of domination. Unlike Tina Pippin, when Julia Esquivel, a Guatemalan refugee, looks into the eye of Babylon/Rome, she does not see a wo/man. Rather she sees U.S. imperial power that has been and still is so destructive of all native peoples:

> In the third year of the massacres
> by Lucas and the other coyotes
> against the poor of Guatemala
> I was led by the Spirit into the desert
> And on the eve
> of Thanksgiving Day
> I had a vision of Babylon:
> the city sprang forth arrogantly. . .
> Each day false prophets
> invited the inhabitants
> of the Unchaste City

to kneel before the idols of gluttony
money
and death:
Idolaters of all nations
were being converted to the American way of life. . .
The Spirit told me
in the River of death
flows the blood of many peoples. . .
the blood of the Indian's ancestors
who lived on those lands, of those who
even now are kept hostage in the Great Mountain
and on the Black Hills of Dakota
by the guardians of the beast. . . .[90]

This poetic interpretation of Revelation's Babylon vision does not use gender but a postcolonial analysis of imperialism as its analytic lens. It foregrounds the experience of colonial oppression and death-dealing political-religious power. Although Esquivel does not engage in a critical exegetical reading but in an imaginative-poetic one, the theoretical issues undergirding such a reading of Revelation in terms of imperialism can be brought into conversation with a feminist gender reading.

In sum, I have juxtaposed two different feminist strategies of reading Rev. 17–18 in particular and the female images of the book in general. One reading practice subscribes to an ideological-archetypal gender politics; the other reads gender in contextual-rhetorical-political terms. A rhetorics and ethics of inquiry can alert us to the fact that the disagreement between these reading practices is not exegetical-textual but rather rhetorical-hermeneutical. Whereas a scientific-positivist paradigm would argue for one interpretation over the other as the only correct one, a rhetorical paradigm seeks to understand why and on what grounds different interpretations privilege different rhetorical markers in the text. The determination of which interpretation is most appropriate, however, cannot be settled on purely exegetical grounds but only in terms of a rhetorics and ethics of inquiry. Both feminist reading strategies highlight important aspects of the rhetorical discourse of Revelation.

While a feminist reading of Revelation solely in terms of gender underscores the ways the discursive sex/gender system determines the rhetoric of Revelation and our own readings of it, an interpretation of it in terms of the "imperial" code insists that gender is not a discrete category but that it is inflected by other relations of domination such as race, status, religion, and colonial imperialism. It points out that Western middle-class wo/men readers will activate the sex/gender system but not that of class, race, or ethnicity. They privilege gender markers when reading Revelation, whereas oppressed and marginalized readers stress the political language and rhetoric of the book. Both readings must remain dialectically related to each other if they should fruitfully correct each other. Such a correction and fine-tuning of the feminist lens and interpretive focus is especially necessary for those who read from the social location of Western elite-male status and privilege. A rhetorics of inquiry must therefore be accompanied by an ethics of inquiry that is able to assess critically the scholarly frameworks and interpretive patterns that determine all interpretation of Revelation in light of its utopian vision of justice and well-being for all.

NOTES

1. I want to thank Julie Miller for her editorial assistance in preparing this chapter.

2. See Stephen D. O'Leary, *Arguing the Apocalypse: A Theory of Millennial Rhetoric* (New York: Oxford University Press, 1994.)

3. I owe special thanks to Michael West of Fortress Press for making this new edition possible.

4. For the most recent extensive discussion of the interpretation of Revelation, see Arthur W. Wainwright, *Mysterious Apocalypse: Interpreting the Book of Revelation* (Nashville: Abingdon Press, 1993); and the review article of Traugott Holtz, "Literatur zur Johannesapokalypse 1980-1996," *Theologische Rundschau* 62/3 (1997) 368-413. Holtz seems not to comprehend the rhetorical paradigm shift in Apocalypse research, however. Interestingly, his comprehensive bibliography does not list my commentary *Revelation: Vision of a Just World* (Minneapolis: Fortress, 1991). For a more general overview in English see Frederick J. Murphy, "The Book of Revelation," *Currents in Research* 2(1994) 181-225.

5. Bruce Malina, *On the Genre and Message of Revelation: Star Visions and Sky Journeys* (Peabody, Mass.: Hendrickson Publishers, 1995), insists, however, on such a "how it actually was" historical reading of Revelation. While I agree that it is important to reconstruct the historical situation of the book, I would argue that we "reconstruct" the mindset of the author or the beliefs of the ancients only in and through our contemporary linguistic and theoretical assumptions. Hence Malina is not critically aware that his reconstruction of the first-century Mediterranean universe often reads like a counter-caricature to what he believes the modern U.S. American understanding of the world is. See also his very instructive essay "Rhetorical Criticism and Social-Scientific Criticism: Why Won't Romanticism Leave us Alone?" in Stanley E. Porter and Thomas H. Olbricht, *Rhetoric, Scripture and Theology: Essays from the 1994 Pretoria Conference* (Sheffield: Academic Press, 1996) 72-101, where he identifies himself as "a member of that small, literary challenged, band of socio-rational empiricists." He defines socio-rational empiricists as "those who are socialized to believe that lightening, by whatever signifier one might signify it, will have an effect on us if it directly strikes us" (72n.1). While I agree with Malina that

a reality is signified by the signifier "struck by lightening," I disagree with him in that we have direct access to this reality. His polemics against "feminism, deconstructionism, fundamentalism and hermeneutics" (in that order!) as Gnosticism and Romanticism indicates the authoritarian character of his own position. "What all of these have in common," in his view, "is that they all dismiss the concrete, physical, situation-conditioned, culturally based orientation of the first telling of the Christian story, much like Gnosticism in antiquity." Yet this advocacy of literalist empiricism overlooks that a socio-historical feminist analysis, for instance, questions the culturally conditioned rhetorical constructions of texts and interpretations because it is very much concerned with the concrete, physical presence of wo/men in history.

6. For this paradigm shift see Elisabeth Schüssler Fiorenza, *Bread Not Stone: The Challenge of Feminist Biblical Interpretation* (Boston: Beacon Press, 1984); and Fernando F. Segovia, "'And They Began to Speak in Other Tongues': Competing Methods of Contemporary Biblical Criticism," in F. F. Segovia and M. A. Tolbert, eds., *Reading from This Place, vol. 1: Social Location and Biblical Interpretation in Global Perspective* (Minneapolis: Fortress Press, 1995) 1-32; and *idem,* "Introduction: Pedagogical Discourses and Practices in Contemporary Biblical Criticism," in Fernando F. Segovia and Mary Ann Tolbert, eds., *Teaching the Bible: The Discourses and Politics of Biblical Pedagogy* (Maryknoll: Orbis Books, 1998) 1-28.

7. I have taken over this expression from John Bender and David E. Wellbery, eds., *The Ends of Rhetoric: History, Theory, Practice* (Stanford: Stanford University Press, 1990) 25: "Rhetoric today is neither a unified doctrine nor a coherent set of discursive practices. Rather it is a transdisciplinary field of practice and intellectual concern, a field that draws on conceptual resources of a radically heterogeneous nature and does not assume the stable shape of a system or method of education. . . . The classical rhetorical tradition rarefied speech and fixed it within a gridwork of limitations: it was a rule-governed domain whose procedures themselves were delimited by the institutions that organized interaction and domination in traditional European society. Rhetoricality by contrast is bound to no specific set of institutions. . . . It allows for no explanatory metadiscourse that is not already itself rhetorical. Rhetoric is no longer the title of a doctrine and practice, nor a form of cultural memory; it becomes instead something like the condition of our existence."

8. I use this expression in conjunction with Hebrew Bible in order to overcome the supersessionism implied by the nomenclature "Old and New Testaments."

9. See the forthcoming collection of essays edited by David Barr that documents the work of the Reading the Apocalypse Seminar.

10. For a fuller development of the argument for a rhetorical approach see my book *Revelation: Vision of a Just World* (Minneapolis: Fortress Press, 1991).

11. See Elisabeth Schüssler Fiorenza, "Challenging the Rhetorical Half-Turn: Feminist and Rhetorical Biblical Criticism," in *Rhetoric, Scripture and Theology,* 28-54; and Dirk J. Smit, "Theology as Rhetoric? Or Guess Who's Coming to Dinner," ibid., 393-423.

12. See my dissertation, *Priester für Gott: Studien zum Herrschafts- und Priestermotiv in der Apokalypse* (Münster: Aschendorff, 1972), which has been much utilized but has never been translated into English.

13. For the advocacy of a postmodern rhetorical approach in biblical studies in terms of the New Rhetorics, see The Bible and Culture Collective, *The Postmodern*

Bible (New Haven: Yale University Press, 1995) 149-77. This volume is dedicated to Wilhelm Wuellner, who has pioneered the New Rhetoric in Christian Testament studies.

14. See John J. Collins, ed., *Apocalypse: The Morphology of a Genre* (Semeia 14; Missoula, Mont.: Scholars Press, 1979), and the reception of it.

15. See, e.g., the dissertation of M. Karrer, *Die Johannesoffenbarung als Brief: Studien zu ihrem literarischen und theologischen Ort* (Göttingen: Vandenhoeck & Ruprecht, 1986), which has elaborated and corroborated this thesis.

16. See also *Vision of a Just World* 130-39.

17. Adela Yarbro Collins, *Crisis and Catharsis: The Power of the Apocalypse* (Philadelphia: Westminster Press, 1984).

18. Leonard Thompson, *The Book of Revelation: Apocalypse and Empire* (Oxford: Oxford University Press, 1990) 185-95, argues that John's dualistic rhetoric is not primarily directed against Rome but seeks to establish "binary opposition and boundary formation—to distinguish insiders from outsiders." His work is part of a depoliticizing trend in Revelation research that has gained widespread acceptance. In a similar fashion Stephen L. Cook, *Prophecy and Apocalypticism: The Postexilic Social Setting* (Minneapolis: Fortress Press, 1995), challenges the conventional "conventicle" approach pioneered by Otto Plöger and Paul Hanson, which assumes that apocalyptic writings stem from the losers in political power struggles, and argues that apocalyptic texts "are *not* products of groups that are alienated, marginalized, or even relatively deprived" (2). This depoliticizing trend in apocalyptic research needs to be problematized and discussed critically in light of the conservative political use of Revelation in particular and of apocalyptic symbolism in general.

19. For the understanding of Revelation as sectarian, see David A. deSilva, "The Revelation to John: A Case Study in Apocalyptic Propaganda and the Maintenance of Sectarian Identity," *Sociological Analysis* 53/4 (1992) 375-95; see also his "The Social Setting of the Revelation to John: Conflicts within, Fears without," *WJT* 54 (1992) 273-302.

20. Harry O. Maier, "Staging the Gaze: Early Christian Apocalypses and Narrative Self-Representation," *Harvard Theological Review* 90/2 (1997) 149f.

21. See Paul B. Duff, "Whoever Is Not with Me Is against Me: Witchcraft Accusation and the Revelation of John," paper presented in the SBL Reading the Apocalypse Seminar, New Orleans, 1996.

22. It is curious that in his fascinating new narrative commentary *Tales of the End* (Santa Rosa: Polebridge Press, 1998), David Barr distances himself from my argument that Revelation has adopted a "perspective from below," the perspective of those who were poor, powerless, and in constant fear of denunciation, but then goes on to state that "it is worth remembering that the writing is addressed to the urban poor" (165). Although Barr uses a narrative rather than a rhetorical analysis, his reference to the correspondence of Trajan for illuminating the rhetorical situation of the book, his characterization of its aim as "consistent resistance," and his integration of the sectarian argument into an overall political one, are interpretive strategies similar to those I have elaborated in my work.

23. To reflect the ambiguity and inclusivity of the term, I write it in this broken form. See Denise Riley, *Am I That Name? Feminism and the Category of "Wo/men" in History* (Minneapolis: University of Minnesota Press, 1988).

24. See especially Tina Pippin, *Death and Desire: The Rhetoric of Gender in the Apocalypse of John* (Literary Currents in Biblical Interpretation; Louisville: Westminster/John Knox Press, 1992).

25. Tina Pippin, "The Heroine and the Whore: Fantasy and the Female in the Apocalypse of John," *Semeia* 60 (1992) 69.

26. Tina Pippin, "The Revelation to John," in *Searching the Scriptures, vol. 2* (New York: Crossroad, 1994) 119.

27. For this thesis, see Tina Pippin, "Eros and the End: Reading for Gender in the Apocalypse of John," *Semeia* 59 (1992) 193-210, 195: "The new Jerusalem is a woman, but women are not included in the utopian city. God's future world excludes women but not before marginalizing them first."

28. Lorraine Code, *Rhetorical Spaces: Essays on Gendered Locations* (New York: Routledge, 1995) x.

29. Cheryl Glenn, *Rhetoric Retold: Regendering the Tradition from Antiquity through the Renaissance* (Carbondale: Southern Illinois University Press, 1997) 1: "Rhetoric always inscribes the relation of language and power at a particular moment."

30. In speaking of a rhetorics of inquiry, I adopt W. Wuellner's suggestion of distinguishing between rhetorics as theory and rhetoric as practice.

31. John S. Nelson, Allan Megill, Donald N. McCloskey, "Rhetoric of Inquiry," in Allan Megill and Donald McCloskey, eds., *The Rhetoric of the Human Sciences: Language and Argument in Scholarship and Public Affairs* (Madison: University of Wisconsin Press, 1987) 4.

32. See Ricca Edmondson, *Rhetoric in Sociology* (London: MacMillan Press, 1984).

33. Robert M. Royalty Jr., "The Rhetoric of Revelation," *SBL 1997 Seminar Papers* (Atlanta: Scholars Press, 1997) 596-617. Similarly John T. Kirby, "The Rhetorical Situation of Rev 1-3," *NTS* 34 (1988) 197-207.

34. Susan Shapiro, "Rhetoric as Ideology Critique: The Gadamer-Habermas Debate Reinvented," *Journal of the American Academy of Religion* 62/1 (1994) 123-50.

35. Susan Jarrattt, "The First Sophists and Feminism: Discourse of the 'Other,'" *Hypatia* 5 (1990) 29.

36. For this characterization, see M. Calvin McGee and J. R. Lyne, "What Are Nice Fellows like You Doing in a Place like This?" in *The Rhetoric of the Human Sciences*, 381-83.

37. Patricia Parker, *Literary Fat Ladies: Rhetoric, Gender, Property* (London: Methuen, 1987) 109.

38. Elisabeth Schüssler Fiorenza, "Challenging the Rhetorical Half-Turn," 28-53.

39. See especially the introduction and conclusion to Nancy Sorkin Rabinowitz and Amy Richlin, eds., *Feminist Theory and the Classics* (New York: Routledge, 1993), for the institutionalization of classics as modern "gentleman" disciplines dedicated to the study of philology, text, and history—pure and simple.

40. McGee and Lyne, "What Are Nice Fellows like You Doing in a Place like This?" 382.

41. Susan C. Jarratt, "The First Sophists," 28.

42. Cf. A. H. M. Jones, *Athenian Democracy* (Baltimore: Johns Hopkins, 1957); Susan Moller Okin, *Women in Western Political Thought* (Princeton, N.J.: Princeton University Press, 1979) 73-98; Page duBois, *Centaurs and Amazons: Women and the Prehistory of the Great Chain of Being* (Ann Arbor: University of Michigan Press, 1982).

43. Leonard L. Thompson, *The Book of Revelation: Apocalypse and Empire,* 206. Yet the analysis of the rhetorical situation does not "mirror its originating situation" but rather complexifies it.

44. Jan Feckes III, *Isaiah and Prophetic Traditions in the Book of Revelation* (Sheffield: Sheffield University Press, 1994) completely misunderstands my proposal that John uses in a rhetorical and not exegetical fashion the Hebrew Bible and apocalyptic traditions as "language" to express his own vision.

45. On the question of language see Mary Vetterling-Braggin, ed., *Sexist Language: A Modern Philosophical Analysis* (Littlefield: Adams and Co., 1981). On the problem of "natural" versus "grammatical" gender, see Dennis Baron, *Grammar and Gender* (New Haven: Yale University Press, 1986). Similar observations can be made for race classifications; cf. Gloria A. Marshall, "Racial Classifications: Popular and Scientific," in Sandra Harding, ed., *The "Racial" Economy of Science: Toward a Democratic Future* (Bloomington: Indiana University Press, 1993) 116-27.

46. Brice R. Wachterhauser, ed., *Hermeneutics and Modern Philosophy* (Albany: State University of New York Press, 1986) 30.

47. Following A. K. Halliday, *Language as Social Semiotics* (Baltimore: University Park Press, 1978); John E. Hurtgen, *Anti-Language in the Apocalypse of John* (Lewiston: Mellen Biblical Press, 1994) 50-51, defines anti-language as follows: "Anti-language is the language of social resistance. It is a language like any other language, that is, it functions to express and maintain the social structure. . . . For groups who perceive themselves as relegated to the outer margins of society (the Apocalypse of John fits here), anti-language offers one form of protest against the standard society to which it stands opposed." According to Halliday (165-66), anti-language is determined by *relexicalization,* that is, new words for old, and *overlexicalization,* that is, multiple words for the same concept, both of which are characteristic for the language of Revelation.

48. Allen Dwight Callahan, "The Language of Apocalypse," *Harvard Theological Review* 88/4 (1995) 453-70.

49. Theophus Smith, *Conjuring Culture: Biblical Formations of Black Culture* (New York: Oxford Press, 1994) 133.

50. Allen Dwight Callahan, "The Language of Apocalypse," 464; see also Pablo Richard, *Apocalypse: A People's Commentary on the Book of Revelation* (Maryknoll, N.Y.: Orbis Books, 1995) 175: "Finally Revelation is having a decisive influence especially in the so-called Third World (the poor countries and the poor within those countries) in the reconstruction of liberation theologies. . . . The Book of Revelation is helping to create a new historical and liberating language. . . . Revelation is coming to be the preferred book of the Base Christian Communities and of all the ecclesial movements that hope to transform the present situation and reform the church, movements that are born among the poor, the oppressed and the excluded (both women and men)."

51. For the exploration and literature on this epistemological debate, see my books *But She Said: Feminist Practices of Biblical Interpretation* (Boston: Beacon Press, 1992); *Jesus: Miriam's Child and Sophia's Prophet: Critical Issues in Feminist Christology* (New York: Crossroad, 1994); and *Sharing Her Word: Feminist Biblical Interpretation in Context* (Boston: Beacon Press, 1998).

52. For the theoretical elaboration of this expression, see Rosemary Hennessy, *Materialist Feminism and the Politics of Discourse* (New York: Routledge, 1993); and my book *Jesus: Miriam's Child*.

53. For the definition and elaboration of this neologism see *But She Said* and *Sharing Her Word*.

54. For a deconstructive reading of Revelation's androcentric G*d language, see the article of Stephen D. Moore, "The Beatific Vision as a Posing Exhibition: Revelation's Hypermasculine Deity," *JSNT* 60 (1995) 27-55.

55. M. A. K. Halliday, "Anti-languages," *American Anthropologist* 78 (1976) 570-84.

56. Susan R. Garrett, "Revelation," *The Women's Bible Commentary*, ed. Carol A. Newsom and Sharon H. Ringe (Louisville, Ky.: Westminster/John Knox, 1992) 377.

57. For a trenchant feminist critique of Carl Gustav Jung's theory of archetypes see Naomi Goldenberg, *Important Directions for a Feminist Critique of Religion in the Works of Sigmund Freud and Carl Jung* (Ann Arbor, Mich.: University Microfilms, 1977).

58. Tina Pippin, *Death and Desire*, 47.

59. Tina Pippin, "Reading for Gender in the Apocalypse of John," 195.

60. For the feminine coding of idolatry in later theological work, see Susan Shapiro, "The Feminization of Idolatry: Reading Jewish Philosopher Moses Maimonides for His Views on Rhetoric, Gender, and Idolatry," *Harvard Divinity Bulletin* 27/4 (1998) 27-28; see also her "A Matter of Discipline: Reading for Gender in Jewish Philosophy," in Miriam Peskowitz and Laura Levitt, eds., *Judaism since Gender* (New York: Routledge, 1997)158-73.

61. Tina Pippin, *Death and Desire*, 55.

62. For a political reading of Rev. 17–18, see Klaus Wengst, "Babylon the Great and the New Jerusalem: The Visionary View of Political Reality in the Revelation of John," in Henning Graf Reventlow, Yair Hoffman, and Benjamin Uffenheimer, eds., *Politics and Theopolitics in the Bible and Postbiblical Literature* (Sheffield: Sheffield University Press, 1994) 189-202.

63. For the imperial context of Revelation, see also D. Aune, "The Form and Function of the Proclamations to the Seven Churches (Rev 2-3)," *NTS* 36 (1990) 182-204; idem, "The Influence of Roman Imperial Court Ceremonial on the Apocalypse of John," *BR* 28 (1983) 5-26; and the most recent discussion by Heinz Giesen, "Das Römische Reich im Spiegel der Johannes-Apokalypse," *ANRW* 2/26 (1996) 2501-614; H. J. Klauck, "Das Sendschreiben nach Pergamon und der Kaiserkult in der Johannesoffenbarung," *Biblica* 73 (1992) 153-82.

64. The study of gender has amply documented that gender images do not need to refer to actual wo/men or men.

65. Susan M. Elliott, "Who Is Addressed in Revelation 18:6-7?" *BR* 40 (1995) 98-113.

66. In order to mark the inadequacy of our language to speak about the divine, I write G*d in such a broken form. For a discussion of the term G*d, see Francis Schüssler Fiorenza and Gordon Kaufman, "God," in Mark C. Taylor, ed., *Critical Terms for Religious Studies* (Chicago: University of Chicago Press, 1998) 136-59.

67. When this is read literally, we have here a marriage between an animal and a wo/man. However, scholars do not read "lamb" as "animal" but see it as a figuration of Christ.

68. Jean Pierre Ruiz, *Ezekiel in the Apocalypse: The Transformation of Prophetic Language in Revelation 16:17—19:10* (New York: Peter Lang, 1989).

69. For a feminist discussion of this language tradition of idolatry as prostitution and the rhetoric of Israel as harlot, see Renita Weems, *Battered Love: Marriage, Sex and Violence in the Hebrew Prophets* (Minneapolis: Fortress Press, 1995).

70. Adela Yarbro Collins, "Feminine Symbolism in the Book of Revelation," *Biblical Interpretation* 1/1 (1993) 27.

71. Ibid., 30.

72. See J. Nelson Kraybill, *Imperial Cult and Commerce in John's Apocalypse* (Sheffield: Sheffield Academic Press, 1996) 102-43.

73. Pablo Richard, *Apocalypse* 120, suggests the following translation of 14:4a: "these are those who did not contaminate themselves with idolatry, for they are clean of heart." However, as I have pointed out above, "idolatry" must not be mis-read in a purely religious, modern sense but must be understood as economic, political, and religious perfidy.

74. See Judith Plaskow, *Standing Again at Sinai* (San Francisco: Harper & Row, 1990), who has problematized Exod. 19:15: "Be ready on the third day; do not go near a woman." According to her, for a feminist this is one of the most disturbing verses in the Bible because wo/men are rendered invisible at the central moment in Jewish history.

75. For the polemics against his Jewish compatriots, see Peder Borgen, "Polemic in the Book of Revelation," in C. Evans and D. Hagner, eds., *Anti-Semitism and Early Christianity* (Minneapolis: Fortress Press, 1993) 199-211; Luke T. Johnson, "The New Testament Anti-Jewish Slander and the Conventions of Ancient Polemic," *JBL* 108/3 (1989) 419-41.

76. Barbara Rossing, *The Choice between Two Cities: A Wisdom Topos in the Apocalypse*, doctoral diss., Harvard University, 1998. For a more deconstructive reading of the Wisdom language in Revelation, see Tina Pippin, "Wisdom and Apocalyptic in the Apocalypse of John: Desiring Sophia," in Leo Purdue, ed., *In Search of Wisdom* (Louisville: Westminster/John Knox, 1993) 285-95.

77. Roger Fowler, *Linguistic Criticism* (Oxford: University Press, 1986) 146, points to "the dialectical semantics" of anti-language at work.

78. See Edith McEwan Humphrey, *The Ladies and the Cities: Transformation and Apocalyptic Identity in Joseph and Aseneth, 4 Ezra, the Apocalypse and the Shepherd of Hermas* (Sheffield: Sheffield Academic Press, 1995) 103-11, who argues against Collins's dis-association of the woman of chapters 12 and 21 (Adela Yarbro Collins, *Combat Myth in the Book of Revelation* [Missoula, Mont.: Scholars Press, 1976] 233-35) that the two figures "have a close relationship, but not an exact identity" (110). However, she does not explore the links between the three "queen" figures in Revelation.

79. However, it must not be overlooked that the feminine metaphor of the bride, which serves to allude to Synoptic messianic banquet traditions, is quickly replaced by that of the city, the New Jerusalem. Contra Jan Fekkes III, "Revelation 19–21 and Isaian Nuptial Imagery," *JBL* 10/2 (1990) 283, who argues that Rev 21:18-21 are a continuation of the bride scheme.

80. See Collins, *Combat Myth.*

81. In her "Response to Tina Pippin, 'Eros and the End,'" *Ideological Criticism of Biblical Texts* (Semeia; Atlanta: Scholars Press, 1992) 220, Jane Schaberg comments: "Helped by the wings of the great eagle (12:14) and by the earth (v.16), she almost seems like a character from the Native American traditions. She represents a third option: she does not follow the beast, nor is she a martyr/companion/bride of the

Lamb. Refusing this either/or she flees. She has become interesting in a new way."
However, Schaberg overlooks this positive understanding of the "earth" in Revelation (see also the hymn at 11:18, where judgment is announced as "destroying the destroyers of the earth") when she claims that reverence for the earth is missing from Revelation (223).

82. See Ronald Mellor, *Thea Roma: The Worship of the Goddess Roma in the Greek World* (Göttingen: Vandenhoeck & Ruprecht, 1975). See also his "The Goddess Roma," in Wolfgang Haase, ed., *Aufstieg und Niedergang der römischen Welt* II, 17.2 (New York: de Gruyter, 1981) 950-1030.

83. S. R. F. Price, *Rituals and Power: The Roman Imperial Cult in Asia Minor* (Cambridge: Cambridge University Press, 1984); see also Steven J. Friesen, *Neokoros: Ephesus, Asia and the Cult of the Flavian Emperors* (Leiden: E. J. Brill, 1993).

84. See Claudia Suter Rehmann, *Geh frage die Gebärerin: feministisch-befreiungstheologische Untersuchungen zum Gebärmotiv in der Apokalyptik* (Gütersloh: Gütersloher Verlagshaus, 1995).

85. Pippin stresses that the New Jerusalem is a controlled and subdued female figure (see her "Reading for Gender in the Apocalypse of John," 195). However, there is no evidence for this in the text, which does not stress wifely subordination but splendor, bliss, and well-being.

86. Pablo Richard, *Apocalypse*, 172: This "is not the end of history, but rather a new creation within history. It is a transcendent world, not because it is beyond history, but rather a new creation within history. This new creation is the final achievement of our history."

87. Note that here the masculine-feminine dualism is interrupted through the figuration of Christ as an animal.

88. For this expression, see my book *Jesus: Miriam's Child*.

89. Elisabeth Schüssler Fiorenza, "The Followers of the Lamb: Visionary Rhetoric and Social-Political Situation," in F. Segovia, ed., *Discipleship in the New Testament* (Philadelphia: Fortress Press, 1985), reprinted as chap. 7.

90. From Julia Esquivel, *Threatened with Resurrection: Prayers and Poems from an Exiled Guatemalan* (Elgin, Ill.: The Brethren Press, 1982) 79-91.

Index of Passages

OLD TESTAMENT

Genesis
49:9-10—80 n. 46,
    180 n. 47

Exodus
Book of—162
15—102, 135
19:6—72, 123, 131
    n. 61
29:38-46—95
33:20-23—52

Leviticus
4:32—95

Numbers
25:1-18—127
    nn. 15-16
25:12—116
31:16—116

Deuteronomy
32—102, 135

1 Samuel
12:6—72

1 Kings
12:31—72, 80
    n. 41, 131 n. 61
13:33-34—72

2 Kings
19:20-34—200
    n. 20

Psalms
23:1-3—99
33:3—80 n. 43
96:1—80 n. 43
98:1—80 n. 43
114:9—80 n. 43
139:1—80 n. 43

Isaiah
11:1—180 n. 47
11:9-12—200 n. 20
11:10—80 n. 46,
    180 n. 47
23—24—200 n. 20
25:7-10—200 n. 20
40:10—100
40:11—99
43:4—71, 79 n. 27
44:6—64 n. 109
48:12—64 n. 109
53—95, 96
55:1—100
63:1-2—98
63:3—162

Jeremiah
2:13—100

Ezekiel
Book of—67
    n. 154, 162
29:6—111 n. 51
47:1-12—100

Daniel
Book of—54, 59
    n. 36, 66 nn. 147,
    151; 106
2:28(LXX)—49
7—162
7:13—102
7:22-23—81 n. 60
8:26—56
10—162
12:1—63 n. 96

Joel
2:32—200 n. 20
4:13—162

Amos
1:1-2—170

Jonah
1—180 n. 61

Micah
4:6-8—200 n. 20

Zephaniah
3:13—200 n. 20

Zechariah
12—66 n. 151
12:10—93, 95, 102
12:10-14—102
13:1—100
14—66 n. 151
14:8—100

APOCRYPHA AND
PSEUDEPIGRAPHA

*Apocalypse
of Abraham*
30—63 n. 96

*1 Apocalypse
of Baruch*
25—63 n. 96
27—63 n. 96
29—63 n. 96
48:31-41—63 n. 96
70—63 n. 96

*2 Apocalypse
of Baruch*
40:3—81 n. 59
35—40—59 n. 37
40:1-2—81 n. 56,
    200 n. 21
53—71—59 n. 37

*Apocalypse
of Peter*
    —63 n. 92

Enoch (Ethiopic)
    —41

1 Enoch
1:2—56 n. 5
9:5—98
10:1ff.—63 n. 96
47:1—63 n. 89
81:5-7—153 n. 21
85—90—59 n. 37
91:12-17—39, 59

237

n. 37
93—59 n. 37
93:3–9—39
93:19—56 n. 56
97:3–5—63 n. 89
99:3—63 n. 89
99:4ff.—63 n. 96
104:12—56 n. 56

2 Enoch
33:9—56 n. 56

4 Esdras
—48
2:42–47—200
n. 21
4:36–37—48
4:51–5:13—63
n. 96
5:55—64 n. 119,
138
6:11–25—63 n. 96
7:127–29—105
9:1–3—63 n. 96
11:2–3—59 n. 37
11:46—81 n. 59
11ff.—60 n. 53
12:31, 32—80
n. 46
13:14–24—63 n. 96
13:25–50—81
n. 56, 200 n. 21
12:42—153 n. 21
14:22, 26—153
n. 21

Gospel of Thomas
—75, 105
Logion 2—119
Logion 18—129
n. 43

Jubilees
23—63 n. 96
32:21–26—153
n. 21

Psalms of Solomon
17:42ff.—99

*Sibylline
Oracles*
2:154ff.—63 n. 96
5:214—81 n. 59

Sirach
24:21—100
36:10—63 n. 89
51:24—100

*Testament
of Joseph*
19:8—95, 109

*Testament
of Levi*
16—18—59 n. 37

*Wisdom
of Solomon*
9:5—100
19:15—98

DEAD SEA
SCROLLS

Qumran
—112 n. 73

1QM 19.8—81
n. 60

1QpHab
2,5–10—136
7,4–5—136

1QSb 5.21—81
n. 60

4 Qpatr 3—80
n. 46

NEW TESTAMENT

Matthew
Book of—38, 141
7:15—104
10:32—104, 148
11:15—105
12:8—103
13:9—105
13:24–43—103
13:43—105
19:28—80 n. 47,
104
22:1–13—104
23:3—113 n. 77
23:25—104

24—103
24:3—104
24:15—105
24:30—102–3
24:42—103
24:50—103
25:1–13—104
25:13—103
26:28—79 n. 30
28:20—113 n. 77

Mark
Book of—38, 62
n. 83
2:19—104
3:14–19—72, 80
n. 39
3:14—80 n. 39
3:17—87
4:9—105
4:23—105
7:7–13—111 n. 65
7:9—113 n. 77
7:16—105
13—38, 59 n. 34,
62 n. 83, 63
n. 96, 64 n. 113,
65 n. 140, 103,
169, 179 n. 39
13:4—39
13:10—49–50, 103
13:14–23—111
n. 65
13:14–17—39
13:14—105
13:18—105
13:22—104
13:24–27—111
n. 65
13:29—104
13:35, 37—103
14:58—99
15:29—99

Luke
Book of—38, 59
n. 32, 60 n. 47,
64 n. 113, 92–
94, 148, 156
n. 6
8:8—105
10—11—39

11:39—104
11:50—104
12:8—104, 148
12:35–39—104
12:39–40—103
13:28—103
14:35—105
21—38, 103
21:5–7—39
21:8—39, 103
21:9—39
21—24—60 n. 47
21:11–12—39
21:12–19—39
21:24—39, 66
n. 148, 103
21:25—39
21:27–28—39
21:29–31—39
21:34–36—39
22:28–30—80
n. 47, 104

John
Book of—85, 87,
88, 91, 93–101
1—20—90
1:1—95
1:14—95, 97, 99,
110 n. 49
1:16—110 n. 49
1:29—95, 96, 97
1:36—95, 96
2:19—95, 99
2:21—95, 99
3:11—110 n. 45
3:13—112 n. 67
3:29—104
4:14—95, 100
4:20–26—95
4:20–24—99
6:35—95, 100
6:39, 40—113 n. 82
6:44, 54—113 n. 82
7:17–18—100
7:37–38—95
7:37—100
8:44—128 n. 25
10:2, 11—99
10:12, 14—99
10:16—99
11:24—113 n. 82
12:48—113 n. 82

14:2f—113 n. 82
14:4—201 n. 28
14:24—113 n. 77
14:26—112 n. 71
16:33—105
17:8, 14—113 n. 77
17:17—113 n. 77
18:36-38—195
19:24—135
19:35—102, 110
n. 45
19:37—95, 102
21—90-91
21:16-17—110 n. 47
21:16—99
21:24—110 n. 45

Acts
Book of—92-93,
140-41, 156
n. 62
2:36—72
6:1-2—89
6:5—126 n. 5
6:14—99
10:5—113 n. 77
13:2—105, 154
n. 31
13:14-43—135
15:20, 29—127
n. 16
20:29-30—128
n. 20
21:11—154 n. 31
21:25—113 n. 77,
127 n. 16

Romans
Book of—35
1:17, 18—155 n. 56
2:5—155 n. 56
3:24-26—72, 79
nn. 31, 34; 110
3:25—79 n. 28
5:9—79 n. 28
5:17—75
6—130 n. 56
8:18—155 n. 56
8:19—155 n. 56
8:23—81 n. 55
8:29—70, 78 n. 15

11:3—129 n. 41
11:33—119, 129
n. 41
12:1—131 n. 57
13:1-7—195
13:11-14—155 n. 42
13:11—103
15:12—80 n. 46
16:15—81 n. 55
16:25—155 n. 56

1 Corinthians
Book of—113
n. 80, 117-19,
151
1:7—150, 155 n. 56
1:30—79 n. 31
2:10—119, 129
n. 41, 155 n. 56
3:13—155 n. 56
4:8—75, 119
5:7—73, 80 n. 50,
97
6:11—79 n. 32
6:12-20—119
7:29—103
8:1—9:23—119
9:1—150
10:6—110
10:8—127 n. 15
10:14-22—119
10:23—11:1—119
11:25—79 n. 28,
110
13—14—129 n. 39
14:6—150, 155
n. 56
14:26—155 n. 56
14:30—155 n. 56
15:8—150
15:16—81 n. 55
15:20—70, 78
n. 15, 81 n. 55,
153 n. 16

2 Corinthians
6:14—7:1—77 n. 11
6:18—77 n. 11
12:1-10—155 n. 59
12:1—150, 155
n. 56
12:7—151, 155
n. 56

Galatians
Book of—35, 149
1:1—150
1:5—79 n. 22
1:12—150, 155
n. 56
1:16—150, 155
n. 56
1:15-16—150
2:2—150, 155
n. 56
2:19-20—79 n. 24
2:20—71
3:23—155 n. 56

Ephesians
Book of—141, 147
1:5-6—71
1:7—72, 79 n. 28
1:17—155 n. 56
2:4ff.—71
3:3—155 n. 56
3:5—155 n. 56
5:2—70 n. 26
5:25ff.—71, 79
n. 25

Philemon
2:17—62 n. 87
4:4-6—155 n. 42
4:5—103

Colossians
Book of—141, 148
1:15-20—78 n. 14
1:18—70, 78 n. 14,
96, 153 n. 16

1 Thessalonians
5:1—155 n. 42
5:2-3—103

2 Thessalonians
Book of—156 n. 62
1:7—150, 155 n. 56
2:3-10—104
2:3, 6, 8—155
n. 56
2:16—71, 79
nn. 24, 25

1 Timothy
2:2-3—195

4:1—105, 154 n. 31
6:13-14—113 n. 77

2 Timothy
2:11-12—75, 104
2:18—119
4:2—128 n. 22
4:6—62 n. 87
4:8—104

Titus
1:9—128 n. 22

Hebrews
Book of—89
4:12-13—98
9:12—72
9:14—79 n. 28
10:23-31—155
n. 42
13:9—128 n. 22

James
1:1—155 n. 60
1:12—104
1:18—81 n. 55
5:7-11—155 n. 42
5:9—104

1 Peter
Book of—141, 147,
202 n. 45
1:5—155 n. 56
1:7—150, 155 n. 56
1:12—155 n. 56
1:13—150, 155
n. 56
1:18—73, 79 n. 28
1:19—72, 97
2:9—72
2:17—195, 202
n. 45
4:7—147
4:11—77 n. 9
4:13—150, 155
n. 56
4:17—147
5:1—155 n. 56
5:13—132 n. 69

2 Peter
1:1—155 n. 60
3:10—103

1–3 John
—90–93, 141

1 John
Book of—87, 89,
    92–93, 112
    n. 73, 113 n. 80
1:1–2—96
1:7—96
1:9—96
1:12—101
2:13—105
2:18–19—155 n. 42
3:1–2—101
3:5—96
4:4—105
4:10—96
5:2—101
5:4–5—105

2 John
1—113 n. 80
9—10—128 n. 22

Jude
1—155 n. 60
8, 11—127 n. 13

Revelation
1—11—22, 38, 58
1—4—105
1—3—31 n. 76,
    35, 62 n. 83,
    161
1:1–11—167
1:1–8—170, 175
1:1–3—170
1:1—35, 49, 56,
    126 n. 4, 130
    n. 48, 150, 164,
    173
1:2—56, 110 n. 45,
    130 n. 48, 150
1:3—19, 35, 49,
    56, 103, 130
    n. 48
1:4–3:22—177
1:4–8—28 n. 35
1:4–6—35, 150,
    170, 178 n. 23
1:4—64 n. 108, 70,
    77 nn. 8, 11, 98,
    126 n. 4, 180

n. 48
1:5–6—68–72, 75,
    77 n. 5, 78–79,
    97, 123, 148
1:5—28 n. 35, 78
    n. 18, 79 n. 32,
    150, 153 n. 16
1:6—50, 52, 61
    n. 78, 64 n. 117,
    67 n. 156, 77
    n. 9, 78 n. 18,
    123, 164
1:7—70, 102, 103,
    148, 164
1:8—56, 64 n. 108,
    70, 77 n. 11, 130
    n. 48, 164
1:9–3:22—169,
    173–74, 175
1:9–3:21—198
1:9–20—19, 62
    n. 83
1:9—41, 78 n. 18,
    110 n. 45, 126
    n. 4, 196
1:10—173
1:11—180 n. 53
1:12–20—162, 165,
    171, 174
1:12–3:22—52,
    145
1:12—173, 180
    n. 63
1:13—104, 148,
    180 n. 63
1:14—175
1:15–16—75
1:15—79 n. 32
1:16—98, 175
1:17–18—96
1:17—64 n. 109, 95
1:18—153 n. 16
1:19—58, 173
1:20—165, 180
    n. 63
2—3—13, 23, 37,
    58, 134, 165,
    171
2:1–7—115
2:1—165
2:2—165
2:5—65 n. 125
2:6—118

2:7—65 nn. 125,
    129; 165
2:8—64 n. 109,
    153 n. 16, 165
2:9—118, 165
2:10–11—118
2:10—65 n. 125,
    104
2:11—65 n. 129,
    165
2:12–17—115
2:12—165, 175
2:13—165, 180
    n. 48
2:14—65 n. 125,
    106, 116, 118,
    144
2:15—116
2:16—49, 65
    n. 125, 98, 118
2:17—65 n. 129,
    80 n. 43, 98,
    165, 175
2:18–29—115
2:18—98, 165
2:19—165
2:20–25—127 n. 16
2:20—65 n. 125,
    106, 116, 118
2:23—144
2:24–25—106, 145
2:24—116
2:25—65 n. 125
2:26—65 n. 129,
    105
2:27–28—131 n. 65
2:27—98, 99, 175
2:29—165
3:1—77 n. 8, 165
3:2–3—65 n. 125,
    103
3:2—165
3:3—49, 103
3:5–8—104
3:5—45, 65 n. 129,
    148
3:6—165
3:7—165
3:8—165
3:9—71, 79 n. 27,
    105, 116, 118,
    191
3:10—48, 63 n. 91

3:11—49, 65 n. 125
3:12—80 n. 43, 99,
    189
3:13—165, 193
3:14—98, 165
3:15—165
3:17—119
3:18—74
3:20—49, 104
3:21—65 n. 129,
    73, 80 n. 47,
    104, 105, 131
    n. 65, 173, 180
    n. 48
3:22—165
4—22—13, 21, 58
4:1–22:5—30
    n. 75, 46, 201
    n. 25
4:1–19:10—175
4—16—52
4—12—161
4—11—38
4—9—198
4—7—62 n. 83
4—5—62 n. 83,
    165, 173, 178
    n. 11
4:1–22:5—173
4:1–9:21—174,
    175
4:1–5:14—167
4—53, 131 n. 68
4:1—173, 174
4:2—173
4:5—77 n. 8, 173
4:8–11—173
4:8—64 n. 108, 77
    n. 11, 164
4:9–11—164
5—6—111 n. 65
5—52–53, 56, 73,
    162, 189, 200
    n. 19
5:1–5—65 n. 137,
    178 n. 11
5:2—73
5:3–14—121
5:5—73, 105, 180
    nn. 47, 49
5:6—42, 77 n. 8,
    96
5:8–14—173

5:9–12—164
5:9–10—68–70,
  73–76, 77 n. 5,
  96, 97, 123, 148
5:9—201 n. 26
5:10—50, 61 n. 77,
  64 n. 117, 67
  n. 156, 123
5:11–12—189
5:13–14—164
5:13—77 n. 9
6:1–7:17—162
6:1–17—167
6:6–9—191
6:9–11–46–47, 50
6:9—48, 110 n. 45
6:10—49, 63 n. 91,
  164
6:11—48
6:12–17—63 n. 93
6:16—164, 180
  n. 48
6:17—47
7:1–8:4—167
7—177 n. 9, 189
7:1–17—171
7:1–8—48, 58
7:9–12—173
7:9—180 n. 48
7:10–12—164
7:10—76 n. 3, 180
  n. 48
7:11–12—189
7:11—180 n. 48
7:13–17—165
7:13—54
7:14—45, 61 n. 77,
  109
7:15—95, 99, 180
  n. 48
7:16–17—9, 48
7:17—95, 99, 100,
  110 n. 47, 180
  n. 48, 190
7:25—54
8:1–11:14—162
8:1–63 n. 93
8:3–80 n. 48
8–14—62 n. 83
8:2–5—53
8:2—172
8:3–5—48, 99,
  172

8:5—9:21—167
8:5—173
8:6—9:21—172
8:6—172
8:13—54, 63 n. 91
9:20–21—165
10:1–15:5—188
10:1–15:4—53,
  55, 174, 176–
  77, 192
10—14—169, 198
10—13—177 n. 9
10—52–53, 54, 62
  n. 83, 65 n. 142
10:1–15:14—175
10:1–11:14—162,
  172
10:1–11:2—165
10:1–13—65 n. 135
10:3–4—155 n. 59
10:6—49, 58
10:7—136
11:1–15:4—66
  n. 151
11—20, 54, 55, 59
  n. 29
11:1–19—54
11:1–14—54
11:1–2—48, 54,
  99, 111 n. 51
11:2–14—167
11:2—103
11:4—66 n. 144,
  180 n. 63
11:5–6—144
11:7—50
11:10—56, 63 n. 91
11:14—54, 99
11:15–19—54, 55,
  56, 63 n. 93,
  167, 171–72,
  174, 175, 189
11:15–18—47
11:15—131 n. 68,
  164, 173
11:16—180 n. 48
11:17–18—164
11:17—77 n. 11
11:18—47, 49, 196
11:19—173
12—22–22, 59
  n. 26, 161
12–18—37

12:1–15:5—54
12–14—56, 111
  n. 65, 172
12–13—54, 66
  n. 153
12—13, 14, 17, 28
  n. 41, 57 n. 16,
  58, 65 n. 142,
  171
12:1–14:5—162
12:1–17—167
12:1–66 n. 153
12:3—98
12:5–14—54
12:5–42, 56, 99,
  180 n. 48
12:6—54
12:9—124
12:10–12—76 n. 3,
  164, 189
12:10—171
12:12—49, 99
12:13—66 n. 153
12:14—55, 66
  n. 153
12:15—54
12:17—47, 110
  n. 45
13—19, 98, 103,
  181, 189, 193
13:1–18—167
13:1–7—144
13:1–55, 98
13:2–4—191
13:2–180 n. 48
13:3–55, 103, 124
13:4–8—165
13:4–6—189
13:4–55, 164
13:5—54
13:6—99
13:7—103
13:8–63 n. 91,
  103, 124–25
13:9—105, 178
  n. 22
13:10–15—24
13:10—23, 125,
  132 n. 72, 190
13:11–18—103
13:11–103, 104
13:13—104
13:14—63 n. 91

13:16–17—125
13:17—74
13:18—165, 201
  n. 35
14—172
14:1–7—167
14:1–5—81 n. 56,
  171, 181–84,
  186, 188, 190,
  191
14:1–3—189, 191
14:1—181
14:2–3—181
14:3—74, 164, 180
  n. 48
14:4–5—165, 181,
  189
14:4—74
14:5—97
14:6–20—55, 171
14:6–13—189
14:6–11—189
14:6–10—56
14:6—49, 63 n. 93,
  103
14:7—48, 124
14:8–15:1—167
14:8—7, 48, 181
14:9–20—162
14:9–11—47, 181
14:9—164
14:10—47
14:12–13—189
14:12—23, 182
14:13—105, 143,
  182
14:14–20—103, 191
14:14—148, 171
14:15—99, 104
14:17—99
14:18—47
15—22—62 n. 83
15:1–19:10—198
15:5–19:10—162
15—16—47
15:1–8—172
15:1—54, 172,
  174–75
15:2–8—54, 167
15:2–5—58
15:2–4—55, 171,
  172, 188, 189,
  198

15:3-4—96, 164, 173
15:3—98, 102, 135
15:4—52, 63 n. 93
15:5—19:10—7, 175
15:5—16:21—174
15:5-8—53, 99, 172
15:10—98
15:13—77 n. 11
16:1-21—172
16:1-20—167
16:1—99
16:4-7—28 n. 36
16:4-6—28 n. 36
16:5-7—164
16:5—103
16:7—48, 77 n. 9, 98
16:9—48
16:10—98, 180 n. 48
16:11—189
16:13—103, 191
16:14—47
16:15—49, 164
16:17-20—63 n. 93
16:17—99, 189
16:18—173
16:19—47, 66 n. 153, 172
16:21—189
17:1—22:9—172, 174
17—20—47, 171
17—18—185, 190
17:1—20:15—174
17:1—19:10—172, 174, 180 n. 56
17—18—7, 47, 48, 66 n. 153, 162
17—19, 20, 66 n. 153, 124, 177 n. 9
17:1-18—167
17:1—56, 66 n. 153, 172
17:2—66 n. 153
17:3—66 n. 153, 173
17:4—104
17:7-18—165

17:8—63 n. 91
17:9-16—20
17:9-12—41, 60 n. 51, 126 n. 1
17:10—42, 60 n. 53
17:14—96, 98, 189
17:15—66 n. 153
18—6, 20, 31 n. 77, 202 n. 57
18:1-24—164
18:9-20—47, 189
18:13—47
18:20—7, 48, 164
18:24—7, 104
19:1-16—167
19:1-9—171
19:1-8—55, 173
19:1-5—189
19:1-4—164
19:1—76 n. 3
19:2—48, 98
19:4-5—180 n. 48
19:5-8—164
19:6—77 n. 11
19:7-8—104
19:9—164
19:10—110 n. 45, 145, 189
19:11—22:9—169, 174, 175
19:11—22:5—67 n. 154, 162, 198
19:11-21—47, 111 n. 65
19:11—21:8—172
19:11-21—180 n. 56
19:11-20—162
19:11-16—98, 171, 174, 175
19:11—48, 174
19:12—175
19:13—95, 97-98, 162
19:15—47, 175
19:16—121
19:17—20:15—167
19:20—103, 191
20—22—27 n. 29, 65 n. 127
20:1-3—47
20:3—49
20:4-6—45, 56,

81 n. 60, 81 n. 56, 123, 132 n. 74, 171, 177, 189
20:4—110 n. 45, 180 n. 48
20:6—67 n. 156, 77 n. 6, 131 n. 64, 164
20:7-10—47
20:10—103, 191
20:11-15—67 n. 154, 162
20:11-13—47
20:11-12—180 n. 48
20:14-15—47
21—22—28 n. 40, 52, 65 n. 128, 128 n. 30
21:1—22:5—167, 189
21—58 n. 23, 66 n. 153, 111 n. 53
21:1-8—52, 65 n. 128
21:1-2—80 n. 43
21:2—162
21:3-4—9
21:3—95
21:4—76
21:5—80 n. 43, 98, 180 n. 48
21:6-7—101
21:6—95, 100-101
21:7—131 n. 65, 191
21:8—65 n. 129, 165
21:9—22:9—173
21:9—22:5—28 n. 39, 52
21:9-27—65 n. 128, 162
21:9-11—190
21:9—66 n. 153
21:10—65 n. 129
21:14—13, 52
21:22—77 n. 11, 95, 99
21:24—65 n. 129, 78 n. 18
21:27—165
22:1-5—48, 65

n. 128
22:1—95, 180 n. 48
22:2—65 n. 129
22:3-5—99, 131 n. 66, 189
22:3—180 n. 48
22:4—65 n. 129
22:5—45, 52, 65 n. 129, 81 n. 60, 123
22:6ff.—31 n. 76
22:6—49, 56, 98, 130 n. 48
22:7—56, 130 n. 48, 164-65
22:8—49, 56, 126 n. 4, 130 n. 48
22:9—145-46
22:10-21—175
22:10—49, 103, 130 n. 48
22:12—49, 155 n. 42
22:13—56, 64 n. 109, 130 n. 48
22:14—164-65
22:15—191
22:16—80 n. 46, 146, 161
22:17—95, 100, 105, 154 n. 31
22:18-20—164
22:20—35, 42, 49, 110 n. 45, 161
22:21—149, 161

EARLY CHRISTIAN
LITERATURE

Barnabas
4:9—155 n. 42
21:3—155 n. 42

2 Clement
12:1—155 n. 42
16:3—155 n. 42

Didache
—141, 143-44
10:6—100
11.8.16—115
15:1-2—143

Hermas
  Mandates
  IX.11–15—115
  11.5,6—54 n. 31

Justin
  Dialogus cum
  Trypho
  81:4—108 n. 7

Eusebius *(Ecclesi-*
astical History) —87
  H.E.
  3.18—126 n. 1

4.15—129 n. 37

Hippolytus
  De Resurectione
  fr. 1—129 n. 42

Ignatius
  Letter to the
  Ephesians
  6:2—116
  7:1; 8:1—116
  9:1—116
  9:2—197
  11:1—155 n. 42

Letter to the
Philadelphians
  —143
  7:1–2—154 n. 30
  7:2—105

Iraeneus
  Adversus
  Haereses
  —108 n. 8, 126
  n. 1, 128 n. 21

Polycarp
  —141

Martyrdom of
Polycarp
  12.2—129 n. 37
  13.2—129 n. 37

Papias
  —87, 91
  5:2—75
  7:1–2—128 n. 25
  7:1—119